INDIA AND ITS PEOPLE:

ANCIENT AND MODERN

INDIA AND ITS PEOPLE:

ANCIENT AND MODERN.

WITH

A VIEW OF THE SEPOY MUTINY:

EMBRACING AN ACCOUNT OF

THE CONQUESTS IN INDIA BY THE ENGLISH,

THEIR POLICY AND ITS RESULTS

THE MORAL, RELIGIOUS, AND POLITICAL CONDITION OF THE PEOPLE: THEIR SUPERSTITIONS, RITES, AND CUSTOMS.

HOLLIS READ

GYAN

Published by

Gyan Publishing House
5, Ansari Road
Daryaganj, New Delhi-110002
Phone: 011-47034999, 9811692060
E-mail: books@gyanbooks.com

Distribution Network
gyanbooks.com
India, USA, Canada, UK, Australia, France

ISBN: 978-81-212-8830-9 (PB)
First Published,1858

2nd Impression 2023

Printed at: Gyan Press, Delhi.

INDIA AND ITS PEOPLE ANCIENT AND MODERN
Author: Hollis Read

INDIA AND ITS PEOPLE:

ANCIENT AND MODERN.

WITH

A VIEW OF THE SEPOY MUTINY:

EMBRACING AN ACCOUNT OF

THE CONQUESTS IN INDIA BY THE ENGLISH,

THEIR POLICY AND ITS RESULTS

ALSO,

THE MORAL, RELIGIOUS, AND POLITICAL CONDITION OF THE PEOPLE:
THEIR SUPERSTITIONS, RITES, AND CUSTOMS.

BY

REV. HOLLIS READ,

AMERICAN MISSIONARY TO INDIA.

ILLUSTRATED WITH NUMEROUS ENGRAVINGS.

COLUMBUS:
PUBLISHED AND SOLD EXCLUSIVELY BY SUBSCRIPTION,
BY J. & H. MILLER.
1858.

CONTENTS.

CHAPTER VII.

CHAPTER VIII.

CHAPTER IX.

CHAPTER X.

CHAPTER XI.

CHAPTER XII.

CHAPTER XIII.

CHAPTER XIV.

CHAPTER XV.

CHAPTER XVI.

CHAPTER XVII.

CHAPTER XVIII.

CHAPTER XIX.

CHAPTER XX.

CHAPTER XXI.

CHAPTER XXII.

CHAPTER XXIII.

CHAPTER XXIV.

CHAPTER XXV.

Drawn by W. Daniell, R.A. Engraved by R. Brandard.

Boa Constrictor & boat Crew

PREFACE.

All false religions may be traced to an Asiatic pedigree. The parent stock is a practical Atheism, developing itself in a melancholy *perversion of the knowledge* of the true God, "changing the glory of the incorruptible God into an image made like to corruptible man, and to birds and four-footed beasts and creeping things." The two great fountains of religious error from which, for near 6,000 years, streams of death have been flowing, are Brahmunism and Boodhism. These streams, though modified by almost every conceivable circumstance, as intellectual culture, the spirit of the age, the social and political condition of a people, national and provincial character, and the prevailing philosophy of the times, and oftentimes so changed as to seem, to the superficial observer, to bear little affinity to their original, nevertheless are issues from the same corrupt fountain.

Brahmunism is a colossal system of practical gnosticism — a warfare on poor defenseless matter — the laceration and mortification of the body — a religion of rites and forms and penances. Boodhism is an equally luxurious growth of gnosticisms, as developing the *ascetic principle* — a religion of abstraction, whose chief aim is to rid the spirit from bodily connections and propensities, that it may lose itself in the great pervading Spirit of the Universe.

Take as a specimen whatever form of false religion you please, and you will find it a republication, or new blending, or modification of the elements of one of these two mighty systems. It may be more especially the child of the one or the other of its parents — may abound more in the *penitential* or the *expiatory* — mockery or a love of a gaudy religious external may preponderate, yet its lineal descent may be traced in no ambiguous line to the palmy East. If it be neither Brahmunism or Boodism, it is both, as recast in the mould of the age in which you find it, and combined in different proportions and adapted to "the times."

It is in reference to such a view of the great schemes which Satan has originated and nurtured (in the form of false religions) by which to deceive the nations, that I put forth the accompanying volume. It is designed, as one object aimed at, to be a PLAIN AND PRACTICAL ILLUSTRATION OF BRAHMUNISM. And whoever will study this monstrous system of error in referrence to a right understanding of modern systems of false belief, will find his position peculiarly favorable to acquaint himself with the philosophy of all religious error. He will see that Error, as well as Truth, has its system, its lineal descent, its history and its philosophy — that all the different forms of Error are but parts of one great whole, and this whole but an exact counterfeit of Truth itself.

The memoir is submitted to the perusal of the public, to exhibit the character of a Hindoo Brahmun, both before and after his heart had been subdued by divine grace; and with the hope that it may encourage the friends of missions to the heathen, and silence the cavils of the skeptical. His conversion, life, labors and death, is a merciful token from the great head of the church, that the Brahminical priesthood, though so sunk in all that is morally degrading, may yet be a "holy priesthood." The power and grace of God here displayed, force on us the conviction that the conversion of the heathen is an event confidently and rationally to be expected. To disbelieve here, is more absurd than to believe.

It is not pretended that the case of Babajee was a common one. His zeal for the conversion of his countrymen, his energy of character, his disinterestedness and spiritual attainments, distinguish him from most converts from Paganism. He seems selected, by sovereign grace, to show the riches of God's mercy, for the honor of his name among the heathen, for the conformation of his promises to his church, and the encouragement of missionaries abroad and their patrons at home.

The historical notices in which the volume somewhat abounds, will, I flatter myself, not prove its less interesting portion, but will furnish the general reader with so much information on topics not well known, as shall repay the perusal.

I have throughout this volume attempted an UNDISGUISED exhibition of Hindooism. This I have, in many instances, found to be impossible, without sometimes transgressing those STRICT rules of delicacy — amounting sometimes, perhaps, to SQUEAMISHNESS — which, in our country, the present age has prescribed. I have, as far as possible, avoided all indelicacy of language. More than this could not be done, without omitting entirely to speak on several subjects which, more thau any other, go to develop the real character of Hindooism. I could have said, as most writers on these subjects have said, that "delicacy forbids me," &c. But I have always regarded such apologies as miserable substitutes for the information which I was seeking concerning the national and religious character of a great nation of Pagans. The reader need not, however, suppose that I have unblushingly told ALL. There still remains behind the curtain all those things which "may not so much as be named among you."

I have likewise pursued the same course in my accounts of missionary operations in India. My only endeavor, in both cases, has been to present a FAIR picture, without giving an undue prominence either to light or shade. H. R.

INDIA AND ITS PEOPLE.

CHAPTER I.

Introducotry remarks—Ancient India—Trade with the West—Solomon—Tadmor of the Wilderness, its Magnificence and Ruins—Conquests of India—Silk-Worms first brought to Europe.

I CANNOT think of the Old World without enthusiasm. I cannot look back on its once familiar scenes and not cherish a pleasing remembrance of a land where Paradise was; where the first human family opened their ravished eyes in innocence on the unblemished beauty of this lower world; where have transpired most of the mighty events which have kept the world in motion, and where yet remain the monuments of human greatness and folly. It is now in ruins. Its once fertile soil languishes for the want of the industry and skill of man. Its costly temples, tombs, and aqueducts are in ruins. Its gorgeous palaces, which were once the busy theatres of all that was great and proud and brilliant—its spacious halls, and courts and armories, are in ruins. Man, too, is in ruins. He is but the wreck of the noble being God placed in Eden. Mind is there in ruins. Bleak desolation has swept over it. It is but the stinted, withered plant of its noble original. But the direst of all its ruins, is that of man's moral and immortal part. Here virtue weeps and religion hides her head.

India has always been a country of rare interest—at times, of enchantment. Here have been the scenes of the mightiest martial exploits. Empires more extensive and mighty, more brilliant and lasting than ever flourished elsewhere, existed here before the first frail bark plowed the dark waters of the Atlantic, or the red man of this New World had been molested in the chase. It is the land of many a fairy tale which is scarcely an exaggeration of real life.

The natural productions of India, the works of art, the beauty and grandeur of its scenery, the unvarying and unique manners of its inhabitants, make it one of the most interesting regions on the face of the earth.

By India is meant the territory that lies between the Indus river on the west and the Brahmapootra on the east; Cape Comorin on the south and the Himalaya mountains on the north; including a surface of 1,800 miles from north to south, and 1,500 in its greatest breadth from east to west. A remarkable feature is that it presents such a variety of climate in so narrow a compass of latitude—and this, too, so far south. Its various degrees of elevation produce every variety of climate, from the intense cold and eternal snow of the polar regions, to the burning sands and scorching heats of the torrid zone. The tops of the Himalayas are covered with perpetual snow; the plains of the Deckan are scorched by a burning sun. Consequently India yields the productions of every land.

Though much of India be level, yet it presents some of the most picturesque and sublime mountains in the world. Such are the Himalayas on the north, and the Ghauts on the west.—One immense plain extends through its whole width, watered on the east by the Ganges and the Jumna, and is the most fertile land in the world.

Such, in some of its general features, is the country to which I now ask the reader's attention. Accompany me through the subsequent chapters, and if I cannot please you with fictions, I will endeavor to interest you with facts, such as have fallen under my observation during a five years residence in that great and interesting country.

I am not ignorant that the limited intercourse between India and America very much precludes us as a people from having any very accurate or minute acquaintance with that country. There is but a vague knowledge of the country, and, in general, a still more vague knowledge of the people. Reports, journals, letters have done what in this way could be done. But the heterogeneous mass of information thus communicated, lies scattered through the innumerable volumes, pamphlets and newspapers, which the religious press has sent forth the past twenty years, and the public are scarcely the wiser. It is not possible for me, wholly, to supply the deficiency. I may not expect to present in a connected form so *much* information as has already, in *detached* portions, been thrown before the American public, and overlooked or forgotten by them. Yet I may contribute a humble share to supply an important desideratum at the present stage of our benevolent enterprises.

The Hindoos claim an almost unbounded antiquity. They will modestly tell you they are the most ancient, honorable, learned, holy nation on the face of the earth. They believe their country occupies the centre of the world, which is one great plain, and the other nations of the earth are placed about it in concentric circles. They trace back their history to an immense antiquity, and assert that all Hindoostan, from the Indus to the confines of China, formed one vast empire.

Indian history may be divided into three periods: the period before the conquest of the Mohammedans; the period of the reign of the Mohammedans; and that since the nations of Europe have held large possessions in India.

The history of the first of these periods is so enveloped in the mists of fable that it is difficult to distiuguish truth from fiction. Indeed, we are not sure that we know anything of the *early* history of India — though we do know something of her history earlier than Greece flourished, or the foundations of Rome were laid, or the Hebrew Commonwealth had arrived at the acme of her glory. When Europe was darkened in barbarism, and England with the abode of the Druids, and her people scarcely towered in intellectual stature above the Hottentots, and

America was an unknown forest, traversed only by the wild man, India was an old country, covered with mighty nations, and peopled by men of comparative refinement and civilization. We cannot trace the origin and the early progress of the arts, the sciences and institutions of Ancient India. We find her a full grown nation at our first introduction. The records of her childhood and youth are lost, probably past all recovery.

Yet I do not think it quite true that no traces of the history of this ancient people have come down to us. The Hindoo himself—his peculiar genius and cast of mind—furnishes us a key by which we may unlock the mystic door, and cull from the legendary store a few genuine materials. The Hindoo invests every thing with the marvelous. Truth and honesty are too tame and insipid. To say that some renowned king lived a thousand years ago, made conquests, established a great empire, administered his government with justice, protected Hindooism, fed the Brahmuns, abounded in charity to the poor, reigned thirty years, and died at the age of sixty, would be too insipid a tale to command the perusal of any one. The hero, therefore, must be invested with a divine character. It must be said he was an incarnation of the Deity; that he flourished two millions of years ago; that he was in stature like the cocoa-nut tree; that he lived a thousand years; fought with the giants; imprisoned thirty-three millions of gods; tore mountains from their foundations to construct a bridge over the sea; gave lacks of rupees to the Brahmuns; became a terror to Indra, the king of the gods, on account of his piety; paid court to the sun, and received from him some invaluable boon; and, like Virgil's hero, descended to the infernal regions, and visited the manes of his fathers.* The Hindoo, though the most incredulous about historical truth, feels no difficulty in believing such kind of history. Such are his habits of thinking, and such the character of his sacred books, that he seems quite incapable of believing the naked truth. Hence it is that the accounts which the

* Such is the history of the *great* king Vicram, of central India.

Hindoos have of the creation, of the deluge, of the subsequent peopling of the earth, and of the rise and progress of the Indian empire, are so wrapped up in the most incredible fictions, that, at first view, we are ready to say there is not a particle of truth to be found in this whole heterogeneous mass of rubbish.

The Hindoos divide time into four periods, which are called yoogs: the last of which periods (the one in which we are now living) is called the Kalee yoog; the present year (1858) is the 4958th year of this yoog. What occurred among mortals during the three first periods of the world, we know not; no records remain. Tradition here steps in, as usual, and pretends to supply the deficiency. We learn, however, little from her, except that virtue and truth prevailed in the first period, and men lived one hundred thousand years. In the second period, only three parts of the creation obeyed the oracles of God, and men lived ten thousand years. In the third period, half the creation became corrupt, and the age of man was limited to a thousand years. During the last period, man has departed from the recitude of his fathers,—only a fourth part regard the dictates of God, and human life is curtailed to one hundred years. The commencement of the Kalee yoog, it will be seen, does not materially differ from the Mosaic date of the creation.

The founder of the first empire in India, appears, from the Maha Burut, (an Indian poem,) to have been Krishna. This event took place soon after the commencement of the Kalee yoog. Krishna and his posterity reigned four hundred years. In his reign, learning is said to have flourished, and the people were divided into castes. Then followed a succession of sixteen or eighteen dynasties. The empire of the Hindoos over India came down entire, till about one hundred and seventy years before Christ, when it was dissolved by civil discord and war. Princes and governors of different provinces assumed the appearance of independent sovereigns, and took the name of emperors. Still, there was never afterwards a regular succession of kings. India, though no longer united in one great empire, was still powerful and rich. No foreign invasion had exhausted her resources. If we may judge from the wealth, comforts, and luxuries of life, which the first conquerors found, we must believe that India was once a land favored of Heaven, above almost any nation on the face of the earth. And may we not indulge the pleasing supposition that she once honored and adored the Author of her blessings? But, alas! ungrateful India! thy present degradation betrays thy guilt! Thou hast forsaken the Lord thy God! Thou hast not hearkened to his voice, to observe to do all his commandments, and his statutes, which he has commanded thee; thou has turned aside after other gods to serve them; and all the curses pronounced against rebellious Israel have fallen on thee! "Thou art cursed in the city and in the field; thou art cursed in thy basket and thy store; thou art cursed in the fruit of thy body, in the fruit of thy flocks, and in thy lands; thou art cursed when thou comest in, and when thou goest out! The Lord has sent upon thee cursing, vexation, and rebuke, in all that thou wouldst do! — The pestilence cleaves to thee! The Lord has smitten thee with consumption, with fever, with extreme burning, and with the sword, and with blasting and mildew, and they will pursue thee till thou perish!"

It seems not certain that sacred history contains any direct account of India. Allusions are doubtless made to an extensive trade with that country in the days of Solomon. This wise, rich and enterprising prince conducted an extensive foreign commerce. He had ships on the Mediterranean and Red Seas, the latter of which traded with Ophir and Javan, countries which, judging from their products — as "gold, peacocks, apes, spices, ivory, ebony, precious cloths, embroidered work, chests of apparel bound with cords"—must have been in India.

Ships in this trade, called ships of Tarshish, sailed from Ezion-geber on the Red Sea. But this sea, on account of contrary winds, not being navigable more than half the year, commerce met a sad check, which induced this ambitious prince to seek another route by which to procure the rich manufactures and luxuries of the East. Such a route was found by the way of the Persian Gulf and the Euphrates, and thence by caravans over the desert to Judea. And to facilitate the passage of caravans over this arid desert, Solomon built "Tadmor in the Wilderness," both as a vast store-house for goods, and a resting place for caravans.

You will not regret stopping a few moments in this extraordinary city. It is now in ruins; but these are enduring memorials of its former magnificence. It was situated 60 miles from the Euphrates and 200 from the Mediterranean, and surrounded on every side by a sandy desert. A strange location for a city; yet not so replete with folly as that of scores in our western wilds. This was no "paper city." It was what its name so beautifully imports — *a palm tree* in the desert —a spot on which the eye was regaled with all the beauty and splendor of the East, and the taste gratified with all the luxuries of the oriental world.

"Its ruins extend over a space ten miles in length by five in width, and may challenge any others in the world," says Buckingham, "for costly splendor. There are traces of avenues five and six miles in extent, with immense rows of Corinthian columns, and the many remains of vast temples." Athens, Rome, or Thebes do not exhibit a mass of ruins so magnificent. Yet it enjoyed none of the ordinary resources of wealth. It had neither agriculture, shipping, mining, nor manufactures. But it was the grand thoroughfare of the eastern and western worlds, at a time when India was proverbially the land of opulence. It was simply the spot where buyers and sellers on a magnificent scale met, and caravans of 50,000 or 100,000 camels were receiving their supplies and preparing for their journey westward. Though its means of wealth were singular, they were neither few nor small.

But whence the pre-eminence this city of the desert may claim in architectural beauty and grandeur? The answer is, that no other city ever brought together such an assemblage of wealthy and enterprising men. Tadmor was then the depot of the only great and rich trade in the world, and there has not since been a more lucrative one. And as they could not, in the midst of a sandy desert, enjoy the luxury of villas, parks, gardens, artificial lakes, fountains and shady walks, with statuary and arbors, they could only gratify the love which opulence begets for display, in the erection of superb and costly edifices. Hence those stupendous architectural monuments whose ruins are to this day to be classed among the wonders of the world.*

This overland trade with India, once so successfully prosecuted by the wise king of Israel, was never abandoned till after the discovery of a maritime passage to the fairy lands of the East by the Cape of Good Hope.

The *Phenicians* visited India at a very early period, and perhaps were the first to introduce the rich produce of that country into Europe. Theirs was an overland trade, carried on by the means of the camel, an animal so admirably fitted to traverse deserts and support heat and fatigue as to have got the name "ship of the desert." No sooner had Tyre become opulent and powerful by this traffic, than her neighbors sought to share in the trade. The Persians, Arabians, and Jews, as already mentioned; the Greeks, Romans, and Egyptians, each in their turn participated largely in the lucrative traffic with India—and each in their turn enjoyed the rich monopoly, and became enriched and enfeebled by the luxuries of the East. This was the chief source of the wealth and power of *Venice*. She carried on the trade principally by the aid of the Moors, a name applied generally to those Arabs who had become masters of the Ethiopian, Arabian and Indian Seas. Genoa and Florence were also replenished from the East. From the

* These ruins till recently remained unknown. Near the close of the last century, some gentlemen of the English factory at Aleppo, incited by wonderful accounts of the ruins at Palmyra, ventured, spite the dangers and fatigue of the journey through the desert, to visit them. "A fertile spot, of some miles in extent, rose before them like an island out of a vast plain of sand, covered with the remains of temples, porticoes, aqueducts and other public works, which, in magnificence and splendor, and some of them in elegance, were not unworthy of Athens or Rome in their most prosperous days." At present a few miserable huts of beggarly Arabs are scattered in the courts of its stately temples, or deform its elegant porticoes, exhibiting a humiliating contrast to its ancient magnificence.

time of Alexander the Great (who we shall see figures in the history of ancient India) to the discovery of a passage by the Cape, the chief seat of this trade was Alexandria, in Egypt. This became on the southern route (by the Red Sea) what Tadmor was on the northern. Hither the spices, gums, aromatics, silks, and precious stones of India were brought by the Red Sea to Bernice, thence conveyed overland to the Nile and re-shipped to Alexandria; and from this mighty emporium of Indian commodities, distributed over Europe.

These sketches suffice to show that India was an opulent, old, civilized nation at least 3,000 years ago. She had then brought the arts — and the sciences as their bases — to a state of perfection unknown elsewhere.

A moment's reflection here will give us a stupendous idea of the former wealth of India. Was there a time in Judea when gold was, for plenteousness, as brass, and silver as stones, and cedars as the sycamore tree — when Solomon made 200 targets and 600 shields of beaten gold, and a great ivory throne overlaid with pure gold, with six steps and a footstool of gold — all whose drinking vessels and all the vessels of the house of the forest of Lebanon were of pure gold? — none were of silver, for that was not anything accounted of in the days of Solomon? It was when the ships of Tarshish, "once in three years," brought home their precious cargoes from India — it was when they were "replenished from the East." Was there a time when *Tyre* was the *crowning city, whose merchants were princes and whose traffickers were the honorable of the earth?* It was when she became the store-house of the wealth of the Indies. Whence but from the same fountain, the treasures that garnished the throne of Greece, or laid the foundation of the wealth of Rome, or called into existence, as in a day, Genoa, Venice, and Florence, and made them prosper and increase and maintain their independence amidst mighty empires? Whence did the Portuguese, the French and the Dutch derive their greatest wealth? And whence but through their agents in Leaden Hall street, have the English that superabundant wealth which makes England so proud, so mighty a nation?

We may trace the history of ancient India through another line. I refer to conquests. As you may suppose, ambition early fixed his insatiable eye on such a land. She early became, and has not ceased to be, an object for conquest to all who have fought for the prize of empires.

It has always been the misfortune of that ill-fated nation to be visited only to be fleeced of her wealth. Till recently, she scarcely arrested the attention of the philosopher or the historian. So intent on gain were the early monopolists of her trade, that no one stopped to tell us of her manners, customs, laws, religion or literature.

The earliest reputed conqueror of India was Sesostris, an Egyptian king who lived near 3,500 years ago. Next we hear of a famous attack on India by *Semiramis*, the celebrated queen of Assyria or Bayblon. She spent three years in preparation — is said to have led on an army of one million of soldiers, and was met by a force equally numerous. The king of India — for India was then one empire — met the haughty queen on the banks of the Indus, opposed her passage, gave battle and gained a decisive victory. Next, India is assailed and subdued by Darius, the Persian.

We now come to a period on which the light of history has more profusely cast her beams. Alexander, the Macedonian and the conqueror of the world, turned his victorious arms towards India 327 years before Christ. Fired by the hope of gain, excited by the success of the *Tyrians*, he determined to secure the commerce to himself. He therefore built the town of Alexandria, in Egypt, as a depot, and proceeded on his route to India, which had so long been in his eye the fairy land — conquered Persia — traversed the wild regions of Central Asia — crossed the Indus — encountered and overcome Porus, a powerful Hindoo prince, with his formidable army of Rajpoots — overrun the Punjaub, the finest country in India. His progress being checked, both by the periodical rains and the mutinous spirit of his army, he was compelled to return to Persia.

Alexander opened to Europe a much more ample knowledge of India than had hitherto been obtained. He had in his army and among his principal officers men of learning and research. Such were Ptolemy, Aristobulus and Nearchus; the journal of the latter only has outlived the ravages of time.

From him we learn that India was, at that remote period, as populous, fertile, highly civilized, and more opulent than at any time since; and that her manners and institutions were almost precisely the same. These suffer no change from the lapse of time. The people of India neither know nor will be taught the meaning of the word *fashion*. Change in the cut of a coat, the form of a dress, the shape of a hat or the poise of a bonnet, are unintelligable terms to an Indian. All such matters were with him fixed by *law*, the unalterable law of *custom*, thousands of years ago. Each caste, profession or employment has its own, which changes not. We have ample proof of this in the records of Alexander's invasion. These give us, in substance, the following items of information respecting the manners, customs, dress, appearance and religion of the people of India more than 2,000 years ago:

"They are delicate and slender in form—complexion dark—hair black but uncurled—their garments principally of cotton—live on vegetable food—are divided into sects and classes, called castes—marriages of mere children, and the prohibition of marriages between different castes—men wearing ear-rings and parti-colored shoes—the custom of wives burning themselves with the bodies of their deceased husbands." And their religious and social institutions were then almost precisely what we find them at the present time. Each caste bound on his turban and wore his cloth in the same manner—had shoes of the same shape—worshiped the same idols in the same way—daubed his forehead with the same kind of paint and with the same marks which the men of his caste do 2,000 years later.

The conquests of Alexander were followed up by Seleucus,

one of his successors. He advanced considerably beyond the limits of Alexander's progress, and conciliated the sovereign of a powerful nation on the Ganges (Sandracottus), by sending an embassador to his court. This delicate task he confided to Megasthene, who, having been in the army of Alexander, was well versed in a knowledge of the country. He was the first European who traversed India in its full breadth — the first who beheld the mighty Ganges. To him we are principally indebted for all the knowledge we have of the internal policy of India in its early history.

His hostory is valuable for the truth it contains, and amusing from his love of the marvelous, in which he sometimes indulges. He mingled with his facts many extravagant fictions. He tells us of men with ears so large they could wrap themselves up in them — of men with only one eye — without mouths — without noses — with long feet — with toes turned back — of men only three spans in hight — of wild men with heads in the shape of a wedge — of ants as large as foxes, which dig up gold — wool growing on trees like fruit — and many other things quite as probable. Nor is it a matter of great surprise that one who has penetrated so far beyond the goal of all former travelers into so extraordinary a country, should sometimes trespass on the credulity of his friends.

India was subject to no further conquests from Europe, till the invasion of the Portuguese by the way of the Cape, near the close of the fifteenth century.

One event during this period considerably affected the communication between Europe and the East, and wrought an important and lasting change in the commercial world: I mean the introduction of silk-worms into Europe. This happened A. D. 557.

The Persians were at this time the rival power of the Greeks. The use of silk, both in dress and furniture, had become so general in the court of the Greek emperors at Constantinople, who now imitated and surpassed the sovereigns of Asia in splendor and magnificence, that it had become with them an indispensable demand. The Persians so improved the advantages they enjoyed, of being able to cut off both the caravans by the northern route and those by the way of the Persian Gulf, as to secure the monopoly of nearly the whole commerce to themselves.

After some fruitless attempts to wrest this trade from the hands of his rival, Justinian, the Greek emperor, secured the object of his wishes in a most unexpected manner.

Two Persian monks, employed as missionaries in the East, penetrate as far as China. There they observe the labors of the *silk-worm*, and become acquainted with the skill of the Chinese in manufacturing the productions of this wonderful little insect into a great variety of elegant fabrics. They repair to Constantinople, explain to the emperor the origin of silk and the various ways of preparing and manufacturing it; mysteries unknown or imperfectly understood in Europe.—Encouraged by his liberal promises, they undertook to bring to his capital a quantity of these insects; which they do by conveying the eggs in a hollow cane. These were hatched, fed with the leaves of the wild mulberry—they multiply and worked as in China. From this small beginning, the culture of silk spread over Europe, and diminished very considerably commerce with the East.

A reflection will very naturally close this chapter. India has from generation to generation supplied Christendom with her *luxuries*. From her we have received spices, aromatics, silks, and the precious metals. As we have received her *pearls*, have we sent her the "pearl of great price?" As we have reveled in her *luxuries*, have we given her "the one thing *needful*?" As we have received her odoriferous gums, precious aromatics, her healing unguents, have we sent her in return the Balm in Gilead, the oil of joy, the good tidings of Him that cometh with healing in his wings?

CHAPTER II.

Conquests of India by the Mohammedans, and the Empire of the Great Moguls.

The next great event was the conquest of India by the Mohammedans. This introduces us to the second period of Indian history. The first invasion by the Moslems took place about the year 1000 A. D., and perhaps no period, ancient or modern, is so full of thrilling incidents. Prowess in arms, extraordinary military achievements, brilliant conquests, imperial magnificence—surpassing the glory of Babylon or Nineveh, and empire co-extensive with all India—gorgeous palaces, temples, mosques, tombs, aqueducts, and every stupendous work of art, salute the bewildered vision as we unroll the canvass of the next 700 years. No period of history opens to the reader a wider or more attractive field.

We here emerge from the fogs of fiction and mythology, and hail the more certain light of the Persian historian, Ferishta. He is regarded a faithful chronicler of the period of which we are now to speak.

But who were those mighty, furious conquerors, who came down on India like a wolf on the fold, laying waste her thousand cities, breaking down her temples, pillaging her treasures, carrying away her gold and precious stones, and everywhere marking their course with blood? Such an inquiry leads us back a step.

The rise, and the rapid and irresistible progress of Mohammed, produced a complete revolution among the nations of the East. A new empire rose in Arabia, which was destined soon to roll its resistless waves over most of Asia, Africa, and Europe. The banners of the crescent waved amidst the hills of Spain, and led a countless army to victory among the mountains of Independent Tartary. The torrid regions of the equator and the frigid lands of the poles trembled beneath the mighty tread of the Prophet.

HUMAYUN.

Mohammed unsheathed the sword and clothed himself with the mystic power of the Koran in the year of the Christian era 622; designing, no doubt, to lay the foundation for universal empire. The capital of this mighty dominion, mighty not only in the vision of the Prophet's mighty mind, but, within a few years from its origin, mighty in reality, was first fixed in Arabia. Thence it was removed to Damascus, and thence to Bagdat, whence for centuries went forth the power of the false Prophet to the ends of the earth.

The califate extended as far east as Independent Tartary. This country, though so far distant from the central power, was early subjugated by Moslem arms, and became an important province. The Tartars were rude and savage, roaming hordes of shepherds and warriors, who neither lived in houses nor cultivated the ground. Yet their subjugation to Bagdat wrought in them an extraordinary transformation. They soon formed a regular government, cultivated their large and fertile plains, cherished the arts, and congregated in cities. This province was the first to break away from the grand califate, and, after a few intermediate steps of revolution, to form a kingdom, which soon proved a powerful rival to Bagdat itself. These brave Tartars first extended their empire over Persia, and finally carried their victorious arms to the very walls of Bagdat, and the vicegerent of the Prophet, whose arm had made the earth tremble, is obliged to yield to the terms of a Tartar prince. Other provinces of Central Asia are added to this new and rising empire. The Afghans, a rude, fierce, warlike, athletic race, inhabiting the mountainous regions between Persia and India, were brought under the same yoke; and the city of Ghizni, that ancient seat of empire, which for centuries after spread her broad mantle over nearly all Asia, was selected as the capital. Had this selection been made solely in reference to the future subjugation of India, it was altogether judicious, for it commanded the grand entrance to India.

At this point we shall do well to pause a moment and look about us.

It is the site of magnificent ruins. Eight centuries ago, and Ghizni was already an ancient city of barbarous Afghans; then suddenly became and remained for four centuries the capital of a proud and powerful empire—enriched and adorned by a race of princes, who, for wealth, and pride, and power, the world has never seen their like. Here the riches of India were lavished in all that taste could devise, or passion desire, or luxury crave. But her glory has long since departed; her magnificent piles, her superb works of art, have long been leveled with the dust; and, except some scattered masses of misshapen ruins, not a monument remains of Ghizni's former grandeur.

Though a city among the mountains in the interior of Persia, 600 or 700 miles from the sea coast, Ghizni was the radiating point of that military glory which shone over all Asia—the centre of a power which soon found all Hindoostan too straight to contain it.

This empire, destined in coming years to play so conspicuous a part in the affairs of Asia, became consolidated in the reign of Mahmoud, who mounted the throne of Ghizni in the year A. D. 997. He was one of the most extraordinary characters that ever ruled in Asia, or, indeed, that figures in the annals of conquerors. His empire, called the Ghiznian, afterwards the Patan or Afghan, was made up of a confederacy of Tartars, Usbecks, Afghans, Persians, and all the fierce, hardy, warlike tribes that inhabited the mountains of Central Asia. Its importance in Asia was like that of Turkey at present in Europe. Aware of this, the British government have not deemed their vast dominions in the East safe from invasion till they had secured this ancient key-stone to the arch of empire.

For wealth, splendor, and power, it had rivaled imperial Bagdat, and for the tombs of its many saints it had acquired a sanctity scarcely inferior to the holy Medina. It was the tower from which the fierce Moslems descended twelve times to ravage the plains of India—from which, in succeeding ages, host after host poured streams of desolation over the fertile plains of Hindoostan. But the gleam of the British bayonet struck terror in the heart of the present degenerate race of Ghizni, and in a few days the uncircumcised feet of a foreign foe tread on the marble pavements and the dilapidated mosaics of Moslem grandeur, and the British flag waves on the falling walls of Ghizni.

It was in the year 1000 that *Mahmoud* made his descent on India. Ostensibly, he was actuated by an indomitable zeal to extend the Mohammedan faith; really, by an unconquerable love of glory and wealth. Having made a vow to heaven that if ever he should be left to tranquility in his own dominions he would turn his arms against the idolaters of Hindoostan, he set out with 10,000 of his chosen horse, encountered Jeipal, king of Lahore, supported by an army four times his number, joined battle, and was victorious. Mahmoud returned, inflated with glory and laden with immense wealth. For, apart from the ordinary booty, there were about the neck of the conquered rajah, sixteen strings of jewels, each of which was valued at 180,000 rupees—the whole equal to £300,000, or $1,500,000.

In four successive expeditions, the work of subjugation went on, former conquests were secured, rebellions quelled, tribute collected, many a bloody battle fought, and stupendous wealth borne away. The siege of Birne is too notable to be slightly passed over. The conqueror directed his steps to this celebrated fort, breaking down idols, destroying temples, and spreading desolation wherever he went. Birne was built, as is common in India, on the top of a high hill; and here the Hindoos had, on account of its strength, deposited the wealth consecrated to their idols in all the neighboring provinces. There is said to have been a greater quantity of silver, gold, precious stones, and pearls, than the royal treasure of any prince on earth had possessed. The garrison having been drawn into the open field, the defenseless fortress fell an easy prey.

This mighty contender for the "faith," returned to Ghizni ladened with 700,000 golden dinars, 700 maunds of gold and silver plate, (each maund at least 28 pounds,) 40 maunds of pure gold in ingots, 2000 maunds of silver bullion, and 20 maunds of various jewels, and prepared a magnificent feast, at which he displayed his wealth in golden thrones and other rich ornaments. The whole was arrayed in a great plain without the city of Ghizni; and after the feast princely presents were distributed to the multitude.

Entrenched in his native mountains, where he shone in gold, and his palaces sparkled with the richest profusion of gems ever brought together, he pounced like a tiger on his prey, and bore his rich booty back to his strong domains. He flew from fort to fort, from one temple to another, robbed them of their treasures, demolished their strongholds, put the inhabitants under tribute, while, like a fiery meteor, he rolled his terrific car onward. Delhi fell before him; the beautiful valley of Cashmere yielded to the invading spears of the conqueror, and city after city opened their gates to the fierce Moslem. At the head of an immense army of his favorite Tartars, he attacked Kanouge, one of the most renowned capitals of India. Oriental writers give the most glowing and extravagant account of the wealth, the splendor, and luxury of this ancient city. It could present no effectual resistance to the Afghan bands of Mahmoud; yet, after three days, he was prepared for new prey. Having conquered several other places on the Ganges, where he now was, he heard of the wealth and fame of the holy city of Muttra, situated on the Jumna. Thither he turned his victorious spears, and, with little opposition, he found its treasures at his feet. Its temples, more splendid than he had yet seen, were filled with gigantic idols of pure gold, having eyes of rubies, and one had in it a sapphire of enormous size. Besides these, there were found, says Ferishta, one hundred idols of silver, which loaded a hundred camels with bullion.

The last and most celebrated expedition which Mahmoud made into India, was undertaken in the year 1024. He now directed his arms towards the rich and fertile country of Guzerat. The object toward which his avarice and ambition was now turned, was the famous temple of Samnaut, on the shore of the Indian Ocean. This was the richest shrine in India; and so strongly fortified, and so stoutly defended was it, that it nearly cost the conqueror a complete defeat. The details possess much interest, but cannot be given at length.

Never had the brave Tartar contested a battle so severely. He fought two days, but without success. The attack was renewed on the third, and now were the Moslems near being overpowered, when Mahmoud, in person, appealed to the religious zeal of his troops, leaped from his horse in the midst of the conflict, and implored, on his knees, aid from heaven in his attempt to destroy the infidels, and earnestly called on his chiefs to advance to martyrdom or conquest. The victory was theirs; and soon the brave Tartar stood before the giant god, beating him to pieces with his own hands. The Brahmuns at this moment rushed forward with a petition, backed with several crores (tens of millions) of rupees, that he would desist. But the idol, he said, was his, and he chose rather to be a *breaker* than a *seller* of idols. The next blow he struck opened the interior of the image, which, to his astonishment, had been left hollow, that it might serve as the secret depository of the wealth of the temple. Out poured pearls, rubies, and diamonds, to an amount far exceeding in value the sum offered for its preservation.

Such was the introduction of Mohammedanism and of the Mohammedan powers in India. They came, they saw, they conquered. Nothing in modern times has equaled the ferocity and desperation of the first Mohammedan conquests in India. Urged on by a mad enthusiasm, intoxicated with the hope of rich booty, and inspired with the promise of beatitude in pardise, if they died fighting with infidels, they pounced like tigers on their prey. A fertile country was left desolate; flourishing cities, heaps of ruins; and rivers, sacred to their fathers, flowed with the blood of their countrymen; palaces were burnt, temples pillaged, and the public works of ages destroyed in a day. Suffice it to say, the Moslems were soon the lords of the land, and despots over the unoffending Hindoos. The mosque was reared on the ruins of the temple; the crescent waved in the place of well-known banners of their native land; Islamism became their national religion, and the only road to place and preferment. The Hindoos from this hour became bondmen and slaves to foreign masters. Their chains have been riveted on them, by a succession of conquerors, till freedom, patriotism, and national virtue have quite disappeared from the land. But all the calamities which were so unsparingly inflicted by the infuriated zeal of the Moslems, was but the beginning of sorrow to the devoted Hindoo. These were but the commencement of a series of wars and rapines, which were to lay waste the land, impoverish the country, and drive to the verge of desperation a once prosperous and comparatively happy people. The carcass had begun to be torn, and now new flights of birds of prey and passage were attracted from the west. Soon they were seen hovering over their prey. The Portuguese, the Dutch, the French, and the English have all in their turn satiated their rapacity on the unoffending natives of India.

Mahmoud dies—but not so the Mohammedan power in India. The Ghiznian Empire falls into decay, or, rather, is transferred to the east of the Indus, where it struck deeper its roots and spread wider its branches. Delhi became the seat of empire, and for seven centuries remained the capital of Moslem power in Hindoostan.

The work of conquest went on, kings were made and unmade, rebellions rose and were quelled, new territories in Bengal and the Deckan were acquired, and all the vicissitudes of a great empire transpiring; but we must pass these in silence.

The conquest of the Deckan, or southern portion of Hindoostan, and the establishment there of Mohammedan power, is too characteristic of the times, and the conquerors, and of their government, not to be allowed a passing notice.

The Moslems first turned their hostile spears towards the Deckan in the year 1292, led on by the brave Alla, nephew of the emperor. Hitherto the Deckan had suffered little from their northern invaders. It had enjoyed an independent government, the capital of which was Deoghire, now known as Dawlatabad, which means the depository of riches. This is an immensely stronghold, on the top of a hill several hundred feet high, the only entrance to which is by an underground passage, excavated in the solid rock, and secured at different distances by iron gates, in the inside of which were kept in readiness large piles of dried fuel, that, in case of the approach of an enemy, the wood might be piled against the gates and fired, and the assailants given a *warm* reception.

Ramdeo was, at the time of the invasion, the reigning prince. The character of the contending parties, the wealth and weakness of the Hindoos, and the rapaciousness and cruelty of the Mohammedans, are too strongly marked in this invasion not to be noticed.

The arms of the Mohammedans had now for more than two centuries been victorious in Hindoostan. The terror of their approach struck a panic in every heart. The rumor of an advancing army reached the capital of Ramdeo, and Alla, with a numerous host, was besieging the supposed impregnable fortress. Resistance was vain, and the panic-struck prince offered terms. Alla accepts fifty maunds of pure gold, a large quantity of pearls and jewels, fifty elephants, and one thousand horses. On these conditions he retreats. But the son of Ramdeo, returning at this time with an army to the capital, attacks the retreating foe, without the order or knowledge of his father. Enraged at this supposed perfidy, the Tartars give battle to the idolaters, disperse them with great slaughter, and will not now stay the work of destruction, or spare the kingdom, but on the following almost incredible conditions: That Alla should receive, on evacuating the country, six hundred maunds of pure gold, seven maunds of pearls, two maunds of diamonds, rubies, emeralds and sapphires; a thousand maunds of silver, four thousand pieces of silk, and a long list of other precious commodities, which surpass all belief, together with the cession of Elichpoor and its dependencies. Laden with this rich booty, Alla returned, murdered his emperor, Ferose II., who had come to pay him a friendly visit, and assumed the royal umbrella.

Here I must be indulged in a short digression, for the sake of delineating more fully the character of this extraordinary man.

Alla mounts the throne of Delhi in 1295; is twice invaded by the Moguls; meets them with an army of 300,000 horse and 2700 elephants; repulses them with great slaughter; forms the plan of establishing a new religion, that, by a union of Mohammedanism and idolatry, it might be made universal. He also devises a scheme for universal conquest and empire; but is dissuaded from both these visionary plans by the sage Alla ul Muluck. When he mounted the throne, he could neither read nor write; yet he was the constant and beneficent friend of literature and science, patronized men of letters, and, while on the imperial throne of the East, himself took lessons in the first elements of learning.

Becoming alarmed for the stability of his vast empire, on account of frequent conspiracies and insurrections, he demanded of his Omrahs (nobles) the cause of the prevailing disorders. They declared that they believed the public use of wine and strong drink—which had, contrary to the religious practice of Moslems, been introduced among the rulers and people—to be the fruitful source of these disorders; "for," said they, "when men form themselves into societies, for the purpose of drinking, their minds are disclosed to one another, while the strength of the liquor, fermenting their blood, precipitates them into the most desperate undertakings." He then published an edict against the use of wine and strong liquors, upon pain of death. He himself set the example to his subjects, and emptied his cellars into the streets. In this, says the historian, he was followed by all ranks of people, so that for some days the common sewers flowed with wine. He endeavored to equalize property by laying taxes on the rich. His pomp, wealth, and power was never equaled by any prince in Hindoostan; his household servants were 17,000. In one day he massacred in the streets of Delhi 15,000 Mogul slaves. He is, perhaps, but a fair specimen of the first conquerors of India. Their character presents an extraordinary compound of the brave, the savage, the noble, the cruel, the generous, the avaricious, the devout, the profane.

Now follow a succession of emperors, who make some con-

TAMERLANE.

quests—suppress rebellions—build palaces and mosques—found cities and overthrow those that others have founded—die by assassination; and their successors, as perhaps they did, wade to the throne through the blood of rival brothers and kindred.

The Patan or Afghan Empire prospered, with such vicissitudes of fortune as all despotisms are subject to, until the year 1397, when it encountered one of those mighty convulsions which shake empires to their foundation, and, perhaps, out of their ruins erect others more powerful and magnificent. I refer to the conquest of India by *Timour Bey*, more familiarly known by the name of Tamerlane.

The Moslem throne had trembled at the passing by of the conquering car of *Ghengis Khan*, more than a century and a half before. That fearful destroyer, who had extended his empire from China to the centre of Europe, was too intent on other prey to seize on India. His power was felt, but rather as a reflex influence than in its direct terror. The waters of all Asia were disturbed, yet India only felt the power of the receding wave.

But not so with Tamerlane. Of the same Mogul stock, and a remote descendant of Ghengis, he rose from a small beginning till he aspired to nothing short of universal empire. Having subjugated a great part of Asia, and spread the terror of his name to the ends of the earth, he made his fearful descent on Hindoostan in the year 1397. This invasion seems to have been wholly unprovoked, and undertaken for no other purpose than a love of conquest. Wherever he came on his route, his march was marked with devastation and blood. Having captured, on his way to Delhi, the city and fort of Batnier, he ordered the execution of 500 of the principal captives, and committed such atrocities as to drive the Hindoos into a frenzy of desperation. They set fire to the fortress over their own heads, killed their own wives and children, then rushed forth on their besiegers, to sell their lives as dear as possible. Every individual perished; yet not till thousands of the Moguls had fallen by their hands. This so exasperated Tamerlane, that he ordered the general massacre of the whole population.

He now prepared for the grand design of his invasion—the capture of Delhi. All was terror before him; all was devastation behind him. Finding himself encumbered with an enormous multitude of captives, he issued the bloody mandate for a general butchery, and 100,000 were put to death at a single time.

Delhi fell before him. The emperor, after a weak and ineffectual resistance, fled to Guzerat, and Timour remained master of his capital. The city was given up to a general pillage; and to such desperation were the inhabitants of this great and rich metropolis driven, that, having dispatched their wives and children, they rushed on the deadly spears of the foe. The streets of Delhi streamed with blood; and the unresisting natives were doomed to death, or a miserable captivity.

Thus rolled this burning meteor over India, spreading consternation and ruin on every side, till intelligence reached him of the movements of the Sultan of the Ottoman Empire against him, when he recrossed the Indus, and hastened to other prey.

It is not a little remarkable that this great conqueror was at no pains to secure his vast conquest. He established no dominion in India; and his whole vast empire, embracing nearly all of Asia, was soon dissolved into its original elements. In the mean time, India was restoring itself from the terrible shock of the Mogul; and its government revived again at Delhi in the hands of the same dynasty.

Though Mogul power had been so awfully exemplified, yet no Mogul sat on the throne of India for nearly 200 years. The first was a lineal descendant of Timour, of the fifth generation, by the name of *Baber*. Oriental history scarcely presents a character of so varied fortune, or thrilling interest. From being the petty prince of a small mountain territory, he became master of a great part of Asia, and finally, by the force of his arms, seated himself on the throne of Delhi, in the year 1525. Here commenced the empire of the *Great Moguls*, which existed in all its oriental magnificence till undermined and diminished, and finally overthrown, by the irresistible conquests of the British rulers of India.

BABER.

ACBUR.

They were an illustrious line of emperors—some for war and conquest—some for the erection of palaces and public buildings—some for the promotion of learning and good government. One distinguished his reign by extending a road for travelers from the Ganges to the Indus—a distance of 3000 miles. It was bordered by fruit trees on either side, supplied with caravansaries at every stage, and with a well of water every two miles; and travelers were accommodated at public expense.

Acbur, who received, and, more than any one perhaps that ever mounted the throne of Delhi, deserved, the name of "Great," commenced a prosperous reign of fifty-one years in the year 1556. His reign is spoken of as marked with much justice and lenity. A scholar himself, he patronized learned men at his court. Having heard of the introduction into the southern part of India of a new religion called Christianity, he expressed a wish to be made acquainted with it, and accordingly three missionaries were requested to come from Goa to the Mogul court for this purpose. The emperor received them with all honor—treated them courteously—examined their books, which, by his request, they had brought—entertained them for fifteen years, and gave them full permission to hold public controversy with the Mollahs or Mohammedan doctors. Though he did not answer the hopes at first raised, that he might embrace the new religion, yet, in two other instances, he renewed his request for Christian missionaries to reside at his court. They did little more than, at each time, to present him with a splendid cross and the image of their lady.

Prince Selim, the son of Acbur, succeeded to the throne, with the high-sounding title of *Jehanghire*, or *conqueror of the world.* Jehanghire commenced his reign in crime. His affections had been engaged in behalf of a young Tartar girl, whom his noble father had refused him, because she was betrothed to another. She was the daughter of poor, though noble, parents; born in a lonely desert, as they were on their way from Tartary to seek their fortune in Hindoostan. The family had risen, were introduced at court, and now sharing the royal favor. No sooner had Selim become Jehanghire, than he adopted the most barbarous measures to persecute unto death the noble spouse of this beautiful flower of the desert. The gallant officer, now her husband, fell, after many a noble fight, by the hand of forty armed ruffians, and Mher ul Nissa (the sun of women), or Noor Mahal, as afterward called, was borne in triumph to the emperor. She finally became a favorite queen of the emperor, ruled him and his empire for more than a quarter of a century, and was the most extraordinary woman ever known in Asia.

The story is long and captivating, and in some of its incidents more like a fairy tale than a reality in human life. But my limits are too narrow for its detail.

This reign was also distinguished by the arrival of the first English embassadors to negotiate the opening of a trade with India, which was the entering wedge to that extensive commerce and stupendous empire which now spreads over the whole of Hindoostan.

During the reign of Jehanghire, the Deckan remained his tributary—half subdued, half independent, but always rebellious. The complete subjugation of the country, however, was left for that extraordinary character in Indian history, Aurungzebe. He, the last of his illustrious race, was the "Great Mogul," who sat on the throne of Delhi when the "East India Company" commenced their career in Hindoostan, and who is so often mentioned in the early history of British India. He was the great-grandson of Acbur, and the son and successor of the emperor Shah Jehan. He is known, also, in history, by the title of Allumghire, conqueror of the world.* He is, as I said, called great; and so he was—great in war, great in council, great in his pretensions to devotion, great in wading through the blood of his family to the throne, and greatest of all in duplicity, dissimulation and hypocrisy. He commenced his public career, when only thirteen years old, as viceroy of the Deckan, under Shah Jehan,

* Shah Jehan means king of the world—Jehanghire, lord of the world. Ornament of the world, sun of women, light of the seraglio, are terms of respect applied to honorable females.

his father. The different provinces were now subdued, and brought under a more complete subjection than had been done in any former reign. The capital was, in 1634, transferred from Dawlatabad to the neighboring town of Gurka, which, becoming the favorite residence of Aurungzebe, during his viceroyalty in the Deckan, received the name of Aurungabad.

During the long and prosperous reign of Aurungzebe at Delhi, which continued fifty years, and concluded with his death in 1707, the Deckan remained a province of his vast empire. A formidable power was now rising in western India, which, during the last years of his reign, occupied all his resources, and could only be kept in check by his extraordinary mind. The Mahrathas, a people comparatively of recent origin, and known only as pirates on the coast, or marauding tribes in the interior, gave him great trouble. Although overawed till the death of Aurungzebe, they then seized on most of the southern portions of his dominions, and set up a new empire in the western provinces of the Deckan. Nizam ul Muluck took the eastern portion, which is still held by his successors.

Sewajee, a name well known in Indian history, was the first who consolidated the Mahratha empire, by combining the efforts of the different military and predatory chiefs. He was born in 1626, and died in 1680. The Mahrathas very soon became possessed of the most formidable empire in India. In the year 1740, we find them in possession of the whole of the Deckan, and of the south of India. Their dominions, eastward, were bounded by the sea, and stretched north and south from Agra to Cape Comorin. They had ransacked and burnt Delhi, the capital of the Mogul Empire. The conquests of the Mahrathas were of the worst possible character. They never lost their predatory habits. They acted the part of robbers — not of conquerors — who overcame, not to aggrandize themselves by possession, but to enrich themselves by plunder. They swept over the country like devouring locusts; they conquered, massacred, plundered, burnt, and only left behind them the most dreary desolation. Their empire, though for sometime formidable, and at different periods extensive, continued to wane till its final overthow by the English, in 1817.

I have given only the outlines of a history, which it would require some volumes to fill up. But this is sufficient for my present purpose. The predatory spirit of the Mahrathas is now broken. They are a peaceable, inoffensive people. Though many of the chiefs of their tribes are still living, and possessed of their hereditary estates, there seems no apprehension of a revolt. The people in general are extremely poor. The cultivators are hard working and industrious, and appear to be possessed of some integrity. Still, indolence, the hereditary disease of the Hindoo, characterizes the majority of the people. The higher orders of the people are daily sinking in importance. Their hereditary possessions are wasting away without the hope of recovery. The Brahmuns are struggling to maintain their superiority, but in vain. Blind as the people are to their gross impositions, and corrupt as is the character of their priests, and slow as the multitude are to learn from foreigners a lesson which they ought to have known long ago without teaching, they seem not unlikely to be compelled, by their poverty, and the many ills which they suffer, to throw off a yoke which has galled their race from time immemorial. The Brahmuns in their turn complain of the degeneracy of the times, and long for, but despair of, the return of that "golden age" when the poor Hindoo thought it an honor to kiss the dust of his feet, and would not pass him without an offering. If craftiness, address and consummate management could extort money, (where one would suppose none was to be had,) the Brahmun might still be pampered on the hard-earned pittance of the poor; or if pride, and high pretensions to sanctity, and unblushing claims to divinity, could insure the respect and adoration of the unthinking multitude, the Brahmun would not fail to bo honored and adored, as he was wont to be in the golden age. God grant that the unhallowed spell may soon be broken—that the pride of the one, and the blind superstition of the other, may be forgotten in that universal benevolence, which breathes peace and good will to all.

Of the European nations who have shared in the plunder of India, and who have, and who still hold possessions there, the English are by far the most prominent. The power of the other European nations has long since been on the wane, and is now reduced to the government of a few small provinces. I avoid entering into any detail of the *means* which have been adopted by these several nations to gain possessions in India. The history "of their unparalleled crimes, violated treaties, bloodshed, treachery and devastation," will stand recorded in the book of God's unerring memory, and cannot fail to be made manifest in the day of divine retribution.

The dominion of the English extends from the Indus to China, and from the Himalaya mountains to Cape Comorin. Within these extended boundaries, there are, it is true, several nations who fancy themselves independent, and they are said to be so. Some of these are termed allies, some independent, and others dependent states. But they differ very little, except in name, and in the degree of their dependence. They are directly or indirectly subservient to the East India Company. Let them but *act* as if they *were* independent states, and they would soon awake from their pleasant delusion. We have a specimen of their real condition in the case of the Rajah of Sattara.* He fancies himself an independent prince; has an English *Resident* placed at his capital; is required to keep up a specified military force, to be *officered* by Englishmen. This is what is called a subsidized force. The same is to be found among all the *independent* princes of India. The policy on the part of the invaders, in imposing on their dependents this subsidized force, is a consummate piece of worldly wisdom, and is well understood by the English. In this way they virtually secure the army of those who might become their opponents. They secure the patronage for the most lucrative offices in these states, which, in England, is so highly valued, as to make this one of the greatest advantages

*He has since been deposed, and has followed Barjee Row on his pilgrimage to Benares.

derived from their Eastern possessions. By allowing these states, many of which are not fertile, and but sparsely peopled, to govern themselves, they derive more advantages than they would be likely to realize were they to assume the reins of government over them. The Rajah of Sattara is not allowed to go out of his own capital, or to see an Englishman, not even an officer of his own army, if he be an Englishman, without permission from the Resident. The truth is, these princes only retain the shadow of power; and this will vanish when the interest or the will of the East India Company shall require it. The Residents are kings; the princes are vassals.

The possessions of the English, in India, are more extensive than is generally supposed. Their dominion, in the manner I have described, embraces a population of about one hundred and fifty millions. Their vast territories have, heretofore, been divided into three portions, called Presidencies, viz: Bengal, Madras and Bombay. A new Presidency has recently been added, in the north of India, the capital of which is Agra. Each of these has its governor. The Governor of Bengal is the Governor-General of all India; and the other governors are subordinate to him. He enjoys an income, and supports a state dignity, scarcely inferior to that of the king of England. His palace, in external appearance at least, far surpasses St. James' in London, and is not inferior to the new palace. All the heads of government are princes; and Calcutta, the capital of all India, is well named the City of Palaces. The revenue of India, which is enormous, and which burdens the poor natives beyond any thing which they can much longer endure, is said to be inadequate to the expenses of government. The soil is the immediate property of the government, which the people cultivate as vassals.

A vast army is, of course, required to insure the peaceful possession of such a country. The majority of the soldiers are Sepoys, enlisted in the country, disciplined in European tactics, and invariably officered by Englishmen. No native is allowed to hold any office of trust, or of much profit. The military force is diffused over the whole country. Every stronghold is secured, and every large town, or other important place, is garrisoned. Hence, in whatever part of India we go, we meet with people of our own color and language, in different ranks of life, but all connected with the government. We find, at every important military station, Christian churches and chaplains, and nominal Christians, and a few real Christians. We also find, in these insulated spots, which are like little smiling islands in the midst of the dark ocean, comfortable and elegant houses, beautiful gardens, refined and intelligent gentlemen and ladies, European markets, roads, bridges, carriages, and all that goes to make up the comforts and elegancies of life. What a contrast between the conquerors and the conquered!

An important acquisition, which the English made in India, was that of the Mahratha country, in the Deckan. This was done in the year 1818. The prince of the Mahratha states being in his minority, the government was administered by the Peshwa, (prime minister.) The Peshwa had confined the young prince in the fort at Sattara, under the pretext that he was *non compos mentis;* and had assumed the reins of government himself. It is unnecessary to detail the causes that led to the war which terminated in the subjugation of those states to the British rule, and sent Barjee Row, the Peshwa, on a long pilgrimage to the holy city of Benares, with a pension of 800,000 rupees a year! Barjee Row no doubt deserved, on account of the infamous course of policy which he adopted, both towards the English and native governments, a severe chastisement. But whether the English were right in judging that his misrule and his treachery afforded a just ground for them to substitute what *they* thought a better form of government, I leave for the politician to decide. The fact is before us, that they did it; and in this conquest, added another large tract of territory to their already overgrown possessions, and again replenished their coffers with the wealth of the Peshwa. But in this, as in all their conquests, there is a semblance of virtue and justice. They espoused the cause of the rightful heir to the throne, and put down the usurper. But what did they do with the usurper? and what with the lawful heir of the Mahratha states? The former they sent to Benares, the holy city of all India, with a rich pension of 800,000 rupees ($400,000) a year; and to the latter they gave Sattara, his former prison, with a small province adjacent. Here for a time he wore the crown, while another wielded the sceptre.

The famous NENA SAHIB is none other than the adopted son of the Peshwa; at the death of whom, he claimed the pension of the Peshwa. The refusal on the part of the East India Government to continue it to the claimant is, no doubt, the chief grievance which has for years been festering in the mind of this prostrate prince, till it has at length burst forth in deeds of revenge and savage cruelty unparalleled in the annals of history.

CHAPTER III.

Modern India — India of the last century — Conquest of the English — English Policy, and the Unchristian Character of the English Government—India of 1857–8 —The Mutiny of the Mutineers.

ALL eyes are, at the present moment, again anxiously turned towards the great East. There the mighty hand that rules the world, is signally at work. India and China, the two great Oriental nations, are again in commotion, presaging revolution and change. Events are now transpiring there, the recital of which fills us with horror, and quite puts at fault all our preconceived notions of the designs and workings of Providence. We have been wont, admiringly, to follow the stately steppings of the great controlling power, in the singular progress of advancement, in that wonderful country, from its discovery by De Gama, around the Cape of Good Hope, to its present prosperous and (as we had supposed) consolidated condition of the British Empire; and to mark, from step to step, the rise and fall of one empire after another, until the great civilizing race, the Anglo-Saxon stock, came; and with the religion, science, arts and institutions, which elevate, enlighten and purify, seemed to have obtained a peaceful and permanent possession.

But how soon is all human sagacity staggered! We stand amazed at the dreadful developments of the present hour! They seem to contradict all our pleasing anticipations, that that great and idolatrous land, which we had seen so strangely transferred, first from Pagan to Mohammedan rule, then from Mohammedan to the Christian faith, should speedily be numbered among the nations that belong to Immanuel, and rejoice in the light of the Sun of Righteousness! A dark cloud has risen! The tempest of war has broken, with dreadful violence, on that ancient land!

The English had subjected to their rule nearly all those extensive and rich, populous and superstitious lands; had opened wide the door for the ingress of western civilization, learning and religion; had given full protection to the missionary of every name, and seemed to hold out an undoubted promise that those dark realms of idolatry, and those sickly regions of the crescent, would soon be illumined by the Sun of Righteousness. The Morning Star had risen, and we rejoiced in songs of victory over the supposed downfall of the last stronghold of idolatry. What, then, is this strange sound that reaches our ears? It is the sound of war! The standard of rebellion has been raised! A "mutiny!" the most violent, atrocious and bloody, has suddenly broken out among the native soldiery; and English officers, and civilians, their wives and their children, are made the victims of the most unrelenting and shameless cruelty. The tortures, maiming, scalping, flaying alive, murdering by piece meal, and brutalities innumerable, which are indiscriminately practiced on every class of Europeans, surpass all description. We are astonished at the strange fertility of conception which has given birth to such monstrous atrocities. The North American Indians were mere tyros in the infernal arts of torture and shameless barbarity, compared with these Indians of the East. But I will reserve details for another part of this chapter, that I may speak of India as she has appeared since the first introduction of Christianity, and especially in the part she has played in the drama of the last hundred years.

The discovery of a passage to India by the Cape of Good Hope, began a new era in the history of the East. The Portuguese soon began to acquire territory, and to exercise dominion over the nations; and they shortly found themselves in possession of all India, and of nearly all southern Asia, from the Red Sea to the Chinese Ocean. They took possession in the name of the Pontifex Maximus of Rome. Thus more than one-half of the population of the globe, and a yet larger proportion of the wealth and civilization and civil power of the world, passed into the hands of this power.

But this magnificent empire soon passed away. In less than a century its glory had departed; and the Dutch, and the French, in turn, became its successor. As late as the middle of the last century, so strong had the power of the French become in India, that an Indo-French empire seemed not improbable, but no one would have then dreamed of an Indo-English empire.

Previous to this period, a few English merchants and adventurers had asked a little land on the Hoogly river, where they might deposit their merchandise, as collected from the natives, and thence ship it to England. Then they needed a few Sepoys to protect their persons, premises and property. This the reigning prince granted. But they required a little more land and a few more Sepoys; and as difficulties arose with their neighbors, or depredations were committed by lawless bands, they applied for further protection and more room. Native princes at length became jealous and troublesome neighbors; and now they required a *few more* Sepoys, in order to help themselves to a little more territory, until the rich and vast empire of the Great Mogul was dismembered, and piece-meal fell into the hands of the English. And thus it has been, only by increasing a large army by a few more Sepoys, and annexing to their already extensive dominions a *little more*, that they have subjected all India to their sway.

Much of India's history is told, in a few words, in the following paragraph, cut from the Albany Journal:

"India is a country that has never belonged to its natives. Two thousand years ago Alexander and his Greeks led dusky captives in golden fetters from them to Athens. After him it became the prize of Parthian bows and Scythian spears. Then came Mohammed and his Persians from Ghuznee, to teach, by scimitar, the new theology, "Allah il Allah, and Mohammed is his Prophet." Then the Afghans drove out the Persians. Then the Tartars drove out the Afghans. Then came Timour, the terrible Tartar, and the long and princely line of Great Moguls—Baber and Acbur, Jehanghire and Aurungzebe. The Mogul Empire got, like the British, too big to hold together. Down went the throne at Delhi, and up sprang a crop of viceroys, nizams, kings, shahs, rajahs, newaubs and nabobs, all over the provinces. About this time H. B. M. East India Company came to trade, and stayed to rule. By cajoling one prince, threatening another, invading a third, and 'protecting' a fourth, they got the whole concern into the hands of John Bull, and the lion and the unicorn. If the Sepoys succeed in securing a native Hindoo dynasty now, it will be the first they ever had."

Occasions for war were never wanting. A native prince became troublesome, and he must be put out of the way, and his territory be annexed to the conquering power; or a prince already in alliance becomes refractory, and he must be humbled; or there is misrule or oppression, or usurpation of one native ruler against another, and the English must, in mercy or justice, interfere and set all at rights. If the strong oppress the weak, the English must, forsooth, become the arbiter; and not the quiet arbiter only. They must interpose their powerful arm, and rebuke the wrong-doer by espousing the cause of the one reputed to be right. The result of these rectifying processes—more or less plausible—has usually been that the English have taken to themselves the lion's share. And thus their rule had become undisputed over nearly all the nations between the river Indus and the Burampootra, and Cape Comorin and the Himalaya mountains. So completely subjugated had all these tribes and nations become, and so apparently submissive and satisfied, that we supposed an insurrection scarcely possible.

But in order that we may obtain any thing like a just appreciation of the character of the present difficulties in India, we need to call up something, at least, of the history of English conquests and dominion in that country. We will open to the records of less than a century ago, and see what the faithful historian has recorded of the doings of his countrymen in that very land. And if it shall appear that they have been "replenished from the east," without having made any adequate return, such as the most obvious dictates of justice would imply that a great and Christian nation should make towards a nation of idolators; if they have held and governed, without let or hindrance, a nation of 150,000,000 of souls, without scarcely making it manifest that they are themselves a Christian people, without scarcely leaving a monument of their own superior advancement and philanthropy behind them, should they be driven from India to-day; and especially if, in their early conquests, they committed wrongs, oppressions and atrocities scarcely, if at all, less barbarous and appalling, and less disgraceful to humanity, than those which do at the present time appall the very heart of barbarism itself, we shall cease to wonder that the great and just One, who "requites" nations, as well as societies and individuals, for all wrong-doing, "according as they have done," should suffer such things to be. Wherever there be oppression, there will sooner or later be retribution. There is no attribute in the God-head that can finally favor the oppressor.

What right had England in India? How came she there? By what means, and for what reasons, did she conquer that country, and why has she for so long a time held possession of it? And what does the faithful page of history declare to be the real character of her conquests? Does not the voice of blood, unrighteously and inhumanly shed—does not the cry of oppression and wrong go up into the ear of Him who avengeth all wrong-doing?

But we would gladly be spared from any such allusions. We cannot reply to such queries without seeming censoriousness on a nation which we would only honor. But it is the English historian that has left the fatal facts on record. Yet we are not ignorant of the great providential mission which the exercise of British rule in India has been made to fulfill. We thank God, and honor that government for it. It is only as British power has weakened, if not demolished, the formidable bulwarks of Brahminical idolatry, that a wide and effectual door has been opened for the introduction of the Gospel; it is only as the same strong arm has been extended over them, that modern missions have been established there and proved so abundantly successful. Education, science and European civilization have been extensively introduced; a better form of government has been established among the abject tribes of Hindoostan than had ever been known there. And more than all, an infinitely better type of religion had followed in the wake of those conquests than had ever blessed that land of idols before. From the beginning there have been delightful specimens of vital piety among the English residents in that country; though during the earlier periods of the English there, it must be confessed, such examples were like angels' visits. During the last half century, there has been a gradual and decided advance in the character of the Christianity of English residents. There now greet you, in every part of the land, chaplains and churches, missionaries and their schools, presses, churches and convents, and you no where meet more delightful specimens of enlarged and liberal piety.

There is, indeed, a providential phase of the history of British India that is truly admirable; yet there is another phase which is neither admirable nor innocent. But it is this aspect of Indian affairs which we must bear in mind if we would understand the true character of the dreadful insurrection which has recently broken out in that country. It is, on the part of the Sepoys, a war of retaliation and revenge—a desperate attempt to throw off a yoke which had from the beginning galled them to the quick.

We are shocked, we stand amazed at the savage character of the warfare now waged by the natives of India against their European rulers. We were altogether unprepared to hear of such atrocities in the nineteenth century; and least of all did we expect that such rare exhibitions of wanton ferocity should be perpetrated by a people so servile and harmless as the Hindoos of the present generation appeared to be. But the dreadful problem seems to find a solution the moment we recur to the early history of British India. God is just; and as a people do, so he will requite them. Thinking men in England, at the present hour, are not slow to see, and are frank to acknowledge, the retributive character of the present horrible warfare in Hindoostan. The Sepoys are but the faithful pupils of their British teachers. The appalling cruelties which the latter are suffering, are awfully similar to the wrongs which their ancestors suffered from the hands of their conquerors.

No one can read the following paragraphs without being painfully struck with the fact, that the refined tortures, which the English have recently suffered, are but the repetition of cruelties which they themselves have been inflicting, for many long and bitter years, upon the victims of their oppression in India; till at last, in their feebleness and extremity, and in the mingled aggravation of human vindictiveness and religious fanaticism, they have turned, with dying desperation, upon their rulers, to throw off the yoke from their necks, or to perish, as they will, in the struggle.

We first quote from the British Standard, edited by the Rev. Dr. Campbell, a distinguished clergyman of London: "Let it never be forgotten, that, in the terrible events which have recently transpired in the East, the English have been the tutors, and the Sepoys the pupils; they have only been exemplifying the lessons taught their fathers and themselves. The difference is simply one of circumstances; the public eye is intently fixed on their doings, while their reasons are concealed. On the strength of history, however, we assert that nothing has, on the present occasion, been done by the mutinous troops that cannot be paralleled, if not exceeded, from the history of England's career in Hindoostan. One of the most noted events of the hour, for its treacherous wickedness, has found a parallel in England's treatment of the Rajah of Bengal."

"The fort was surrendered on express stipulation for the safety, and freedom from search, of the females; but, adds Mills, 'the idea suggested by Mr. Hastings diffused itself but too perfectly amongst the soldiery; and when the princesses, with their relatives and attendants, to the number of three hundred women, besides children, withdrew from the castle, the capitulation was shamefully violated. They were plundered of their effects, and their persons otherwise rudely and disgracefully treated by the licentious people, and officers of the camp.'"

Again, as to modes of raising money, Mr. Patterson, the Company's own commissioner, says: "Those who could not raise the money demanded were most cruelly tortured; cords were drawn tight round their fingers, till the flesh of the four, on each hand, was actually incorporated, and became one solid mass. The fingers were then reparted by wedges of iron and wood driven in between them. Others were tied, two by two, by the feet, and thrown across a wooden bar, upon which they hung with their feet uppermost. They were then beaten on the soles of their feet, with dreadful torture. They were afterwards beat about the head till the blood gushed out at the mouth, nose, and ears. They were often flogged on the naked body with bamboo canes and prickly cactus; above all, with some poisonous weeds, which were of a caustic nature and burnt at every lash."

But what of the treatment of females, as this is the most aggravated feature in the present instance? The commissioner shall again answer:

"The treatment of the females could not be described. Dragged from the inmost recesses of their cells, which the religion of the country had made so many sanctuaries, they were exposed

4

naked to public view. The virgins were carried to the court of justice, where they might naturally have looked for protection, but they now looked for it in vain; for in the face of the ministers of justice, in the face of the spectators, in the face of the sun, these tender and modest virgins were brutally violated. The only difference between their treatment and that of their mothers was, that the former were dishonored in the face of day, the latter in the gloomy recesses of their dungeon."

And, as if this were not enough, the same writer says: "These females had the nipples of their breasts put into cleft bamboos and torn out!"

"What follows," remarks Mr. William Howitt, as he is commenting on such appalling cruelties, "is too shocking and indecent to describe! It is almost impossible, in reading of such frightful and savage enormities, to believe that we are reading of a country under the British Government, and that these unmanly deeds were perpetrated by British agents, and for the purpose of extorting the British revenue."

Another gentleman, for a long time resident in India, speaking of other abuses of British power, says: "I have known respectable officers tied up and flogged before the whole regiment, and then dismissed without any sort of inquiry. They did complain, but the commanding officer was related to Lord Dalhousie, and, of course, there was no redress; one was named Hyder Khan, and his brother, Gaffer Khan, died gloriously at Khalat. Nor are the miserable ryots better off. Their sufferings, their poverty, their degradation, are a matter of public notoriety, and at the bottom of this, as of all disasters attending our Indian rule, is corruption, and again corruption. Corruption in the native officers and agents, encouraged and turned to profit by the European servants of the Company; corruption again among these, winked at by the government at home."

Were not these the language of British gentlemen, who know what they affirm, we should not dare to quote them. It would seem invidious. But if the remembrance of such wrongs has been festering in the breasts of that people, we cannot wonder at the present outbreak. The tortures and shameless brutalities which the victims of the present insurrection are made to suffer, are in revenge for similar outrages committed by them in their former warfares. We open the well accredited "History of British India," by the Hon. Hugh Murray, and meet details, incidentally related, which fully confirm all I have intimated. We find, at an early period of this history, a mission sent out to India "to put an end to the exactions of presents by British officers, who had enriched themselves at the expense of the native powers."*

The nefarious schemes by which the celebrated Warren Hastings (then Governor-General of India) adopted to increase the revenue of his government, and to enable him to prosecute his wars against the native princes, are but too much of a piece with the general policy pursued by the local government, and winked at, if not approved, by the government at home. The great Mogul, after being dethroned and driven from the capital of his great empire, is assigned, under governmental protection, the provinces of Corah and Allahabad. But the wily Governor-General soon finds a pretext to annul all obligations to this fallen prince, and to take possession of those provinces.

And here we must not overlook the significant fact, that these provinces (including Bengal, the seat of a misrule not less oppressive,) are, in awful retribution, now the theatre of the present most appalling scenes of massacre and desolation; while those parts of the country where the British church has done her duty, and Christian missions have fulfilled their benign office, have hitherto been kept, in a great measure, exempt.

The Rajah of Benares, after exactions had been made on him for money, which he could not and would not meet, was thrown into prison and his whole treasure seized. But these exactions, fraudulent and arbitrary as they were, were harmless and decent compared with the extortions which, under torture, drew from the Begums (the mother and grandmother of another prince) the sum of two and a half millions of dollars.

* Vol. i, pp. 278–82.

On his return to England, Hastings was impeached for frauds and treacheries the most gigantic. Burke, with Sheridan and Pitt, espoused the side of the prosecution. The great orator "opened the charge in a speech which lasted four days, in which he represented the conduct of Hastings as a compound of treachery and cruelty disgraceful to the British name, and almost without a parallel in the annals of history." Yet, after the most unheard of evasions, shifts, and delays, the ex-Governor-General was allowed to go unwhipped of justice.

But has not the policy of the British Government in India greatly changed for the better? Are not her servants there, the present rulers of the country, guided by more liberal and just principles? And is not that country at the present day better governed than it had been for eight centuries previous to the conquests of the English? All this we grant. Yet England, when weighed in the balances of a righteous Providence, is found wanting. God has committed to her, as a Christian nation, 150,000,000 of idolaters. He has given her a singular supremacy there; and had her rule in that country been such as became a great and Christian nation—had she used her unparalleled facilities for the civilization, education, and Christianization of those heathen nations, she would, undoubtedly, ere this, have been the honored instrument of the greatest political and moral revolution that has ever yet transpired in our world. India converted, and her 150,000,000 enclosed in the fold of Christianity, would have been sufficiently extraordinary of itself; but this would probably have been but the beginning of good things for all those great and populous nations of the East—the first great development of that noble Anglo-Saxon element, which, we trust, is yet destined to leaven the whole corrupt mass of orientalism. India once Christianized, and a great and independent Christian nation (the greatest in the world) once established there, and India, as an illustrious exemplification of what Christianity can do in renovating the great moral stagnations of the eastern world, and England as the noble agent in such a work, they would, unitedly, assume a position before the whole world the most commanding and influential. Persia, Burmah, Siam, and China, with her 360,000,000 of Pagans, and all the islands of the Indian Archipelago, would soon yield to British power and British benevolence; and soon Paganism and oriental despotism would be no more.

But England has betrayed her great and sacred trust. No nation ever had it in her power to do so great and good a work. Her mission was an illustrious one; and Providence had, in a most remarkable manner, furnished and adapted her to fulfill the mission we have supposed. But she has failed—and now her first great day of reckoning has come; yet we will not despair. When she shall have suffered the righteous judgments of her God—and in these judgments learned righteousness—when she shall be humbled, and repent, and expiate for the past, and be prepared to do her duty as a great Christian nation in time to come, she shall yet bear a conspicuous and a good part in the great revolutionary movements which seem destined soon to change the entire aspect of our world. In her, as the great and leading nation of Anglo-Saxondom, we trust, the sanguine hopes of the world shall yet be realized.

Had England discharged her high and holy responsibilities in India, and stood up in the face of all those nations as a Christian government, and instead of allowing and defending caste, and supporting idol temples and idol worship, and repudiating the Christian religion in the schools which she supports, and excluding the Bible from them, and the missionary from access to her native army, had she stood forth in her Christian character, she would have escaped the reproach of Christendom and the sore rebukes of heaven; she would have been spared the present crushing calamities, which have, like a thunderbolt, fallen upon her. Such an unwelcome conclusion we rather express in the words of one of her own writers. The London Times, looking at these events in the spirit of Christian statesmanship, utters the following high-toned and wholesome truths: "These startling events are a solemn rebuke from the God of providence for our national unfaithfulness in the use of unequaled opportunities for honoring the name of Christ, and promoting the temporal and spiritual welfare of one-sixth of the world's population. The crime on our part, so sternly rebuked, is not proselytism, but profaneness; not the god-like zeal of Christian missionaries, but the selfish blindness of mere money-getting men of the world. Where has this terrible revolt broken out, and under what circumstances? The people among whom the missionaries have labored, have given no visible signs of disaffection. The Madras Presidency, where alone whole districts have been Christianized, escapes, hitherto, scatheless, and the smell of fire has not passed upon it. The seat of the evil is the army of one Presidency alone. By the system of recruiting from high castes alone, that army has been like a government preserve of heathen bigotry. Among these Bengal Sepoys, heathenism is found concentrated and in fullest vigor. Once taken into the pay of the Indian government, they have been shielded from the slightest touch of missionary instruction.

"It is not then, be it observed, where missionary labors have told, that revolt has arisen. No, it is in the Bengal army, a government preserve of high caste Hindooism, where no missionaries, we believe, have ever been permitted to preach for a single hour, or to mitigate, by the gradual and gentle diffusion of Christian truth and morality, those violent prejudices, and that gross moral darkness which has been nursed under military discipline and supplied with Enfield rifles, so as to precipitate at last an explosion of religious excitement and national hatred, under which our Indian Empire, for a moment, rocks to its foundation."

But I have digressed. I had not finished the testimony of England's wrongs in India. To the testimony of the historian I must add that of late residents in that country. Mr. Gutherland, late judge at Surat, in a report to his government, Sept. 29th, 1838, says: "Indeed, the scenes that have been practiced beggar all description. Most vicious and immoral conduct appears to have been carried on in the confidence of security as to consequences; and I unhesitatingly affirm that the administration of civil justice in this place has been openly abused by designing men, to the deterioration of morals, the injury of every grade of the community in their property, while the actual damage done must be very great; bands of wicked men resort to the Adawlut to satisfy their base ends; the same evil means are resorted to to rebut claims as were used to advance them, and, I grieve to say, otherwise good men have often, in their own defense, been obliged to have recourse to them. Conspiracies against property have been conducted in an open manner, and regularly organized bodies existed, of forgers and persons who would swear falsely. This stain on the character of our administration I have used my utmost endeavors to put down; and were I not to do so, I should consider myself to be conniving at acts of wickedness. Cases are supported by forgery and perjury — crimes which, I grieve to say, have been prosecuted in as open a manner as the promotion of just claims by fair means. Thus the wicked practice upon the honest citizen without expense; the Zillah court, by such means, becomes debased to so low a state as to be literally an engine of tyranny and oppression."

This upright, humane, and patriotic testimony, says the Standard, from which we quote, produced on the government no other than the speedy removal of the judge himself who bore it, and the appointment of a successor more to the taste of the times.

While we admitted that the natives have committed the most dreadful barbarities, and greatly provoked the British authorities and the British people, we were constrained to believe that they were led into such conduct by the British in India themselves. And we find that a considerable and influential portion of the people of England, while deeply sympathizing, as we do, with those who have been afflicted by the savage conduct of the native population of India, express most unequivocally similar sentiments to those put forth in this paper.

A handbill, entitled "Vengeance on India!" has been widely circulated in England, by persons of great respectability, containing the following facts: "Sir Charles Metcalf said, while Governor-General of India, 'Such is the insecurity of our tenure of India, that I should not be surprised to awake some morning and find the whole thing blown up!' Mr. Montgomery Martin speaks thus: 'The handwriting is on the wall; if ever a nation deserved punishment, it will be England, should she continue in her present career of injustice to India.' Mr. Mangles, the chairman of the East India Company, when examined before the Committee of the House of Commons, stated that, 'during fourteen years we have taken from India three hundred millions sterling, and have spent in improving it not a million and a half!' The Protestant missionaries of Bengal state, (in a paper presented to the House of Commons last session, by Mr. Kinnaird,) 'Sixty years have sufficed to reduce a fair and fertile region, as large as France, to a condition similar to that under which Ireland suffered so grievously and so long. The vast mass of the population live in a state of the most helpless poverty and wretchedness, aggravated by the inefficiency of the police, and the exactions and cruelties of its officers. A spirit of sullen discontent prevails among the rural population, growing out of an impression that the government is indifferent to the sufferings of the people.'"

The British handbill referred to, further states that "dreadful famines, the result of misgovernment, often occur. In the year 1837–8, five hundred thousand people died of famine in Bengal!"

There is a testimony from another quarter which we may not quite overlook. What do English missionaries say of British policy in India, and its bearing on the present unhappy state of affairs there?

In an interesting speech made at Leeds, England, on behalf of the Baptist Missionary Society, Mr. E. B. H. Underhill, who has recently visited the Society's stations in India, stated some facts on this point which ought to be widely known. While Christianity — the very mention of Christianity — was, he said, forbidden in the government schools, the scholars in them were constantly hearing references to Hindooism, Mohammedanism, and idolatry. Yet of all the boys who had learned English in the Missionary College at Serampore, there was not one who remained an idolater. Hindooism had lost all its influence upon the educated young men of Bengal, who were fully persuaded of the folly of the faith of their fathers. Missionaries are rarely insulted now, and never insulted by the Hindoos. If they are insulted at all, it is by the Mohammedans. In disproof of the idle statement that the mutiny was caused by the missionaries, Mr. Underhill conclusively remarks, that the Indian Government had forbidden the missionaries going to the native regiments to speak to the Sepoys about Christianity; and it had excluded from the cantonments every Christian missionary and Christian Sepoy: "for as soon as a Sepoy became a Christian he was expelled from the army." In fact, the Indian Government had done everything in its power to preserve the Sepoy from the "contamination" of English morality and Christianity. In proof of the friendly feeling entertained towards missionaries by the Hindoos in general, it may be stated that out of seventy missionaries in the northwest provinces, not more than five or six have lost their lives.

The Rev. D. Catuthers, a Scottish clergyman, who has been recently lecturing in America, says:

"This anomalous government—a trading company—exercising civil powers over a subjected and conquered people, was denounced as the worst possible form of despotism, tyranny, and oppression, regardless alike of the civil rights and the religious superstitions of the people; their only object, gain and the means of extension, directed to the sole end of realizing the greatest possible amount of money. The recent outbreak is the natural result of the long-continued series of wrongs and insults heaped upon the people by their foreign rulers."

We omit here, for reasons already suggested, the testimony of the Rev. Mr. Hary, American missionary. He has been extensively heard in Great Britain, when on his return to this country. He speaks responsive to the testimony already adduced.

Thus far for the British Standard, the Bombay judges, and the friends of Christian missions. The conclusion is but too obvious, that, however naturally our sympathies may flow out for England, in this day of her dire calamity, and however ardent our desire that British power may be speedily re-established in that country and a strictly Christian government be administered there, it is but too obvious that England was the first transgressor, and has not ceased to provoke the outrages which her people are now suffering at the hands of her indignant subjects.

We have no pleasure in detailing such facts. England is a great, noble nation, and, as Americans, we are proud to honor her. She has been as the right arm of Providence to carry on a higher order of civilization and a better type of Christianity around the globe; and we hope her mission is not yet finished. Yet she has sinned. Her pride and love of power, her ambition, and avarice have but too often led her to play the oppressor; and we marvel not that the voice of rebuke has at length broke like a thunderbolt upon her head. May she heed the voice that now speaks in such awful tones of cruelty and carnage, repent, learn humility towards the weak and oppressed, and extend a benign and Christian government over all the vast and populous nations of the East. We feel that the downfall, or the crippling of the English Empire, would roll back the wheels of modern progress at least a century.

Had England heeded the warning voice of her great statesman, and ceased her unrighteous doings toward her Indian colonies, she had been saved her present humiliating position, and the appalling disasters which have befallen her unfortunate sons in India. The words of Edmund Burke are yet terribly true of her present sway in that country. He said:

"With regard to Hindoostan, those natives who are unfriendly o us *might with justice declare our conduct to be more allied to Vandalism than to civilization.* If the English were driven from India, they would leave behind them no memorial of a great and enlightened nation; no monument of art, science, or beneficence; no vestige of their having occupied and ruled over the country, *except such traces as the vulture and the tiger leave behind them.*"

The British paper from which we have cited these testimonies—and we have not quoted half of the horrible details—closes its appeal to England in these sublime and, some of them, *inspired* words:

"No more thoughts of 'vengeance,' then, but of humiliation before the GOD OF THE WHOLE EARTH. The language of the Prophet is only such as befits the mouth of England: 'We have sinned and committed iniquity, and have done wickedly: O Lord! to us belongeth confusion of face, to our kings, to our princes, and to our fathers, because we have sinned against Thee: to the Lord our God belong mercies and forgiveness.' Let all England hear the words of the greatest advocate that ever stood at her bar:

"'*We are accustomed to govern India—a country which God never gave us—by means which God will never justify.*'"

Or we may quote from the *Church Missionary Intelligence*, a paragraph from Buchanan, which seems scarcely less than prophetic: "The toleration of all religions, and the zealous extension of our own, is the way to rule and to preserve a conquered kingdom." And we add another: "To countenance false religions, and discourage our own, in the hope of strengthening our influence, and securing the affections of the natives, is the surest way to forfeit the Divine blessing, and deprive ourselves of all we have gained. Kings and governments who act with such infidelity must expect Belshazzar's doom, 'Thou art weighed in the balance and art found wanting: thy kingdom is departed from thee.'

"The nation has now to decide between these two antagonistic principles of government. We have tried the wrong course, and are now reaping its bitter fruits. May the grace of repentance be given us, henceforth to choose the better part."

But there are more specific causes of the mutiny. These, however, with some accounts of the character and the results of this terrific warfare, must be reserved for another chapter. However severe or retributive it may be in its bearings on suffering England, or however savage and inhuman, on the part of the natives, there is an eye that overlooks the whole—there is an arm that directs—an all-wise and benevolent Mind that will bring out of it a result truly great and glorious.

CHAPTER IV.

The savage character of the Mutiny — Nena Sahib — Causes of the Mutiny — What God is bringing out of it, and what will probably be the final results.

We do not propose to enter deeply into the heart-sickening details of the Sepoy war. Yet we need to contemplate certain features of it in order to give a right understanding to its true character. It is singularly cruel, heartless, blood-thirsty. The natives engaged in it seem quite to belie their own character—at least, what, from a long acquaintance, was believed to be their character. The Hindoos, especially, were understood to be a quiet, submissive, amiable, servile people; unresisting, and anything but blood-thirsty. The taking the life even of an animal or insect, seemed as abhorrent to their nature as it is to their religion. They appear in no wise vindictive or cruel. Yet it is horribly characteristic of the present outbreak, that "a singular propensity to cold-blooded murder takes possession of them the moment they gain the power to gratify it." After years of residence among them, and a familiar acquaintance with all classes of the people—their manners, customs, and ostensible feelings towards their European rulers—it is difficult to give full credence to all the appalling accounts which come to us, of their inhuman doings at the present time. They seem instigated and nerved to deeds too infernal to be the conceptions of a human mind. The master whom they so loyally serve has all at once made them more devils than men. Every fresh message that comes from those awful scenes of butchery and outrage, seem to say, "Woe to the inhabitants of the earth, for the devil is come down unto you, having great wrath, because he knoweth he has but a short time."

We are horror-stricken as we read the following paragraphs. Are the perpetrators of such barbarities *men*, or spirits incarnate, let loose for a little season to inflict the last judgments on proud and wicked nations, and on offending men? A correspondent of the New York Times, writing from Hong Kong, says:

"The mutineers have at every place manifested the most fiend-like character, by acts too horrible to relate. They respect neither age nor sex. Every European that they have captured has suffered the same fate—*death*, and sometimes more awful atrocities.

"By the Hindoo religion, the spirits of bad men are said to pass into the bodies of other men or brutes. It would seem that by some such transmigration of souls, if there be a hell upon earth, just now, it is in that benighted and afflicted country, and that it has 'broken loose' and is running riot with an insatiate and ingenious malice that devils might envy.

"Nothing in the annals of war, during this century, can compare with the abominable scenes enacted already in India, and what the future is to bring forth is known only to Him who limiteth the powers of evil, and to whom the future is as the past. They have shown no discrimination, butchering the most inoffensive and defenseless, the holy and self-sacrificing missionary and his household, the meek and amiable native Christian, and the devoted wife and mother, after murdering, before her eyes, her husband and helpless infant, or bearing off her gentle and shrieking daughter, to await a more dreadful fate.

"A more degraded people, as regards sensuality, cruelty, duplicity and avarice, is not to be found; and it is alike for the interest of all civilized nations, that England, the great parent of modern liberty, and that race who are doing the most to spread the Gospel throughout heathen lands, should not be exterminated or overthrown in India. We are, by steam and inter-oceanic communication, brought nearer to the great marts of Europe and America; and, of course, anything affecting civilization and commerce here, is of grave importance in both hemispheres."

After the massacre at Meerut and Cawnpore, the women were turned over to the rabble in the bazaar—stripped, made to walk naked through the city, and then outraged, mutilated and tormented to death. The picture is too horrible for contemplation.

The Bombay Telegraph contains the following account of the recapture of Cawnpore. I give a single extract:

"On the evening of this engagement the column encamped outside the walls of Cawnpore, and on the morning of the 17th our soldiers entered the city. Accustomed as they had been to scenes of slaughter, the spectacle that met their eyes nearly petrified them with horror. They marched straight to a place where they were told 175 women and children were confined, but on their arrival they found they had come too late! They only found the clothes of the poor victims strewn over the blood-stained ground. The scene of the horrible catastrophe was a paved court-yard, and one of the Highlanders, in writing to a cotemporary, says: 'There were two inches of blood upon the pavement, and from the report that we got from the residents of the place, it appears that, after we had beaten the enemy the evening previous, the Sepoys and Sowars entered the place where the unhappy victims were, killed all the ladies, and threw the children alive, as well as the ladies' dead bodies, into a well in the compound. I saw it, and it was an awful sight. It appears from the bodies we saw that the women were stripped of their clothes before they were murdered.' A feeling more terrible than vengeance arises in the heart at reading this, and even the most reverent shudder when they think that Omnipotence could have deemed such an ordeal necessary. The history of the world affords no parallel to the terrible massacres which, during the last four months, have desolated the land. Neither age, sex, nor condition has been spared. Children have been compelled to eat the quivering flesh of their murdered parents, after which they were literally *torn asunder* by the laughing fiends who surrounded them. Men in many instances have been mutilated, and before being absolutely killed, have had to gaze upon the last dishonor of their wives and daughters previous to being put to death. But really we cannot describe the brutalities that have been committed; they pass the boundaries of human belief, and to dwell upon them shakes reason upon its throne. If ever a nation was made the instrument of an insulted Diety, that nation is England; and we trust that she will strike and spare not."

"No tongue," says another writer, "can describe the cruelties which have been perpetrated. We know but little, for government prudently conceals many details; but we know that Sepoys treacherously embraced their European officers at twilight, and barbarously murdered them at midnight. We know that they spared no sex, and pitied no age. We know that they tossed children into the air before the eyes of their parents, and received the descending bodies upon the ends of bayonets, or clove them as they fell with their swords. We know that they cut the quivering flesh from the bodies of living fathers and mothers, and made the children eat it, and then flung the little ones into a burning pile prepared for the purpose. We know that fair women, wives, and virgins, were abused in the foulest manner, and then horribly maimed by the excision of their noses, ears, lips, breasts and hands. We know that Englishmen have been hunted down like beasts, and cut into bits, or tied to cannon and blown into spray. We know that white men and women, of gentle birth and noble character, are lurking in remote jungles, subsisting as they may, till our rainy season fills the river beds, and affords them the only hope of escape to Calcutta. We know that from more proximate parts, fair-haired babes have been brought to that city, whose parents none can discover, and that ladies have wandered down there insane or idiotic, whose mutilations tell the story which they have not mind left coherently to relate. My heart fails me. I cannot enter into further particulars. History has no annals, so for as I have consulted them, that exhibit the diabolical malignity and the enormous atrocities which have stamped with hideousness every stage of this mutiny."

We are justly shocked by "the bloody orgies of these slaughtering savages." There is a cold-blooded barbarity in the outrages they are committing, which we never expected the world would again witness. "These oriental savages even transcend, in the ingenuity and extent of their cruelties, the aboriginal red men in our western forests." Rome alone can boast an unenviable pre-eminence and refinement in the work of torture; children are cut in pieces, joint by joint, before the eyes of their parents, and then the parents are themselves abandoned to the inflamed passions and fury of thousands of men more vindictive and merciless than the tigers of their native jungles.

If it be a fact, as we have supposed, that the peculiar character of the horrible cruelties which have been inflicted by the Sepoys, have been suggested and provoked by similar wrongs inflicted on the natives by their conquerors and rulers, it ought to repress all such ideas of *revenge* as was so liberally breathed by the British press, and is still to some extent burning in the bosom of the English nation. Humiliation and repentance rather become the first transgressors.

But let us look a little more particularly into the immediate causes of this singular outbreak. It has been charged to the "greased cartridges." It has been imputed to some apprehended interference of the government with the religion of the Hindoos, and of the Mohammedans. Missionaries and missions have been brought in for a share among the causes of the revolt. Neither of these, if causes at all, probably had much to do in the matter. The requisition to use certain offensive cartridges no doubt furnished the occasion for the outbreak. It was the tinder that conveyed the spark to a trail already laid. But the causes were of a longer standing. They lay further back — more deeply lodged in grievances of former days.

While speaking of some of these more immediate causes, we will not lose sight of what we have intimated to be the primary and principal cause, namely, the retributive hand of God. England, in India, virtually denied her religion, and now God has, for a time at least, forsaken her. Not only have the European rulers of India appeared before their idolatrous subjects as a people of no religion themselves, but they have been only too ready to extend a patronizing hand over the religion of the country; but not only this, but the government have been at pains to shut out from their schools, and from their army, all knowledge of the Christian religion. It has been a misdemeanor in the army, a crime to be punished by dismission from military service, for a Sepoy to become a Christian. We must not forget that MEERUT, the very spot where the present dreadful mutiny broke out, was the place where, in 1814, the first Sepoy was dismissed from the service on account of his profession of Christianity; refusing to sacrifice his convictions of right and duty, and to do violence to his conscience and his God, at the bidding of his foreign Christian master.

This case is too significant to be passed over without further notice. The Sepoy in question was a Brahmun of good caste. For nine years he struggled between duty and fear—the duty of yielding to his honest convictions and the dictates of conscience, and the fear of encountering the displeasure of his own people, and perhaps the more serious displeasure of the Christian government whose soldier he was. His convictions finally prevailed; and he applied to the chaplain of his regiment for instruction and guidance. The Rev. Mr. Fisher received him gladly, cherished his convictions of duty, and taught him the way of life more perfectly. From his hands he received baptism, and openly confessed Christ as his God and Savior. This produced no great excitement or persecution among his own people. Some of his friends at first plied him with threats and promises to deter him, if possible, from his resolution. To them he replied: "Jesus Christ will be my friend; He will be a friend to all that trust Him. My becoming a Christian cannot make me a bad soldier; and I see no reason to believe that government will cast me off any more than the officers who are Christians." Alas! he did not know with what sort of Christians he would have to deal.

His *Christian* officers and Christian government would not allow the matter to rest so. "The adjutant kindled into indignation (I quote from the London Christian Times) at this unauthorized conversion, and reported to his superior the singular and unprecedented circumstance. The Governor-General, in council, took fire—censured the chaplain for having dared to baptize the Sepoy, and ordered a court martial to be held on the case, in which court the convert boldly, yet modestly, confessed Christ; and then the Marquis of Hastings, acting in his capacity of commander-in-chief, dismissed Prabu Din from his regiment, as disqualified for the service, by his profession of Christianity."

It is in this very Meerut where the outbreak commenced; and these very Sepoys, who have been so carefully guarded from all contact with Christianity, have there pounced, like wild beasts of prey, upon their European benefactors, and spread rapine and slaughter into every nook of the city. "No more Sepoys were known to be converted; but after the vigilance of the Company had done its utmost to keep the very name of Christ out of sight and hearing, those pampered Pagans rose up, in a mass, to wreak death, and worse than death; first upon the Christians of Meerut, and then upon their brethren, wherever to be found." Henceforth Meerut shall have an unenviable fame; first, as the scene of a solemn act of persecution; and, then, "of that most fearful stroke of retribution, under which scores of sufferers endured the mockery of the self-same army in its mutiny." What a signal rebuke of the godlessness and timidity of the men to whom Great Britain "had entrusted the honor of her crown and of her faith!" Mr. Gladstone lately said, in a public speech: "He viewed the Indian insurrection as a Divine judgment, and as teaching the nation a lesson of humility." He admitted that "measures had been undertaken there without a shadow of justice, and which were a perfect scandal to English history."

The Montreal Witness reiterates the same sentiment. A resistless tide of public feeling has set in, rebuking past wrong, and presaging, on the part of England, a juster state of feeling in relation to her East India possessions. The Witness says:

"Had the Sepoys and native princes conducted the war with fairness—using prisoners well, and setting women and children free—the general sympathies of mankind would have been with them. Every nation but Britain would have been on their side, as far, at least, as prudence permitted; and even in Britain a very strong feeling would have favored them."

A concession, this, which betokens that better feeling which is fast rising in England; and promises results, from her present disasters, salutary and far-reaching.

1. No doubt impatience of foreign rule, especially on the part of the Mohammedans and high caste Brahmuns, had much to do in the origin of the present insurrection. The iron rule of the English, a remembrance of past exactions and cruelties, and restiveness under burdens not yet removed, have been rankling in the breasts of the oppressed, till at length they have found a terrific vent.

We are struck with the prophetic spirit of the following lines, written some twenty-five years ago by a brother of George Canning. It appears in a remarkable poem, entitled "*India.*" The writer had enjoyed many advantages for studying the native character. He sums up the result of his official experience at Delhi, Cawnpore and other places, in the following prophetic lines:

"There needs but some surpassing act of wrong
To break the patience that has bent so long;
There need but some short, sudden burst of ire,
May chance to set the general thing on fire;
There need but some fair prospect of relief,
Enough to seize the general belief;
Some holy juggle, some absurd caprice,
To raise one common struggle for release.
* * * * *
Think not that prodigies must rule a state,
That great revulsions spring from something great;
The softest curl that floats on beauty's brow,
The smallest leaf that flutters on the bough,
Is not more lightly easy to derange,
Than *human minds with cause to wish for change.*
Out breaks at once the far-resounding cry,
The standard of revolt is raised on high,
The murky cloud has glided from the sun,
The tale of England's tyranny is done,
And torturing vengeance grins as she destroys,
Till Secil's vespers seem the game of boys."

2. Hatred of the Christian religion, and the hope to exterminate it, root and branch, from their country, has probably contributed a no inconsiderable share in the present rising of the Sepoys. Christianity in India has been as the stone cut out of the mountain without hands. Without power or governmental aid, without observation, and, seemingly, without adequate means, it has strangely increased; slowly, imperceptibly, and surely displacing the gigantic and hoary systems of the ancient religions, and, with a life more and more vigorous, taking possession of the native mind. Superstitions as venerable as time, and usages and institutions that date back far into the mists of ages, are numbered among the works and the things which must pass away. Priestly pride is scandalized; and hating and fearing the rising Star of Bethlehem, priestly power and influence have risen up to crush it. And who will not recognize the hand of retributive justice, in the fact that the Bengal army, from which government made the most sedulous efforts to preserve its Sepoys intact from all Christian influences, was the first to raise the banner of revolt? But in despite of the unchristian policy of a Christian government, and the ungodly example of too many of India's nominally Christian rulers, the religion of the Cross has made such progress as to excite a serious alarm that it will yet supplant both the religion of Brahmu and of the Crescent. Such a presentiment has, for years past, greatly to the chagrin of the priestly craft, possessed the minds of the masses of the people. And no wonder there should be one more desperate strike for the altars and the gods of the ancient faith. Brahmuns, even, were yielding to the conquering banners of Christianity; proud Moslems were being converted, and all castes and nationalities were beginning to bow before the rising Star of Bethlehem. The present Sepoy war is, doubtless, to a considerable extent, a religious war.

3. We discover a reason as well as a cause of the mutiny in the constitution of the Anglo-Indian army, and more especially in the Bengal army. The army in India is composed principally of the natives of the country, called Sepoys, officered by Euro-

peans. These Sepoy forces, at the commencement of the mutiny, amounted to some 300,000; while the number of European soldiers was comparatively a handful. These Sepoy regiments have generally been found faithful. An outbreak at this late day was scarcely thought possible; yet all the elements of insurrection were there, and needed only a sufficiently exciting cause, and some leading spirits, to blow the latent fire into a blaze. And the Bengal army, in which the mutiny began, was a field yet more fearfully adapted to such a revolt. Composed chiefly of Brahmuns and high caste Mohammedans, the wonder is, that an army of such materials did not mutiny before. It was, in some special sense, a godless army—not only godless because composed of Pagans, but godless in the policy of government toward it. It was most cautiously guarded against all Christian influences which might otherwise be brought to bear upon it. There was, therefore, a twofold reason why a rebellion should break out there. The constitution of the army was such as to make it a fit agency for such a rebellion; and the policy of government had been such as to make that rebellion a fit retribution for their time-serving policy. A paragraph, from a late letter of a resident in India, will confirm what I have just said:

"The Bengal native army has always been petted and pampered. It contains a great number of Brahmuns. These men have dictated to their officers, rather than their officers to them. Their unwillingness to go on foreign service, (to Burmah or China, for instance,) because their caste would be lost in crossing the waters, secured them enlistment on the condition that they should not leave their own country. Their officers have been accustomed to boast of the high caste of their men, and scornfully contrast it with the lower caste of the Madras Sepoys. Whence, then, has the insane desire of re-establishing native rule arisen? Has it originated in a population among whom missionaries have statedly labored? No. It sprang from the Bengal native army, the very men who were guarded from missionary contact, whose caste was so tenderly cherished, whose religion was so sedulously protected, and whose heathenish prejudices were so fully fed.

When such prejudices are fostered, they not only themselves grow, but, like the plantain-tree, they put forth new shoots from their roots. New and artificial prejudices are created. Matters wax worse and worse. The Sepoys, of course, see their power. They learn boldness from the pliancy of their masters. What more natural than that the desire of native sovereignty should spring up among such men, gather strength, and at last culminate in rebellion? Fostering the prejudices of the Bengal native army has been the seed of this mutiny. That army has long been notorious for its lax discipline. The spoiled child has grown to be a turbulent man, full of the spirit of disobedience. What wonder that such an army should watch its opportunity, and, when India is almost denuded of European troops, rise and assert its independence?"

4. We may name as another cause of the mutiny, *misgovernment*, and the bad example of European officers and residents in India. It was a gigantic blunder, to say nothing of the enormous moral obliquity, that England did not rule India as it became a great Christian to bear rule in a heathen land. It was a misgovernment—a fatal mistake that has drawn after it consequences of the gravest character. Had the English, as the dominant party in India, not denied their religion, and, by example at least, taught men so—had they respected themselves and honored God as their Sovereign King, he would not have left them to these severe rebukes. Nations, as truly as individuals, are made to feel the truth of the Divine Oracle, "Them that honor me, I will honor."

But the defection is not all of a religious character. The history of British rule in India has been characterized by extortions, exactions, severities and outrages; the remembrance of which has, from generation to generation, been as a fire smoldering in the hidden recesses of the native mind, till at length the heaving volcano has exploded.

In the history of English conquests in India, we meet details of treacheries, massacres, extortions, scarcely less appalling than have disgraced the present warfare of the Sepoys. We are shocked at the idea of mutilating, torturing, cutting off fingers, toes, ears, noses, breasts; cutting up joint by joint, and exposing women and girls naked, and subjecting them to indignities that may not be named, and can scarcely believe that untutored savages are capable of such enormities; yet we are not the less shocked when we learn that, in days that are gone, (but not forgotten,) English officials did things *very much like* them.

But the history of England in India has another phase, less hideous only because less seen; but were its loathsome features to appear, they would yet more shock all the sensibilities of the virtuous mind. The great day of revelations will divulge a history of unblushing concubinage such as the world never knew. When we admit into the account the long list of transgressions on this score—the long-continued and systematic invasions on female virtue, and too often on the sanctity of the family—we are not surprised that the day of reckoning should come, and that their own countrywomen should be made to suffer a like fate. Sad it is, that, in this dispensation of partial adjustments, the innocent should suffer for the guilty. But so it is. All will be adjusted at last on the principles of the strictest justice and the most enlarged benevolence.

5. Long-continued disaffection, and the unheeded grievances of native princes and chiefs, has had much to do as a cause of the present revolt. After being conquered under one pretext or another, some have been pensioned off by government, and sent to some place of pilgrimage, or other holy place; others have been allowed to retain the show of royalty, without its power or independence, or been otherwise disposed of, so as to be the least troublesome, and the most profitable, to their foreign masters. But what is worse, the government is freely accused (by their own countrymen) of not acting in good faith in fulfilling, toward the prostrate princes, the stipulations of their own treaties. Their claims have too often been disregarded; obligations to them have, on the slightest pretext, been repudiated; and, as they became weaker and less to be feared, provinces and pensions, which had been assigned them, were withheld; and the claim-

ants were not unfrequently subjected to the most expensive and vexatious processes, before they were brought to the humiliating and provoking conclusion, that their claims were but the claims of the weak against the strong. "Such has been the case," says an English writer, "of NENA SAHIB; and such has been the case of the Rajah of Coorg; of the Ranee of Jhansi, where another frightful massacre took place; and such has been the case with numbers of Indians of rank, with whom we have not dealt either wisely or well. Far be it from us to offer even the shadow of an apology for the authors of the atrocities which have plunged nearly half of the nation into mourning; but, at the same time, we cannot forbear expressing our opinion, which is now generally felt and acknowledged, that to the gross mismanagement of our Indian Empire, and the manifest injustice of which the East India Company has been so frequently guilty, may be mainly attributed the deplorable state of affairs which now exist.

"The grievance of Nena Sahib was simply this: The East India Company guaranteed to the late Peshwa, his heirs and successors, a certain pension. The Peshwa died without heirs born of his body; but, previous to his death, he adopted Sreenath (Nena Sahib). Now, according to the Hindoo law, an adopted son is entitled to all the rights and privileges of an heir begotten of the body of the deceased. According to the Hindoo law, Nena Sahib was entitled to the pension of the Peshwa; but the claim, as before stated, was not allowed. It is a pity that the East India Company have not been consistent in their decisions upon this head. In some, indeed in very many cases, (where the pension has been very considerable, or the amount of territory to be 'absorbed' extremely profitable,) the Hindoo law has been shelved, and the claimant favored with a letter from the Secretary to Government, informing him that the 'Governor-General in Council has dismissed his petition, but that the ordinary channels of redress are open to him.' He sends home an agent, who haunts the India-house and the Board of Control.

At both places he is 'referred to the local government'—the local government which has already decided against him."

Nena Sahib, the present commander-in-chief of the Sepoy forces, and the author of atrocities more horrible than we had supposed humanity capable of in the present age of civilization and human progress, stands as one of these unsuccessful claimants. He had spent large sums of money in the unsuccessful prosecution of his claim in England; and chagrined, irritated, and smarting under a sense of injustice, of which he saw no redress under British rule, he bottled his wrath till the day of vengeance came—and what a day of vengeance has he made it! In vain you search the annals of history for deeds more appalling. Other native princes have waited for this day, that they, too, might pay off in blood, pillage, and torture, some old family grudge of an hundred years' festering.

Having mentioned Nena Sahib, it will not be amiss to say a word more. This man, so notorious in the annals of cruelty and bloodshed, is a veritable pupil of the government schools—the genuine handiwork of the East India Company's policy in that country. In such men as the Nena, the government are reaping what they have been sowing. He is just what this policy has made him. Rev. Mr. Williams, Baptist Missionary from Bengal, in a speech before a missionary meeting at Southampton, said that he knew Nena Sahib intimately, and bore testimony to his mental accomplishments, and to his polished and gentlemanly manners. Nena Sahib was educated in one of the English Government schools in India, where almost every book is studied but the Bible, and everything taught but Christianity. The greatest enemies to British rule, and to the spread of the Gospel, in India, were men like Nena Sahib and others, who have been educated in the government colleges; most of whom were professedly deists, but in reality atheists.

CHAPTER V.

What God is bringing out of the Sepoy mutiny, and what will probably be the final results.

But we take yet another view of England's disasters, and of India's vengeance, in the late war.

What is God bringing out of it? and *what will He finally bring out of it?* All who see in these civil, social and moral earthquakes and bursting volcanoes, a supreme overruling agent, so controlling the whole as to bring out of it results most wise and benevolent, will have no doubt that such shall be the end of their present dreadful warfare. Already, indeed, do we see such results, and these we may take as the sure harbingers of other results yet more far-reaching and beneficent.

Already the English nation feels rebuked and humbled. She sees the retributive hand reached out over her, and she trembles. The nation mourns, and looks with fearful misgivings at the things that may shortly come upon her. She is brought to confess her sins, and, by humiliation and prayer, to seek the return of Heaven's favor. Should England reconquer India, (as we hope with the whole heart she will,) we may expect her future rule in that country will be permeated, as it never has been, with the high and pure principles of political wisdom and justice, and the practice of that holy faith, which have made England what she is. May she never forget again that it is righteousness that exalteth a nation, and that sin is a reproach to any people. In saying this, we do not forget the burning reproach that rests like the incubus of political death and moral perdition on our own dear America. May all England pray for us, and the Lord have mercy on us!

England has been notoriously a proud nation, as well as oppressive. Her present position is fitted to humble her, and make her feel her dependence on the King of Nations.

The church, of every name, in the British relm, is receiving, too, salutary lessons. The conviction rushes upon her, that, if she had done her duty toward that benighted land — if she had employed to the extent she ought the unwonted facilities which Providence had put in her hands for the renovation of that people — these things never would have happened. The difficulties in India have not risen from native Christians, but from those from whom Christianity has been sedulously excluded. A pure Christianity alone can secure to England the loyalty of India. Late transactions have done much to force this conviction on the English mind. And not only is the present state of things in India fitted to humble the English church and to rouse her to renewed efforts for the evangelization of that great country, but the American church, the Christian church universal, is taught a similar lesson. All Christendom is concerned in the conversion of India to Christ; and had she done her duty, the world would have been spared one of the awfulest spectacles ever witnessed.

Again, the *character* of the present race of the heathen has been fearfully unfolded in the bloody transactions of the present revolt. We are startled at such exhibitions of cold-blooded ferocity; and are made vividly to see what the world would be, should such a people be allowed to have dominion. Never had the truly philanthropic mind a stronger argument for the speedy evangelizing of the whole world. If such be the character of the Hindoos, whom we have supposed to be a very quiet, inoffensive people, what might we expect, when their turn shall come to rise, will be the strength and malignity of the more ignorant and savage portions of the heathen world? All Christendom will now see, that, in self-defense, as well as a matter of duty, she must convert the heathen.

Another good result which has already come out of the Indian catastrophe is, that India and her people, her religion and institutions, her wants and her woes, are better *known*. In America, little has ever been known of India in any respect — not enough to have created any general interest in her history or literature; and in England she has scarcely been better known, except as avarice and ambition have introduced her to notice. A new interest is now thrown over the whole country and all that belongs to it. Maps are consulted, books read, and travelers questioned, and their narratives read, as never before. Every source of information is now eagerly resorted to, and the whole reading world have probably more than doubled their amount of acquaintance with India in a single year; and knowing India, the church will feel a new interest in, and may be expected to be roused to new energy for, her conversion to Christianity. We had thought to make a quiet and easy work of it. But the "strong man" will not yield up his long-cherished possessions so easy. The great battle is to be fought — Gog and Mogog to be met and vanquished.

God has doubtless large and benevolent purposes to answer through these commotions and bloodshed. When all parties shall have been humbled and duly punished, British pride rebuked, and the English and American church be humbled and roused to the importance of the conversion of India, we may expect that India will be restored to England, or given to a nation that will better fulfill her destiny there; at least, we may feel assured that the result shall be for the furtherance of the Gospel. The only safeguard to English dominion and authority in India, is the thorough Christianization of the whole country.

Another result of the war will probably be a *great destruction* of the native population, the annihilation of Mohammedan influence and power, and the extinction of caste and all governmental power on the part of the Hindoos. The time may have come for the extinguishment of all that remains of the native prestige, and the final establishment of a higher and a better state of things. They that watch the mighty wheels of Providence in their onward march in human progress, are accustomed to see that there is a "sword" that goeth before Him. The destruction of enemies, of the heathen, has always held a prominent place in the movements of Providence. We may expect it shall be so now.

Already we see no doubtful indications that England is

humbling herself under her chastisements. She is searching out her sin and making confession before her God, and pouring her supplications into the ear of the Lord of the Sabbath. The Queen proclaims a day of fasting, humiliation and prayer, and the nation falls prostrate before the God of Heaven. This day, we are told, was very universally observed, and with great interest and solemnity. For scarcely a town, neighborhood or family are left unscathed by the dreadful calamity; and it is a matter of momentous interest to observe the spirit of the numerous assemblies which convened on that day, and the character of the teachings, and the spirit of the prayers, which occupied the minds of those assembled. From these we may form some judgment as to what shall be the influence of those untoward events on the minds of the British nation, and what shall be the future policy of that nation in India, should it please the Great Disposer of nations to perpetuate the English government in that country. The following paragraphs, taken from English papers, speak no doubtful language as to what was the prevalent feeling on the occasion referred to. And in these we see the star of hope rising above one of the darkest clouds which ever darkened the English horizon. Every indication that the nation is returning to God, is a sure presage of Heaven's returning smile on the nation. One of the leading papers of Great Britain exclaims:

"Are the lessons of history to be forever lost upon us? Have we forgotten the great struggle of the last century with the American Colonies, now the United States? The language then was precisely that which is being so generally held now concerning India. Heaven forbid that it should be attended with similar results! There are deeds beyond the might of armies. The natives of India, notwithstanding their physical weakness and moral impotence, are, if they choose, more than a match, many times over, for all the troops that England can afford to keep up in India. Friendship, not force, a sense of sound advantage, not a sense of iron power, are the feelings on which we must rely. The tendency of every passion is to produce its like.

Cries of 'vengeance!' will only awaken feelings of hatred and abhorrence, in much increased intensity! Few can fight, but all can detest; and detestation is a plant that will grow through out every rod of the soil in India."

On the great fast day the sin of misgovernment was mos freely and sincerely confessed, and especially in reference to the treatment which had been bestowed on the cause of Christianity in India. On this subject the London Patriot says:

"That our Indian Government has been unfaithful to the paramount claims of Christianity; that, at the bidding of a miserable political expediency, it has consented, if not to abjure its religion, at least to hide it, and place all possible obstacles in the way of its advancement, no one can deny; and to such an extent has this been done, that, had it not been for the inherent vitality of Christianity, it must, as far as the natives are concerned, have been completely extinguished and destroyed."

The same paper quotes from a sermon, and approves of the following comprehensive and eloquent passage:

"From the day when the British missionary was compelled to take refuge under a foreign flag, and when he was conveyed from the ship to the jail for the great crime of coming to India to preach Christianity, to the dismissal of the Sepoy from the Bengal army because he became a Christian, and thence to the present hour, the uniform policy of the East India Company has been one of hostility to missions. In the great conflict between Christianity and Paganism, its help has uniformly been arrayed on the side of the latter. Hindooism has its subsidies out of the government treasury, and Mohammedanism has its subsidies, but Christianity has been prohibited from opening its mouth. The Company have rebuilt idol temples, and re-decorated pagodas; it has compelled Christian soldiers to officiate at Pagan festivals, and Christian officers to collect Pagan revenues — compelling men like Sir Peregrine Maitland to leave its service on account of its identification with idolatry, and men like Carey and Dr. Judson to leave its shores on account of its opposition to Christian missionaries. It has closed its schools against

Christianity, and prohibited even conversion to it in its service. It is hardly too much to say that our Indian Government has mainly upheld the decaying strength of idolatry and caste, and more than any other power neutralized the moral influence of Christianity. And now that Lord Canning has ventured to become a subscriber to certain Christian societies, it has become the ground of remonstrance in the British House of Lords. Even on the low ground of policy, this has been a blunder as great as, religiously, it has been a sin. It has shorn us of the moral power of religious character and sincerity. It has nurtured the elements which are our most deadly antagonists. That which is morally wrong can never be politically right."

Another English writer on Indian affairs says: "Instead of taking a high stand as a Christian power, and avowing its belief in the religion of the Bible, as the religion for man, it has, with almost laborious care, appeared to aim at producing the impression that Hindooism and Mohammedanism were to be nurtured and conserved. It has acted the part of guardian to heathen temples and shrines. It has collected the revenue for Juggernaut and Krishna, and bestowed upon idols costly gifts. It has drawn up its troops in military array to salute and honor false gods and sanction the grossest idolatry. It has favored caste and sided with the Brahmun. It has discouraged Christianity. Under the plea of full toleration of Hindooism, it has been either regardless of truth or intolerant to Christians."

The Church Missionary Society of England, in an official paper on the state of affairs in India, and the relations of government to the progress of the Gospel there, speak freely of the exceptionable course of the East India Government, and unhesitatingly charge the sin of the present rebellion on the time-serving policy of the British Government. They reiterate, what we have already repeated, that "the instrument of Divine judgment has been the cherished high caste Bengal army, from which the first Sepoy Christian convert was expelled, through caste prejudices, in the year 1819, by order of the Governor-General, after an official inquiry at Meerut, in which the soldier was acquitted of every charge except that of becoming a Christian on conviction. At Meerut the first blood was shed by Sepoys. Whoso is wise shall observe these things, and will mark in this and other peculiarities of the judgment, the reflection of our national sins."

Rev. Dr. J. W. Alexander, in a recent letter from Scotland, states that on the occasion of the recent national fast in Great Britain, the most candid confession of national sins, including the opium business, was fairly uttered. He quotes the following striking rebuke of the Government of India from one of the sermons delivered on that day: "It is calculated that a hundred thousand acres of the richest lands watered by the Ganges are devoted to the growth of the supply of opium. *These are the very regions which the revolt is now desolating.* The profit which the Company derives is very great. For that which costs about $175, they receive $525—the aggregate is about twenty-five millions. This money has come to be, what faith was at the Reformation, the article of a 'standing or falling' government. It is felt that the solvency, and consequently the existence, of the Company depends upon it. The principal portion of this great revenue is extracted from the Chinese. The Government of British India, in league with the vile passions of the Chinese populace, has proved too strong for the Chinese Government. There is not a more humiliating fact on the face of the world or in the history of man than this: it is by becoming the sole and exclusive purveyors to the gigantic vice which is degrading and destroying the Chinese population, that the Government of British India maintain their solvency!"

"The East India Company," says the London Times, "steadily resisted the invasion of Christianity, step by step, into their unhallowed soil. They fought hard, first, against the admission of missionaries, then against regular chaplains, then against a bishop; and when poor Bishop Middleton went at last, he landed, lived, and worked and died, under a constant, unrelenting protest by the authorities, who were determined to show the natives that they had nothing to do with him. The present position of a bishop in India, such as it is, we owe to the great abilities and the singularly engaging qualities of Heber."

And not only the Times, but leading statesmen, members of Parliament, and speakers in all sorts of public meetings, are speaking out without hesitancy, urging the duty of henceforth giving a decided Christian character to British rule in India. "Every vestige of the past exclusive policy," they say, "should be made to disappear, and it should be known that the government is a Christian government, and desires all the people to be Christians." Thus light may spring out of darkness, Christians be awakened to new missionary efforts, and the government be led to shape its legislation, and modify its educational and general policy, so as to favor as much as practicable the interests of Christianity.

These are no doubtful indications that better days are reserved for ill-fated India, and that she shall yet be blessed through the sons of Japhet. At a late Bible meeting at Manchester, a proposal is made to raise £250,000 (more than a million of dollars) for the distribution of 5,000,000 Bibles in India. This looks as if England were awake to her duty to her Indian Empire. "The Christian principle of England has been roused by the discovery of the oft repeated fact that India has been kept in heathenism by the anti-Christian policy of the Company; and now that the truth has burst upon the public mind, the churches of England are rising in their might, demanding an instant change of policy, and preparing to execute, on a grand scale, the work of evangelizing that benighted land."

Others propose that "memorial" churches shall be erected, by general contribution, at Delhi and Cawnpore. With the return of peace, say others, we expect to behold the power of religious zeal exhibited, as it never was before, in giving the Gospel to India. These are noble purposes, and we bid them God-speed. And not this alone; but with open hands and a full heart, let American Christians become the active co-operators in so great and glorious a work.

Considered in a religious point of view, we believe this insurrection will be seen to have involved momentous results. The great obstacles in the way of missions are now removed. The chain of caste will henceforth be comparatively weak. The English Government have seen the consequences of attempting to keep up their rule by the encouragement of superstition. They will no longer deem it necessary to court the native priesthood, by buying splendid robes for Juggernaut, or supporting the Brahmuns that officiate at his shrine. Such men as Col. Wheeler will not again be compelled to relinquish the service, as the penalty of conversing with the Sepoys on the subject of Christ and salvation. The native aristocracy will no longer have the power to persecute, disgrace, and impoverish the native disciples. Missionaries have been called, during the last few years, to pass through sore trials, some of them from quarters they least expected. May not the hand of Providence have been in this thing, fitting them for a coming hour of prosperity?

The cry in England for revenge upon the Sepoys for their perfidious rebellion and fiendish cruelties has died away, and been succeeded by a general utterance of infinitely nobler character. Mercy and not sacrifice, beneficence and not vengeance, is now the prevailing voice; and there is no longer a doubt that the policy of the government will be shaped in accordance with it.

"In Great Britain," says a writer, "the whole Christian community is moved in behalf of India. To avenge the death of Englishmen by giving the Gospel to their murderers! This is noble, Christ-like. It is worthy of England — a noble Christian land. It is worthy of old Scotland, the land of Bibles and the Sabbath."

A large meeting was recently held in Edinburgh, the object of which was to carry forward, with a vastly augmented energy, the evangelization of India. In this effort the "Evangelical Alliance" are making their influence felt, especially in their endeavors to harmonize the labors of the various societies, and thus bring to bear on India the united power of the British church — the concentrated power of British philanthropy.

England has felt the rebuke. The British church has been

smitten, and the wail of woe has reached the American Zion. Missions, houses, and churches have been burnt, schools dispersed, printing establishments destroyed, missionaries murdered, and the labors of years seemingly lost. And what response does the English church give to this singular array of disasters? And what answer does our trans-Atlantic church return? Nobly do they respond,

> "Those ruins must be built again,
> And all that dust must rise."

"Houses, and schools, and churches must," say they, "be rebuilt, and every appliance re-supplied to promote with new energy and efficiency the work of the Lord. And those men — who will go for the men? Who will take the places made vacant by death? Who will fill the martyrs' place?

"The church must meet these new and large demands. Here are the places of more than twenty faithful laborers made vacant by the blast of a single storm, and our sons and daughters must be dedicated and trained to take the field. Perhaps we must go ourselves. Let us lay this awful lesson to heart. It may be that this calamity is the precursor of a mighty blessing. When we are humbled, God will appear for our help, and he will certainly have pity on his afflicted cause."

Every mail from England inspires the hope that the heart of the rebellion is crushed, and ere long tranquility shall be restored, and a more promising opportunity than ever be afforded for the evangelization of the whole country. Such changes in the administration of government shall be made as shall greatly facilitate missionary labors. All Christian communities and societies are preparing to avail themselves of the openings that are sure to be created for diffusing over all Hindoostan, and thence over all Asia, the blessings of the Gospel.

Discern ye not in these things the dawn of a better day for India? The realization of England's Christian philanthropy is likely more than to repair the ruins of a selfish and time-serving government.

We believe that a glorious future awaits that long-forsaken and ill-fated land. Hushed shall be the din of war; the carnage of the battle-field shall be forgotten. Immanuel shall there unfurl his peaceful banners; and those nations, no more inured to the devastations of war, shall become the willing subjects of the Prince of Peace. Faith contemplates these luxurious climes as all vocal with the high praises of our King. Their idol gods cast to the moles and the bats, and the waning crescent sunk into the abyss whence it came, all those populous nations shall bow about the cross and serve the one only God.

It is the voice of faith that has said there is to be yet another invasion, and yet another conquest of British India; and the fame of the Clives, and Wellesleys, and Lakes, of the Havelocks, the Wilsons, and the Neills, shall yet be surpassed. This conquest is to be achieved by railways, telegraphs, power-looms, and steam-plows — by just and equal laws, by schools, by the active promotion of every moral word and work, by the practical exemplification, from the Himalayas to the Indian Ocean, from the Burmese frontier to the banks of the Indus, of those Christian principles and duties which have the promise of the world that now is, as well as of that to come. To this course the British people are impelled by the strongest motives of self-interest, as well as the purest impulses of philanthropy. And we rejoice to see that they have at last become so deeply sensible of the fact. The rebellion, terrible as it has been, will prove a signal blessing, and no misfortune, if the sense of responsibility and spirit of duty which it has awakened shall bear their appropriate fruits in practical action. British statesmen have permitted themselves to be too much occupied in wars and diplomatic arrangements. They have allowed the petty wirework of the little old European continent to occupy a disproportionate share of their attention. Europe is no longer to be the scene of the great controlling events of the race. The theatre of action has been far removed. England has interests to assert in the Old World, and loth should we be to think they were neglected; but England's future greatness and happiness will depend upon the rank she is able to hold in the new political world outside of Europe. When we look back to the struggles of Venice, Genoa, Pisa, and other petty republics of the middle ages, how pigmy do they seem when compared with those of the great continental powers of more modern times! And yet the time is speedily coming, when the struggles, and all the activities and concerns of these modern kingdoms, which are but patches upon the earth's surface, shall be as diminutive, in comparison with the great interests and doings of those Caucasian empires that shall sway the destinies of America, Australia, and Hindoostan.

Such utterances, as I have before quoted, betoken the commencement of a better feeling in England, and hold out the promise of the returning favor of heaven. England has changed her policy towards India, very essentially, since the day when Buchanan "waged war with the government," before he could gain the slightest concession, that the Gospel might, in any form, be preached to the native population of India; and since, at a later day, (1812–13,) Hall, Nott, and Newell fearlessly renewed the battle in a correspondence with the Governor of Bombay; in which they boldly and righteously took the ground that no government could have the RIGHT to shut out the Gospel from any people whatever. It is God's gift to man as a sinner, and no earthly power may for a moment interpose to deprive him of the heavenly boon.

But England must change her policy once more; and when she shall adopt, and, in all fidelity, act upon the policy so fearlessly and righteously forced upon her attention by the first American missionaries in Bombay, she may expect to stand firm in her own political and moral integrity, respected as the representative of the noble Anglo-Saxon stock, and of a great Christian nation; and honored as the instrument of raising up a great nation of idolaters from a low state of moral debasement, to take their position among the enlightened and Christianized nations of the earth.

CHAPTER VI.

Characteristics and Sketches of Hindoostan and the Hindoos in general—Domestic, Social, Civil, Local, Physical and Religious.

It is proposed in the following chapter to bring together various notices of Hindoo character and condition, which shall introduce the reader into a more familiar acquaintance with that singular people. These notices will be numbered according as they come before me in sketches taken on the spot.

1. Their *domestic* character, condition and relations. The masses of the people are very poor—a bare subsistence is all they expect; and this subsistence is such as the poorest class in America would regard as little above the point of absolute starvation. One rupee—about forty-five cents—per month, is as much as the poorer or working classes can realize from their labor to supply food and clothing to an individual. Should a man escape with a small surplus from the hands of the tax-gatherer, he is sure to fall into the jaws of the more voracious priest. Indeed, it is not easy to determine whether their civil or their spiritual despots are most to be dreaded. A two-fold bondage crushes them to the ground. The poverty, degradation, and ignorance of all the lower orders of the people, are the consequences of their systems of government and religion. Give them the power of wealth and education, and let them feel the dignity of manhood, and they could no longer be manacled by priests and tyrants.

Come with me into their dark, dirty, empty, comfortless houses: no neat, tidy house-wife; no intelligent, pretty children; no tables, chairs or couches; no nice carpet, or clean floor; no beds, with linen white and clean; no crockery, glass or cutlery—nothing to delight the eye, or cheer the heart, in these dreary abodes. We no sooner approach the domestic condition and relations of this people, than we find ourselves penetrating a dark corner of Paganism; for the light of woman's countenance does not shine there. This single fact, so often told, and so well known, of the universal degradation of the whole female sex, speaks a volume to the reflecting mind, concerning the domestic relations of the Hindoos. Divest woman of her native dignity and persuasive power, strip her of her natural prerogatives in the domestic circle, and what of domestic happiness and comfort have you left? Convert the mother into a menial, the wife into a servant, and what idea of a family remains? Make marriage a matter of contract and sordid interest, in which the fathers of the infant parties only consult their own profit or convenience, or, perhaps, only their whims, and what prospect is there of conjugal happiness and fidelity?—what pledge of domestic peace and happiness? Forbid second marriages; make widowhood disgraceful and miserable; close your doors against all that large class of girls and women, who have been so unfortunate as to lose their husbands; deprive them of all the means of an honorable subsistence and a happy social existence; doom them, by these cold civilities, to a life of disgrace and misery; or compel them to mount the funeral pile to escape the infamy of a sadder alternative, then ask, if woman may be happy in India? Make woman feel that she is a being of another and an inferior order; that she is made to be trampled on; that she is incapable of mental improvement; that she cannot rise above her present low level; and, finally, that she is below any order of beings that may hope (while retaining her womanhood) to reach the unfading delights of Paradise—familiarize her to such debasing lessons of her humiliation, and where would be the golden dreams of connubial bliss?—where the sweet converse of "kindred souls?"—where all the tender associations, the kindly emotions, which cluster around the dear names of sister! mother! wife? Alas! what is heathenism, when seen in real life!

Instances like the following, which came under my own observation, and which were not uncommon, will illustrate what I have said: "While addressing a native assembly at one of our preaching places, we were disturbed by an uproar in the street near us. In an instant my hearers had all decamped. Some passed out at the door, but more made an unceremonious escape through the windows. After a few moments they returned, and I inquired the cause of the riot. 'Oh, nothing,' replied one, 'only some fellow was whipping his wife!' On looking, I saw a multitude of people passing, at the head of which was the man referred to, driving his poor wife through the town with his shoe, and, at almost every step, beating her with it. The scene did not seem to impress the mind of the crowd that there was any thing singular in it. I did not discover that it excited any sympathy in behalf of the woman."

2. The social condition of the Oriental World has excited no little interest among the nations of the West; and the Hindoos have here contributed their full share to such interest. But the feature of Hindoo society which has attracted most attention, and which distinguishes the social condition of that people from that of any other, is the institution of caste. This determines all social positions and intercourse, and, indeed, regulates every calling, employment and profession—it erects a formidable barrier to all improvement beyond the prescribed limits of caste—it circumscribes the efforts of the aspiring within the narrow limits of their own hereditary occupation—it cripples genius, and holds out no premium to merit or industry. No degree of energy, excellence or virtue—no effort which a man of inferior caste can make—can raise him to the next superior caste; all emulation is nipped in the bud. The laws of caste, as unchangeable as the laws of the Medes and Persians, have determined every man's position before he was born. This cold, exclusive system, is carried into all the varied affairs of life. It prohibits all social intercourse among the different castes—it excludes every man of an inferior caste from the house, the company, the employment, and the table of the man of superior caste—it forever prevents the intermarriage of different castes; and it is, indeed, founded on the principle that the different castes are not indeed beings of the same species of the race.

Thus one portion of the race is *born* to lord it over the other: one is born the head, another the tail. The two can neither eat together, nor drink from the same cup. They can have no social intercourse; and if so much as the *shadow* of a low caste man falls on a priest, the latter is polluted, and must undergo ablution and purification.

The influence which such notions must have on the social and moral condition of a people, can be easily conceived by any one who has a moderate share of discernment into human affairs. One of the most obvious effects of the system is, to pamper the pride of the higher orders and to demean the lower. Hence we find the Brahmuns haughty, insolent, overbearing, dogmatical and despotic; while the common people are base, cringing, mean, spiritless and mercenary. They have no character to support, and are well aware that no efforts of theirs can ever acquire them a character; consequently, they have none to lose. The former are objects of *worship*. The people actually bow down and worship them in the most servile manner; while, on the other hand, the caste of people who form the extreme of the latter, are regarded as so very low that they are not allowed to live in the same village, or to step into a public temple. Indeed, the Abbe Dubois speaks of a caste of people in southern India, called the Pannah caste, who are so completely excluded from the community of man by the reputed meanness of their birth, that they are not allowed to build houses, or to walk on the public road. They live in caves or dens in the earth, or under some temporary shelter; and, if seen in the public path, they are obliged to make a circuit of a hundred yards around a traveler whom they may have occasion to pass. A Brahmun is polluted if he step on the same mat with a Pannah, or the shadow of the latter fall on him.

3. There is much that has attracted attention in the *civil* condition of the people of India. It is a feature not a little extraordinary, that nearly all the political power, which, directly or indirectly, controls that great and populous country, should be exercised by a nation which inhabits a little island on the opposite side of the globe; that this great mass of people should be kept in subjection so long as they were by a foreign people at such a distance, and this, too, when little but the controlling

power was foreign. The people were absolutely hired to conquer, and then to keep in subjection, themselves! All commissioned officers of the army, and all heads of departments in the civil service, are Europeans; while the great mass of the common soldiery, and all subordinates in the civil services, are natives. The pay and honor belongs to the foreigners; the hard service to the natives. The government is a military despotism. The very soil of the land is the exclusive property of the government. Each of the four presidencies into which the British possessions are divided, has its subordinate governor and bishop, its own army, judiciary and executive; while the whole is under a Governor-General, whose seat of government, as well as the residence of the Lord Bishop, is at Calcutta.

The goverment of India is exceedingly expensive—the revenue, in time of peace, barely meeting the expenditure. Taxation is, of course, oppressive. The army is immense: in time of peace—or rather, I should say, in ordinary times—scarcely less than 300,000 native Sepoy soldiers, and, perhaps, a tenth part of that number of European soldiers. The heads of departments—that is, English officers and functionaries—are paid extravagantly. The salary of the Governor-General is £25,000 ($125,-000) per annum; a member of council receives £8,000 ($40,000); judges, £6,000; commanders-in-chief, about the same. The almost fabulous wealth of ancient India has long since departed; and the real wealth of modern India has long since been made the spoil of her conquerors. Immense sums have gone to England. Very much of the present revenue is realized from a people so absolutely poor that they look not beyond the paying of their taxes and the bare supply of their absolute wants from day to day. Such is the condition of more than 100,000,000 of the natives of India! Besides these, there are 50,000,000 governed by their own native princes; yet none of these are absolutely independent. Some are tributary to the English Government; others are obliged to receive an English Resident at their court, who is more king than counselor, and to keep up an army *officered by Englishmen;* and all are, by treaty or by terror of British power, in some sort of dependence on the will of their foreign invaders. Such *has* been the state of things in India. What *will* be, remains to be seen.

The character of the present government, though it be the government of a great empire, does not differ very essentially from the character of the first little company of merchants which settled on the banks of the Hoogly, near two hundred years ago. No plans of permanent residence, or of benefiting the people of the country, can be supposed to have actuated the individuals composing the Company at that period. That little body, now expanded into colossal dimensions, is still animated by the same spirit. Every Company's servant is still a true representation of his honorable patrons. In no sense does he regard India as his *home.* He comes for a limited period; he longs to have it expire. He has almost as little sympathy with the natives as if he had remained in England; he transmits his fortune there; sends his children there; his interests, his relations, his heart, is in England; and I should only be repeating what many confess, should I say, he leaves his *religion* there.

I need not add that such a state of things, and such a tenure of the soil, can never be favorable to the improvement of the country, and the social and civil progress of the people. Such a government may, as it actually does, *tolerate* the philanthropic and benevolent efforts which others would make to instruct and evangelize the people, but sanctions nothing of the kind. Indeed, the government are bound by treaty not merely to abstain from all interference with the religions of the country, but actually to contribute to the support of temples and holy places, to pay Brahmuns to pray for rain, and many such like fooleries as may be supposed to conciliate native prejudices, or not to offend their superstitions.

Under her present governmental auspices, India is, as she has been for more than eight centuries, like a rented estate, for which the tenant has no further regard but to secure his present profits. The policy of her rulers has been to fleece the land, and to secure the greatest possible amount, and at the least possible return.

And the subordinates, again, as they rent the lands, feel, if possible, less interest to bestow labor on them in reference to any future benefit. Internal improvement, therefore, is scarcely a part of the English policy there. Since their castigation by Burke, they have constructed a few roads, railways and telegraphs; and a few bridges, hospitals and churches would remain, were they driven from India, as foot-prints of their rule. Yet when we consider the extent of their territory, the immense wealth which they have carried from the country, and the hundred million of souls, whose temporal and eternal welfare the Great Disposer of nations has put into their hands, we are constrained to say they have done, comparatively, nothing for that people.

4. In a review of a pleasant, and, as the writer hopes, not altogether a profitless residence in India, reminiscences, *personal, local* and *physical,* are readily reproduced.

Fatalists, as the Hindoos all are, they believe a man is a mere automaton, a machine, without self-agency or accountability. His motives, thoughts, affections, impulses, actions, are not his own. The learned priest will seriously argue that there is really no such thing as merit or demerit, right and wrong. Caste is not an arbitrary or conventional arrangement, but an institution founded in the nature of beings. It naturally, and eternally, divides men into different orders—erects barriers, which no circumstances, education, or progress can break down. The origin of the different orders is radically different, and no efforts of man can change them. One proceeded from the head of Brahmu (the Creator), and of course inherit the wisdom, and excellence, and sanctity of its divine Original! These are the priests. Another originated from the arms and breasts of the imaginary Brahmu; and therefore possess, in an eminent degree, the strength of the Supreme. These are designated as the protectors of the race, or the kings and soldiers. The third class originated in the loins of Great Brahmu—indicating that they are to supply the world with the means of subsistence. These are merchants, shop-keepers, and the like. And the last, and the least of all, are the poor Shroodras, who proceeded from the feet of the Creator. These are all that large class of laborers, servants, and working-men of all descriptions.

The Shroodras, comprehending the great mass of the common people, are divided and subdivided into as many castes as there are different kinds of labor. Hence the institution of caste is, practically, but little else (except in reference to the Brahmuns) than a hereditary division of labor, enforced by a pretended divine sanction. Such notions cling to every man there as a part of his being, and may, therefore, be regarded as personal.

Other natural traits of Hindoo character are, indolence, falsehood, subtlety and treachery. Labor is everywhere in the East regarded as a sore evil and a disgrace. No one will perform manual labor, unless compelled to it by actual necessity. If a man has an income of only five rupees per month, he would give two of these for a servant, and half starve himself and family on the remainder, rather than do his own work; and this servant will perhaps pay one-half of his small stipend to some one poorer than himself to do his work for him. To eat, drink, smoke, lounge, and sleep two-thirds of the time, and then to spend the remainder of the day in idleness, or in listening to some gross tale or bawdy song, is, in the estimation of the sensual idolater, the *summum bonum* of all human happiness. Nothing sooner attracts the attention of the newly arrived in India, or impresses him more unfavorably of the native character, than the throngs of idle people which he everywhere encounters, and at all times of the day. The number employed, at any one time, is comparatively so small that he would suppose the people were having a holiday.

This national indolence has been charged to the climate. To some extent it is doubtless so; yet it is rather the legitimate result of heathenism. A cold, lifeless system of Paganism offers no premium to industry. No value is set on *time*. The comforts and elegancies of life are, if not unknown, unappreciated. Domestic happiness is a term without a meaning. Public spirit and patriotism are but names. Political despotism and a most accomplished system of priestcraft annihilate everything belonging to the common man but his bare existence. And what incitements has he to industry? And, besides, the people have no right in the soil, and, consequently, feel no interest to make improvements, and to better their condition; for all that a despotic government leaves, a voracious priesthood is sure to take. Few as the wants of the mass of the people are, no necessity is felt on the present system to increase them. Every man's rank and character being established by immutable law, sovereign custom, and religious sanction, no industry or virtue of his can change them. The social, the more tender, refined and benevolent feelings of our natures not being there developed, the consequent incentives to industry and virtue are not brought into action.

Would we benefit these heathen people, we must first of all supply incentives to industry—we must apply a remedy suited to the disease. This remedy is found only in Christianity. This restores to man the *condition of a man*. It opens before him ten thousand motives to industry, of which Paganism knows nothing. It *allures* him to labor, and assures him of the fruits of his labor. No more shall the hand of the sower recoil, because "one may sow and another reap." While a bare subsistence — the mere sustenance of the *animal* — is the highest and almost the only object aimed at or desired; and while this is furnished, as in warm countries, by the labors of only a small portion of the day, the people are not likely to be reclaimed from their vitiating habits of idleness.

Idleness is the mother of vice everywhere; but I shall not attempt to describe the progeny in so fertile a soil as India.

Nor are dishonesty, falsehood, dissimulation and subtlety less prominent traits of native character. It may be said of them, as of the Cretans, they are always *liars!* They justify falsehood, and deem it comely if the end be good. Expediency seems their only standard of right and wrong. This is the first lesson of *morality* which the infant mind receives; and, as he grows to maturity, a vitiated moral sense does not lead him to correct the errors of his early teachings. Deception becomes a habit; and no people acquire it more readily, or become greater adepts. Dissimulation and subtlety seem the spontaneous growth of the Indian mind; and in these unlovely arts the Brahmuns surpass all others. The duplicity of a Hindoo priest puts to the blush the most refined system of civilized hypocrisy. In social intercourse, in commercial dealings, in argument, honesty is but a name.

Physically, the Hindoos do not differ essentially from European races, except in the color of their skin. They have the European features—are doubtless of the Caucasian variety—have straight hair, slender, well-formed bodies, somewhat below the common stature. This may be attributed partly to climate, and perhaps more to their light vegetable diet. Persons of high caste are not only fairer in complexion, but smaller in stature, and more delicate in form, than the lower and laboring classes. The latter, to some extent, use animal food. The women of the lower orders are generally stout and strong, and capable of nearly as much hard labor as the men.

5. No theme, perhaps, occupies the attention of writers on India more than the religions of the country. Brahmunism is the prevailing religion of the Hindoos; and it is that with which we are at present concerned. Bhoodism is the prevailing religion in the countries beyond the Ganges and in China; and Mohammedanism, a religion of less ancient date, is practiced by a large class of people in all those countries.

Brahmunism is not so gross and absolutely false, as it is sophistical, frigid and transcendental. Its mythology indicates more of perverted intellect than of absolute ignorance. It is at very antipodes of Christianity. The one breathes good will to man. It is in its very nature to remove evil, and to impart unadulterated good. It is a sun that dispels darkness. It is a river which fertilizes the barren field; a fountain, whose streams flow forth to irrigate the parched desert; a tree, whose leaves are for the healing of the nations, whose fruits shall gladden the hearts of many, and under whose shadow the weary may rest. It is an ocean, on whose bosom are wafted the treasures of heaven. The other is a system of cold, unmixed selfishness. Practically, it is a most unblushing system of priestcraft. Its rites, practices, precepts, all tend to a single point, the aggrandizement of the priesthood. It imparts neither light, nor life, nor love. It brings no relief to the needy, no joy to the sorrowful, no balm to the wounded spirit, no hope to the desponding. It rivets the chains of the captive, closes the prison doors against all aspirations for light and liberty, and seals up the lips of instruction. It vitiates the fountain of moral principle, and dries up the streams of human happiness, and leaves man a cold-hearted, selfish, hopeless being. It nurtures sin by religious sanctions, and entails it on its miserable votaries; but makes no effectual provisions for its removal. It offers no remedy for the miseries of this life, nor affords a gleam of light to guide the benighted soul to the realms of eternal day.

Pilgrimages, holy days and holy places, constitute a larger portion of the religion of this people, and are sources of more corruption and misery, than is generally known. Most pilgrimages are undertaken doubtless at the instigation of priests, and for the benefit of a more lazy set of the same order, who subsist at the holy place on their unrighteous impositions on pilgrims. A long pilgrimage is the occasion of an immense deal of suffering and wretchedness, and many leave their homes never to return. To a family that could scarcely live at home on their scanty resources, a three months' journey could be no trifle, even were there no Brahminical impositions to filch from them their last *pice*, or no disease or desolating pestilence to be encountered amidst the filthy, half-fed and half-clothed crowds which throng the holy place. These are calamities which almost always accompany a pilgrimage. Tens of thousands, sometimes hundreds of thousands, without shelter, without a competent supply of even the coarsest food, badly clad and intolerably filthy, are for weeks, or months, crowded together in the narrow limits of one dirty village. Here they are fleeced by the priests, under the pretext that the efficacy of their pilgrimage depends on their paying good fees for Brahminical prayers and the performance of religious rites, and for the privilege of

VIEW OF THE CITY OF BROOSA.

bathing in the sacred stream, or for worshiping the renowned deity of the place. The cholera seldom fails to cut down the wretched multitude with pitiless havoc.

But these holy places are not merely, and perhaps not principally, the resorts of pilgrims for religious purposes. They are the rendezvous of the vilest of the vile, congregated here not to pay their adorations to the god of the place or to the sacred stream, but to compass their own base purposes, and add another list to the long catalogue of human crimes. The gambler, the cheat, the libertine and prostitute are prominent characters in these motley multitudes.

The same is essentially true of the celebration of holy days, and days of public worship of the gods. At best, these are but days of amusement and frivolity, and only tend to debase and corrupt the minds of the people. On these occasions no restraint is laid on children and youth. They attend and mingle freely in all these scenes of foolery, vice and low obscenity, without any one to raise the note of alarm, or to teach them to hate what is so instinctively hateful. Their fathers and mothers, and the reputedly wise and holy, bear a part in rites and observances the most childish, if not abominable; and why should they not follow in their footsteps?

Hindooism has no heart. It scarcely, if at all, affects the moral feelings of the man. A man may be very religious, and yet indulge any corrupt passion flesh is heir to. His holiness consists in a stock in trade which he has accummulated by acts of penance or of worship, the quantity always being in proportion to the bodily exercise or infliction of pain. Nor need he personally accumulate righteousness. He may do it by proxy, or buy of him who has to sell. Religion is a *business* to be performed by its appropriate class or caste of men, subject to similar restrictions of caste as any other business. It is the work of the priest. A person of any other caste has nothing to do with religion, except to perform a few unmeaning ceremonies, submit to any imposed penances, and pay his money. He depends for the atonement of his sins, for righteousness and the salvation of his soul, on a class of men who do these things for hire. Righteousness is bought and sold like any other commodity. A late Hindoo prince in one day paid a devotee 25,000 rupees ($12,000) for his righteousness. Priests and devotees go through the different duties of religion *officially*, without the least appearance of seriousness; and the people having little or nothing to do in the matter, and being taught that they cannot understand it, concern themselves but little on the subject. By religion is meant pilgrimages, processions, penances, prostrations to idols, presents to Brahmuns, repetitions of names, counting of beads, observances of holy days, and such like mummeries. With all the talk of the wise and holy about *divine contemplation*, abstraction, absorption in the deity, nothing is so difficult to teach this people as the *spirituality* of our religion. In all their religious notions and habits, they never connect religion with the heart.

Credulity is a marked feature in the Hindoo's belief. He scarcely pretends to believe because his reason is convinced, for reason has nothing to do with his religion. Nor does he practice the rites and observe the ceremonies of his religion because he sees in them any suitableness to his condition as a sinner, or any adaptedness to his wants in this world or the world to come. But he so believes and practices because his fathers did so before him. *This* he regards as an incontrovertible answer to all you can urge against his religion. He thinks it presumption to call in question the wisdom of his wiser and holier forefathers. He has no more need of *reason* in his religion than he has of heart.

Hindooism, I said, is priestcraft, and the priests are notorious for their duplicity and avarice. The people are the dupes of the most designing, voracious set of men. Their sacred writings, their national legends, the oral teachings of the priests, custom, caste, every influence that can be brought to act on the fears and superstitions of an ignorant people, are brought into play for this purpose. The people are dependent on the priests for everything—not in matters of religious belief and practice alone, but in all the affairs of common life. The Brahmuns hold the keys of all knowledge and mystery. They can as effectually open and shut the hidden stores of happiness or wealth, as they can the treasures of heaven. Hence the perfect subserviency of the people to the priests. They revere them as gods, fall down and worship them, make them offerings, and lick the dust of their feet.

The religious character of the Hindoo may be, also, inferred from the number and character of his *gods*. Nominally, there are 33,000,000. It is nearer the truth to say they are pantheists. They worship everything but the true God, and believe anything but the truth. They adore the sun, moon and stars; they worship through the medium of images of wood, stone, iron, brass, silver or gold, a great variety of imaginary deities, superior and inferior. Under every green tree and on every high hill may be seen the disgusting emblems of idolatry. Sometimes the idol is but an uncarved stone, or a shapeless piece of wood, daubed at the top with a little red paint; sometimes it is of elegant workmanship, and presents an imposing appearance. Often are these fabled deities richly ornamented, and seated in an elegant temple, attended by a great company of priests, bathed with Ganges water, which may have been brought overland a thousand miles, clothed in gaudy attire, perfumed, decked with garlands of flowers, supplied with food and offerings of money, attended by servants who wave the fan over their heads to cool them or drive away the flies, and are worshiped by people as stupid and unconcerned about the act performed as the dumb idols.

Once a year these idols are taken from their places, seated on cars of enormous size and splendor, and drawn through the streets, amidst the shouts and acclamations of the multitude. Great pains are taken to keep up the character of these gods and to inspire the multitude with awe. It is pretended by the priests that miracles are from time to time wrought by them, and that they occasionally utter oracles to the priests. These things, however, are always done in the darkness of the night, and we in vain seek other testimony than that of the designing priesthood. Indeed, the multitude are not permited to enter the temples at all, and seldom or never see the god, except on his annual festival.

The tree, the blade of grass, the vegetable, the flower, the grain, are objects of adoration. They worship the reptile, the serpent and the fish. They pay divine honors to the birds of the air and to the beasts of the field. They adore the ox, the cow and the horse. Whatever is useful and conducive to their comfort or gratification, and whatever they fear, they make the objects of their worship. How debasing is idolatry! The noblest part of man is thus brought down from the contemplation of the grand and ennobling realities of heaven, and is confined to the contemplation of a piece of wood, or a stone, or a loathsome reptile. But this is not all: the influence of idolatry is not only degrading, not only *belittleing* to the *mind*, but it vitiates the *heart*. It benumbs the kindlier feelings of our natures, and dries up all those sweet fountains of life which send forth their streams to refresh and gladden the weary pilgrim on his way through this wilderness world.

They attribute to their gods all the vile passions of human nature: lying, deception, thefts, adulteries, intrigues, and all manner of sins. What can we expect the votaries of such gods will be? They may emulate their gods, they may be like them. But who ever thinks it incumbent on him to be better than his god? The Hindoo may find an apology for any sin he may wish to commit, in the precept of his Bible or the character of his god.

The Hindoos, however, are not a very religious people, even in their own acceptation of the term. They worship their gods at option, observe festivals and holidays as pastimes, and go through the drudgery of rites and observances, either for the sake of a livelihood or for a name. Their bigotry does not often appear, except when elicited by opposition. They find in Hindooism a counterpart of their own corrupt hearts. It imposes no restraints on their passions, it demands no sacrifices which the most depraved heart cannot render, and therefore they prefer their religion to any other. But a few unmeaning acts, a few heartless observances, make up the religion of this wretched people. Enmity to God, hatred to holiness, is really the prominent characteristic of the Hindoo. No argument is necessary to show that nothing but the Gospel of Jesus Christ can supply the desired antidote. The disease lies deep in the heart. Nothing can reach it but Gospel truth. Give the heathen the Gospel, and you at once throw open to them a fountain which alone can wash them from the moral pollutions of a hundred generations. In view of the religious character of the heathen, what, Christian reader, seems to be your duty in reference to the work of the world's conversion? Have you done all you ought to do — all you can do? This question will recur at the great day with an awful solemnity.

Their heaven is a place of unbridled sensuality, with the physical susceptibility on their part of perpetual indulgence. After a series of transmigrations, in which they may be successful or unsuccessful in bringing their righteousness to preponderate over their sin, and so pass accordingly into a higher or a lower state of existence, the soul at length finds rest in one of the seven heavens. So absurd and contradictory are all their theories of a future state, and so trifling and carnal are all their notions on this subject, as to afford nothing on which the mind can repose. Their darkened souls can never be cheered with the hope of a glorious immortality. All beyond the grave is dark, unknown. I have often listened to their various theories of a future state, but have never met with one who, if he were not prevented by pride to sustain his argument, would not confess that neither he nor any one knew anything "what will be beyond the grave." Neither fears nor hopes seem often to sustain or depress them in the hour of death. Most that can be said is, they have a dark foreboding of the future — a dread to cease to live and to enter on an *unknown* state of existence.

Dark indeed are the *prospects* of the heathen world. Not a ray of light penetrates the dark abyss which stretches out beyond the river of death. We follow him to the furthest precincts of revealed light. We see him enter the portals of eternal darkness, thence we hear a voice saying, "No idolater shall enter the kingdom of heaven." Here we must leave the poor heathen. Little would it avail in the mind of the devoted saint, if he could, by any process of reasoning, convince himself that here and there *one* out of the hundreds of millions of heathen might feel his way, guided by the dim lamp of nature, to the realms of eternal day. Could he, indeed, know that there are a few pious heathen, (a fact by no means established,) this would form but a sorry excuse for neglecting the millions who must perish without the Gospel.

Another feature of the religious character of the Hindoo, which has an important practical bearing on his life, and presents a no slight obstacle in the way of his moral and religious improvement, is his inveterate *fatalism*. On this subject the Hindoo writings teach that it is "the Great Spirit which is diffused through every form of animated matter; that actions of every kind are *his;* that he is the charioteer, and the body the chariot; that it is the highest attainment of human wisdom to realize the fact, that the human soul and Brahmu are one and the same. By this doctrine, all accountability is destroyed, and liability to punishment rendered preposterous. How often has the author heard it urged by the most sensible Hindoos, that the moving cause of every action, however flagitious, is God; that man is an instrument upon which God plays what tune he pleases. Another modification of this doctrine is that of *fate*, unchangeable destiny; embraced, without a dissentient voice, by all the Hindoos. Thus the Deity, on his throne, is insulted as the author of all crimes; and men are emboldened to rush forward in the swiftest career of iniquity."

The Hindoos are the most cold-blooded fatalists in the world. Every occurrence in life is the result of dire necessity. If they are prosperous, it is fate. If they are in distress, it is fate. To lie, cheat, or steal, is fate. To be idle, dissipated, impoverished, and imprisoned, is fate. The poor sufferer apparently feels no remorse that his own sin has brought misery on him. He only curses his hard fate. The thief or the robber is detected, convicted, and condemned to prison or chains for life. He apparently never regards himself as suffering the just penalty of the violated law. He submits with the uttermost coolness to his lot, as being the irresistible decision of fate, over which he could have no control, and in which he has no responsibility. The murderer is arraigned, tried, and sentenced to the gallows. He confesses no guilt, and manifests the most perfect indifference. The intention, the act of murder, the detection, the sentence, and the execution, are all alike the consequences of incorrigible fate, in which he had no direction, agency, or responsibility. Declaring his innocency to the last, he goes to the gallows as coolly as he would go to his dinner, and launches into eternity as regardless of futurity as the brutes. All with him is fate. The application which natives frequently make of this term is sometimes really laughable. A child, who was usually very peevish and noisy, was one day crying incessantly, to the great annoyance of all in the house. A hamal (bearer) who took care of him, and was much attached to him, hearing the complaints which were brought against his little charge, felt called on to defend him from all censure on that subject. "The child is not to be blamed for crying," said he, "*it is his fate to cry.*"

It will not be an unbefitting close of this chapter to inquire what has been done, and what is doing, to save India from the demoralization of her religion, and the vortex of her despotism? I have said that the prevalence of a pure Christianity is the only remedy. Had this been applied in time—had the East India Government done what it could to favor the introduction of Christianity and all its benign institutions into her populous provinces of the East, and had the Christian church followed up, to the full extent of her ability, the unprecedented openings which Providence had thus made—had she employed the facilities which were in so extraordinary a manner put into her hands, India would probably have been saved her present calamities, and the government been spared an atrocious and expensive war, and the kingdom of Christ secured one of its richest conquests.

But what has been done, and what are the available resources which Christianity at the present time possesses for further conquests in that great field? I cannot, probably, answer the question better than by transcribing a statistical paragraph from an article in a late number of the Calcutta Review. The article seems to be got up by an intelligent writer in the country, and comes to us indorsed by our late excellent missionary, Mr. Hume, of Bombay. It is believed to contain reliable, as it certainly does encouraging, facts as to what has been effected by missionary effort in India and Ceylon, in the last half century. It must be borne in mind, while reading this extract, that the larger part of these results have been gained within a few years. It was an immensely difficult work, and one which required a long time, to prepare the ground and get in the seed, the first fruits of which are beginning to appear. When it is said that "five thousand have been received into the churches on evidence of their conversion," it is not meant to throw discredit on the conversion of the remaining number; but we are probably to understand, that while many have been taken into a nominal connection with the church by baptism, which has been readily done by the missionaries of some societies, especially in Southern India, yet none of these have been admitted to full communion, till, in the judgment of charity, they could be regarded as real Christians.

"At the close of 1850, fifty years after the modern English and American societies had begun their labor in Hindoostan, and thirty years since they have been carried on in full efficiency, the STATIONS, at which the Gospel is preached in India and Ceylon, are *two hundred and sixty in number*, and engage the services of FOUR HUNDRED AND FORTY-THREE MISSIONARIES, belonging to *twenty-two* missionary societies. Of these missionaries, TWENTY-TWO ARE ORDAINED NATIVES. Assisted by SIX HUNDRED AND EIGHTY-EIGHT NATIVE PREACHERS, they proclaim the word of God in the bazaars and markets, not only at their several stations, but in the districts around them. They have thus spread far and wide the doctrines of Christianity, and have made a considerable impression even upon the unconverted population. They

SCHOOLHOUSE IN INDIA.

have founded *three hundred and nine* NATIVE CHURCHES, containing *seventeen thousand three hundred and fifty-six* MEMBERS, or COMMUNICANTS, of whom *five thousand* were admitted on the evidence of their being converted. These church members form the nucleus of a NATIVE CHRISTIAN COMMUNITY, comprising ONE HUNDRED AND TWELVE THOUSAND individuals, who regularly enjoy the blessings of Bible instruction, both for young and old. The efforts of missionaries in the cause of education, are now directed to *thirteen hundred and forty-five* DAY SCHOOLS, in which *eighty-three thousand seven hundred boys* are instructed through the medium of their own vernacular language; to *seventy-three* BOARDING SCHOOLS, containing *nineteen hundred and ninety-two boys*, chiefly Christian, who reside upon the missionaries' premises, and are trained up under their eye; and to *one hundred and twenty-eight* DAY SCHOOLS, with *fourteen thousand boys and students*, receiving a sound scriptural education, through the medium of the English language. Their efforts in FEMALE EDUCATION embrace *three hundred and fifty-four* DAY SCHOOLS, with *eleven thousand five hundred girls;* and *ninety-one* BOARDING SCHOOLS, with *two thousand four hundred and fifty girls*, taught almost exclusively in the vernacular languages. The BIBLE has been wholly translated into *ten languages*, and the New Testament into *five* others, not reckoning the Serampore versions. In these ten languages, a considerable Christian literature has been produced, and also from *twenty* to *fifty* tracts, suitable for distribution among the Hindoo and Mussulman population. Missionaries have also established, and now maintain, *twenty-five* printing establishments. While preaching the Gospel regularly in these numerous tongues of India, missionaries maintain ENGLISH SERVICES in *fifty-nine* chapels, for the edification of our own countrymen. The total cost of this vast missionary agency, during the past year, amounted to ONE HUNDRED AND EIGHTY-SEVEN THOUSAND POUNDS; of which *thirty-three thousand five hundred pounds* were contributed in this country; not by the native Christian community, but by Europeans."

We glean from a similar source a variety of facts, of a general and far-reaching character, which we may safely take as prognostics of the rising star of India. The demon of war may sorely scourge her first; but when the smoke of the battle-field shall have cleared away, and the ruins of war shall be repaired, and peace again smile, we divine great and good things for India. The rich temples of Brahmu shall become the sanctuaries of a great people devoted to the service of the living God.

Within a few years what elements of progress have been introduced into India—aside, I mean, from the direct agencies of Christianity.

Among these are the construction of railroads, the introduction of the magnetic telegraph, the greatly increased power of the press, steam navigation on her great rivers, the more rapid transmission of the mail to Europe, improvements in postal arrangements, reforms of the marriage law and of the law of inheritance, and a growing interest in female education. Caste, too, has, to some encouraging extent, loosened its hold on the habits of the people. America is now within six weeks of India, and soon England will be within twenty days' distance, and America within thirty days. Such proximity to two such nations must have a powerful agency in bringing about important changes in the character and institutions of that country.

There is hope for India; and there are strange forebodings in the Hindoo mind, (as there is in the mind of the Moslem,) which justify our hopes. "A strong impression," says one, "is prevailing, that there is soon to be a serious defection from the ranks of Hindooism. In Bombay, for some months there has been an unusual degree of excitement and alarm in view of the progress of Christianity, and the springing up of a more liberal and reforming spirit in certain quarters among themselves. It is well known that many of the better educated young men have lost all confidence in Hindooism, while not a few are intellectually convinced of the truth of Christianity. Numerous reports have been circulated, that on such or such a day, or in a few days, ten, fifteen, twenty, or more, were to be baptized. This blind fear that an impending fatal blow is soon to be received by Hindooism, is further increased by the new law, which secures the right of property, &c., to converts. All the struggles which they shall now make will but hasten the time of the Gospel's triumph."

CHAPTER VII.

The Deckan — Its extent — Tenure of lands — Face of the country — Climate, seasons, soil, productions — Walled towns — Open country — Flocks and herds — No roads — Modes of conveyance — Rivers — Chief towns — Sketch of Poona.

THE Deckan has already become the principal field for the benevolent operation of the American churches in Western India. Not only does it present a wide and extensive field, but there are fewer obstacles to the pleasant and successful prosecution of missions by Americans. A brief historical sketch will, therefore, be acceptable to the inquiring reader; for every thing which goes to elucidate the history of a heathen nation, is a step gained towards its Christianization. Christians cannot be brought to *act* for the emancipation of India till a corresponding *feeling* be excited; and this feeling will not exist till there be a corresponding knowledge of the character, condition, and history of the people for whom they are called to feel and act. We by no means despair that the Lord has yet a great work for his people to do in India. The cloud will be removed, and a better day dawn.

The word Deckan, Dashina, or south country, is a term of somewhat indefinite import; it was formerly applied by Hindoo geographers to all the countries which lie south of the Nerbuddah river. But the Mohammedans, holding no permanent possessions south of the river Krishna, applied the name Deckan to the countries which were situated between these two rivers, and extending from the Indian Ocean on the west to the bay of Bengal on the east. Since the conquests by the English, the term has undergone another limitation. What now is generally understood by the Deckan, is that part of the above mentioned territory which is owned by the English. This is bounded on the north and the south by the Nerbuddah and the Krishna rivers; on the west by the Ghaut Mountains, and on the east by the Godavery river, which separates it from the territories of the Nizam of Hydrabad; including the districts of Poona, Ahmednuggur, Cankish, Darwar, and the possession of the Rajah of Sattara.

Deckan, thus limited, has a population of ten or twelve millions, three-fourths of whom speak the Mahratha language. This territory comprises on area of 70,000 square miles, and contains, according to Hamilton's Indian Gazeteer, 9,481 towns and villages, 7,229 of which belong to the British Government. And here the inquiry will naturally arise, to whom do the others belong? It may, therefore, be well here to explain the peculiar manner in which this part of the country is possessed. Governments within governments are common, I believe, throughout India. The origin of such a state of things seems to have been this: martial chieftains, and others deserving well of the state, were rewarded, by their prince, with the government of a certain number of cities or villages, according to their bravery, or the number of troops which they had furnished, or the services which they had otherwise rendered. As one of these chieftains increased the number of his villages, he increased his army and extended his power, and in time became an independent prince. This was the case with Sindia and Holkar, who were once generals in the Peshwa's army. They fought *for* him, till he had enabled them to fight *against* him; then they fought for themselves, and established dominions in Central India, still holding the possessions which had been given them by the Peshwa in the Deckan.

We will, for the sake of illustrating this subject, take for an example the district or collectorate of Ahmednuggur. This contains 6,000 or 8,000 square miles, and 2,647 towns and villages. One hundred and eight of these are *enams*, that is, they have been given as a present to families or individuals, in consideration of some important service which the parties have rendered to government; one hundred and ninety-eight are jarghires (freeholds); one hundred and seventy-nine belong to Sindia, eighty to Holkar, and forty-four to the Nizam of Hydrabad. These different persons *own* their respective villages, and exercise in them their several governments, independent of each other. There is also another description of land and village proprietors, whose tenure, to the ear of an American, appears somewhat curious. Lands and villages are owned by Hindoo gods. These places, which are not a few in number, have, at some former period, been given by their respective owners to their favorite deities; and the revenue of each village is, from this time, devoted to the supposed benefit of its god. This is expended in the different services at the temple, as bathing the god, burning incense, fanning the idol, sweeping the temple, and such like; in sacrifices, feastings, and processions; and in the support of as great a number of Brahmuns, and *wives of the god*, as the revenue will allow. The reader will have a better idea of these religious establishments, when he has read the seventeenth chapter of this volume.

Hence it is that the traveler or the missionary is heard to speak of being in the possession of different native princes, in the same region of country, and in the same day. In traveling twenty miles, we may preach in one village belonging to the English, another to Sindia, a third to Holkar, and a fourth the property of Gunputtee or Khundoba. This state of things existed under the native government, and has been permitted to remain by the English as they found it. Something similar seems alluded to in the New Testament. The servants to whom a nobleman committed his goods, were rewarded by their masters according to their fidelity; one with "ten cities," another "with five cities." One half of the villages in the vicinity of Ahmednuggur are subject to Sindia or Holkar, whose capitals are in Central India. The suttee has been abolished under the rule of the British Government, but not in the dominions of these princes. Hence it is that the suttee is performed in the very heart of the English possessions, but not under their government. One of these horrid scenes took place, in February, 1834, within five miles of Ahmednuggur, and no notice was taken of it by the English Government. Five widows, the wives of one chief, were burnt, about the same time, within twenty-five miles of Bombay. Perhaps the English authorities cannot, consistently with their stipulations with these governments that they will not interfere with their religion, directly control these things; but as they *can* control where policy requires, why may they not when right and humanity demand?

The indulgence which Brahmunism has received from the existing government, is, in my opinion, reprehensible in the highest degree. There are many good men, both in England and in the service of government in India, who are sadly grieved at it, but are unable to apply the remedy. Treaties were entered into, and stipulations were made with the different native powers, when they yielded to British domination, which put it beyond the power of the present Executive to pursue that stern Christian policy, which, as a Christian nation, to a nation of idolaters, they are most solemnly bound to pursue. The present government is reduced to the sad alternative of violating a most *unchristian* treaty, or of regarding it. They have received large sums of money as the price of idolatry, as in the case of the pilgrim-tax; and perhaps still larger sums go out from their treasury every year for the support of Hindooism, as in the case of the revenues allowed to different temples. As a sort of *offset* against some of these things, they support schools for the natives, on the principles of free toleration, not allowing religion of *any* kind to be taught in them. As the teachers are idolaters and priests, and the scholars are idolaters, and need no teaching to keep them so, the *free toleration* amounts only to this, that *Christianity* shall not be taught in them. I have had an opportunity of seeing how the principle of these schools operates, both in Ahmednuggur and other places, and have found these schools more opposed to Christianity than those wholly under the patronage of the Hindoos themselves.

The Deckan has an elevation above the sea-coast of about 2,000 feet. It may be called an extensive table-land of the Eastern and Western Ghauts. In traveling from Bombay to Ahmednuggur, we pass over the low and level lands of the Concon, which are either occupied as rice fields, or contain large groves of cocoa-nut trees, and ascend these rugged mountains on the west, by a winding road to Kandalla, a village at the top of the Ghauts, and a place of some celebrity as a convalescent station for European invalids. This road is a work of enormous magnitude, and does honor to the enterprise of the English Government, at whose expense it was constructed. The view from the top of the Ghauts is magnificent. In the back ground rolls the western ocean, stretching to the limits of human vision, and losing itself in the distant view of the blue sky. Under your feet, but nearly two thousand feet below, commences an extensive plain, intersected by numerous streamlets, divided by deep furrows into rice fields, or covered with groves of the straight, slender, and stately cocoa-nut tree, or diversified with the mango tree, with its thick and beautiful foliage, and its wide-spreading branches. Other portions are overrun with an underwood, and present, from this distant and elevated point, a covering of eternal green. The rugged mountains themselves afford the most sublime scenery. They form a pleasing contrast with the surrounding country. Here we seem to get out of India, and once more to behold the scenery and to breathe the atmosphere of our native land. During the rainy season, the natural grandeur of this scenery is greatly enhanced by the torrents of water which fall on these hights, and rush down, in their forced channels, over the perpendicular rocks into the plain below. I have from one point counted more than twenty of these cascades, dashing over precipices of some hundred feet, and falling into one common basin beneath.

As the traveler winds his way through these frightful cliffs, he sees men and beasts of burden, borne down by their heavy loads, struggling to attain his point of elevation; or he may see, almost over his own head, but on a different bend of the same zigzag road, a company of travelers bending their course to the summit. Here he breathes a cool and salubrious air, and regales himself with the pure water of a mountain spring. As he proceeds onwards towards Ahmednuggur, by the way of Poona, without *descending*, he travels over an immense plain, diversified by gentle undulations, or broken up by small abrupt hills and valleys, and intersected by a great number of streams and rivulets, which take their rise among the Ghauts. He also crosses, if it be in the dry season, the almost empty channels of four or five rivers, of the magnitude of the Hudson, the Connecticut, the Delaware. During the rainy seasons, these channels are full, and perhaps overflow their banks. (Job 6 : 15 – 20.)

For eight months in the year, that is, during the dry season, the Deckan presents but little more than one unbroken waste of barrenness and desolation. No hedges or fences; no houses, except in the villages; no vegetation, except here and there a field about a well, or reservoir of water, called a garden, and artificially watered; and scarcely a tree to cheer the prospect, except it be a fruit tree, or a shade tree about a village. The country presents a dreariness of aspect which must be seen to be described. From November till about the first of July, the country presents but one dismal aspect of parched earth and barren rock. (Isa. 15: 6.) But on the return of the rains, about the middle of June, grass, flowers, vines, weeds, and a most luxuriant vegetation of every description, spring up, as if by magic; and the fields, which a few days before seemed as destitute of the root or seed of vegetation as the ash-heap, are now covered with green herbage. The barren rock seems to have vegetated. All nature smiles. The flocks and the herds are no longer obliged to thrust their noses into the earth, that they may crop the dried stems of the grass, or extract the very root. They are now led out to *green* pastures, (Psalm 23 : 2,) and soon satisfied from the abundant herbage, they lie down by the "side of still waters," whither the shepherd or the herdsman has guided them, or repose under the shade of the mango.

The eight *dry* months include both the cool and the hot

BAMBOO TREE.

seasons. The cool season commences with November, and the hot season with March. The atmosphere in the Deckan, during the cool season, is dry, clear, and cool. The variations of heat and cold during the twenty-four hours are much greater than in Bombay; and, in consequence, the climate is not so favorable at this particular season of the year as it is on the sea-coast. The extremes of cold and heat, from twelve at night to twelve at noon, are about 45° and 80°. Seldom, however, does the mercury fall below 50°, or rise above 70° or 75°.

From the first of March the weather becomes warm; but not always uncomfortably so, till the commencement of the *hot winds*, about the tenth of the month. These winds are a kind of sirocco, and resemble in a degree the heated air from the mouth of a burning furnace. There is nothing, however, pestilential in them. Europeans, if they are strong and healthy, do not suffer from this season; and those who are debilitated probably do not suffer on account of these winds, but rather on account of the great degree of heat. The mercury of the thermometer almost daily ranges from 90° to 100°. This is greater, perhaps, than the heat of the same season in Bombay. But there is this difference: the nights in Bombay are as oppressive as the days; while in the Deckan, the nights, during a greater part of the season, are *comparatively* cool. Hence we throw our houses open of a night, as far as our fears of thieves and robbers will allow of it; and by breathing the refreshing air a few hours, we recover, in a degree, from the lassitude of an oppressive day. At eight or nine in the morning, we close every door and window, and, as far as possible, shut out the heated atmosphere. In this way, a room which has thick walls, and not connected with the roof of the house, may be kept comparatively, not always, tolerably cool. At four or five in the afternoon, our prison doors are thrown open, and we go forth to our duties without. We can also do the same of a morning. The extreme heat of this season is moderated in Bombay by the *sea-breeze*, which daily blows during the same hours as the hot winds in the

Deckan. These winds are rendered *hot* by their passage over a great extent of heated land.

The remaining season is called the *wet* or rainy season. This commences about the middle of June, and continues three or three and a half months. Except in these months, a shower of rain, or a mist, seldom moistens the parched earth. On the sea-coast, the rains during this season are almost incessant. Day after day the water falls in torrents, until the tanks and reservoirs of water are overflowing, and many of the fields are inundated. The heavens are shrouded in blackness; the atmosphere, if not streaming with the descending flood, is damp and gloomy; the whole surface of the ground is mud and water; every thing is covered with rust or mould; and nothing but the "bow in the cloud" can satisfy the mind that Bombay and the whole Concon is not about to sink into a watery grave. It need not be said that the sea-coast is an uncomfortable as well as an unhealthful place in the rainy season.

But not so the Deckan. This is our most delightful and salubrious season. There we have alternate rain and sunshine. Genial showers, with intervals of clear weather, sometimes of two or three days, water the fields and nourish the springing vegetation. All nature wears a most lovely aspect, and only man withholds the expression of his gratitude to the Great Author of all his mercies. The quantity of rain which falls in Ahmednuggur, is probably less than a third part of what falls in Bombay. Hence Europeans, as far as their business will allow or their means will permit, endeavor to spend the rainy season east of the Ghauts. Poona is the most common place of resort.

The month following the rainy season, that is, October, may be regarded, in all this part of India, as the most unhealthful month in the year. Its insalubrity arises principally from the hot weather, and the rapid decay of vegetable matter. The quick and luxurious growth of vegetation, which covered the whole face of the country, now vanishes more rapidly than it appeared. The saturated earth, again exposed to the rays of a tropical sun, sends up its vapors, and these become impregnated by the noxious miasma of the decaying vegetation. But, as has been said, the quantity of rain is moderate in the Deckan, when compared with that of the sea-coast, and consequently the vegetation is proportionably less. Hence this month in the Deckan is much more salubrious than in the Concon. Persons disposed to liver complaints, or subject to rheumatism, are perhaps the only persons who are not likely to enjoy better health here than in Bombay, or any part of the Concon.

The soil of the Deckan in general is not fertile. If well watered and properly cultivated, it produces well. The cultivation in general is very miserable; and not a sixth part of the land is cultivated at all. The soil is not suited to rice. Wheat may be grown in abundance. Bajree, zoondlee and gram are the staple productions of the Deckan, and supply the place of rice in the Concon. Flax is grown; but the only part used is the seed, from which oil is made. The stalks are fine and short. Hemp is also a common production, from which ropes, etc., are manufactured. From the tops of the hemp, the natives make an intoxicating drink. The tops are plucked when green, and after being dried, are steeped in water and drunken. This is called *bhang*. Nearly all European vegetables flourish, if properly cultivated. Oranges, limes, plantains, bananas, shaddocks, guavas, grapes, peaches, melons, and citrons, only require attention to be produced in great abundance. The land is never manured. When the soil is exhausted, it can only be recovered by allowing it to remain fallow a few years. There being no wood in the Deckan, the manure is consumed for fuel.

The people in the Deckan do not live on their farms, or scattered over the country, but compactly in villages. This practice probably originated from the insecurity which they have experienced on account of robbers and plunderers, with whom the country was formerly, and is still to some measure, infested. The number, size, wealth, and population of the villages which the traveler meets at any given distance, depend very much on the fertility of that part of the country. The distance from one village to another is seldom less than two miles, or more than six. The number of houses varies from 10 or 12 to 3,000 or 4,000. Every village is surrounded by a wall, and secured by one or more gates. The wall is sixteen or eighteen feet high; the lower part is built of stone, and the upper part of sun-dried bricks. Nobody, except outcasts, who are not allowed to live in the village, resides outside the walls, and no one will spend the night without the gates, if he can avoid it. A little before sunset, the people, who, in small villages, are mostly cultivators, may be seen coming from the fields in every direction, bringing their farming utensils and driving their flocks and herds into the village. Nothing is allowed to remain without. When the inhabitants have returned, and all is secure, which is usually before nine o'clock, the gates are closed, and kept during the night, by persons of the Mhar caste, who are the hereditary porters of the village. In the small villages, the people are all cultivators. In the larger villages, there are Brahmuns, shop-keepers, artists, etc. Every village, unless it be very small and poor, contains a temple, a chawdee, (resting-place for travelers, and place of resort for public business,) and a public tank. In large villages, these public places are numerous.

Another feature of the Deckan is, that there are neither fences, roads, nor bridges. This, however, is not peculiar to the Deckan. Cows, sheep, goats, and buffaloes are driven out from the villages in the morning by their respective keepers, who attend them during the day, "leading them by the side of still waters, and causing them to lie down in green pastures." The shepherd is always accompanied by his faithful dog; carries a long stick, and wears over his head and shoulders a coarse blanket. He lives on the most familiar terms with his flock; they know his voice, they follow him wherever he calls them; he brings back those which stray, watches over the feeble, and takes care of the young; "he gathers the lambs with his arms, and carries them in his bosom, and gently leads those that are with young." The pasture-grounds are for the common use of all. The shepherd and herdsman lead their flocks and herds wherever they choose, except over the tilled fields. These are

SYRIAN GOATS.

not separated from the grazing lands by any fence or other barrier, but are guarded during the time of the ripening of the crop, or of the harvest, for the twofold purpose of securing the grain from the grazing cattle, and from the depredation of birds and wild beasts. A rude scaffold is built for this purpose in the centre of the field, and a temporary hut (Isa. 1: 8) for the accommodation of the watchman. This office is generally performed by a lad, the son of the husbandman, or some one employed by him for the purpose. The wild beasts which prey on the fields are, for the most part, the wild hog, the bear, and deer. Those which disturb the flocks and herds are, the tiger, the leopard, the bear, the wolf, the fox, and jackal.

The villagers generally possess large numbers of cattle; and but for their superstitious notions of abstaining from the eating of flesh, these cattle would be valuable. As it is, however, they are of very little value. Their cows and goats yield but a small quantity of milk; the wool of their sheep is extremely coarse, and of very little account. Their oxen turn to good account, in the cultivation of their farms, for carrying burdens, and for riding and driving in the carriage. Those accustomed to the latter services, trot over the plain like horses, and are governed by a rope in the nose or on the horns. Buffaloes are used in every respect as bullocks, or neat cattle; though more common than cows for milk, they are less frequently used than oxen for service. The buffalo is the ugliest animal in India. He is of a dirty brown color, high bones, and very long horns, sometimes pointing toward the ground, sometimes running nearly parallel with his back. Their horns grow at random, without the least form or beauty. The buffalo yields richer milk and more in quantity than the cow. Still, the latter is generally preferred. Camels are much used for carrying burdens. European travelers prefer them to any other conveyance. Natives ride them, European residents seldom. Asses are very common about villages, where they are employed to carry bricks, stone, dirt, &c., but are not much used for traveling. They are regarded as an animal of very *low caste*, and their employment is similar to that of the working class of women. No greater indignity can be put on a Brahmun than to set him on an ass. This is sometimes done as a punishment for petty offenses. The Deckan abounds in horses. They are small, called tattoos, and used chiefly for riding and carrying loads. The price of a horse is about ten dollars. An ox is worth six dollars, a cow about four; a sheep or a goat half or three quarters of a dollar. The natives never eat beef, and very few eat mutton. They live principally on bread made of a cheap grain, which they eat with a vegetable curry, or with Chili peppers. Half a dollar will support a man on this fare for a month. And their clothing is proportionably cheap.

Except the government road from Bombay to Ahmednuggur, there are no roads in this part of the country but foot paths or bridle roads, crooked and difficult to be followed. A stranger cannot go from one village to another without a guide. While the natives formerly expended enormous sums, both of public money and private munificence, in building and adorning temples, digging tanks, and constructing holy places on their sacred streams, it never seems once to have occurred to them that roads and bridges would be a public benefit, or a private convenience. They traversed the country on horseback or on foot, and conveyed the produce of the country to market on bullocks. These travel about ten miles a day, in companies of hundreds, sometimes of thousands. The men who perform this service are called "Bringaries," or carriers of grain. This is their profession through life. They travel from one part of the country to another in large bodies, with their wives, children, dogs, and all they possess. They carry grain, or other merchandise, not on their own account, but as agents for others. The men go armed with swords, shields, and matchlocks, against robbers; and sometimes, if the country be insecure, they employ a guard of Bheels. The Bringaries are employed to supply armies when in the field with provisions; and it is not a little remarkable, that two contending armies allow them to pass and repass without molestation, though they may be known to be victualing the enemy's camp. They travel during the day about ten miles, allowing their bul-

MODE OF TRAVELING IN INDIA.

locks to graze by the way. At night they encamp in a plain, unlade their bullocks, form a wall of defense on three sides, by means of the bags of grain, and place their families, their household furniture, and their cattle in the centre. The latter are arranged in a line, and connected together by means of ropes or chains. Around the whole they place their dogs, who give the earliest notice of the approach of intruders; and if they be in an insecure part of the country, one of the Bringaries stands sentry.

During more than half the year, the largest rivers in the Deckan—rivers as large as the Connecticut and Hudson—are fordable. On the approach of rains, they are swollen and fill their broad channels. They are then crossed in boats. These boats, except where the government have provided them, are frequently only such as the traveler constructs for himself on the spot. He takes a sleeping cot, (native bedstead, which is strung with broad tape,) and binds on a sufficient quantity of gourd shells to make it buoyant under the weight to be put on it; or the same object is gained by attaching four inverted earthen vessels to the corners of the cot. Europeans, even ladies, have often been obliged to cross large rivers on this frail craft.

The principal town in the Deckan is Poona. Ahmednuggur is the second place of importance. In the next rank may be placed Seroor, Malagaum, and Sholapoor, which are military stations of the British Government; Nassic, which is a missionary station of the church of England, and Junere, which, though not the residence of Europeans, is the next most desirable spot for the establishment of a mission. One person who shall occupy this station should be a physician. Poona and Ahmednuggur excepted, I need say no more of these towns, than that they are central locations, mostly situated on principal roads; and they contain from 10,000 to 40,000 inhabitants.

Poona was the capital of the Peshwa and of the Mahratha Empire, situated about thirty miles east of the Ghauts, north lat. 18° 30′. Considered as a capital of dominions so extensive, Poona was never large. It did not contain, in the days of the Peshwa, more than about 100,000 inhabitants, and its native population has probably not increased since. Another singular feature of Poona is, that it was never fortified with a wall like the other towns and villages in the Deckan. It is situated in an open, defenseless plain, two thousand feet above the level of the sea, and at the junction of the rivers Moota and Moola. These rivers, after their junction, form the Mootamoola, which runs into the Beema. This river afterwards forms a junction with the Krishna, which falls into the Bay of Bengal, thus forming, during the rainy season, a water communication from within seventy-five miles of the western coast of India to Madras or Calcutta. Though not fortified by walls, or by natural defense, Poona was still a very convenient capital. There are, in the vicinity, several hill fortresses, to which, in case of an attack, the people fled with the archives and the valuables of the place, after having set fire to the city.

Poona contains several rather elegant buildings, truly elegant after their style. With the European taste of convenience and beauty, we regard the low entrance, the narrow flight of steps, and the small windows, or rather loop-holes, of the palaces at Poona, as anything but elegant or comfortable. Nor are we better pleased with gildings and gaudy paintings on the walls. Still we admire their dimensions, their architecture, and their Asiatic splendor. Two or three of these palaces, which were built by the last Peshwa, and fancifully named after the days of the week, are still standing; one is now occupied for an English school, and another is devoted to the purposes of government. It is said to have been the original design of the Peshwa to erect seven palaces, to be called Sunday, Monday, &c. Whether they were all to have been in Poona is uncertain. When he was dethroned, he was erecting a palace at Phoolshair, fifteen miles distant, which still remains incomplete.

The streets of Poona, which are narrow, crooked, and badly paved, are also fancifully named after mythological personages, adding the termination warree, (street,) and the members of the Hindoo pantheon are represented by paintings on the exterior of the houses. So that as one traverses the streets, he may read the history of the Brahminical deities.

A complete and most beautiful view of Poona, with its palaces, its numerous temples pointing their unhallowed spires to heaven, its gardens, orchards of mango trees, and plantations, its cantonments, and European settlements, and the extensive plains stretching on every side to the horizon, and interrupted only by a garden, a tope of trees, or a little hillock, may be had from Parwuttee Hill, about a mile west of the town. This hill itself is a most picturesque, charming spot, rising, in the midst of a fertile plain, to the hight of a few hundred feet, and covered at the top with a rich and elegant establishment of temples, and other idolatrous buildings. These, when illuminated on certain festivals, afford the spectator, in the city, a most brilliant and beautiful spectacle. In descending from this delightful spot, by a broad flight of stone steps, you see at the bottom a large square field, inclosed with high brick walls. This is the field in which the Peshwa used, annually, to assemble the Brahmuns from all parts of the country, and give them alms on a certain feast day. Begging their way, from all parts of India, they came to Poona, when they were marked and shut into this field. They were then called out, one at a time, and the gratuity bestowed. The Peshwa is said also to have offered premiums to the competitors for literary merit. An examination was annually held at Parwuttee, when the successful were rewarded with medals, sums of money, or other prizes, according to their respective attainments.

There was another annual assemblage at Poona, near the same time with the one above mentioned, of a more imposing, but of a less amiable, character. I mean the festival of the Dussura (doorga pooga). On this occasion, the great Mahratha chiefs were in the habit of assembling at Poona, accompanied by prodigious bodies of their followers, for the celebration of this festival, preparatory to their predatory incursions. Having propitiated the goddess with offerings, and sacrifices of sheep, and consecrated their horses, by offering to each of them a victim, they set out on their plundering expeditions in the surrounding country, making little distinction, in their robberies, between friend and foe.

But Poona is changed. It fell under the power of British arms in 1817. One day the banners of the Peshwa waved over his palace, and the streets of Poona were crowded with the proudest and bravest army in India. The next day that army was repulsed and scattered; the Peshwa, a fugitive in his own country, hunted from fortress to fortress, like a dog driven from his kennel. The English flag was waving over the royal mansion, and an English collector of revenue occupied the palace of the haughty Bajee Row. The oriental magnificence of his court vanished in a day; the native town fell into comparative insignificance, and the graceful turban, and the stately elephant, and all the glittering trappings of Asiatic grandeur, gave place to the military cap, the hat, the horse, and the less gaudy equipage of the European. All the great functionaries of the former government were reduced to the condition of dependents, or they voluntarily abandoned their country to seek a better fortune elsewhere, or followed Bajee Row to his exile. The European cantonments have grown into a town, adorned with an English church, laid out in elegant streets, which are inclosed with hedges of the milk bush, or the prickly pear, with English houses, surrounded with beautiful gardens, which are inclosed with hedges, and yield nearly every European vegetable, and every kind of tropical fruit. Poona contains a bazaar, which supplies the inhabitants with every production of the country, and almost every comfort and luxury of Europe or China. Few places in India can vie with Poona for the beauty of its situation, or the salubrity of its climate.

It is still the metropolis of the Deckan. It is preferred as a residence, by learned Brahmuns and rich natives, and is a favorite resort of devotees, and no less a favorite resort for Europeans. All who can leave Bombay during the rainy season, take up their residence at Poona. The quantity of rain which falls here is small, when compared with that at Bombay. There is at Poona a Sanskrit college, patronized by the government, but wholly under the control of the natives. Here Brahmuns are taught their ancient and sacred language, which few among the priests at this day understand.

The military force at Poona is necessarily considerable. It generally amounts to about two regiments of European infantry, a corps of horse artillery, a corps of engineers, and two or three regiments of native Sepoys. These are all officered by Europeans. No native, whatever may be his character as a soldier, can hold a commission. The number of European soldiers at Poona is about 2,000, and the whole number of European gentlemen, including officers and civilians, public functionaries and private residents, may be 200. There are two chaplains and two churches, and two Scottish missionaries, who, besides their various labors among the Hindoos, preach regularly in English, and have a Presbyterian church of a goodly number of members.* This is composed of soldiers, and such gentlemen and ladies as have been educated in the Scottish church, or from preference have since joined it.

CHAPTER VIII.

Ahmednuggur taken by the English—Its ancient grandeur—Present condition—Ruins—Fortifications in the Deckan—Hill Forts—Excavated Temples—Moral condition of the People—Missionary field.

WE shall introduce the reader to the city of Ahmednuggur, not on account of its own importance, but because it was the more immediate scene of the writer's observations and labors, and because it affords a good specimen of an internal city of India, and is the centre of an extensive and successful field of missionary operations by the American Board.

* The mission has since been reduced to one member.

Ahmednuggur is a town eighty-three miles northeast of Poona. It was built by Ahmed Nizam Shah, from whom it has its name, in 1493. He made it the capital of an independent state of the same name. This dynasty continued till the year 1600, when, in the events of revolution, it became a province of the Mogul Empire, in the reign of the renowned Emperor Acbur. It continued under the government of the sovereigns of Delhi, till the death of Aurungzebe, in 1707, when it was seized on by the Mahrathas, and made a part of the Peshwa's dominions, till 1797, when he was forced to cede it to the Dowlet Row Sindia, who, in his turn, was forced to yield it to the superior claim of the British bayonet, in 1803. The city was taken by General Wellesley, the late Duke of Wellington. The fort has ever since been retained by the English. The city, however, was ceded to the Peshwa in the following year, who seems to have possessed it till the overthrow of his empire by the English, in 1817. Since that period it has remained a part of the dominion of the Honorable Company, and an important military and civil station. From its central position in the Deckan, and its proximity to the territories of the Nizam of Hydrabad, on the east, it is a place of great importance in the defense of the country. It has no natural fortifications, nor is there any hill fortress in the vicinity; its fort, half a mile from the town, is a place of great strength, and capable of sustaining a long siege. The town is situated in an open plain, which forms, with circular ranges of hills, an amphitheatre of about fifteen miles in diameter.

The population, wealth and appearance of Ahmednuggur has, within these few years, considerably increased. This has been chiefly owing to the great accession of merchants, artisans and laborers, who have been drawn thither on account of the military force, and the civil corps, which have been stationed there. The native population is estimated at 50,000; and the number of Europeans, including about 800 soldiers, is between 900 and 1,000. No European (with two or three exceptions) lives within the wall of the town. Their houses, surrounded for the most part by beautiful gardens, are scattered about the environs of the town, some to the distance of three miles, and generally situated on rising grounds, for the benefit of a cool and pure air. Carriage roads have been constructed from the fort, in which stands the church, to the dwelling of nearly every European. The roads, bridges, barracks, hospitals, mess-houses, English dwellings, and every work of foreign artifice, which has, within these few years, been constructed by the English, form a singular contrast with the native huts of the poor, or the massy, expensive and uncomfortable houses of the more wealthy. These are improvements which have added much to the importance of the place. Still, Ahmednuggur is far, very far, inferior in point of wealth and grandeur to what she was in the days of her Mohammedan masters. Nearly a century and a half has now elapsed since those mighty conquerors possessed the city, and to this day, almost every rod of ground bears some testimony to the grandeur of their dynasty. Palaces, mosques, tombs, gardens, aqueducts, tanks, public buildings, and private buildings, of great magnificence, are every where to be seen, both in the city and for several miles on either side; some in perfect repair, some in ruins, and others falling to decay; but all indicate a state of grandeur and wealth which is no where to be seen at the present day. The most perfect specimens of the remains are the mosques and the tombs. Some of these are as entire as if they were but of yesterday. There are two relics of Moslem grandeur, which, in particular, demand the attention of the traveler. The one is the Palace at Fariah Bhag, three miles from town; and the other Salabat Khan's Tomb, six miles distant, and on the summit of the highest hill in the neighborhood.

The palace, which is an octagon of immense dimensions, stands on an artificial island, in the centre of a beautiful artificial lake of some acres. The lake, again, is in the centre of a large garden, which contains three or four hundred acres of excellent land, and appears, from the numerous fruit and flower trees still remaining, to have been an Eden, in which the eye was regaled and the taste gratified with all the beauty and luxury of the East. An artificial rivulet, fed from a river at some miles distant, watered the garden and supplied the lake; and fountains were playing at different distances from the gate of the garden to the palace, and others in front of the principal entrance to it. By whom this noble pile was built, at what period, or to what purpose it was devoted, does not appear. The whole central part of the edifice is a rotundo, terminating in a vast dome, a little higher than the common roof, which is flat, and forms a promenade. On the four principal sides, in the second story, there are four inclosed rooms, about forty feet by twenty. The remainder of the building consists of open apartments, which look toward the garden, in every direction, through arches. There was originally neither bridge nor causeway to the palace. The only communication was by water. The present causeway is of recent construction. The rivulet still feeds the lake, and the garden is still a fertile field. The palace and farm, as it is now called, is rented by government as a place for rearing silk-worms and the manufacture of silk.

The Tomb of Salabat Khan is likewise an octagon, and a huge pile of masonry. Above the basement, in which repose the ashes of the Khan, and of some of his family, the structure is three stories high, and each story, I should judge, thirty feet. The centre, like that of the palace, is one immense arch, extending quite to the top of the edifice, and the spaces between this arch, or rotundo, and the outer wall, form, in reference to the former, three galleries, one above another. The whole, though apparently unfinished, is a work of great labor and expense, and remains a very striking monument of human pride and folly.

Ahmednuggur is surrounded by a wall about fifteen feet high, constructed partly of stone and partly of sun-dried bricks, and is entered by eight gates, which are closed of a night and kept by Sepoys. The town, like most of the villages and towns in the Deckan, presents a most dismal appearance to the stranger. The streets, for the most part, are narrow, crooked and dirty; and the houses low, flat-roofed, and covered with earth. Grass may be seen growing on their roofs, and the sluggish ass grazing there, or the roguish goat leaping from roof to roof in search of the best pasture. The Mohammedans bear a much greater proportion to the Hindoo population than is usual in India. There still remain here a few families of high birth, who hold a part of the estates of their forefathers; but in general they are reduced to poverty and degradation. I know not how they restrain their indignation, when they witness the desecration of the tombs, the temples and the dwellings of their fathers. Many of these are fitted up as dwellings for Europeans. Christians, whom they affect to despise, proudly and thoughtlessly trample on the graves of their fathers. Others are converted into stables, shops, offices, prisons, hospitals and manufactories. Even the more humble monuments in their common burying-places have been leveled to the ground, for the sake of the stones, to be used in the erection of houses for Europeans. Their glory has departed. Ichabod is written on every thing which once showed how great and how proud the Moslems were.

I have alluded to the natural fortifications of the Deckan. These are too remarkable to be passed unnoticed. The Deckan may properly be called one immense plain. But it is not unfrequently diversified by beautiful rising grounds, varying in hight and size, from the little graceful hillock to the mountain of several hundred feet. Most of these have a smooth table-land on their summits, and the larger ones are encircled with a belt of rock just below their tops. This rock is, by nature, scarped nearly perpendicularly, so as to render the ascent generally impassable, except by artificial means. The warlike Mahrathas did not lose sight of this mode of defense to their country. Winding or zigzag roads are formed on the surface of the hill, by which the ascent is comparatively easy, as far as the rocky belt. A pass is then cut through the rock, by which men, and sometimes horses, could ascend by flights of steps to the summit. Sometimes this passage is subterraneous, as at Dawlatabad; in which case, the strength of the fort is considerably increased. If the rock, in any place, be defective, the breach is supplied by a wall. A garrison is posted on the top, and batteries planted on the walls.

As a description of one of these fortifications is, with a few exceptions, a description of the whole, I shall only speak of one which I have ascended and minutely observed. This is in the vicinity of Junere, forty miles to the north of the city of Poona. There is but one path which leads to the summit, and this winds nearly half way around the surface of the hill, before reaching the encircling rock, and is so narrow that two men can scarcely walk abreast. Almost every foot of this path is exposed to the unobstructed fire of the battery above. We were not convinced of the great strength of the place till we arrived at the gate near the commencement of the rocky belt which forms the chief defense of the fort. As the huge gate, set with great iron spikes, or covered with thick sheets of iron, grated on its rusty hinges, one was reminded of Milton's description of the infernal gate. We then began to ascend the steps, and passed successively through *five* similar gates, all of which seem to bid defiance against any power which can be brought to act against them in their peculiar situation. Nothing but the well-directed shells of the English could ever have caused a garrison here to surrender. On the top are decaying barracks, houses, magazines, and reservoirs of excellent water. Nearly all these forts are in the hands of the English, but very few of them are garrisoned.

The excavated temples of this part of the country are, perhaps, still greater objects of curiosity to the common traveler than the hill forts. They are very numerous. The principal ones are at Carlee, Junere and Ellora. The latter are the most magnificent, and are said to be unrivaled by any human work on the face of the earth, the pyramids of Egypt not excepted. Some of these are more than a hundred feet in length, by fifty broad, and three stories high. As I cannot describe the whole, for they are very numerous, and of a great variety of forms and dimensions, I will endeavor to give some idea of one here called Keylas. This, though superior to the others, does not, in its general features, greatly differ from them, except that it is a temple *externally*, as well as internally. That is, after the temple was excavated, with doors, porticoes, altars and images, and the whole internal part complete, the portion of the mountain above it was removed, so as to form a temple externally, with dome, spire and court-yard; and the whole one entire piece, and of the same rock, every part remaining unmoved, as nature created the mountain. The first object in excavating these temples was, to select the side of a hill where was a solid rock, without rent or fissure. It was then scarped down till there remained a perpendicular side to the rock high enough for the gate-way. Then proceeded the work of excavation from the top of the intended room downwards, leaving portions of the rock for pillars of support to the roof, for idols, and any purpose as required. The pillars are carved and ornamented with figures of men, beasts and fictitious animals. Figures of every description, and some of them shockingly obscene, are carved on the walls. But it is not my object here to describe the caves, but only to tell you that they exist in the Deckan.

I have said that the physical aspect of the Deckan is bleak and barren. Would to God that its moral aspect were not more so. Here are temples, priests, holy places, altars, sacrifices, holy days, gods many and lords many; but no temple is here reared to the worship of Jehovah; no priest, as a good shepherd, brings the wandering sheep into the fold; no place is sacred to the praises of the Most High; no sacrifice is made to the only living and true God; no day is hailed as a welcome cessation from labor, and a day of holy rest, when the soul may find repose on the precious promises of God's word. From the cradle to the grave, generations after generations of this wretched people worship they know not what, and believe they know not why.

But, blessed be God, there now appears a redeeming spirit for this deluded race. It is not yet fifteen years since missionaries were prohibited from entering the Deckan. An attempt was made about that time to distribute books and tracts in Poona and its vicinity. Two natives, one a Jew, were dispatched for that purpose. They came to the city of Poona, and there commenced their work. The Brahmuns no sooner ascertained the nature of their embassy, and the character of their books, than they preferred complaints against them to the English Collector, the chief magistrate of the city. He ardently espoused the cause of the Brahmuns, seized the books, and imprisoned the missionaries. It is *said* that he indulged, in the presence of the natives, in bitter imprecations against the missionaries in Bombay, who were the agents in this affair; and told the people that they were abused by this attempt against their religion, and assured them that they should have redress. The books were indignantly kicked about the streets, and finally sent back to Bombay, with the two assistant missionaries, under a guard of soldiers. The whole was done, no doubt, under the pretense of non-interference with the religion of these newly acquired subjects, and from an apprehension of a revolt, if any attempts to introduce Christianity should be allowed. The *policg* of government might, at that time, *seem* to require this precaution. But where is the *Christian principle* which allows a Christian nation to conquer and to hold possession of an idolatrous nation on terms like these? The Great Judge and Disposer of nations will vindicate or condemn. He is not an idle spectator among the nations of the earth.

Four or five years elapsed before any further attempts seem to have been made to introduce the gospel at Poona. An attempt was then made by the Scottish mission. Two of their number made a preaching tour as far as Poona. They preached in the streets, distributed tracts, and held public discussions. Complaints against them were brought to the Collector, the gentleman above named. He had not been sustained by the Bombay Government in the violent measures he had pursued in the former instance, and he now saw fit to adopt a more lenient course. He inquired of the complainants what the missionaries did, that rendered them so offensive—if they resorted to any violence, or used any compulsion in their attempts to propagate Christianity? They answered no; but that they *talked* and *argued* continually against Hindooism and in favor of Christianity, and distributed books. Well, said the magistrate, I will allow you the same privilege. Go *talk*, and *argue*, and overthrow their religion, if you can.

Since that period, the apprehensions of the government have

been greatly allayed; and the missionaries have been allowed to traverse the country in any direction they choose. Missionary stations have since been formed at Poona, Ahmednugger, and Nassic; and tours for preaching the gospel, and the distributing of tracts and books, have been made from Candish to Goa, from the Ghauts to Jalna and Sholapoor. These, however, are but scoutings and skirmishings in an enemy's country. Only a small part of the towns and villages have been so much as *once* visited by a missionary; and probably not a fourth part of the population where the missionaries reside has even heard of the doctrines of the cross. It is better to consider here what *remains to be done*, than what has been done.

We will make Ahmednuggur the point from which, as a centre, we will look abroad over the spiritual waste of the Mahratha country. On every side appears a vast moral desert. Looking westward, we see a single missionary station at Poona, eighty-three miles distant. Here there is one Scottish missionary. To the northeast, there is the station at Nassic, 100 miles, and two missionaries of the church of England. Casting the eye to the north, it meets not with a cheering spot till it stretches beyond the confines of India, and not then, unless the station at Mongolia should fall in the range. Bearing to the northeast, we find missionaries at Delhi, 830 miles; at Agra, 750; at Allahabad, 500; and Benares, 550 miles. To the east, there is not a missionary this side of the Bengal Presidency. At Nagpoor, 300 miles, there is a single chaplain, but not a missionary till we reach Orissa. To the southeast, there are no preachers of the gospel this side of Hydrabad. A chaplain resides there, but no missionary. At the south, we find the first missionaries at Belgaum, 300 miles. Taking the above named places as limits, the area included can be scarcely less than 800 miles by 1000 square; and contains a population probably of 40,000,000; one-fourth of whom speak the Mahratha language.

Such is the extent of the unevangelized regions in the interior of India, and for the most part comprised within the limits of the Deckan. And it should not be overlooked, that many of the places named above as *limits* may again be regarded as *centres*, having about them as wide an extent of unevangelized country as Ahmednuggur. Of the thousands of towns and villages comprehended in this region of country, by far the greater number has never yet been visited by a Christian missionary. Previous to the establishment of the American mission at Ahmednuggur, in December, 1831, members of the Scottish mission had, in two instances, made preaching tours as far east as that city. The gospel has now for more than four years been preached daily at Ahmednuggur, and great quantities of tracts, books, and portions of the Scriptures have been distributed both in the city and through the adjacent country. More than a hundred and fifty villages in the Ahmednuggur district have been visited by Christian missionaries; three tours have been made into the dominions of the Nizam of Hydrabad, as far east as Jalna; and other tours have been made to the west and to the south through the Poona district, and also through the territory of the Raja of Sattara. When we consider how many villages there are in the Deckan, which have never yet received a single visit from a missionary, and how few of the inhabitants of those which have been visited, not more probably than one-tenth, sometimes not a hundredth, ever come near a missionary to hear his message, we shall again exclaim, "Surely darkness covers that land, and gross darkness the people."

If the heart of the Christian sickens when he contemplates the general fact that so vast a population is, in the 19th century, still enveloped in the accumulated darkness of ages, and, for the most part, without the *means* of being enlightened, how much more must his sympathies be enlisted, when he looks more minutely into their moral condition, when he contemplates the bondage of superstition, the abominations, the cruelties, and the general wretchedness which idolatry has, from generation to generation, entailed on this mighty mass of human beings. The debt which the church of Christ owes to these forty millions is no less imperious because the sufferers do not themselves present their claims. The starving, diseased beggar may not be able to plead his case before you in person. But who will say that he, on this account, has no claims on your charity, no demands on your humanity? Such is the nature of the *claims* of the heathen. Their cry for help is heard in the sad tale of their miseries. Their appeal to your compassion comes in the disgusting story of their abominations.

The simple fact that this extensive inland country has, within these few years, been thrown open to the labors of missionaries, ought doubtless to be regarded as a divine intimation that the long night of death, which has for centuries brooded over this land, is now about to disappear, and the Sun of Righteousness ere long is to arise, and to make this "region and shadow of death" as a city that needeth not the light, because the Lord God is the light thereof. It ought to speak with a voice that shall thrill the heart of every Christian.

I have said the whole Mahratha country, and perhaps I may say the whole of India, is laid open to missionary labors. Missionaries, however, would not be allowed to *reside* in every part of the country. They may travel, preach, and distribute books any where, if they have English protection; and they may settle in any part of the Company's possessions, with the permission of government, which is almost certain to be obtained. In this the native inhabitants of the place have no voice. They may neither encourage nor wish the missionaries to settle among them. If the government permit, there is no one who can prevent it. In this way missionaries may settle any where in the Mahratha country, with the same prospect of success as is experienced, or is anticipated, at Poona or Ahmednuggur. They have no obstacles to fear but such as arise from the stupidity and prejudices of the natives, and from their aversion to hear the truths of the gospel. It is doubtful, in my opinion, whether this field will be open in any other sense, until it shall be occupied as it now is. There can, properly speaking, be no *demand* for the gospel, in any better sense of the term, till it shall be known, embraced, and appreciated. Should the door, which, in the providence of God, is now open to the interior of the peninsula, not be entered, we know not how soon it may be closed; and years may roll away, and other countless millions sink to perdition, before the same door shall be opened again. Whether missions in this part of the country would be attended with any more *visible success* than has been experienced in other parts of Western India, does not affect the question of our duty, nor is it needful for us to know. This is only known, and can only be affected by Him who gives efficacy to *means*. That the gospel should be *preached* to every creature, is a simple *command, binding on us*. We must stand or fall in the judgment of our Divine Master, not according to the *conversion* of every nation, but according to our efforts to *evangelize* every nation. Hence, it may be urged, that guilt attaches itself to the Christian world, and to *every individual Christian*, if every field is not occupied as soon as, by the providence of God, it is laid open.

CHAPTER IX.

Brahmunism, illustrated in the Life and Character of Babajee — Early life of Babajee — His connection with Missionaries — His conversion — Renunciation of Caste — Force of habit — Obstacles to Hindoos' Conversion.

We are here very naturally led to inquire *what Brahmunism*, the prevailing religion of that country, is? It were palpable injustice to our sketch not to answer such a question. For the country does not afford a subject of more solemn interest—a question of more practical importance to the philanthropist and Christian. The inquiring reader will therefore desire to know what this colossal system is; what power it exercises over the minds of the people; what obstacles it presents to the spread of the Gospel; what kind of personage a Brahmun is; what control he holds over the popular mind; what he is by nature, and what he may and has become by Divine grace. That I may answer such questions, and many others calculated to introduce the reader at once into the penetralia of Brahmunism, I shall here introduce a somewhat extended account of the Brahmun Babajee. The memoir itself is believed to be of sufficient interest to warrant its introduction. It is here designed, however, only to furnish an extended illustration of several points, immensly interesting, at least to all such as are looking to that great and ancient country with the eye of a Christian, a philanthropist, a historian or a philosopher. And perhaps we can in no other way summon to our aid a happier illustration of the power of Divine grace than in the conversion and subsequent Christian character of this same Brahmun.

Brahmuuism is perhaps as complete a consummation of priestcraft as the world affords. It very appropriately takes its name from the Brahmun or priest. Though they still exalt themselves above every other caste of men, not exeepting kings and princes, the extraordinary pretensions of the Brahmuns of the present day, their arrogance and subtlety, their avarice, duplicity and selfishness, their pretended learning and real ignorance, are but the shadows of the claims put forth by the priesthood, under whose auspices was inflicted on India the present system of Brahmunism. This system is but a stupendous monument of what the genius of man is capable of affecting, when left to the guidance of unassisted reason. Here the rationalist and infidel may gaze and admire what the human mind can do without the aid of Divine Revelation. This great Babylon is the legitimate product of human skill.

Hindooism, from the foundation to the top-stone, is one cold system of selfishness. The ultimate object of all is the aggrandizement of the priesthood; and the grand means by which this is accomplished, is the mental thraldom of the people. Their sacred books, which contain the details of this astonishing system of imposture, and which have been written with consummate ingenuity and diabolical skill, are locked up in a language unknown and forbidden to the people, and may only be read and explained by the Brahmuns. All the learning of the nation is monopolized by these same priests; and the other castes are either prohibited, or, as far as possible, prevented, from aspiring to the "dangerous pre-eminence" of learning. Custom and caste and superstition have been made, by the subtle priests, to conjoin in discouraging all attempts, which the common people might be disposed to make, to disenthral themselves from their hereditary ignorance. And the usages of caste, again, as well as prejudice, prevent the Hindoos from traveling; and consequently cut them off from all the advantages which they might otherwise gain by visiting foreign nations, and comparing other institutions with their own.

And nothing, perhaps, tends more to perpetuate the mental bondage of the Hindoos, than the ignorance, and the consequent degradation, which Brahmunism has entailed on the female sex. We very justly attribute to the female part of our community a great share of the mental exaltation, the refinement, and the active benevolence which bless our society. But in India woman is nothing. She exerts no influence on society, nor can she ever exert any under the present state of things. A long and continued degradation has rendered the Hindoo woman unqualified to share in the intercourse of the other sex; and iron-handed prejudice forbids her to become qualified. A sad experience has so long taught her that she is inferior, and, by nature, degraded, that she now seems fully to believe that she is so, and submits, without a murmur, to be treated as a being of an inferior species.

These things, without mentioning innumerable other instances which might be adduced as reasons for the mental degradation of the Hindoos, exert a powerful influence to bring all things in subserviency to the Brahmuns. The more the religious system of this people is examined, the more the conviction will force itself on us that the aggrandizement, and the pecuniary advantage of the priesthood, are the ultimate objects of the whole. These sentiments are every where taught in their sacred books, and constitute a principal part of the Brahmuns' instructions.

In their domestic and social relations, nothing can be done

without a Brahmun. No one else can determine on lucky and unlucky days, of which they have an endless number, or explain signs, omens, visions and dreams. No one but a Brahmun may read and explain the sacred books, or even touch them. Nor may any other person officiate in their myriads of rites and ceremonies which make up their religion. All offerings to the gods are appropriated by these priests—giving to the Brahmuns is the most effectual way of propitiating the gods and procuring the pardon of sin. Penances and pilgrimages are enjoined; but the most severe penance may be commuted for a present to the Brahmun; and the chief end of a pilgrimage is, in the mind of the priest, the advantage to the idle Brahmuns who officiate at the holy place.

The Brahmun is revered as a god, the people fall down before him, make him offerings, and lick the very dust of his feet. They believe the Brahmun, on account of his righteousness, and by means of his enchantments, may control both men and gods.

Hence the proud pre-eminence of the Brahmun. In all things he domineers over an ignorant multitude. He works on their fears; turns every prejudice and superstition to his own account; checks every innovation or improvement; enforces his injunctions and accomplishes his purposes by the tyranny of custom and caste, and under the insidious garb of religion. The pride and dissimulation of a Brahmun, his intrigue and dishonesty, are proverbial.

This view of Brahmunism and the Brahmuns will be abundantly illustrated and sustained in the life and character of Babajee, and the power of Divine grace will be as richly and beautifully illustrated in his subsequent conversion, brief Christian course, and triumphant death. Should the writer succeed, as he hopes, in developing, through this biographical vehicle, what may be called the philosophy of that great satanic delusion, the reader will not peruse the following chapters without profit.

We know little of Babajee's early years. His mother sacrificed herself on the funeral pile of her husband, when he was but four years old, depriving him at this tender age of even the miserable guidance heathen parentage may afford. His only brother becoming a religious mendicant, the family inheritance fell to Babajee. What became of it I know not.

When twenty-eight or nine years old, we find him in the service of the Scottish mission as a pundit, or teacher of the Mahratha language, where he remained two or three years, and gained probably his first knowledge of salvation by Christ. As might be expected from a person of his naturally ingenuous mind, he was at times not only persuaded of the folly and insufficiency of Hindooism, but practically convinced of the truth and excellency of Christianity. Sometimes he appeared penitent, and wept an account of sin. This state of mind seldom continued long. His relapses, however, were rather towards skepticism than back to idolatry. He came to Bombay about the year 1823, and from that time to his death was much in the service of the American mission.

In this connection, he improved to some extent the means he had of becoming acquainted with Christianity. An event occurred in May, 1828, which had no doubt much to do in opening his eyes to the absurdity, as well as the tyranny, of Hindooism. The mission at that time made a condition of service that their pundits, school teachers, and all in their service should rise and remain standing during the time of prayer at the chapel. A combination was formed to resist the regulation, and all but Babajee refused to comply with it. He said there was nothing in the regulation improper in itself, or contrary to the Hindoo sacred books; and though threatened with the loss of caste in case of compliance, he promised to rise and stand on the following Sabbath. He fulfilled his promise. This brought down on his head a storm of Brahminical indignation. Council after council was held to condemn and cast him out. In one of these assemblies, as he afterwards told me, where there were present not less than a thousand Brahmuns, he appealed to their reason and common sense, and pointed out to them the absurdity, as well as the unkindness of their persecuting him with such severity, for doing what was neither improper in itself, nor contrary to the requisitions of their shastras, nor to the usages of the people in the worship of their own gods. He also declared in that assembly, that there were many Brahmuns there present, with whom he had actually *eaten beef*, and *drunken brandy*, and caroused for whole nights together. For such *flagrant* transgressions, these Brahmuns had not been cast out, or even censured, but were esteemed as priests of the first respectability, while he was arraigned without the charge of any such transgression. Eating beef, and drinking brandy, are things for which a Brahmun ought (even according to the Hindoo shastras) to lose caste, and for which he would be considered an outcast, if it were known to the people. He here referred to a private society of Brahmuns, and others of high caste, who drink and revel together without distinction of caste.

The indignation of this profane priesthood had now risen to so violent a pitch against this defenseless Brahmun, and so humiliating were the penances required of him, that the mission deemed it advisable for him to leave Bombay till the storm should be overpassed. After his return, little seems to have been said on the subject. The whole affair was well fitted to give him a disgust for the foolery and despotism of caste, and to open his eyes to the corruption of the priesthood. It produced, however, no saving effect.

In the spring of 1831, the writer found him out of employ, having been discharged for profligate habits and unfaithfulness in his business. The punishment inflicted by the dismissal being deemed sufficient to insure his better conduct, I engaged him as a pundit. He was for some time attentive to his business, and always anxious his pupil should make rapid progress in acquiring the language. Though sometimes obliged to admonish him for irregularity, and oftener for advancing infidel sentiments, his kind, open and generous heart I could not but admire. After the lapse of six months, being about to leave Bombay to make a long tour on the continent, I discharged our Brahmun, not intending to employ him again, unless there should be a reasonable hope he would serve me more faithfully than he had done.

Just at this time Mr. Graves returned from the Neilgherry Hills. The repetition of the instruction Babajee had so often heard from him, and the renewed appeals now made to his conscience, sunk deep into his soul and awoke him from his lethargy, and he was soon brought to the foot of sovereign mercy, to plead for pardon. He used often to say, "The Christian religion is very strict and severe." He alluded especially to its cognizance of the thoughts and motives. He had many convictions in favor of the Christian religion; and the more because of its purity and his own conscious impurity. Yet on some occasions he reasoned against it most stubbornly. At other times he was overwhelmed with tears and acknowledged his obligation to embrace it. "On one occasion," says Mr. Graves, "he was so deeply impressed, that, with his consent and wish, I prayed with and for him. He knelt and was deeply affected. Yet those impressions subsided, or were subdued by his opposition to them, so that he seemed unfeeling; and I had almost entirely relinquished the hope of his conversion. But not knowing what might prosper, after my return from the Neilgherry Hills, when he called on me, I felt disposed to address him seriously. He seemed very sedate, and I felt unusual freedom and pity. But the substance of all that I pressed upon his consideration, was the importance of deciding at that time, for *eternity*, what religion he would positively choose. 'Have you fully and finally, for eternity, decided respecting the Christian religion? Are you sure you shall have no wish or occasion to reconsider? Do attend to it now, in such a manner that you would be willing to have the decision unalterable forever. You have eternity before you; you may cause yourself joy or sorrow to all eternity, as you fix your decision right or wrong. I entreat you to decide, so that you will not wish to change the decision forever. And then practice cheerfully and heartily, according to that decision. There is a right and a wrong. Search them out—choose the good and refuse the evil. Your opportunity to decide favorably to your interest, will soon certainly close for eternity. You cannot change after death. You are now to act for an interminable time. Do not miss.' Such, as well as I can recollect, was the substance of my address. He seemed rather serious, and disinclined to say anything of consequence in reply, and presently took his leave. But that night he could not sleep. He felt persuaded that the Christian religion was true, and that he had lived in a constant violation of the dictates of his conscience, in his idolatry and wickedness; and he resolved that, whatever might be the consequences, the next day should fix forever his separation from both. Accordingly, in the morning, he left everything but a drinking vessel, which he brought with him to our house. When he came, he cheerfully said that his mind was then made up, according to my advice. I was scarcely prepared for such a declaration from him, and could scarcely understand or believe it. However, I at length gave him my hand, after hearing a little explanation, and invited him into a private room, where I prayed with him, that his mind might be solemnized, and that he might understand and feel what he professed to do. After me, he prayed on his knees, in the first person singular; acknowledging that he was worthy to be utterly and eternally rejected, yet entreating God the Father, Son and Holy Ghost, to receive him on the ground of grace in Christ alone, and to purify and accept him forever. Such a solemn self-dedication and confession astonished me, as totally beyond my anticipation, and such as I had scarcely, if ever, witnessed. I could not but think it sincere. He immediately relinquished caste, and all his connections, expecting nothing but reproach, as he afterwards often said, and not looking for any earthly good whatever. But you know how happily he was disappointed, by the softening down of the enmity of his friends, and their conviction, to some extent at least, that he was sincere and cordial, if not in the right. For my own part, such was the fullness of my conviction of his sincerity, that I dared not long defer his baptism, and felt myself called upon to admire the change, and praise the Lord on his behalf. And his serious and steady perseverance afterwards, gave me no occasion to change my opinion. I still feel myself called upon to acknowledge and admire the visibility of the Divine hand, in effecting so obvious and great a change. May the Lord multiply such trophies of grace, and receive all the praise."

No one, acquainted with the force of early habits, will be astonished to be told that it is not the business of months, and, in many cases, not even of years, to enable a native convert to divest himself entierly of all those ten thousand superstitions and absurdities which he imbibed with his mother's milk. Notions about lucky and unlucky days, omens, signs, dreams, ghosts, hobgoblins, things pure and impure, ablutions, penances, usages of caste, and an innumerable list of minor observances, as inconceivable by the Christian as common and inveterate with the Hindoo, are engrafted on the mind from its earliest infancy. To think to eradicate them by human expedients, is to think to form a new creation. No one, acquainted with the Hindoo character, will affirm that a Hindoo may, by mere human efforts, ever be brought to relinquish what has, by education and habit, become his nature. Poverty, which in this country means the want of those things which are absolutely necessary for mere subsistence, pressing him on one hand, or avarice exciting him on the other, may induce him, externally, to cast off his superstitions, and to feign a compliance with the sentiments and usages of those from whom he hopes to gain the object of his desires; but a cordial abandonment of his own religion, not to say the conversion of his heart, and a radical change from those usages, practices, and superstitions, which are alike repugnant to reason, common sense, and revelation, can only be effected by the almighty power of God. Overlooking such agency, it is no wonder that so many nominal Christians, and none more than those who are best acquainted with the character of the Hindoo, affirm that the Hindoos cannot be converted to Christianity, nor any radical change be produced among them. Leaving Divine Omnipotency out of the account, my opinion will fully coalesce with theirs. But once bring into the account the idea of Divine agency, which I here most fully and joyfully admit, and the sure promises of God, on which I rely as the only basis on which we can ground the conversion of the Hindoos, and the question is in an instant changed from one of entire despondency to one of hope. We then at once see that they can be brought, not only to conform to the external rites of Christianity, but to exemplify its virtues in uprightness of intention, refinement of feeling, purity of heart and holiness of life.

It is lamentable, and ought to humble us before God, and make us feel our dependence on sovereign grace, to confess that such instances of conversion have as yet been rare in this part of India; still enough has been done to convince the missionary and his patrons, that the grace of God is abundantly sufficient to overcome every obstacle which the depravity of men, in its cunning devices, has thrown in the way of the conversion of this people. Babajee may be presented to the friends of missions as a very striking example. The obstacles, in his case, were as great as are to be looked for any where. I knew him well before his conversion, and assure the reader no exception can be made in his favor. He was as learned and as ignorant, as false and subtle, as devoid of moral rectitude, and regardless of the rights and happiness of others, as any of the hollow-hearted fraternity. Nor does any thing appear in his childhood, or early education, conducing to the extraordinary change which afterward took place. From his infancy, he had been acquainted with all the ordinary means of licentiousness and corruption which are to be met with among a most licentious and corrupt people; and for the last ten years he had been acquainted with what, in reference to the heathen, forms a no less barrier to the prevalence of Christianity, the ungodly lives of Europeans. He saw many of the representatives of Christianity, in India, indulging in sins which put to shame the heathen themselves. He could see no connection between the pure doctrines of the Gospel and the ungodly walk of the greater part of those who profess to be the disciples of its Author; and, therefore, very naturally concluded that Christianity, like the system of the Vedas, is some Utopian notion of virtue, got up by a designing priesthood, but not designed to be reduced to practice, except by a few ascetics. He had also seen that a large number of the nominal converts to Christianity differ but little from their heathen neighbors, except, having thrown off the few restraints which caste and superstition imposed, they enjoy greater license to indulge in all kinds of vice. None of these things had escaped the discerning eye of Babajee. One day, when I was urging on him the claims of Christianity, he replied, "Your system is very good, and so is ours, if stripped of corruptions and additions; but nobody practices according to either system. You say, one God only must be worshiped, and so say we. In order to enable an ignorant people to worship this invisible God, whose greatness they cannot comprehend, and whose purity they cannot appreciate, we introduce inferior deities to aid them; but the great majority of Christians are satisfied without worshiping anything." His conclusion was, that the world is extremely depraved: and so deep is the disease, that no remedy can reach it. Such having been his circumstances, and such the state of his mind, the conclusion is forced on me that Babajee was, through the free and sovereign grace of God, a chosen vessel of mercy, on which God designed, from the beginning, to "make known the riches of his glory," for the confirmation of his promises, for the encouragement of missionaries, and for a pledge of salvation to the Hindoos.

CHAPTER X.

Babajee's Marriage — Removes to Ahmednuggur — His account of his Conversion— Eagerness for Instruction — Private Character, delineated by way of contrast.

PREVIOUS to his conversion, Babajee had been living for several years, illicitly, with one of those unfortunate females, who, having lost their betrothed husbands in childhood, are forbidden by the laws of caste again to marry. Such women are often taken by Brahmuns, and treated as wives. In most cases, however, they become common prostitutes. Hence, no doubt, the reason that the terms widow and prostitute are synonymous. Babajee and Audee (the name of the young widow) lived together, with the understanding that each should perform their relative duties as husband and wife; and, apparently, they cherished for each other as strong a conjugal affection as is to be expected in such a state of society. On embracing Christianity, Babajee immediately felt the impropriety of remaining in his present condition with this woman. He, therefore, communicated to us the particulars of the case, and requested he might now be lawfully married to her. This being ascertained to be the wish of both parties, the mission saw fit to comply with the request, and they were accordingly married.

The day following, he left Bombay, with his now lawfully wedded wife, to accompany the brethren who had been set apart to form a mission at Ahmednuggur. He now appeared peculiarly animated with the prospect before him. The Deckan, till recently closed against all missionary labor, now opened a field of rich Christian adventure. His only wish, from this time, seemed to be, that he might live for the good of his countrymen, and, in every possible way, lighten the burdens, and strengthen the hands, and encourage the hearts, of those devoted to the welfare of the heathen. The reader will here be more interested to learn from Babajee himself what were his views and feelings, and what the struggles of conscience against the heart, for some time before he resolved to embrace the offer of salvation, as made known in the Gospel. The following paper was written some weeks after his arrival at Ahmednuggur; and as it illustrates more accurately than I can do the process which the mind of a Brahmun must pass through, before it can reach the goal of truth, it is inserted. Like most of his written papers, it bears no other title than

"BABAJEE, A SERVANT OF JESUS CHRIST.

"This is the controversy which I had with my mind before I became a Christian. I reasoned thus: O, my soul! art thou sinful or not? Then the soul replied, Yes, I am sinful, and am still committing sin. Then, I said, if thou remainest in sin, what will be thy reward? My soul said, If I die in sin I must suffer punishment in hell for ever. Then, continued I, does it seem good to thee to endure eternal punishment? The soul replied, It does not seem good. If it does not, what then art thou doing to escape the just recompense of sin? In the Hindoo religion, I am only worshiping idols, and calling over the names of Row, Vishnoo, Krishna, and our numerous other deities. But what does this profit? This looks like a system devised by men. The religion ordained by God is for *all* men. What! replied my mind, are all men, then, of one caste? Discarding such a thought as profane, I again reasoned: there are eighteen castes; be it so.* Of what caste, then, is my *soul?* Spirit *has* no caste. In the body only am I of the Brahmun caste. To obtain salvation by Hindooism, I must walk according to the religion God has given to my caste. Do I fulfill the requirements of our own sacred books? Rising at early dawn, do I, as prescribed, perform the sacred bathing and the appointed oblation to the sun? I am found guilty at the very threshold. But another question: Is a man allowed by our shastras to commit adultery? Now, O my soul! thou art found wanting. Thou art this moment living in the practice of this sin. It is, indeed, a sin; and, in committing it, I am defiled and fallen. But all Brahmuns do the same thing, and no one regards them polluted on that account. Why, then, am I? Ah! the Brahmuns do not pronounce him who commits lewdness an apostate and outcast, lest they condemn themselves. But this is certain: whoever breaks the Divine commands is fallen in the sight of God, and the consequence of this transgression is punishment in hell! Let me not share with him. I must then walk according to the shastras. But this I cannot do. I am a sinner from my birth, and cannot, therefore, work out a proper righteousness. A man may, for once, fulfill the requirements of our shastras; yet he does no more than his duty—gets no merit by it, though the neglect would incur guilt.

* The Hindoos believe there are, in the East, eighteen castes of *turban* men; also eighteen castes of topee wallas, or *hat-men*, in Europe.

"Hence, it appears evident, that by ceremonies prescribed in the shastras, by the worshiping of idols, by vain repetitions of muntras, by holy bathing, by religious austerities, and such like expedients, freedom from sin, and blessedness after death, can never be obtained. What then shall I do? What will rescue me from this ocean of sin? Alas! nothing that I can do can save me from the punishment of sin.

"When my mind was thus distressed, I resolved to cast aside every system of religion, forsake the world, and flee to a gooroo.* I then employed a Brahmun, by the name of Wasadeo, as my gooroo; of him I learned the muntras.† These I repeated no less than three thousand times. For a time my mind was satisfied. But soon I began to reason with myself again. Is my gooroo without sin? If not, how can a sinful gooroo save a sinful disciple? What now shall I do? Where shall I find a sinless gooroo? Alas! alas! among the whole human race there is not a sinless man to be found. For all men from their birth are sinful. Then I brought to mind the instructions I had heard, how that the Almighty, all-wise, ever just, merciful, and holy God, in order to make an atonement for the sins of men, took on him the nature of man, and became incarnate in the world. The name of this incarnation is the anointed Savior, Jesus Christ. He now sits at the right hand of God, making intercession for all who repent and believe on his name. While in this world he endured, for more than thirty years, many sufferings for the sins of the people. He obeyed the Divine commands, and, for the sake of man, he, who was Almighty, became of no reputation, and gave his life for sinners. The wicked people charged him with fault, but no guilt was found in him. He was altogether holy, and could therefore make an atonement for sin.

*A gooroo is a spiritual guide, and with the Hindoos a sanctifier and savior. Almost every man employs his gooroo. According to the Hindoo books, he must be sinless.

†Muntras are charms, or incantations, which are muttered over by the Brahmuns. By these they pretend to bring the Divinity into an image; and do various other things equally probable.

He is the way, and by him only can I enter the kingdom of bliss. It is said in our shastras that the good works of a sardoo (saint) are his way to heaven. But what are described to be the marks of a sardoo? They are these: equity, compassion, self-denial, freedom from anger, and disregard of caste. But such a man is not to be found; for all men are deceitful and deceived, covetous, lascivious. Therefore, O my soul! despise thyself, and flee for refuge to God, the Savior Jesus Christ, and he will make you worthy by the Holy Spirit. Hast thou ever heard of him of whom I now speak? Yes, I have often heard of him, and read his shastras. And what do you think of him? I believe the Christian shastras to be true, and Jesus Christ the true Savior of the world. Why not then believe on him? Should I believe on him and be baptized, should I not be defiled? According to the Christian shastras, the things which defile a man are these: evil thoughts, murders, adulteries, fornication, theft, lying, deceit, and such like things. By loving unholy objects, my mind has become polluted.

"I have despised the goodness of God, which should have led me to repentance. What shall I now do to be saved? I then determined that I would renounce all worldly hope, cast off the fear of the people, repent, and flee to Jesus Christ, and cry with my whole heart to God the Father, Son, and Holy Ghost, three in one, that he would have mercy on me. I fully resolved to go to Jesus, to be baptized, and partake of the Lord's Supper, and to keep myself from sin. I then prayed to the living God, and communed with my own heart. I resolved to go to Graves Sahib, tell him my whole heart, and ask baptism. I begged that I might remain with him, as I did not like to go to my own dwelling. After having examined me, and tried me for a few days, his Christian brother, Hervey Sahib, baptized me in the name of the Father, the Son, and the Holy Ghost, three in one; and the same day I partook of the Lord's Supper. In the good instructions which Graves Sahib then gave me, he said, 'Think not that your work is done, for the obligation under which you are now laid to labor for your countrymen is very great.' From that time I have examined myself, to see if I walked according to the Gospel. If I find myself acting or thinking contrary to my Savior and my God, I repent, forsake it, and ask forgiveness. When I do right, I know this is through the influence of the Holy Spirit, and for this I thank God. Moreover, I leave myself in the hands of God, through the mercy of Jesus Christ."

From his arrival in Ahmednugger, Babajee became an efficient member in the mission. He had already acquired a considerable knowledge of the Scriptures; indeed, he possessed a pretty good theoretical acquaintance with Christianity before he knew its spiritual intent. But now he sought Divine assistance, and gave himself up to seek the truth as revealed through Jesus Christ. He seized on every new truth to which his mind was directed, or which discovered itself to him in his reading or meditation, with an avidity truly astonishing. It was gratifying to see with what delight he would hang on your lips, while relating to him some portion of sacred history which had not yet been translated; or illustrating some particular doctrine, with which he was but partially or not at all acquainted; or while directing his mind to some eminent examples of Christian fortitude or devotedness. He grasped the truth with peculiar eagerness, and seldom would allow even a suggestion, or an incidental mention of any one truth, which he did not well understand, to pass, till he had, by further inquiry, not only made himself master of it, but made it subservient to his own benefit by self-application. Nor would he stop here. He, more peculiarly than any person I have ever met, had the the happy talent, or rather, I should say, the invaluable spiritual gift, of communicating to others, and of enforcing on their consciences, every truth which he had himself acquired.

In his demeanor, as a man or as a Christian, he was modest, gentle and affectionate, kind-hearted and ingenuous, conscientious and upright in his secular dealings, fervent and active in his piety, frequently fertile in devising, and always willing and ready in co-operating to accomplish any plan of usefulness. To say that he had no errors, would be to say that he was not human; or to say that he did not sometimes fall into errors which would, at first view, excite the surprise of the good people in a Christian land, would be to affirm what no one acquainted with the perversity of the Hindoo's heart would expect from one just emerged from Paganism. From his conversion to his death, the writer does not recollect an instance when a hint, or gentle rebuke, was ever received unkindly, or was not found sufficient to correct an error, though that error were the result of long habit, or the offspring of wrong instruction in childhood.

It was a long time before he fully comprehended the length and the breadth of the fourth command. That the Sabbath is a day of rest from all secular avocations, and should be in a special manner devoted to the worship of God, both public and private, he well understood; but he did not so fully comprehend that it should be sanctified *to the end*, to the utter exclusion of idleness, sleeping, worldly conversation, and such like intrusions on holy time. Unfavorable as this may at first appear to one educated in a Christian land, he will greatly moderate his censure when he reflects that the idea which the Hindoo attaches to a holy day, bears no analogy to the notion which the devout Christian entertains of the Sabbath. These holy days, which amount in all to more than three months out of the twelve, are, for the most part, professedly days of worship, but, in reality, days of revelings and debauchery; and it is but making a moderate allowance for the force of habit, to conceive that the mind of a Brahmun, which had for more than thirty years been nurtured in the most degrading notions of its obligations to the Supreme Being, should, even when partially enlightened by Divine grace, still incline to identify the sacred day of the Christian with its miserable substitutes, the holy days of the Hindoos. These are but days of idleness and amusement.

In justice to Babajee, however, I should add that these remarks apply to him with less force than to any convert which I have known in this part of India.

Nor ought we to wonder, should converts from Paganism be found lamentably deficient in industrious habits. Diligence in business is almost as rare a quality among the Hindoos as fervency of spirit in serving the Lord. They seem to know nothing of the value of time. This, added to their natural indolence, forms one of the most obstinate barriers to their improvement. It is only dire necessity, or sensual gratification, that impels them to action. The Arabian Prophet well understood these traits of character in the people of the East, when he made the enjoyment of heaven to consist principally in inactivity and sensual gratification. To eat and drink, smoke the hookar, lounge in perfect listlessness, sleep, and wallow in beastly indulgence, seem to form in the mind of the generality of Hindoos the acme of bliss. This native indolence of character is confirmed by long habit, and fostered by a great variety of long-established customs; and though Divine grace may produce a more visible change in them than is generally observed in the conversion of nominal Christians, yet there is, in this respect, a most lamentable deficiency in all converts which have fallen under my notice in India.

The subject of this memoir, if weighed in the balance of Christian diligence in America, would be found wanting; but when tried by the heathen standard, or when compared with any thing I have seen among native converts, he was truly an example worthy of imitation.

I have spoken of Babajee's *eagerness in pursuit of truth.* This is by no means a natural trait of Brahmunism or the Brahmuns. Of the great number with whom I have conversed on different topics, connected with religion and science, I cannot say I have found one who showed a decided wish to know *what is true and what false.* At the time, I have sometimes thought differently; but the result has showed that an interested motive lay at the bottom of any seeming interest manifested for truth. They stupidly believe, or pretend to believe, everything handed down from their forefathers. When asked *why* they believe this or that, they reply, that investigation or discussion is no part of their duty; for every thing needful for them to believe was piously examined and settled by the good men of old; and that it ill becomes them of this degenerate age to question the wisdom of their more holy and erudite ancestors. Ask them why they believe there is one sea of ghee, one of milk, another of honey, &c., or why they believe sin may be expiated by bathing, pilgrimage, feasting Brahmuns, or by penance? They reply, so our shastras say, and surely our sage and pious fathers understood these matters. They will tell you, too, that "as a man believeth, so is he." If he believeth a stone, or tree, or any visible object, to be a god, to him it is a god; or if he believeth a sinful being to be his Savior, or a bad man to be a good man, to him it becomes so.

The Brahmun shows a strange moral obtuseness. He calls good evil, and evil good; light darkness, and darkness light. Lying is good, if it result in immediate benefit; to speak the truth is evil, if it terminate in immediate loss. Meats and drinks, divers washings and corporeal inflictions, make up their righteousness, while sin is really but a transgression of the laws of caste. To lie, steal, cheat, deceive, commit adultery, and wallow like swine in the filth of moral turpitude, is too trifling a thing to be named; it is only what their gods did before them. But to eat with a man of another caste, however respectable he may be, or to drink out of the same cup, is a sin only pardonble by a large sum of money! A Brahmun becomes polluted by eating with his prostitute, but not by cohabiting with her, although she be of low caste.

The *anxiety* and *disinterestedness* which Babajee manifested in his *efforts for the welfare of his countrymen*, both in this world and the world to come, are traits which we in vain search for among the Hindoo priesthood. Disinterestedness and gratitude are ideas, to express which there are no corresponding terms in the Indian languages; and it may be questioned whether any such ideas exist in a native's mind. However this may be, it is a lamentable fact, that efforts of any kind are very seldom or never made for the spiritual benefit of their fellow beings. How can a gleam of benevolence warm the heart of one who fancies that the shadow of a man of low caste pollutes him; and who will affirm, as I have heard them, that he would not lay hold on such a one to pull him out of a ditch, though this were the only means to save the poor man's life? They most industriously conceal from the people the books which they regard as divine, asserting, as if written in them, any thing which best suits their own purposes. There probably never was, since the creation of the world, so complete and gross a system of priestcraft as Hindooism. Not a precept is inculcated, not a ceremony is palmed on the people, that does not, directly or indirectly, go to aggrandize or profit the priesthood. The poor wretch is told to make a pilgrimage, and is promised in consequence a large stock of merit. This is to feed a set of lazy Brahmuns, and to support a train of vile prostitutes, who keep the holy place. For the poor man may rest assured that he will never have the satisfaction of knowing that the object of his pilgrimage is accomplshed, and that he may now return home, till his money is gone. Almost every event in the common occurrences of life, must be attended with some silly ceremony. This is that the Brahmun may get a fee. The mental improvement, much less the eternal welfare of the people, forms no part of a Brahmun's wishes and plans in reference to his flock. As far as he manifests any concern about them, it is to keep them involved in the gross darkness of ignorance. When the drunkard becomes sober, or the profane man devout, or the highway robber an honest man, he does not exhibit a more decided change of heart, than the Brahmun does when his breast glows with benevolence towards his kind. Being themselves supremely selfish, they cannot conceive how any one should be otherwise. Hence the idea that the missionary enterprise is a disinterested thing, solely for their own benefit, appears to them perfectly preposterous. It is to be doubted whether one of a thousand of those who know something of the nature of missionary efforts, yet believes that there is not behind the curtain some grand scheme of aggrandizement, both to missionary societies and to their missionaries. Formerly, they supposed them connected with government. We cannot, when we look into a native's mind, wonder that he should entertain such notions of all plans of benevolence; and we cannot expect that he will appreciate in another a quality which he is conscious he does not possess himself, and which, from experience and observation, he knows does not exist among those with whom he associates. Though he cannot see in what way missionaries or their friends are to be benefited by their thankless labors among them, yet, reasoning from the only premises he possesses, he doubts not that pecuniary benefit or worldly aggrandizement is the moving principle. Some, affecting to be more sagacious and charitable, suppose the missionary work an affair of *merit* or penance, perhaps of indulgence, and they congratulate themselves as the promoters of our spiritual good.

It is scarcely too much to say, that Babajee's whole soul seemed bound up in the welfare of his people. He would weep over their perversity, entreat them with the affection of a brother, pour out his soul to God for their salvation, and beseech the Lord to preserve the missionaries who are laboring for their good, and to increase their number. In his private conversations with the people, which were many, and his daily instructions at our religious services, he always pressed the truth on their attention, with a tenderness and force which was truly admirable.

The facility with which he renounced any custom or prejudice, or any usage of caste, as soon as he discovered it to be contrary to the Christian religion, is no less indicative of a radical change. For no one who knows the Hindoos will allow that this is a natural trait. To forego any of the silly rites of caste, to eat from the hands of a person of another order, to admit an innovation, or even to adopt an improvement, is as repugnant in a heathen land, as the opposite is in a Christian land. I cannot better illustrate this part of the subject, than by a reference to what has actually fallen under my obeservation in the case of Brahmuns who have been employed by us at Ahmednuggur as pundits. One objected to a man of low caste coming into the room where he was, and would not allow the table to be laid, or a piece of meat to be brought into his presence. Another was polluted by passing over a mat on which a Mhar had stepped. The same person asked leave of absence for three days, to purify himself from a pollution with which he had become infected by a Mhar passing through a room where he was sitting, the room being matted. Once he was called before a council of Brahmuns, and charged with taking from my hand, and eating, a banana. The same men petitioned to have a low wall built across our mud chapel, at which they were required to attend Divine worship while in our service, that they might be the more effectually secured from the people of low caste, who were also present. These prejudices, born with them, and engrafted in their very nature, may sometimes deserve more indulgence than they receive. The nominal Christian has no such sacrifices to make before he becomes a convert; and should some of these relics of Paganism remain after conversion, it is only what might be looked for. In this, however, Babajee formed an exception. He would eat with foreigners, and had almost continually some one of low caste about his house. More than once he bade several of the inmates of the poor-house, persons of the lowest caste, to dinner, and partook with them himself. He seemed to have wholly freed his mind from the notions of lucky and unlucky days, omens, hobgoblins, and the like; a deliverance of vast magnitude for a Hindoo. But nothing showed more decidedly the complete conquest which he had gained over the superstitions and customs of the country, than that which appeared in reference to touching the dead, especially the corpse of a low caste person. In two instances he prepared the body for burial, and assisted in carrying the corpse from the house. The cheerful and unhesitating manner in which he did a duty, which no Brahmun in the country would do for the price of his caste, or perhaps the price of his life, excited the wonder of Dajaba, who had been a professor of Christianity more than five years, without being able to bring his mind to so willing a performance of a duty of this kind.

In scarcely any way did Babajee evidence more clearly a radical change of heart, than in his uniform *adherence to the truth.*

This, in a Christian country, would not, I am aware, be allowed as any decisive evidence; for there the liar is stigmatized by an enlightened public opinion. But nothing of this exists in a heathen land. It was never more true of the Cretans than it is of the Hindoos, "that they are always" and all "liars." The only exception to be made in favor, or rather against the Brahmuns, is, that they practice the abominable vice with a little more grace and subtlety. Both in precept and practice, they allow that a man may lie, if he can be more benefited by a falsehood than by the truth. The people are also taught, from their sacred books, that if the interest of a Brahmun, or the welfare of a cow, require it, they ought to lie, and that such a lie is no sin. From the Maharaja (the great king) down through every grade of his subjects, every man speaks the truth or utters falsehood just as he fancies will best comport with his own interest. The native prince makes treaties, to break them; pledges his faith, to violate it the moment it suits his interest or convenience. This same disregard to all engagements and bargains, runs down through all ranks of natives. You can expect a native to fulfill an engagement, only as far as he is impelled by interest or fear of authority.

An example or two will suffice to show how the most learned and respectable among the priesthood can lie. A Brahmun, by the name of Ragoba, has been employed by us as a Mahratha pundit nearly two years. He is a mild, gentlemanly man, regards himself very wise and holy, and shows, to say the least, more pride to be thought a man of truth and integrity, than any Brahmun with whom I have been acquainted. As an indispensable condition of service, he is required to attend at our preaching-place on the Sabbath, and the prayer-meeting on the first Monday of the month. Being, of course, averse to this, he invented every excuse to avoid it. After some time, his excuses became more frequent; and I (for he was then in my service) had too much reason to believe he was deceiving me by gross falsehood. At one time, he mistook the hour, or his family were sick; at another time, a father or brother from a distance had called on him, and he could not neglect the tenderest offices of friendship; again, he had heard of the death of a relative at another village, and was unclean, and could not, in consequence, appear in public. So improbable did his excuses become, that I finally told him that I should no longer regard them. After a few Sabbaths, he was absent again. I had but just returned from the morning service, when he came to me with a tale of woe, which softened all my severity. The image of grief sat on his countenance, and his whole demeanor made me repent of my rigor. He was tacitly excused before he spoke. My conscience reproved me, that the poor man should think it necessary to obtain my approbation, to enjoy the melancholy pleasure of spending the few hours which were afforded over all that remained of his only and beloved son. "Yes," said he, "my only son is dead; he died this very morning. I hope you will excuse my absence, and allow me to pay the last mark of respect to his remains this evening." The manner in which he spoke, indeed his whole deportment, confirmed the truth of his words. His grief, thought I, is not that superficial, half-felt grief, which sometimes appears in the countenance of an indifferent father only, on the days of the death and burial of his child. But it is rather that deep, solemn, and almost heart-rending grief, which a tender mother feels when the darling of her bosom is snatched away by death. I sought without delay to make the best amends I could, for the wound which I had, unintentionally, inflicted. I opened my Mahratha Testament, and poured into his wounded spirit the balm which flows from that blessed fountain. He appeared more calm, and acknowledged the superior excellency of the Christian Scriptures in the hour of distress. Thankful for the comfort which I had administered, he went away. After the days of mourning and purification had passed, he returned to his employment. Though he had by this time resolved the whole into truthful *fate*, and bowed to the shrine of his hard destiny, he was evidently still a man of grief. I accordingly referred to the subject with all due delicacy, and endeavored to improve the occasion to his spiritual benefit. Judge then of my surprise, when I tell you, that I have the consolation of knowing that the child is still living: indeed, he was never dead!

It will not be irrelevant to mention, under this head, the unfairness and prevarication which a Brahmun will use in argument. I have seldom conversed in good earnest with one of this class, that is, conversed with him in such a manner as to press upon him the peculiarities of the Christian religion, so that he could not but see that it was done at the expense of his own favorite scheme, when he would not, to gain his end, prevaricate, turn, twist, contradict himself, deny that he had ever said what but a moment before he uttered, resort to gross falsehoods, and use any means which best suited his present exigency. To gain their point with an opponent, or to answer their selfish ends with the people, they will assert, as written in their shastras, any thing they please; and what they affirm to be divine truth to-day, they will, on the same principle, deny to-morrow. Babajee, by his uniform practice of unhesitatingly and unequivocally speaking the truth, differed from what he once was, in the same degree that he did from the men of his tribe. For he was, like them, a child of the same father. (John viii. 44.) As closely connected with the preceding, I may next mention,

His simplicity of character, as a grace which eminently adorned our Hindoo Christian, but one, too, for which he was in no wise indebted to Hindooism. The term will but ill apply to any class of people which I have met in India. They are, as a people, double-tongued, double-minded, subtle, and deceitful, every man according to his ability. To speak of a simple-hearted, artless Brahmun, would be like speaking of a sober drunkard, or a pious infidel. Never does the subtlety of the Brahmun appear more pre-eminently hateful, than in the ten thousand artful manœuvres which he is constantly practicing to keep the eyes of the people closed from the light, and to induce them to keep up the observance of those silly rites which secure his own honor, and gain him a livelihood. The example given above, very strikingly illustrates this part of the subject too. But a few others will be here tolerated. To defeat our efforts for female education, the Brahmuns intimated to the parents of the girls, who were at first drawn into school by the force of presents, that our object in organizing girls' schools, was to collect together as many as we could, then take them off to our own country, or sell them as slaves. A teacher who had been dismissed for illicit intercourse with one of the older girls, in order to prevent any other person from succeeding in the school, (which already was but just tolerated by the people,) propagated the same story, accompanied with other fabrications, which quite destroyed the school. Nothing is too absurd for the credulity of the people. They were all frightened, and kept their children at home.

To prevent the success of any plan of ours, to get service for themselves, or to get a recommendation to a gentleman in the service of government, they are proverbially clever in all the expedients of craft, flattery, significant insinuations, frauds, and falsehoods. If they wish to prevent some poor man from receiving a book, or hearing our doctrine, they have only to say, "some calamity will fall on you;" and holding in their own hands all the dark mysteries of signs, omens, and inauspicious days on the one hand, and relying on the credulity of the people on the other, they find it no difficult task to sway the minds of a superstitious and ignorant populace as they please. They gravely open the *Punchang*, (Hindoo calendar,) and declare that a work must be undertaken on such a day, or that the consequence of such and such undertaking will be prosperous or disastrous; or that a marriage must be immediately celebrated or delayed, according to their fancy, or, more generally, according as it best suits their own interest. In this way they keep up an influence over the minds of the people, not only ridiculously absurd, but very advantageous to themselves, and ruinous to the people. If, again, they wish to incur our favor, they will call on us, speak in the most flattering terms of our labors, (though we know them, at the same time, to be exceedingly bitter against us,) eulogize Christianity, profess their belief in it, and beg that we will put them in a way to be instructed in its doctrines. All this is done with a perfect grace, and with all the appearance of sincerity.

The instances here alluded to have fallen under my own observation, and will be given in detail in another chapter.

Honesty in secular affairs, furnishes another point of contrast. Most of the secular business of the mission, together with the daily distribution at the poor-house, was in Babajee's hands. He never wanted opportunity, if he had been disposed, to practice on us acts of dishonesty almost every day. The usages of the country, too, would have justified him in such a manner as, in many cases, to spare his own character in the eyes of the people, and to prevent its coming to our ears. As this is known to be a most vulnerable point in the character of a heathen convert, the strictest vigilance was observed towards him, lest the confidence which the weak state of our mission at the time obliged us to repose in him, should be abused, or a temptation thereby placed before him, to ensnare his soul into the easy-besetting sin of the heathen. But I am most happy to say, that I never detected him in attempting to defraud me of a single pice, nor had any reason to think he ever did it. No one that ever heard the name Hindoo, will pretend to call this a national trait, or the result of Hindooism. Cheating, defrauding, and embezzling are limited in this country, only by the ability of the native, and the means which he has to practice them. The usages of the country allow this to a certain extent; but a native is not likely to stop short at the limits of sanctioned dishonesty, if he have the power and opportunity of going further. This only forms a pretext to go any length he chooses. For example, if a man in your service be intrusted with a sum of money, great or small, for the purchase of articles, his first object is, to pocket part of it, in the exchange of silver for copper: then he overcharges for the articles; and lastly, if possible, cheats in weight or measure. The puntogee (school teacher) brings a false account of his scholars, and demands his pay accordingly. The laborer, the cooly, (porter,) the merchant, or mechanic, if he sees you are impelled by necessity or distress to call in his aid, has no bowels of compassion. I am disposed to think that the natives do practice more dishonesty on foreigners than they do on their own people. They have an idea that Europeans, being their conquerors, must be rich, and can well afford what their wants demand, or what their avarice craves. And as the former are foreigners, and have but an imperfect knowledge of their language and customs, they do not want opportunities to indulge their propensity. The native servant undoubtedly finds it much less difficult to justify himself for defrauding a European master, than he would a Hindoo or Mussulman.

The circumstances of Babajee were such, that he might often have improved them to his advantage. In several instances, he refused bribes which were offered him, (a practice very common where a native has the superintendence of any business,) if he would induce me to give such an amount for a certain piece of work, or such a sum for a certain article. According to the customs of the country, every overseer of business, in which workmen are employed, demands and receives a small share of the daily wages of each person. He also gets a per centage on every rupee expended in materials for the work, besides divers little or great immunities, as the rupees pass through his hands. Babajee, of his own accord, set his face at once against all these customs. He regarded them as fraudulent in themselves, and contrary to the usages of the Christian religion.

CHAPTER XI.

His tender Conscience — Docile Temper — Humility — Self-Examination — Dependence on God — Conquest over Covetousness — A letter to other Converts — Loves the Bible — Feels for his Countrymen — Letter to Mr. Allen.

WHILE the foregoing particulars undoubtedly deserve in the present case all the prominence which has been given to them as marks of a radical change of heart, I should be doing unpardonable injustice to his piety, were I to pass over the more direct, and, for the time being, the more satisfactory evidences. It is true, the tree must finally stand, or fall, according as it brings forth good or bad fruit; but as there can be no well-grounded hope that a tree, however sightly it may for a time appear to the eye, should continue to flourish and bear fruit, unless it be well rooted in a good soil, and refreshed by the genial dews and rains of heaven, it becomes, by no means, the least interesting part of our task to seek to enter into the more secret recesses of his neart, and there inquire from whence *originated* the above-mentioned traits of Christian character, which so much distinguished him from his heathen countrymen.

He possessed a tender conscience. If, from slothfulness or inadvertence, or from the force of former habit, he neglected his daily devotions, or did or said any thing which might give an unfavorable impression of the religion which he possessed, or if, in his more public instructions, he unwittingly advanced a sentiment not in accordance with scripture doctrine, on being reminded of his error, he always manifested the deepest concern lest he had given the enemy occasion to blaspheme, or misguided some benighted soul who might otherwise have been led to seek after the truth.

He had a docile, child-like temper. This was far removed from the silly credulity which emphatically makes the Hindoo the dupe of any one who will say a marvelous thing. But once, after a thorough examination, having renounced his ancient system of belief, with all its farrago of inconsistencies, he implicitly took the Bible as his counsel and his guide. Like an amiable child who loves and reveres his father, and knows that his kind parent, though he may sometimes cross his favorite plans, only seeks his ultimate good, so Babajee adopted the missionaries with whom he was connected as his parents, and ever yielded to them the most filial love and obedience. His heart was much in the duty of preaching the Gospel from village to village. He never appeared so happy as when traveling from place to place, and declaring to new multitudes of heathen, every day, the before unheard of riches of Jesus Christ. As he was at that time my only associate in the mission, we could not both conveniently be absent from Nuggur at the same time; nor could Babajee travel alone. The Brahmuns would not deign to be taught by one of their own number whom they regarded as an outcast, unless they saw him under the protection of some one to whom nature had given a skin of the same color with their rulers. Considered as a servant of such a one, they are not disparaged by hearing him. Such is the case, too, in a greater or less degree, with the common people, who are, in these matters, much influenced by their priests. Though extremely desirable that he should accompany the missionary on these tours, still it was not always expedient. In this, as in matters of less moment, he would submit with cheerful and filial obedience, and never allow his disappointment to relax his labors at home.

Humility, without which the pure and undefiled religion of the meek and lowly Jesus will not deign to dwell in the heart of man, beautifully adorned the walk of our Hindoo brother. His voluntary and entire renunciation of caste, which, in its humiliating consequences, dashed to the ground the boasted fabric of Brahminical infallibility, and left the demigod* but a poor, sinful, self-destroyed *man*, affords of itself a pretty satisfactory proof that he possessed this amiable grace; for, by this one act, he at once and for ever forfeited every thing which in this life is dear to man—his home, family, countrymen, the priesthood in which he had gloried, were now to him worse than annihilated; for they not only remained to him as monuments of his former folly, but they afforded the Brahmuns ample occasions for abusing and despising him. Not even the common hospitality of a father or a brother, or the ordinary compassion which is shown to the meanest beast, could he now claim. But it is not to the patience, the humility and cheerfulness, with which he supported himself when thus circumstanced, to which I now refer. It is rather to that distrust of self, that feeling of unworthiness, that sensitive

* The Brahmuns regard themselves not only as the peculiar favorites of heaven, but, in consequence of the honorable descent *from the mouth* of the Creator, as a superior order of beings. They believe themselves as much superior to other men, as God is superior to the Brahmuns—that is, they hold a station middle way between God and man.

concern lest he should do or say something prejudicial to the cause of Christ, or dishonoring to God, which satisfied the mind that Babajee's humility was not the humility of the hypocrite.

He wholly *disclaimed all hope of righteousness through the merit of works*, and trusted only in the meritorious righteousness of Jesus. Justification by faith was a subject on which he dwelt much in his instructions to the people. He dwelt much, too, in his private conversation, on the deceitfulness and exceeding depravity of his heart, and often expressed his fears that he might be left to fall into gross sin. The most prominent thing in his addresses at the throne of grace was, confession of sin. He seldom spoke of his former course of life, or of his present innate corruption, without tears. Whether he was beset by Satan with any peculiar temptations which do not fall to the common lot of the godly, I am unable to say; but true it was, that he very frequently spoke of the devices, the intimations, the suggestions of an evil spirit, in such vivid terms, as always to give me the impression that he had grappled with him in no ordinary way.

He often expressed his meditations and prayers on paper. I quote a few sentences as examples: "O, my soul! cast off all desire for worldly pleasures; seize on the hope of eternal happiness; and, in the name of the Savior, pray to God, and thou shalt receive. Ask for such things as these: wisdom, peace of mind, compassion, forgiveness, hatred of sin, knowledge, love to God, love for the worship of God, faith in Jesus Christ, repentance, the indwelling of the Holy Spirit—ask to dwell with God, and to enjoy him forever. I have no righteousness; I cannot walk in the right way; I continually stumble. But God is a sovereign, and knoweth all things. Therefore, what is most fit for us, he will surely give. Hence we ought to love him with our whole mind and heart. Merciful God! hear my prayer; I am sinful, polluted and fallen; clean me by the blood of Jesus Christ. I was born in sin, my works are all sinful, I am sin. Love me, O God! deliver me from destruction—give me a pure heart, and let not evil thoughts arise. Let not sin predominate in my heart. Deliver me from pride, covetousness, the displeasure of the good, and the desire of worldly good. But may all my hopes be in the happiness of the world to come: this can only be through help in Jesus Christ; for I have no power of my own by which I should walk in the right way. I am, by nature, only deserving of pain; but then, merciful God! make me worthy of happiness and of thy love. O! thou ocean of mercy, I am a sinful man. I cannot worship thee aright; keep me and guide me, according to the truth."

This distrust of self, naturally begat a corresponding dependence on God. He seemed to feel, in a remarkable degree, that every good and every perfect gift is from above, and cometh down from the father of lights. He did not here satisfy himself with the general expression, that it is in God that we live, move and have our being; but he regarded, in an uncommon degree, his daily food, raiment, protection, happiness, the use of his senses, the continuation of health, the opportunities which the present day afforded him of being useful to his countrymen, as special blessings from the hand of God. He would often specify particulars like these in his prayers, when his heart would glow with gratitude to the great Giver, and cast itself in sweet reliance on Him who giveth and upbraideth not. He had a happy talent, both in his prayers and instructions, of specifying and drawing useful lessons from what, in common language, are called little things. The birds of the air, the beasts of the field, the starting vegetation, the opening flower, the maturing of grain and fruits, the blessing of water, of air, of rain to fructify the earth, of day and night, and of the vicissitudes of the seasons, all furnished him with ample illustrations of the unbounded goodness and mercy of God toward His creatures. When addressing the Brahmuns, he would frequently point to a tree, a flower, or any sensible object which might be before him, and inquire, Is that the workmanship of Shiva or Vishnoo? Can your thirty-three millions of gods produce an object like that? or, if made to their hands, can they preserve it for a moment? Why, then, will you pass by Him who created, preserves and pervades all things, and worship the lowest works of his hands? If addressing the poor, the halt, the blind and maimed of the asylum, he would frequently point to a sparrow or an insect, and say, "Behold how insignificant a thing is the peculiar care of God! And will he not provide for you, if you love and serve him? Seek ye not what ye shall eat, or what ye shall drink, neither be of doubtful mind; for all these things do the *heathen* seek after."

Babajee too well understood the character of his countrymen, not to perceive that covetousness is the rock on which they are likely to make shipwreck of faith. He seemed to watch over his own heart, and smother the rising desires of avarice with great vigilance. He never expressed the least dissatisfaction respecting his monthly allowance; but gratefully received it as a means which God afforded him, through the benevolence of foreigners, to do good to his deluded people. He often declared, (what every missionary too well knows to be true,) that there is no stronger temptation to a Hindoo to change his religion than the hope of worldly gain; and it is lamentable to say, that the greater part of those, concerning whom we hoped that better motives induced them to embrace Christianity, exhibit, in this respect, a grievous deficiency. Instead of gratitude to God, and gratitude to the missionaries, who have, for their benefit, forsaken all that was dear in country and home, voluntarily taken up their residence in an insalubrious climate, and are fast wearing out their life for their good, they not only expect a support, but not unfrequently manifest the most trying dissatisfaction that they are not better supported. They often feel as if they have conferred a great favor on the missionary by renouncing their own religion, and assisting him in his missionary labors among themselves; and that he ought not to be slow in acknowledging their services by a good reward. Here it should be remarked, that the state of things as yet, in this part of India, is such as almost to compel the missionary to keep his converts in his service. This strengthens the impression that converts are to receive a support, and not unfrequently leads to disappointment, that the allowance is not more, and the labors less. It is pleasing to be able to make Babajee an exception. He not only sought to keep himself unspotted from the world, but he was not slow to sound the alarm to others.

Babajee loved the Bible. He had, as stated before, obtained a general knowledge of the New Testament previous to his conversion. Now he studied the sacred oracles spiritually, admiring their intrinsic excellence, and their peculiar adaptation to the wants of man, in all ages and nations. He was particularly interested in a religious service which we held at our table every evening, immediately after tea. It was for prayer and mutual instruction. We first read a chapter in the New Testament, each reading a few verses in turn, prayed, Babajee, Dajaba, and myself, alternately, and then took up some subject for discussion, or I related some portion of the Old Testament history which has not yet been translated. The lively interest with which he seized every new fact, the avidity with which he grasped every new idea, afforded his teacher a rich compensation for all the rebuffs and discouragements which he was daily meeting from the opposition, the listlessness and indifference of the people from without.

I have said that Babajee manifested a very great interest for the spiritual welfare of his own people, and only desired to live that he might be an instrument of good to them. This he regarded as his field of labor; still, his heart, in the true spirit of Christian benevolence, was enlarged, and he encircled in its desires the whole human family. His prayers were scarcely more frequent or more fervent for the people of Hindoostan than they were for the Chinese, the European, the African, or the American. In imagination, he would often bring in the day of millennial glory, and behold, with delight, all nations, and tongues, and kindreds, bowing to the sceptre of Jesus, ascribing "blessing and honor, glory and power, unto him that sitteth on the throne, and to the Lamb, for ever and ever." He listened with peculiar interest to the accounts which were given him of the efforts which are making at the present day to diffuse the blessings of Christianity throughout the world; and heard with still greater pleasure what progress the light of truth has, within these few years, made into the dark dominions of idolatry. This light, he would say, which is now pouring in upon the nations from every quarter, must ere long illuminate India. The history of the recent benevolent movements in America, for the distribution of the word of God, the propagation of the Gospel both at home and abroad, in connection with the account of the rise and progress of the American Republic, greatly excited his admiration. He would say, "that is a land of promise, a chosen inheritance of God."

The last internal evidence which I shall mention, that this idolater had become a child of God, is the desire which he manifested *to be freed from sin.* He believed that genuine happiness can only originate from holiness; and that sin is the procuring cause of all human evil. To be delivered from sin, was, in his estimation, a passport to supreme happiness. Assurance of hope, and perfection in holiness, he thought attainable, and not only a consummation devoutly to be wished, but to be continually sought with prayer and fasting. In scarcely any thing did he differ more from the heathen around him, than in his views of death. He often spoke of it as the fruition of all the Christian's hopes, not to be dreaded but desired. The idolater, he would say, regards death as the greatest possible evil; for in it he can see nothing but loss and destruction. But to himself it opened the portals of heaven, and showed him an exceeding and eternal weight of glory.

The foregoing remarks will be better illustrated by the following letter:

"Babajee, called by the will of God to be a servant of Jesus Christ, to the church of God in Bombay, and to all in every place who are called holy, through the Lord Jesus Christ. Mercy and peace from God our Father, and the Lord Jesus Christ be with you. Amen!

"Brethren, render unto the Lord Jesus, whom you have received, all due honor. Deceive not yourselves and others by taking again the 'old man,' whom ye have crucified, and plunging again into carnal delights and sensuality. If you still indulge in pastimes, delight in exhibitions of folly, and practice the arts of deception, it will come to pass that when the heathen see such conduct, they will reproach you and us; they will reproach our teachers and our Redeemer. For this reason, I entreat that your demeanor be not sensual. For they who only please the senses are carnal, and the carnal cannot please God. The spirit of Christ is not in those carnal desires which men, while in the body, seek to fulfill. And whosoever hath not the spirit of Christ, he is not of God, but of the devil; and if he be not of God, he will be a partaker of the everlasting pains of hell. Before becoming Christians, you indeed walked according to the flesh. And now you profess to have cast off the natural man, and to have become Christians. Let me ask you, have you done this in mind, or only in body and in name? Beloved brethren, whosoever in appearance and name only becomes a Chistian, but whose mind is not Christian, the Holy Spirit has no abode in his heart; he is not, therefore, worthy of salvation: it were better that a mill-stone were tied to his neck, and he cast into the sea. Whoever liveth according to the flesh, is worthy of death. Brethren, if through the Spirit ye do mortify the deeds of the flesh, ye shall live; 'for as many as are led by the spirit of God, they are the sons of God.' If ye are called of Christ, behold our Savior, and, like him, become separated from the world. He indulged in no vain amusements or gratifications. He was a sojourner in this world. Direct your mind to him and reflect. Was he carnal or spiritual? If you find that he was spiritual, then honor him in spirit and in truth, and with your whole strength, and take upon you his name. Whosoever nameth the name of Christ, let him examine himself. For he that doth not anxiously try himself, shall not continue to the end. That you may continue to the end, and be acceptable to Christ, is my desire. This I ask of you, that you may preserve yourselves through the aid of the Holy Ghost, be saved, and eternally happy. He that examines his own heart, understands what the 'minding of the things of the spirit' meaneth, and he ordereth his conversation cautiously before the people. Moreover, brethren, as you are now Christ's, you must teach his commandments. Still, I assure you that your *daily walk* is of more importance than mere verbal instruction. *This*, in my opinion, is more useful to bring men to believe: therefore, it is written to you, 'Be not angry, but, on deliberation, choose what seemeth good,' and reject what is evil. Ye are joined to the church of Christ; walk, therefore, according to the laws of the church and of God, that you may not bring a stigma on the church. For, if your conduct before the people be not good, they will indeed suppose that all Christians are hypocrites."

The following correspondence too well illustrates Babajee's growing piety and increasing desire of usefulness to be omitted. It breathes much of the spirit of the writer. The brother, the Christian, I had almost said the apostle, is here seen, animated in his work by motives the most noble that can warm the heart of man; exhorting his brethren to mutual love, self-denial, diligence, humility, and fervor in the work of the Lord; humble and docile as a child, but strong in the faith as a full grown man in Christ. The animated style, simple language, and softened spirit which prevades the whole, is a pleasing specimen of his daily deportment among a crooked and perverse generation.

LETTER TO MR. ALLEN.

"To the most excellent Allen Sahib, blessed of God through Jesus Christ, Babajee, a door-keeper of the house of God, who stands at the door humbly begging for the bread and water of life, sendeth greeting: I entreat that you will send me a letter of instruction and exhortation, that a poor servant of Jesus Christ may be confirmed in the true faith. The chief intelligence which I have to communicate is, that my love of this world, by the exercise of faith in Jesus Christ, is continually diminishing, and that my love to God is increasing more and more, and that my old man is, on account of sin, crucified with the body of Christ. I confide myself entirely to him. I take hold of the hand of my heavenly Father. Whithersoever he leadeth, there will I go. All the right feelings which I have are of the Holy Spirit. I search the Gospel of Jesus Christ, and daily examine myself concerning what I do, and what I ought to do. I am distressed on account of sin, and repent, and daily ask of God forgiveness for all my past sins. As the watchman puts on his armor, and vigilantly performs his duty, so I put on the armor of self-examination, and daily endeavor to watch over myself. I fully believe that I cannot be saved by my own works, but by faith in Jesus Christ. This is my hope. Formerly I was an adulterer, false, deceitful, and an idolater. In these things I then took delight; but now, through the grace of Jesus Christ, I am disgusted, yea, I hate them. Now I love whatever I believe to be pleasing to God, and hate what is offensive to him. I endeavor to avoid what is forbidden in the sacred Scriptures. I pray and implore the assistance of God, and search the Scriptures daily, that I may be able to give instruction, according to the command of Christ. I gratefully acknowledge the loving kindness of God, and am not unmindful of the kindness of those by whose instrumentality I have been converted. The instructions of Graves Sahib, that true worshiper of God, are particularly grateful to me; for by them the knotty doubts of the mind are solved, and the heart gradually is made pure. By his means my soul was first distressed on account of sin; by faith in Jesus Christ I was again made joyful.

"Since leaving Bombay for Ahmednuggur, I have instructed my wife in the word of God. Before the death of Mr. Hervey she reviled me, and scornfully rejected Christ. From that time she became penitent, began to pray, and asked baptism. I hope her heart is now renewed.

"In the latter part of June, I made a short preaching tour, when I visited five or seven villages, and told the people of Jesus Christ. I now feel that if I am to live long in this world, I desire to live only for Christ. If I am to go to another world, I desire to live with him for ever there.

"Oh, my brother! I cannot love Christ as I ought; for by

reason of sin I am weak. While an enemy of God, he, through mercy, that I might be saved, assumed a vile, perishable human body, and did for me what I was bound to do for myself. Had I died in my sins, and perished, God would still be glorified in the multitude of his creatures. I am indeed bound to love God, who is love. May he, who has done so much for my salvation, enable me to love him.

"I am ignorant, sinful, depraved. By my own works I cannot be saved. I cast myself into the arms of God my Father. If it be his will, he will save me. If he do not save me, I cannot be saved. If he do not keep me from evil, I must fall into evil.

"Brothers Dajaba and Moraba are with you. Confirm them in the right way. I desire that they may well instruct the Hindoo people. I pray that they may be *new men.* To teach us who are ignorant, to confirm us in the right way, and bring us to believe on Jesus Christ, is your proper work. We are *infants*, and must have the milk of the word. We cannot bear strong meat, if you give it us. Wherefore, feed us with milk, and we shall, by little and little, be strengthened into manhood, and, becoming men, we may be fed with meat. Then shall we become strong in the faith, and be saved by Jesus Christ. May peace and comfort from the Triune God, Father, Son, and Holy Ghost, be with you for ever. Amen!

"O God! merciful Father, I am sinful, ignorant and foolish; I have written, because my brother desired it; but I have not been able to write in a proper manner. I desire that this letter may not be useless. I ask not on my own account, but for the sake of Jesus Christ, that the writing of this letter may be of some utility."

"To the Rev. Mr. Graves, well-wisher of our people, and to Madam Graves, both of the same parent in Christ, I, Christian, Babajee, and my wife, write. Peace and comfort from our Lord Jesus Christ be with you. Amen!

"We are tender plants, planted through the mercy of Jesus

Christ, by your hands. That these plants may grow, become trees, and bear much fruit, they must be moistened at the roots, and sprinkled with water from above. I write unto you, that, from your instrumentality, we may derive assistance, whereby we may increase in love and faith, and bring forth fruit, double, treble, quadruple, and a thousand fold."

LETTER TO DAJABA.

"Babajee, a servant of the Lord Jesus Christ, by the will of God our Savior, and of the Lord Jesus Christ our hope, to Dajaba, a beloved child of God through faith: Grace, mercy, and peace, humility, pardon, joy, and comfort, be to you from God our Father, and from the Lord Jesus Christ.

"Dajaba, my beloved brother, the letter which you so kindly sent me by Mr. Read, was received in good time. I cannot express the pleasure which I felt in the perusal of it. By such letters my faith in Christ will be strengthened.

"God has begotten us through the Holy Ghost, according to his purpose, and on account of the righteousness of Jesus Christ: therefore we are dearer to each other than brethren. Among brothers there is often strife, deception, mutual abuse, unfaithfulness, disputes about their fathers' property. But among us, who have been born of the Holy Spirit, there must be no deception, or strife, or covetousness. We must become *gosawees** through Jesus Christ; not, however, such gosawees as are daily seen about us here. We must be true gosawees; that is, have the mastery over our passions. We must eradicate and cast from us all worldly hopes, and hope only in God, and leave ourselves entirely in his hands: then God, our Father, will, through Jesus Christ, account us as innocent. You observed, my brother, in your letter, (and it is in accordance with the Christian shas-

* A gosawee is a devotee who has forsaken the world, goes about almost naked, his body besmeared with ashes, lives on the charity of the people, and professes to be very holy. He pretends to instruct the people in a knowledge of God; but really does no more than to repeat the names of the gods, and mutter over some unintelligible jargon, which the stupid populace suppose to be muntras or incantations.

tras,) that '*we are the body of Christ,*' and ought therefore to love one another.

"Above all, my brother, read much, pray much, be humble, communicate instruction, rebuke with soft words any thing wrong which you may discover in our brethren or sisters; and, by the grace of God, peace be with you."

The following letter was addressed to Mr. Graves, while recently in America:

"Our will-wisher and respected father, Mr. Graves, and respected mother, Mrs. Graves, Babajee, a servant of Jesus Christ, with his wife, presents a great salutation, and begs to write a letter of respect. We have given ourselves an offering, through Christ, into the hand of God the Father; and, through faith, by the Spirit, we remain in the hope of being justified by the righteousness of Jesus Christ. And we who are new-born, are like ignorant children; but may we become mature in faith, and stand against the wiles of the devil, the slanderer, to fight against him! May God array us with his heavenly armor! that is, may he bind our loins about with truth; put upon us the breast-plate of righteousness, and cause our feet to be shod with the preparation of the gospel of peace; and, above all, put into our hands the shield of faith, wherewith we may be able to quench all the fiery darts of the wicked one. May he also put upon our heads the hemlet of salvation, and put into our hands the sword of the Spirit, which is the word of God! And may he keep us, always praying with all prayer and supplication, at all times in the Spirit! And for the same purpose, that we may be awake with all diligence, in prayer for all saints. We ask you both to remember us, as well as yourselves, in prayer to God. May there be peace and love, with faith, among all the brethren, from God the Father, and the Lord Jesus Christ. May grace be with all who love our Lord Jesus Christ in sincerity. Amen!

"Please present to the church the salutation of me, a fallen one."

CHAPTER XII.

Hindooism Debasing — Papers illustrating Babajee's Mode of Thinking — Occasion of Writing them — Hindoo Notions of God.

The inquiring reader will desire to know what is the mode of thinking and reasoning of a man who has, for forty years, been fed on the fooleries of Hindoo superstition. He had drawn in with his mother's milk the deadly bane of idolatry; all his early impressions, and notions of right and wrong, were formed on a false standard. At forty years old he begins to reason — finds all his views, feelings, and opinions, concerning religion and moral duty, wrong — his heart corrupt, his understanding darkened, his conscience stupefied, and all his laborious and costly atonements unavailing; all that had been done, was to be undone. It is impossible for one reared in a Christian land, fully to estimate the influence which a heathen education exerts on the mental faculties and the moral feelings of the idolater. We talk, and very justly, too, of the infinite advantage of a right early education; and when we contrast the character of the man thus educated with that of him who grows up amidst the deadly influences of infidelity, or of thoughtless gayety, or the contempt of all moral obligations, we sēe a *difference* which gives us some remote idea of the influence of the education received by a heathen child. Yet the most profligate family in Christendom are, more or less, under restraints imposed by Christianity. They are not debased by the worship of a stone or a reptile. They have many right views of God, and of duty — many good maxims and customs which cannot fail to produce some influence, though latent it may be, on the mind. Hence the worst man in a Christian land possesses an advantage over the best in a heathen land.

These remarks will enable the reader more justly to appreciate the following specimens of Babajee's theological views. I add them, not for the merit which they contain in themselves, but, as I have done many other things in this sketch, to show, for the encouragement of the friends of missions, what a bigoted Hindoo may become, under the teachings of the Holy Spirit; and, seeing this, that they may give more liberally, and pray more fervently, that God would supply the place of his departed servant with a thousand as faithful and devout.

PROOFS OF CREATION WITHOUT THE AID OF SCRIPTURE.

"If you say the universe was from eternity, let me ask, are not men, beasts, birds, &c., of the creation? Surely these are a part of creation. This being allowed, who will say that the universe is from eternity? These, which are a part of the universe, are not from eternity. Furthermore, if all things are from eternity, how comes it to pass that they are subject to *change?* Hence it appears that the universe was *created.*

"My second proof is this: It is known to be a principle that when water is made turbid by agitation, the heavier particles will, by the power of their own gravity, fall, and collect at the bottom, while the light particles rise. According to this principle, the earth seems to have been *formed.* For, by digging into the earth there are found to be layers of earth, stone, &c., one above another. The same is found to be true on the tops of the highest mountains. On the summits of these mountains are found petrifactions of shells and fish. Hence it appears not only that the earth was *created,* but that it was formed out of a thick watery consistence.

"The third argument is drawn from the import of the word *shrustee* (universe). This is a significant term, viz: *that which is created.* The term shrustee cannot, therefore, be applied to that which is from eternity. If this term may properly be applied only to things which appear, then it is evident they were created.

"Fourthly, it is said in the Rig-veda, 'Before the creation of the universe the Spirit existed alone.' Hence it appears that the universe is not eternal, but was created by Jehovah, who is from everlasting to everlasting. With him there is neither beginning nor end.

"The fifth argument is this: If the world had existed from eternity, the earth would ere this have become one great plain, by means of rains. But we still see many very high mountains."

EXISTENCE OF GOD.

"Do you say there is no God? Then hear: I exist, you exist, and we are conscious of our existence. We have the faculty of speaking, hearing, walking, and thinking; we have understanding, reflection, and knowledge. Whence are all these? And who formed us in the womb? Who protected and nourished us then? Our mother had no such power. Who then did preserve us? Who afterwards nourished our limbs, by means of food taken in at the mouth? Did our mother? Who forms the chicken in the shell? If you cannot answer, I will tell you. He who gave us existence and protected us in the womb—he alone is God, and self-existent.

"I mention another proof: By *whose power is this globe kept in the firmament?* If you say by its *own*, then I reply, the earth is but an inanimate body, and it does not contain in itself the power of remaining in the expanse of the heavens. If you throw a stone or a piece of earth into the air, does it by any power in itself remain in the air, or does it fall? By whose power, then, is the earth sustained? If you cannot reply, I will tell you. It is upheld by the Almighty God. This is a clear proof of the existence of God.

"The skill displayed in the contrivance of the human body, furnishes another argument of the existence of God. For example, the joints of the hands and feet will not *turn back*. Here appears a happy *design*. Were it otherwise, one could not lay hold of an object with the hand, or do any kind of business. He made the mouth, but did not put it in the hinder part of the head, for whatever is put into the mouth must be put in by the hand, in front. Eyes were made for the body; and in the eye are films, or humors, in which there is no blood, but water. The design displayed in this appears to be, that the light must enter through the water, and by this means external objects be made to appear. The eyes were not placed in the back part of the head—for, in that case, no one could see what he does with his hands.

"God gave to man two ears. These he did not place in the forehead, or in any place but on the side of the head. In this there appears *design*, that he may hear sound from every direction. Hence, from the skill and intelligence displayed in the construction of the human body, it appears there is an infinite and all-wise Being."

THE ETERNITY OF GOD.

"Something exists, and therefore something must have existed without a beginning; and if that something exists without a beginning, then will it not exist eternally? From this *something* the universe originated. For it is certain there is no power in the material universe to create itself. Hence it appears that there was an agent. Moreover, all things in the universe continue to move on with the same regularity and precision as they formerly did. From this it is evident there must still be a governor; and if He *is*, and *was*, he will be a governor to all eternity. Another argument which might be adduced, is, that *God is a Spirit*, and therefore will not cease to be."

The above is the commencement of a series of papers which Babajee began to write on theological subjects. The specimens here given will suffice to show what were his notions of a Deity; and when the above views of the Supreme Being are compared with the vague, incongruous, and unworthy notions entertained by the Hindoos in general; and when it is considered that these are the views of one who but a few months ago emerged from the depths of a most debasing system of idolatry, the pious reader will magnify the grace of God, which alone brought him from nature's darkness into His marvelous light. The following extracts are taken principally from "Mr. Ward's View of the Hindoos," and as they very correctly illustrate the indefinite and unworthy notions of the idolaters of India in reference to the

Deity, as well as the revolting character of their own inferior divinities, I here quote them, in order to bring out the contrast:

"No question occurs so frequently in the Hindoo shastras as this: What is God? To know whether He exists or not, page upon page has been written, and this question has been agitated in every period of Hindoo history, wherever two or three pundits happened to meet, with a solicitude, but, at the same time, with an uncertainty, which carries us at once to the apostolic declaration, 'the world by wisdom knew not God.' Some pundits call Him the invisible and ever-blessed; others conceive of him as possessing form; others have the idea that he exists like an inconceivably small atom; sometimes he is male, at other times female; sometimes both male and female, producing a world by conjugal union; sometimes the elements assume his place, and at other times he is a deified hero. Thus in three hundred and thirty millions of forms, or names, this nation, in the emphatical language of St. Paul, has been, from age to age, 'feeling after' the Supreme Being, like men groping 'in the region and shadow of death;' and, after so many centuries, the question is as much undetermined as ever, what is God?

"One day, in conversation with the Sanskritu head pundit of the college of Fort William, on the subject of God, this man, who is truly learned in his own shastras, gave the author, from one of their books, the following parable: 'In a certain country there existed a village of blind men, who had heard of an amazing animal called the elephant, of the shape of which, however, they could procure no idea. One day an elephant passed through the place; the villagers crowded to the spot where the animal was standing; and one of them seized his trunk, another his ear, another his tail, another one of his legs. After thus endeavoring to gratify their curiosity, they returned into the village, and sitting down together, began to communicate their ideas on the shape of the elephant to the villagers. The man who had seized his trunk said, he thought this animal must be like the body of the plantain tree; he who had touched his ear, was of opinion that he was like the winnowing fan; the man who had laid hold of his tail said, he thought he must resemble a snake; and he who had caught his leg, declared he must be like a pillar. An old blind man of some judgment was present, who, though greatly perplexed in attempting to reconcile these jarring notions, at length said: You have all been to examine this animal; and what you report, therefore, cannot be false. I suppose, then, that the part resembling the plantain tree must be his trunk; what you thought similar to a fan, must be his ear; the part like a snake, must be the tail; and that like a pillar, must be his leg. In this way, the old man, uniting all their conjectures, made out something of the form of the elephant.' Respecting God, added the pundit, we are all blind; none of us have seen him; those who wrote the shastras, like the old blind man, have collected all the reasonings and conjectures of mankind together, and have endeavored to form some idea of the nature of the Divine Being. It is an irresistible argument in favor of the majesty, simplicity, and truth of the Holy Scriptures, that nothing of this uncertainty has been left on the mind of the most illiterate Christian. However mysterious the subject, we never hear such a question started in Christian countries: What is God?

"The doctrine of a plurality of gods, with their consequent intrigues, criminal amours, quarrels, and stratagems to counteract each other, has produced the most fatal effects on the minds of men. Can we expect a people to be better than their gods? Brahmu was inflamed with evil desires towards his own daughter. Vishnoo, when incarnate as Bamunu, deceived king Bulee, and deprived him of his kingdom. Shiva's wife was constantly jealous on account of his amours, and charged him with associating with the women of a low caste: the story of Shiva and Mohinee, a female form of Vishnoo, is shockingly indelicate. Vrihusputee, the spiritual guide of the gods, committed a rape on his eldest brother's wife. Indru was guilty of dishonoring the wife of his spiritual guide. Sooryu ravished a virgin named Koontee. Yumu, in a passion, kicked his own mother, who cursed him, and afflicted him with a swelled leg, which to this day the worms are constantly devouring. Ugnee was inflamed with evil desires towards six virgins, the daughters of as many sages, but was overawed by the presence of his wife. Buluramu was a great drunkard. Vayoo was cursed by Dukshu for making his daughters crooked when they refused his embraces. He is also charged with a scandalous connection with a female monkey. When Vuroonn was walking in his own heaven, he was so smitten with the charms of Oorvushee, a courtezan, that, after a long contest, she was scarcely able to extricate herself from him. Krishna's thefts, wars, and adulteries, are so numerous, that his whole history seems to be one uninterrupted series. In the images of Kalee, she is represented as treading on the breast of her husband. Lukshmee and Luruswatee, the wives of Vishnoo, were continually quarreling. It is worthy of inquiry, how the world is governed by these gods, more wicked than men, that we may be able to judge how far they can be the object of faith, hope, and affection. Let us open the Hindoo sacred writings; here we see the Creator and Preserver perpetually counteracting each other. Sometimes the Preserver is destroying, and at other times the Destroyer is preserving. On a certain occasion, Shiva granted to the great enemy of the gods, Ravanu, a blessing, which set all their heavens in an uproar, and drove the three hundred and thirty millions of gods into a state of desperation. Brahmu created Koombhukurnu, a monster larger than the whole island of Lunka, but was obliged to doom him to an almost perpetual sleep, to prevent his producing a universal famine. This god is often represented as bestowing a blessing, to remove the effects of which Vishnoo is obliged to become incarnate; nay, these effects have not in some cases been removed till all the gods have been thrown into confusion, and all the elements seized and turned against the Creator, the Preserver, and the Reproducer. When some giant, blessed by Brahmu, has destroyed the creation, Vishnoo and Shiva have been applied to; but they have confessed they could do nothing for the tottering universe.

"Reverence for the gods, especially among the poor, as might be expected, does not exceed their merits; yet it is a shocking fact, that language like the following should be used respecting what the Hindoos suppose to be the providence which governs the world. When it thunders awfullly, respectable Hindoos say, 'Oh! the gods are giving us a bad day;' the lowest orders say, 'The rascally gods are dying.' During a heavy rain, a woman of respectable caste frequently says, 'Let the gods perish! my clothes are all wet.' A man of low caste, says, 'These rascally gods are sending more rain.'

"In witnessing such a state of gross ignorance, on a subject of infinite moment to men, how forcibly do we feel the truth and the wisdom of the declartion of the Divine Author of the Christian religion, 'This is life eternal, to know Thee, the only true God.'"

There were among his papers thoughts on justification, and on regeneration, which do him equal credit. We give an extract from the latter:

REGENERATION.

"'Jesus answering said unto him, Except a man be born again, he cannot see the kingdom of heaven."

"All men are sinners, and therefore cannot worship a holy God acceptably. For a holy God can only be worshiped in holiness and truth. Therefore, unless there be a regeneration of the heart, neither you, nor I, nor any one, can worship God acceptably. Without purity of heart, no expedient for obtaining eternal blessednes will be of any avail. But the heart is full of uncleanness, as it is written in Romans i: 29–32. How can a mind rendered *impure* by such things worship the PURE God? It cannot be. Therefore, from such impurity our minds must be cleansed. Ye worshipers of idols! what method have you for purifying the heart? One may repeat names, mortify his body, dwell in the wilderness, give in charity, go on pilgrimage to holy places, wrap himself in meditation, bathe, worship, and sacrifice: if his heart be not pure, it is all in vain. These remedies can be of no use to sinners in cleansing the heart. The Hindoo has no idea of religion as connected with purity of heart. He has much to say of persons being holy or unholy, pure or impure; but as this refers only to ceremonial cleanness, the heart has nothing to do with it. A liar or an adulterer may be pure, if he have bathed and performed the requsite rites, while the man of *pure heart* may be unholy; and if the heart were once holy, they would not be needed; consequently, they are altogether useless."

The following paper has interested me too much to be allowed to pass unnoticed. If I have not perused it with undue partiality, the pious Christian, and the minister of the Gospel, will derive from it both pleasure and profit. A depraved son of India, and a corrupt priest of Brahmu, may, by the power and grace of God, become his teacher in the momentous concerns of the soul's salvation. These are the effusions of a heart but eighteen months before benighted in idolatry, and led captive by Satan at his will. I am not quite sure that I have in every instance exhibited the exact meaning of the original. The style, idiom, and much of the language, is Sanskrit, written in a measured style of poetry like the Hindoo sacred books.

The character here given of false teachers, or gooroos, is doubtless true to life, when applied to thousands of religious mendicants who deluge the country. Formerly, they went in companies of hundreds, and sometimes of thousands, and devastated the country like a cloud of locusts. When they came to a village, they demanded whatever they chose, and resorted to violence if it were not given. The practice here alluded to of saying muntras in the ear, is very common, and is regarded as very efficacious.

MARKS OF A TRUE (TEACHER) GOOROO.

"A gooroo should be learned in the Scriptures, a wise and skillful teacher, and versed in all sorts of learning. Casting off the pride of human wisdom, he should delight in the commands of God. He should turn his back on the wealth or the wife of his neighbor, and should never speak of the faults or the defects of others. He is sacredly bound to be discreet, merciful, and benevolent. As the sun enlightens and blesses all around, so ought his beneficence and wisdom to impart instruction and happiness. Having secured his own salvation, he should seek the salvation of all about him. He should make his disciples holy. In honor and dishonor, he should be the same. Should a disciple, whom he has taught with much care, forsake him and go to another teacher, he should not indulge his mind in angry or unbecoming feeling. Should the people revile and stone him, he ought to cast before him the shield of forgiveness, and not allow hatred or revenge to arise. His love to his disciples should be like love to a brother. A gooroo should never take a crooked step, or throw a stumbling-block in the way of his disciples. He should keep himself from all hurtful passions, and fix his mind on heavenly things. If fortune smiles, or if in a moment all is dashed to the ground, his mind is neither elated with joy, nor depressed with sorrow. The ant and the universe, the mighty and the mean, the king and the beggar, are alike. The image of the sun appears the same, whether its rays fall into a large or small vessel of water. He is a true gooroo, who, in all his conversation and intercourse with the world, never forgets his station and character, nor loves disputes or useless controversy. The great and the rich of the earth do him honor; but he regards not their praise, and seeks not to be called great. To flatter the great and despise the low, he knows not. He is at peace with himself, delights in the worship of God, and loves the society of the righteous. Adorned with these marks, he becomes a mighty and a complete gooroo. Whoever does not bear about him these marks, has no claim to the qualities of a gooroo. Such a one is false at heart: keep not his company. There is no wisdom in him. As the lizard runs from place to place, stretching out his neck to spy out every object about him, so the hypocritical gooroo saunters from village to village, to make a show of his sanctity, and to answer his own carnal purposes.* They reproach all good men, and teach for the word of God the precepts of man. They decoy the simple from the right way,

* The impositions practiced by those religious mendicants, and by others assuming their garb and habits, are wonderful; and only show more strikingly the wretched-

and, pretending they know every thing, teach the people that first of all they should worship them. Whomsoever they happen to meet, they accost as their disciple, and strive to draw him after them. Like the gabbling of a drunkard, they prate out unmeaning muntras (charms or incantations) into the ear, but ensnare their disciples by their fair words, and threaten them with curses if they do not worship them. They say 'we are wise, and freed from all earthly pollution, and regulate all our actions by the shastras.' They sometimes appear meek; again they are full of lust and anger. They say 'we are in the way of salvation,' but they know not God. They put on a false semblance of virtue, while the deadly disease within is unhealed."

Babajee, during the last months of his life, had been in the habit of writing abhungu, and other poetical pieces, in which he imitated the style of composition, and the manner of delivering

ness of a superstitious nation. Under the semblance of great sanctity and self-denial, or in the practice of severe penance, these vagrants wander about from village to village, and make all things, as far as possible, subservient to themselves. This they often do in no small degree; for the deluded people believe there is great merit in feeding them. Hence they supply their wants while they remain, and give them money to carry away. These devotees go on long pilgrimages, begging their way for thousands of miles; and are, perhaps, at the same time engaged in some profitable traffic in precious metals or Cashmere shawls. The latter they procure very cheap at Cashmere, and the former in Northern India, and manage to carry them among their rags so as to be unsuspected. They sell these at an enormous profit. These arch hypocrites have been found dead by the road, or at some place far from home, and, on examination, their tattered, dirty ungurka has been found to be quilted full of gold mohurs, a coin of the value of fifteen rupees, or more than seven dollars. The finest portion of the city of Poona, which is called Gosaweepoor, was built by these beggars. They are generally called *gosawees*. A Brahmun, whom I have this moment consulted on the subject, says the circumstance of a gosawee's being rich or poor, has no influence on the people in respect to giving them in charity; they regard only their "*moral* greatness."

Natives have formerly, and no doubt do at the present day, assume the garb and habits of the gosawee for a still worse purpose than to extort charity. The thief, the highway robber, the assassin, the spy, and traitor, all, in their turn, have been known to besmear their hair and bodies with ashes, daub their faces with ochre, doff their ordinary apparel, and put on the copperas-colored cloth of the gosawee. They sally forth with the staff in hand, a bell, a string of beads, a necklace of shells, a cocoa-nut or gourd-shell to receive alms, and their besmeared hair flying in the wind. Thus decorated, the pretended gosawee goes forth, sometimes braying like an ass, sometimes howling like a jackall, and enters houses, spying out its riches, and its defense, and reports to the head of the banditti to which he belongs. And, in like manner, they accomplish any dark deed of robbery or murder which they wish. Captain Mackintosh mentions, in his history of the lawless marauders of the Deckan, called Ramoosees, that this is their most common resource for ascertaining the amount of property in any given place, or the means by which it could be obtained. An arch fellow, in the garb of a gosawee, would bring Oomajee, their chief, an account of any treasure which was to be moved, and an estimate of its value.

instruction, which is practiced among the Brahmuns. The abhungu is a metrical composition, in praise of the Deity, and adapted to the *sing-song* tone in which the natives recite the shastras, or rehearse traditions, legends, and the like.

As this practice is so common, and so well suited to convey instruction to the native, in a manner which will interest him, it is, undoubtedly, an important desideratum to be able to turn this to good account. It is not, however, likely to be done with effect, except by a learned native. The foreigner's *imitation* of it would be so remote and barbarous, that the people would scarcely recognize it. As Christianity advances in India, this kind of composition will not unlikely be adopted as a channel for communicating religious truth; and it will at the same time furnish, perhaps, the only proper substitute for the bawdy songs, stories, and legends which so much abound among the natives. They have so long cherished the propensity to recite and listen to these—the habit is so common and inveterate—that converts to Christianity, unless they are furnished with a substitute, will almost inevitably be corrupted by them. Babajee had not overlooked this principle in human nature. Whether the more effectual edification of his people was the motive which moved him, in the first instance, to adopt this mode of composition, or whether it originated from feeling a vacuity in his own mind, arising from the force of habit, is uncertain. He recited these hymns (as I may as well call them) to his more intimate friends, and to small circles of the people, used then at family devotion in his own house, and when unoccupied he was almost continually singing them. I shall here add a few specimens, without any attempt to exhibit the measure or the style of the original, but only to convey the thoughts of the writer. Our English translation of the Psalms of the "sweet singer of Israel," give us scarcely any idea of the beauty of the original Hebrew poetry. So, comparing small things with great, the following translation conveys but a slight notion of the original.

I. — WHO IS JESUS?

Jesus is the King of saints; Jesus is the support of the soul; Jesus is my God. In heaven or in earth, there is no other Savior.

He is the ornament and delight of his saints, a terror to the wicked, pardon to the penitent, and his tender mercies are over all.

Jesus is an ocean of happiness, a sea of love, a firm mountain which cannot be moved.

He is the guide and protector of his people; an inexhaustible fountain in the house of his saints.

II. — CONFESSION.

In vain was my life; my days went to naught when I did not worship thee, O! my Savior.

I squandered my substance in sin; vain and vile were all my offerings to strange gods.

In vain have I called this or that my own; I have thrust my neck in a snare, and there was none to deliver.

When I turned my back on the righteous, I incensed a Holy God, and deprived myself of the gracious fruits of his Spirit.

Who, and what I was, and whither tending, I knew not; all my penances and oblations were vain.

Helpless, worthless, and undone, my soul shall cleave to my Redeemer. This mortal, wonderful body, will soon perish.

Who can understand the subtlety of Death? He smites, he casts into the grave, and gluts his vengeance.

Lo! this vain world I leave; though lost, I am found; I am saved in Christ, the sinner's friend.

III. — THE SAVIOR.

Surely Christ is our Father, our Mother, our Brother.

Fountain of mercy, blessed Jesus, speedily thou relievest the weary and afflicted.

Thou hast saved me through Grace; what shall I render thee? I have nothing to offer.

Lover of the humble! Thou hast freely saved me! Grant me what is fit; do with me as thou wilt.

Envy, anger, and lust, like flames, consume us; disease, sorrow, and death are the portion of our cup.

Therefore will I continually call on thee, thou fountain of Mercy, blessed Jesus!

Manifest thyself to my soul; for I will seek thee with my whole heart.

Speedily receive me, O! thou friend of saints! deliver me in thy great mercy!

IV. — CHRIST A FATHER AND A FRIEND.

Christ is the Father of the fatherless, the mighy God, the Lord of all.

Like a kind father, he inclines his ear and hears when his suppliant children cry.

He knows their thoughts, He sees their wants, His hand is near. In Life, in death, adore the Savior God.

He who looks to Him with undivided heart, shall find honor, peace, and happiness.

Let all the people worship and adore Him! how vain, how vile to worship other gods, the creatures of His hand!

Behold the man consumed by a hundred desires! Can gold, or pride, or lust procure him peace and pardon? But I will cling to Jesus.

Tell me, O! ye people, how a man can be clean in the sight of God! I have searched your shastras, I have tried your gods; but, alas! in vain! Come ye to Jesus; He is the fountain.

CHAPTER XIII.

The Latter Period of his Life—Labors more zealously—Grows in Grace—The value of Native Assistants—Church Organized—Babajee made Elder—Babajee's Sickness and Death—Reflections—A Voice to Christians—To Young Men—A Prayer.

But the days of our beloved disciple were numbered. Too soon for us—too soon for his poor countrymen—he was called away to a higher and a holier work, nearer to his redeeming God. The sun, which rose so clearly, and shone so brightly, was soon to set. It set without a cloud. But for our fond hopes that the Master of the vineyard would spare a laborer, who, in our estimation, was so important to the furtherance of the Gospel among the heathen, we should have indulged a presentiment that he was preparing for a speedy exit from a state of labor and suffering, to a state of rest and glory. During three or four months previous to his death, he had been more than usually zealous for the conversion of his people, more exclusively devoted to his labors, and more elevated and uniform in his religious affections. His views of Christianity seemed daily to become enlarged, and his benevolence more extensive. He now beautifully exemplified the *diffusive* character of our blessed religion. His love became more ardent, his faith drew nearer and nearer to reality, and his hope to fruition. During this period, he indulged the most sanguine hopes that the conversion of India was near.

But we must review this period more particularly. His labors with the people of the poor asylum were almost incessant. He read to them the Scriptures, explained them, repeated verse by verse to those who were blind, that they might treasure up in their hearts portions of the word of God; taught them from room to room, and prayed with them in private. His instructions became more and more impassioned and pointed; his private controversies with the people of his own caste, were more earnest and solemn; and in all things he labored like a man who had much to do in a short time. We had, at this period, several persons who had asked baptism, and were regarded by us as inquirers after the truth. Though a little too credulous in fair professions, he generally showed a discrimination and judgment in testing the character of such, and imparting suitable instructions, which would do honor to teachers of much more religious experience. On the occasion when these candidates were received into the church, Babajee seemed indeed to partake of the feeling of good old Simeon, when he said, "Mine eyes have seen thy salvation, Lord; now lettest thou thy servant depart in peace."

Although four of these were Mhars, (whose shadow, if it so much as pass over a Brahmun, pollutes him,) and two others were diseased with leprosy,* Babajee gave them the most cordial reception, and did not manifest the least scruple to the receiving of them to the full and immediate participation of the Lord's Supper. This involved a more complete renunciation of caste than he had previously been called on to make.

* The reader may not be aware that lepers, as soon as they appear to be past cure, become outcasts. They are disinherited and cast out by their relatives, and almost unavoidably become great sufferers for the want of the most common comforts of life, to say nothing of the bodily pains which they suffer on account of the disease. Nor are lepers the only persons who are cruelly treated on account of infirmity or disease. "The following persons are excluded from inheritance, unless the defect can be removed by medicaments or penance: Any one who is blind, deaf, dumb, unable to walk, leprous, impotent, insane, idiotic," &c.—*Steele's Law and Custom of Caste.*

On preaching tours, made in company with the writer, Babajee's labors were most zealous and indefatigable. His instructions were now more tender, and at the same time more pointed and searching; his prayers more fervent; his hopes more elevated and sanguine, but completely based on the Divine promises; and his anxieties more intense for the salvation of his countrymen. He always bore an important share of the labor of addressing the people in public; but I here speak more particularly of his more private labors, of his private conversations with little groups of natives, which he always managed to gather about him. He explained to them the nature of the Christian religion, removed their objections, and pointed out to them the absurdities and the errors of their own system. The whole lifetime of a foreigner would be insufficient to qualify him to perform this part of missionary labor, so ably as a pious, intelligent Brahmun can do; so well, I may say, as Babajee did. This does not merely suppose a competent acquaintance with their language, but it supposes a knowledge of every thing which makes a Hindoo differ in habits of thinking, in modes of reasoning, in prejudices, superstitions, maxims, or customs, from a foreigner. Foreigners, missionaries from Christian lands, we *must* have, in order to prepare the instruments who are to accomplish the great work which remains to be done in India; but the instruments themselves must be natives of the country.

The last occasion in which I was united with Babajee, for the furtherance of the Gospel, was the organization of our mission church. It was a solemn and interesting occasion. Babajee had been proposed, and unanimously chosen an elder of the church, and was this day ordained to the office. His whole deportment on this occasion appeared the index of a sincere heart, and bespoke a becoming sense of responsibility. His humility, his gentleness, his solemnity, and the tears of joy and penitence which rolled down his cheeks as he knelt before us, furnished the most pleasing evidence that Divine grace can humble the proud Brahmun, and warm his cold heart; that it can infuse sensibility into his unfeeling breast, and implant the matchless graces of love, friendship, and benevolence, in a soil where once flourished nothing but the rank weeds of avarice, hatred, selfishness, and pride.

From this time to his death, Babajee, with the assistance of Dajaba, carried on the operations of the mission, under the direction of Mr. Boggs, who had recently arrived in the country, and could not, of course, afford any direct assistance in the Mahratha services. He conducted our morning and evening service, superintended two schools, and was the overseer of the poor asylum. In addition to the increased labors and cares which my absence threw on him, he undertook to instruct Mr. B. in the Mahratha language. He was perfectly voluntary in these services. The labors of the mission would have been curtailed had he not desired that they should remain as they were. His zeal, no doubt, hurried him on beyond the limits of his strength; and it is not improbable that his increased labors predisposed him to an attack of the cholera. He was naturally of a feeble constitution, and had been but little accustomed to hard study and severe exertion.

His zeal remained unabated. The spirit was indeed willing; but, alas! how soon we were convinced, the flesh was weak. Never were our expectations more raised, never did *we* regard his labors so essential to the successful prosecution of our work. But the great Head of the church had otherwise determined. We were to be rebuked for fixing our hopes too much on *man* for success. Babajee was not necessary to the accomplishment of God's purposes in India, and he removed him to a higher and a happier sphere of action. While in the midst of his work, and when we regarded him as peculiarly qualified for increased usefulness, he was seized with the cholera. He survived the first attack, and attempted to return to his work; but the scourge reappeared after a few days, and executed its dread commission, and left our afflicted mission again to mourn.

His end, as far as we know, was peace. No member of the mission who could speak his language, or understand what he said, was with him during his illness, or at the time of his death. Some days before his death, he lost the use of his speech, and soon after was bereft of reason. It does not appear that any apprehensions were entertained, either by himself or others, that his end was so near, till he became unable to converse. His wife, and others who were with him, say, that up to the time of his delirium, he uniformly expressed an entire confidence in his Redeemer, and an unshaken hope of salvation by his blood. He died on the 17th April, 1833, aged forty-two; lamented by the mission, deeply lamented by his bereaved widow, lamented by the church, by the people of the poor-house, and respected, as far as a person in his circumstances could be, by all. He was highly esteemed by the lower orders of the people; and the Brahmuns, while they no doubt most cordially hated him for having abandoned the religion of his fathers, and not only become a proselyte to another religion, but a teacher of it, could not but respect him as a clever man, and an honest, upright, and sincere outcast. They had, no doubt, many a time predicted his death as a judgment which the angry gods would inflict on him for his impiety, in forsaking the religion of their ancient order; and they now, not unlikely, sought to turn the present occąsion to their own account, and to rivet the fetters on their willing slaves. The event had verified the prediction, and they could now challenge the confidence of the people, and at the same time hold out to all apostates from Brahmunism an example of terror. But why do the heathen rage, and the people imagine a vain thing? He that sitteth in the heavens shall laugh; the Lord shall have them in derision. He will speak to them in his wrath, and vex them in his sore displeasure; while the holy hill of Zion shall arise, and the glory of her King shall fill the whole earth. Come, Lord Jesus, come quickly! Dispel the dark clouds which now hover over the heathen nations, take thine "inheritance," and possess "the uttermost parts of the earth."

But stop, pious reader, and, as you drop a tear over the little spot of earth where repose the bones of Babajee, reflect for whom you mourn. You mourn not for a hero who defied the thunders of war — who was great only in the destruction of his species, and who shall live only in the history of battles and martial triumphs. You mourn not for a statesman, whose marbled monument tells you how great he was—how little he is. You mourn not for a poet, a sage, or an orator. You mourn for a Hindoo Brahmun—for a despised disciple of Jesus Christ, in a dark corner of the earth, whom the world knew not, and of whom the world was not worthy. You mourn for a hero who dared defy more than the warlike hosts of earth—who dared contend, at the sacrifice of every earthly tie, with a contemptuous priesthood and a superstitious people—who dared confront a sneering world. And why should you lament for him? He is one among the millions who have, within the brief period of your remembrance, gone from that benighted land into the world of spirits. He exchanged a state of persecution and of suffering, for a state of joy and everlasting blessedness. They have gone from a land of wretchedness and abominations, to meet the final doom of the idolater. We lament not his happy exchange. We mourn that he is *so soon* snatched away from the harvest which we had hoped he was to gather in. But we bow, for so, Father, it seemed good in thy sight.

But a voice comes from Babajee's grave, which we would do well to heed. I have alluded to the importance, to the seemingly indispensable necessity of native laborers, in order to carry on any extensive operations in India. I have dwelt sufficiently on the important services which Babajee rendered to the mission, during his short Christian career. But there is another aspect in which we ought here to view this subject. I mean the mysterious nature of the dispensation. Babajee was an extraordinary instance of piety and zeal. He was brought into the kingdom of his Redeemer at a late period of his life. His whole soul seemed intent on a single object—*professedly* the grand object of every disciple of Christ. Zeal for the house of God consumed him. He was a light to the Gentiles. He emerged from the dark abyss of idolatry. He shone brightly for a little space. Many saw the light, and a few were guided by its refulgence to the Sun of Righteousness. This light was extinguished. It sunk not again into the abyss, but ascended, burning brighter and brighter, till it was lost in the inextinguishable splendor of the "perfect day."

Eighteen short months measured his Christian existence. But why was his course so short? God so determined, and we respond, Father, thy will be done! But why, I ask with deference, why does God deal with us in this manner? Why did he single out Babajee from the myriads of that corrupt priesthood, and convert him, and fill his heart with benevolence, and zeal, and piety, and permit him to commence a useful career, and so highly raise our hopes; and then, almost at the outset, dash those hopes to the ground? Why does he open such an unbounded field for missionary operations in India, and permit his people to send laborers to that harvest, and then leave them to contend with such difficulties in reference to the heathen themselves, to struggle with so much ill-health, to be removed, and so often to sicken and die? Why does he give us so little *apparent* success, so few converts? why so much defection among these converts? Why does he seem to withhold from that field the *extensive* influences of his blessed Spirit? We may resolve all these questions in his sovereign will. We may say "it is to try the faith of his people," to test our fidelity and perseverance in his service. But there *may* be reasons with which we, as instruments, are more personally and more awfully concerned. God may be displeased. The cloud which hangs over that country may be the cloud of his indignation. The subject demands a most solemn investigation. There may be awful guilt somewhere.

To ascertain where this guilt lies, we must first ascertain where lies the responsibility. The command has gone out that *the work must be done.* Every disciple of Jesus Christ has recognized, in the general terms of his covenant vows, that this command is enjoined on him, and that he will bear the burden of the work to the extent of his ability. Here then is responsibility. It lies, as a whole, on the entire body of Christ's disciples. It lies, individually, on each, and on every member of Christ's church. If this responsibility be not sustained; if every professed follower of Jesus Christ do not put forth his efforts according to "that which he hath;" if he do not obey a most unequivocal command, and do not fulfill the vow which he knowingly and voluntarily made, what reason has he to expect that God will smile on his enterprise? While God works, as he has said he will work, by human instrumentality, how can he expect that missions will prosper, that missionaries will be preserved, and that God will extensively pour out his Spirit, and remove all those mountain-like obstacles which the perversity of the heathen's heart has set up against the conversion of that quarter of the globe?

My Christian friends! you must measure your expectations of the success of missions among the heathen by your own zeal and devotedness to the cause. Your own heart is the index. The amount of piety there, the amount of genuine love to God in your church, of devotedness to Christ throughout the churches of the land, of self-devotion in her ministers, of interest in the monthly prayer-meeting for the general diffusion of the Holy Spirit, will tell you how much reason *you* have to hope that the Hindoos, or any large portions of the heathen world, will soon be converted. Weigh yourselves in this balance, and if you be found wanting, cease to murmur, cease to reproach the almoners of your bounty to the heathen, humble yourselves in the dust, quicken your diligence, cry for help, and begin anew.

But I do not mean to exonerate your missionaries. They bear with you an individual responsibility. They are your covenanted servants; and bound by this compact to be faithful to the confidence which you have reposed in them. They may not have sustained their responsibility; and they may not have acquitted themselves well as your representatives. They may be chargeable with a share of the guilt. They are but men. Charge them with a want of fidelity in the dispensing of the precious treasure which you have committed to them, if they deserve it. Send out better men if you can; but know that *you* cannot throw off the responsibility of this great work.

But comes there no voice from that consecrated spot to the "schools of the prophets?" Yes; I hear it. I have already told you that an increased burden of labor devolved on Babajee a few weeks before his death. The only efficient missionary had been compelled to leave the station on account of ill health; and the only remaining one was at that time unable to labor among a people of a strange tongue. Why did your predecessors suffer our number to become so reduced, that the temporary absence or failure of a single man must suspend our labors, or throw an insupportable burden on a poor native convert? They knew our wants. Appeals for more laborers at that station had been made but a few months previous to this very juncture. And these appeals are now lying in your archives, then little heeded, now forgotten. They sent us but a single man. He arrived, but late. He came to a people of a hard speech, and could then only look on, lament, in vain desire to labor, and return to his books. Some of these very men, who then heard the cry for help, and who ought to have gone to India, may still be seeking some goodly place in America. They *may* not be chargeable with the calamity which befell us in consequence of their neglect; but they may, perhaps, be chargeable with a dereliction in duty.

Do *you* reply, that if you had been candidates for the sacred office at that time, you would have helped us? The case is not altered. Similar difficulties are encountered, similar losses are sustained at the present day, and the same reasons exist why *you* should go to the help of your brethren in India. You have now before you at least *one* disastrous result of that tardy, hesitating spirit, which has so long spell-bound the young men of our theological seminaries, when they have been called on to make a *decision* as to their *personal* duty of engaging in the work of foreign missions. The above is probably not a solitary instance of a disastrous result from the same cause. Pity, then, to your brethren, who are laboring, fainting, struggling, falling, without comrades enough to carry them to their untimely graves, pleads with you to come and help them. Humanity pleads. The perishing condition of the heathen pleads. Obligation to your Savior pleads. *God commands.*

But we will linger no longer about the tomb of our departed

brother. Dust has returned to dust—ashes to ashes. His spirit has returned to God who gave it. His labors on earth are done; his account is closed; he is singing the song of Moses and of the Lamb. His body reposes under the wide-spreading branches of a tamarind tree. May the good seed which he has sown be watered by the dews of Divine grace, and vegetate, and spring up, and become a great tree; and, like the beautiful and ever-green tamarind, may it take deep root, extend its branches, blossom, and bear much fruit. May its leaves be for the healing of that nation, its fruit delight the souls of many, and under its shadow may the weary pilgrims rest!

PRAYER BY BABAJEE.*

"O thou self-existent God! who art worthy to be adored by the whole universe! I am a great sinner. I was born in sin. My heart is naturally full of lust, envy, pride, avarice, hypocrisy, and deceit. My youth was spent in vanity, and my riper years in dissipation and lewdness. Old age approaches; death is in his train. Without thy mercy, O God! I must suffer everlasting punishment in hell.

"O thou Purifier and Restorer of the fallen! I am fallen. I am deserving of the eternal torments of hell. I am like a broken vessel, only fit to be cast out as useless. I ask, merciful God! the pardon of my sins. I do not ask this on account of any good works which I have done; nor on account of any righteousness of my own. I am fallen: thou art the Restorer. For to restore such as I am, thou didst assume a human body. In the person of the Son, thou didst become incarnate, and didst yield up thy life on the cross, to atone for sin. By his perfect obedience to the law, in our stead, he did work out, for us, an everlasting righteousness. I come to thee in the name of Jesus Christ, my Savior, and implore of thee the pardon of all

* This prayer was written out, by Babajee, a few weeks before his death, and will here very appropriately close his memoir. It may be taken as a fair specimen of his confessions and supplications at a Throne of Grace, as far as related to his own spiritual wants. His supplications for others, and for the cause of Christ in general, are equally ardent and simple.

my sins. Have mercy on me. Infuse into my heart thy Holy Spirit, and cleanse me from sin. Eradicate every sinful propensity, and ingraft in my heart the lovely graces of humility, gentleness, compassion, joy, peace, heavenly wisdom, and a holy disposition. Deliver me from sinful thoughts and imaginations; from anger, hypocrisy, pride, covetousness, and worldly infatuation; and enable me to keep thy commandments, and to worship thee in sincerity. Lead me in the right way; teach me thy word; and enable me to preach the Gospel of thy Son with boldness. I can do nothing without thy assistance. I can neither worship thee, nor pray to thee, nor praise, thank, nor glorify thee aright. Therefore, O thou Father of the fatherless, help me, save me — cast me not off, for to whom else shall I go?

"Adorable God! may this body of sin be crucified with the body of Christ. May he dwell in me, and I in him. Soon my soul must leave this earthly tabernacle. May it then, through Jesus Christ, go to thee, there to worship thee forever. In thy service will be all my joy and happiness. All this I ask in the name of Jesus Christ. May I praise and glorify thee for ever and ever. Amen!"

CHAPTER XIV.

Mission at Ahmednuggur — Its Origin and Early History — Lights and Shades — Itineracies — Schools — Female Education — The English Language.

The American mission in Ahmednuggur was commenced in December, 1831. In a tour made chiefly for the purpose of selecting a location for a mission in the Deckan, we found Ahmednuggur a large and increasing town — once the capital of a large Mohammedan kingdom, and but a year or two previous had been selected as a principal civil and military station in the Deckan, second only to Poona. Ahmednuggur possessed the advantages of a good climate, of British protection, and medical aid. It is a central position, situated in the midst of a great number of towns and villages, some of which are of considerable importance. And there were at that time several pious gentlemen at Ahmednuggur, who ardently desired the establishment of a mission there. They afforded us all the encouragement in their power; and it is due to Mr. R——, the collector, to acknowledge — and I feel a pleasure in the acknowledgement — that he most cheerfully consented to the proposed mission. He is the same gentleman who has been already mentioned as the collector at Poona, when the first attempts were made to distribute books in that city, where he adopted a very different policy in reference to missionary operations. His views had changed. He not only consented to our settlement in Ahmednuggur, but he afterwards showed us many kind attentions.

The mission having determined on Ahmednuggur as the location for a new station, Messrs. Graves, Hervey, Babajee, and myself immediately repaired thither. The mission commenced under very favorable auspices. The European residents received us kindly; and the natives were too little acquainted with the nature of missionary operations to receive us otherwise. During the first three or four months, we could preach to large assemblies of natives wherever we chose, either at our own houses or in any part of the town. They were always orderly, and generally attentive. But the novelty soon wore away, our object became known, the *spirituality* of the Gospel was discovered, and, what no doubt was the greatest offense in the eyes of the Brahmuns, it was also discovered that Christianity and Hindooism could have no communion. The uncompromising nature of Christianity is, every where, in the opinion of the heathen, its most forbidding feature.

The Brahmuns began first to treat our instructions with indifference, and then with contempt. On several occasions, they abused us in the streets, and made our labors by the wayside, and in the chief places of concourse, uncomfortable, and oftentimes very trying. They instigated the boys to hoot at us, and pelt us with dirt and stones. Babajee was, at this time, indefatigable and persevering. His labors were indeed "labors of love" for his poor countrymen, and labors, too, of patience and affliction. These indignities, though aimed more particularly at him, did not seem to dishearten him. No part of his character exhibits him in a more pleasing light than his conduct towards the persecuting Brahmuns. When they mocked and reviled, he ceased not to reason with them, to warn them, and to pray for them. He always reasoned with mildness and love, but oftentimes with an earnestness and pungency which greatly annoyed them. Still, they could not but entertain for him a sort of respect, on account of his stern integrity, and for the unabated interest which he manifested in them in spite of all their abuse towards him. They were convinced, I believe, that he was a sincere worshiper of the eternal and invisible God.

Our usefulness was greatly increased by our connection with Babajee; and his, by our countenance and support. We suggested, and he preached; we led the way, and he faithfully followed. In his public labors he could do nothing alone. The people would not for a moment tolerate him, if he attempted to instruct them in public, unaccompanied by a white man. In a more private capacity, and in his own house, he did not suffer the same inconvenience. But for his greater influence here, he was indebted to his connection with the mission. In the present state of Christianity in this part of India, no Hindoo convert, who shall honor his profession, and manifest a becoming zeal for the conversion of his countrymen, would long be allowed to exercise the functions of a missionary, unless he be under the immediate care of foreign missionaries. The supposed connection between missionaries and the English government affords native converts the protection which they require.

The daily preaching of the Gospel in the town and at our own houses, our regular studies, the superintendence of a few schools, and a tour to sixteen villages in the vicinity, filled up the first five months of our residence at Ahmednuggur. Mr. Graves was principally engaged in translating the Scriptures, and

Mr. Hervey and myself in the acquisition of the Mahratha language.

We had thus far gone on prosperously; beginning to indulge the pleasing hope that the long night of spiritual death and of the Divine displeasure was far spent, and that the "day-spring from on high" was about to arise on benighted India. But alas! how short-sighted is man! He knows not what a day may bring forth. In an hour when we thought not of it, almost in the suddenness of a moment, our dear brother Hervey was transferred to a wider field of usefulness — to an unfading state of glory and beatitude in the heavens! Too soon — not for himself, not for the cause of his Redeemer, in general, but too soon for us who mourn — was he released from the toils and trials of a missionary life. Too soon did he quit the scenes which had been imbittered but a year before by the death of his beloved wife. Too soon did he cease to care for his orphan child. His sorrow was turned into joy; and he mingles with angels in their song of praise to God, and to the Lamb, for ever.

On the evening of the 12th of May, the scourge of Asia — the scourge, shall I say, which has since left its native soil, traversed every nation in Europe, and crossed the broad Atlantic, to take vengeance on America, because she has not discharged her debt to the debased nations of the East — laid her cold hand on our beloved fellow-laborer, and marked him for its own. He dined with us at two; called again at half-past five; changed his apparel at six; the cold sweat, the sunken eye, and the ghastly countenance intimated, at seven in the evening, that he was the sure victim of spasmodic cholera. At nine, he was nearly speechless. Having taken leave of the friends about him, and endeavored, in vain, to kiss his little boy, who now started back with horror when brought to his dying father, he survived till four o'clock in the morning, distorted by spasms, and suffering agonies indescribable. Death, on his first approach, surprised him; but having recovered from the first awful shock, his soul became quiet, and he apparently quit the tabernacle of clay, and entered the eternal world with a hope full of glory. This afflictive providence still lies veiled in the mysteries of eternity. We only know that it was right, that it was merciful and kind in our Heavenly Parent, and productive of his glory. We are able to trace, in one instance at least, that mercy was here mingled with judgment. The wife of Babajee had hitherto been a thorn and a vexation to her husband. She had withstood him in his profession and practice of Christianity, and often grieved his soul on account of her blindness of mind and hardness of heart. Not till she saw a *Christian die*, was she impressed with a sense of her danger and of eternal realities. In a few months she was brought to renounce the delusive system of her fathers, and to embrace the religion of a crucified Redeemer. She was baptized, and received into the Mission Church, on the 17th of July, 1832.

By the death of Mr. Hervey, and the removal of Mr. Graves, the labors of this new mission now devolved on Babajee and myself. When we were weak, then were we strong. We were not left without a visible testimony that God is faithful to fulfill his promises. The asylum for the poor, the aged and infirm, which had been established and was supported by voluntary subscriptions among the English residents, had, from the commencement of the mission, been put under our superintendence. This afforded a daily opportunity of administering to the souls of the inmates the bread of life, as well as the meat that perishes. In the months of September and October, several of the poor people became unusually attentive, and gave pleasing evidence that they began to care for the things which pertain to eternal life. As I was one evening, about the middle of October, returning from our five o'clock service, poor lame Kondooba followed me unobserved. The audience, in general, had that evening appeared unusually inattentive, and some of the bystanders had treated us with open contempt. I had but just sat down on the veranda of the house, half in despair, and began to relate to the only earthly object about me who would listen to and appreciate the tale of my trials, the circumstances which had just occurred, and the abuse which I had received from this ungrateful people, when Babajee came up and said, "Sahib, here is a man who wishes to speak with you." To my inquiry, what he desired, he said, "I wish to be baptized." I asked him why he made such a request. He replied, "I am a great sinner; my mind is very dark, and I wish to be saved through Jesus Christ." I asked him if there were no other Savior to whom he could go; reminding him of the Brahminical expedients in such a case. He said, "Jesus Christ is the only Savior — the Savior of the world." "And why are you *now* troubled about sin? what evil do you see in it?" He said, "I am greatly pained on account of sin; I deserve everlasting punishment." "Do you pray?" "I pray for light; my mind is very dark." I cautioned him against regarding baptism as a rite which, in itself, could save him from sin; instructed him more clearly in the rudiments of the Gospel, and exhorted him to pray much, to hear the word of God attentively, and to repent and believe on the Lord Jesus Christ without delay; assuring him, at the same time, that I should be most happy to baptize him, if it should appear that a work of grace was wrought in his soul. As he told me this short and simple tale of his heart, my soul blessed and magnified the Lord, and took fresh courage.

This man was of very low caste, and had been in the poorhouse about four months, during which time he had almost daily heard the word of God; but we knew not that any favorable impression had been made on his mind. His case, coming to notice as it did at that particular time, I cannot but regard as a kind providence, to cheer a lonely missionary in the hour of despondency, and to show him that he is to look *only* to God for success in his labors.

I have been thus particular in speaking of the case of this poor man, because he was the first fruits of my labors in India. The kind reader will excuse the partiality; and when he surveys the nakedness of the land, he will cease to wonder that the missionary in Western India should, after a residence of nearly two years, feel peculiar emotion of joy and gratitude, that *one*, and one, too, so obscure and despicable in the eyes of men, should be brought to listen to his instructions, and to inquire after the way of salvation. I am happy to add, that this poor man, from the period of his first inquiries to the day of his death, nearly three years, did not disappoint the expectations which were first raised concerning him.

On the 18th of November, Kondooba, and two others of the same caste, were baptized, and admitted to the church; all inmates of the poor-house. The occasion was one of deep interest. Babajee wept for joy. He saw the travail of his soul, and seemed for the time to say, "It is enough." We sat down to commemorate the sufferings and death of our risen and ascended Lord. One such occasion repays the missionary for all the sacrifices which he has made. We were joined in this interesting scene by Captain Sandwith, to whose kindness and Christian attention we have often been indebted, and by two other officers of the eighth regiment. There were also present, as spectators, about a hundred natives. Some looked on with apparent interest; others gazed as at some unmeaning ceremony. Among the former were three or four who requested baptism, and were regarded by us as inquirers after the truth. By them the scene was regarded with deep interest, and, I trust, resulted in their good.

From this time most of the inmates of the asylum, with two or three others, became almost constant attendants at our family worship of a morning. A greater degree of inquiry was excited among them during the month of December. We had, for the three preceding months, observed the monthly prayer-meeting, on the evening of the first Monday, in our native congregation. Its object had been explained; and, at our meeting in November, an account had been given of the recent success which has attended missionary labors in different parts of the heathen world, and especially at Ceylon and the Sandwich Islands. I assured them that it is the practice of all, in every country, who love and revere the name of Jesus Christ, to meet on the evening of that day, and to offer up to God their united prayers and supplications for the outpouring of his Spirit, for the whole world, and, especially, for the conversion of the heathen.* And to confirm this, I told them that they would, in an hour or two, see our pious English friends come to our house for that purpose. There seemed something in the idea of this *prager-meeting* which not a little excited their curiosity. And the next morning I was told that those who had been baptized, and one or two others, came to Babajee in the evening, and, referring to what I had said, told him that several persons had met at our house, for the purpose of praying for the heathen, and asked him if they ought not to pray for themselves. Babajee readily assented, and they all joined in supplications for the same glorious object.

The first Monday in January, 1833, I shall always remember with the liveliest feelings of gratitude. On that day God vouchsafed to visit us from on high with a token of his faithfulness to the promise, "Lo! I am with you." The day had been set apart, though unknown to us at the time, by the Presbyterian Church of the United States, and by other bodies of Christians, as a day of fasting and prayer for the heathen world. I find in my journal the following notice of that day: "This has been the most solemn and interesting day I have witnessed in India. At our morning prayers in the native language, three strangers were present, who said they had come to inquire about the 'new way.' I found, on inquiry, that two of these were the parents of a blind man in the asylum, who had requested to be baptized. Our son, said they, has been blind from his birth, but now *he* says that 'he can see.' At ten o'clock, Babajee returned from his morning visit to the poor-house, in an ecstasy of joy, saying, 'The poor people all come about me, inquiring, *what shall we do?* They are all risen up,' continued he, 'and have their loins girt, and are ready.' I appointed a meeting for inquiry at three o'clock to-day, and, to my joy and surprise, there were sixteen present. A heavenly influence, I am persuaded, was with us. Our Christian friends in America must be praying for us."

* I was not then aware how *partially* this meeting is attended in the American churches in general. I had just heard of the very extensive revivals of religion throughout the United States, and believed there *must* be a corresponding missionary spirit. Does the present appearance of our monthly concerts for prayer manifest such a spirit?

These meetings for inquiry, conversation and prayer were continued weekly. Among the inquirers was the aged mother of Dajaba, who, with her son, had come to Ahmednuggur, that he might enjoy the friendship and support of Babajee, in the trials to which he, as a convert to Christianity, was exposed. In Bombay, he had recently suffered much persecution and abuse, and had once been beaten. We also wished him to enjoy the instructions of his younger brother in the faith, and hoped he would catch the fire of his zeal, and be made partaker of the rich spiritual gifts which seemed to be imparted to Babajee. While Babajee lived, our hopes were, in a good degree, realized. His aged mother had been a stubborn idolater, had cruelly persecuted him on his profession of Chistianity, and openly declared that she would live and die in the religion of her fathers. She had some time previously given up her idols; and now she renounced caste, lost her hatred to Christianity, and became, as we hoped, a sincere and humble inquirer after the way of salvation by Jesus Christ.

During this month, one of the most promising of our inquirers died. He was old and decrepit, had a presentiment that he should soon die, and eagerly sought to be baptized. Late one evening I heard that he was more ill, and he begged to be baptized before he died. I assented to the request, and appointed the next morning for the administering of the ordinance, if he should not be better. But he saw not the light of the morning. At the dawn, he was found dead in his room. No one was with him, but he was heard in the adjoining room to cry out for Babajee, and to ask some of his neighbors to go and call him. But no one would take the trouble to go fifty yards to call Babajee, or to inform me! He was heard to call on the name of Jesus, and to speak of baptism. We trust he had obtained mercy through the blood of our Redeemer. We gave his body a Christian burial by the side of the child of another of our inquirers who died three weeks before. The child was buried in the Christian way, at the request of the mother.

On the 10th February, we baptized four more Hindoos, one of

whom was the aged mother of Dajaba. The native congregation was addressed on the subject of our creed; each article explained, and compared with the Hindoos' creed. An unusual attention was given during the discourse and the administration of the ordinance. As the little church sat around the table of the Lord, it afforded a spectacle which angels must contemplate with delight. Here was a beautiful illustration of the power of the Gospel to unite in *one*, persons of all ranks, complexions, and castes. In this little company of ten Hindoos, there were persons of four different castes; two Brahmuns, two Purbhoos, two Mahrathas, and four Mhars. Our hearts rejoiced in the wisdom, the power, and the goodness of God, that he had suffered our eyes to see and our ears to hear what we this day witnessed. Ride forth, glorious Conqueror! till thou shalt gather in *one*, all things in Christ; and make all men see *what is the fellowship of the mystery*, which, from the beginning of the world, hath been hid in God, who created all things by and for Jesus Christ.

Success in his labors can never fail to give the missionary among the heathen the highest degree of satisfaction which he can experience. Yet it should never be forgotten, that, with this success, come some of his most anxious cares, and his severest trials. This will appear evident to every one, the moment he contemplates the material from which a mission church is taken. The convert to Christianity is expected to sustain a character diametrically opposite to the customs and the prejudices, the practice and the education, the views and the feelings, which he imbibed in his earliest infancy. Suppose a work of grace actually began in the heart of a Hindoo, he may fall into sins for which he would, in a Christian land, forfeit his Christian character, and still he may deserve our kind indulgence. Such are the sins of lying and deception, not to mention licentiousness and many others. Children are taught to lie by their own parents, and of course they feel none of those compunctious visitings of conscience, which persons who have been nurtured under the restraints of Christian morality experience when they utter a falsehood. A native of India is so accustomed to use truth and falsehood indiscriminately, as best suits his convenience or his fancy, that he seems almost incapacitated to adhere rigorously to the truth. I would not palliate the crime, but would pardon the missionary for treating the unfortunate creature with indulgence. Even at this early period, we were obliged to discipline one of our members for lying. Being detected, he confessed his fault, asked forgiveness, and received admonition.

The 4th of March also forms an era in the Ahmednuggur mission. We met on that day, according to previous appointment, to organize ourselves into a church, and at the same time to form a society for the promotion of Christian morals. We had heretofore existed as a branch of the Mission Church at Bombay. After mature deliberation, we fixed on the Presbyterian form of government, as best suited to the circumstances of a church among the heathen. A brief confession of faith had been prepared for the occasion. Babajee had been proposed for an elder and Dajaba as a deacon. Having explained the nature of a community called a church, and the duty and privilege of uniting in this capacity, we proceeded to adopt the articles of faith, and to unite ourselves in solemn covenant before God, to aid, comfort, and edify one another. Babajee and Dajaba were then ordained to their respective offices, by prayer and the imposition of hands; and the services closed with thanksgiving to Almighty God, and supplications to the great Shepherd and Bishop of souls, that he would keep this little flock in the midst of this dark, howling wilderness, and make them to lie down in green pastures, and lead them by the side of still waters. The whole services were intensely solemn, and full of interest to all who desire and labor for the salvation of the heathen. The teachers of our schools, the inmates of the asylum, and several from the town, were present. Such occasions, which, to the missionary in India, are "few and far between," are, no doubt, designed, by a good Providence, as a kind of compensation for the trials and discouragements of a missionary life. Faithless mortals we are, that we tire and faint, if God do not almost continually give us some *visible* token that our labors are not in vain. We are not willing to wait, even when we have his word for it, that the faithful ministration of his truth shall *never* be in vain.

These were the brightest days of this infant mission. A cloud hung over us. One of our number had but recently arrived in the country, and the other was obliged to leave on account of ill health. Nor was this so severe a calamity, while Babajee, under the guidance of Mr. B., was prosecuting the ordinary labors of the mission. But, alas! his work was almost done. He fell a victim to the cholera. His death produced a sensation among the members of the church and the inmates of the asylum, which, for a time, we feared would be followed by disastrous consequences. They thought all was lost, and were thrown into despair. They supposed the church must be disbanded, and the mission broken up. This is all perfectly characteristic of the people, and bears some resemblance to the conduct of Christian converts in another part of Asia many centuries ago. When their head was seized and taken away from them, "they all forsook Him and fled." They gave up all for lost.

The operations of the mission went on with much less change than our native friends had thought possible. The poignancy of their grief was soon abated, and their hopes revived. The consequences of Babajee's death, though less disastrous than they had supposed, were still of a serious nature. Our converts were not yet well grounded in the faith. In every thing they were but children, and needed to be led by the hand. The intimate communication between them and us was now, in a great degree, broken off. Babajee had watched over them as a father, and had that near access to their hearts which it is impossible that a foreigner should have. His wife, in particular, had been borne on in her Christian course very much by him. She now oftentimes became restless and dissatisfied, and in several instances gave us occasion to reprove her for unbecoming conduct. She was sometimes seen in the streets adorned with a profusion of jewels, and her face and forehead disfigured with heathenish marks. She generally received our admonitions with kindness, and reformed of the specified fault.

Ill health in the mission families, and other disasters, continued to impede the progress of our work. During our absence to the Hills, our "hired house" was burnt, and we were on this account obliged to live at an undue distance from our labors, and consequently were separated so far from our converts that we could not exercise over them the necessary vigilance. No house could be obtained at that time nearer than three miles from the town.

Of the different means which have been employed at this station, *the direct preaching of the Gospel* has been regarded as by far the most important. It is through *this* that we must look for the salvation of the Hindoos. And, surrounded as we are there by a numerous population in the vicinity, who have never before heard of the Gospel of Jesus Christ, we have regarded *itineracies* as a very prominent department of our labors. During the first three years of the mission, sixteen preaching towns were made, 2,200 miles traveled over, 230 towns and villages visited, most of which had never heard the voice of a missionary before.

I do not mean that preaching at one's own station may ever be regarded as a matter of indifference, or of little importance. It should always be vigorously sustained—and constantly, if the number of the missionaries and assistants be sufficient to sustain it in the absence of those who are able to travel. There is only about one-third part of the year when a missionary can, without great hazard of health and life, be engaged in itineracies. During this period, every missionary ought, in my opinion, to itinerate, whether the regular duties of his station be continued or suspended. He only leaves, for three or four months, a town where his efforts have been expended for eight or nine months, in order to preach in a hundred other towns or villages, where he will be able to present the Gospel to a hundred-fold more heathen, and, oftentimes, under greater advantages than he could in the place of his residence.

The manner of preaching at Ahmednuggur, as to time and place, has been different at different times. For several months after our first arrival, we went daily into the streets, and into places of concourse, such as temples, markets, and travelers' stopping places. We here collected large assemblies, and generally found them orderly and attentive. But when the novelty of the thing had passed off, and, more especially, when the Brahmuns, and the influential part of the community, discovered the object of our labors, they made this mode of preaching so uncomfortable to us, and apparently so useless, that we gradually relinquished it. To suffer ourselves to be treated with indignity, in situations where we could expect no redress, when we had other means of accomplishing our purposes, seemed inconsistent with the dignity of the Gospel, or of its ministers. Had we complained to the proper authorities, the natives might affirm that our collecting public assemblies at their temples, or in the streets, or near their shops or houses, was a nuisance. We therefore procured ground in eligible places, and erected sheds, where we appointed religious services on specified evenings of the week, and on the Sabbath. We went to these places about an hour before sunset, and addressed all who came. Here, being on our own ground, we could adopt and support our own rules; and we generally found it sufficient to say, occasionally, to a company of reckless Brahmuns, who would, not unfrequently, come to cavil or wrangle, that they must remain quiet till the conclusion of the service, when they should have an opportunity to propose questions, and to enter into a dispassionate discussion if they pleased. Sometimes they would remain, but more frequently retire, defeated in the object for which they came.

It only remains to speak of schools. We employed schools in the furtherance of the objects of the mission, as far as we thought it could be done to advantage. We never have entered extensively into this mode of spreading the Gospel. The reason of this will appear in what follows. A school taught by a *heathen teacher*, in order to justify its being supported from missionary funds, should have a most vigilant superintendence. It should be visited by the missionary daily. It is needless to say that a heathen teacher will teach Christianity no farther than he is obliged, in order to retain his place. The regulations of the school system require that the children be taught the catechism, the commandments, prayers, and hymns. These he will of course teach them. But this is a heartless business. A single word from the teacher is enough to do away any impression which might have been made. It should always be a maxim in our efforts to do good, that if we cannot do what we wish, we must do what we can. Acting, or rather overacting, on this maxim, missionaries in this part of India have formerly fallen into an error, in establishing too many schools. The consequence was, that such schools were left very much under the control of their heathen teachers. Some were visited by a missionary once a week, others once a month, and others, which were at a distance, but once or twice a year. Whereas the true policy of such a maxim, undoubtedly, is to have no more schools than can enjoy a constant and vigorous superintendence by the missionary. And he should ever bear it in mind, that the direct preaching of the Gospel is to be his most prominent duty as a Gospel minister.

Female education is in many respects a matter more to be desired by a mission, than the education of boys. Besides the mental improvement in either case, the education of the female sex strikes at an inveterate prejudice, and opens an almost unheard of field of enterprise to the long neglected mind of the Hindoo woman. On this account, we were particularly desirous to establish and support female schools. Were such schools merely of a literary character, an important object is gained in sustaining them. There are, however, the same drawbacks in the prosecution of this part of our system of schools, as have been mentioned in reference to boys' schools; together with an additional one, of still greater difficulty: I mean the want of any desire, on the part of parents, to have their girls educated. They fear it as a calamity; but submit to it on account of the pecuniary benefits which will accrue by way of presents, and otherwise. Where female schools have become common, as is the case in Bombay, the children, doubtless, feel a degree of attachment to their schools; and some of them attend and learn, not by restraint, but with pleasure; and their fathers, not unlikely, feel gratified with their attainments, and wish them to continue in school till claimed by their husbands, at the age of about twelve years. Yet, if additional pay were not given to the teacher of a female school, and presents to the girls in general were not held out as inducements to regular and prompt attendance, there would not, probably, be a female school, after three months, in this part of India. In accordance with this plan, which was probably the only feasible one, we sustained a few female schools in Ahmednuggur. These were supported by the contributions of the English ladies at the station.

The natives of India are very desirous to learn the English language, and fathers wish to have their sons educated in it. Their object, in general, is neither literature, science, a love of study, nor religion—but money. If they have a knowledge of the English language, they may obtain some lucrative situation in the service of government. Such a school will serve to show the people that we are their friends, and are willing to aid them, whenever we can, in their temporal as well as in their spiritual concerns; and it affords, to say the least, as good an opportunity as a Mahratha school for the communication of religious instruction.

The following anecdote will show how exceedingly sensitive the people at Ahmednuggur were, at that time, on the subject of Christianity. The school contained about thirty scholars; but in a day or two it was reduced to fifteen. The cause of the sudden decrease was this: The boys had been supplied, at a very low price, with the American Sunday School spelling-books. Spelling-books, on account of their scarcity, and the demand created by the great desire to learn English, are much sought after; and, consequently, the boys were much pleased when they obtained them. After a few days, they discovered that these books were of a religious character; and the Hindoo boys forthwith left the schools, without assigning any reason. A few days after, some of these boys called on a member of the mission, who inquired why they had left the school. They replied that the new spelling-books contained something about Jesus Christ; and, on that account, they said they could not use them. They were asked to point out any thing in the books which they thought objectionable; and they happened to open at a place where it was written: "Jesus said to them, Come unto me all ye that labor and are heavy laden, and I will give you rest."

The strong-hold of caste must first be loosened, or the people must see themselves compelled to such a course by poverty, or they must feel the influences of Christianity on their hearts, before they will yield to better influences. How soon the latter motive will influence them, is known only to God; but if an angel of deliverance do not spring up from some quarter, frightful poverty will soon drive the people of India to desperation. Should He who directs the hearts and governs the actions of all men, bring them, in their extremity, to those who, in his providence, are sent thither to succor the distressed, then hundreds and thousands may flock to the missionaries, give up their children to be supported and educated, and give up themselves to serve the Father of all their mercies.

Sometimes I seem to see this happy day arrived. But again, fearing that devoted India has not yet drunken her full cup of Divine wrath, I see the work of oppression still going on, till the high and the low, the weak and the strong, in their desperate struggle—some for pride, and more for the bare necessities of life—devour and be devoured. The numerous bands of marauders which still infest every part of the country, afford the desperate every facility for such an awful enterprise. A change must, ere long, take place. While the Divine mercy is withheld, or the Divine indignation is suspended, while the cloud which hangs over India does not burst, we will hope it is a cloud of mercy. It looks black; it is streaked with vivid lightnings; a threatening voice is heard; yet these may be but the awful manifestations of Omnipotence, coming in mercy, but displaying the fierceness of his countenance to a people who have so long abused his mercy, and trampled his honor in the dust. While we *hope* that the change which is working in India will, in the providence of

God, be overruled for her spiritual deliverance, we ought to labor and pray, relying on the sure promises of God that the fervent prayers and the faithful labors of his servants shall never be in vain. We ground our hope on the broad foundation of the Divine promises. Their fulfillment may be deferred, but they cannot fail. The kingdom, and the dominion, and the greatness of the kingdom under the whole heavens, shall be given to the people of the saints of the Most High, whose kingdom shall be an everlasting kingdom, and all dominions shall serve and obey him.

It will suffice to add, that the past success and the present prosperous condition of the Ahmednuggur mission has delightfully realized the hopes of its auspicious beginning.

Already has the Ahmednuggur mission expanded into three separate missions, viz: Ahmednuggur, Seroor, and Kolapoor. While the latter two has each its missionaries, its assistants, its church, schools and teachers, the original mission has its four stations, eleven out-stations, five missionaries, six female assistants, two native pastors, and twenty-nine helpers. And the little church organized in Ahmednuggur in 1833, with about a dozen members, has expanded into the first and second church of Ahmednuggur, and five other churches at out-stations, numbering in all 194 members. The mother church alone numbers eighty-four; and the whole number that have been admitted from the beginning is 215.

A great work has been done in that extreme diocese by verbal preaching. For nearly 100 miles, in every direction, the laborers in that field have faithfully and indefatigably traveled and preached in a thousand towns and villages, and have not failed to reap a rich harvest. Yet I am not sure but they have done as great, and a more permanent work still, through the printed page. They have prepared and diffused a Christian literature through the vernacular languages, which has laid a deep and broad foundation for all time to come. A great preparatory work has been done, and we confidently look for a corresponding glorious result. The missionaries speak of finding everywhere "a growing desire for knowledge throughout their vast field; and of a marked change in the accessibility of the higher castes to the various labors of the missionary."

There are connected with the central mission, primary schools, a high school, and an efficient corps of laborers, who are bringing to bear on a wide field the munitions of the spiritual warfare; and from this favored centre has radiated the light of truth, till the whole region around about is in the way of a successful evangelization. Churches have their native pastors, and are, in their turn, raising up and sending forth teachers and preachers to the regions beyond.

May God bless those indefatigable men and women; and should they, in the fearful commotions which may there betide, before the great Moloch of the land shall yield his possessions of forty centuries, be called, as other of their co-laborers have been, to seal their testimony with a martyr's blood, may they be found armed with a martyr's faith. They know who has said: "Be faithful unto death, and I will give you a crown of life."

CHAPTER XV.

Duplicity of the Hindoos — Danger of misrepresentation in reports concerning them — Two ways of relating facts — A little Note sometimes needed.

In the preparation of this article my object is two-fold: first, to illustrate the character of the natives of India; and, second, to do it in such a manner that the reader may see how easy it is for him to misapprehend their real character, even with the best written documents before him. Bearing in mind these two objects, I shall relate several facts, the most of which fell under my own observation, and the others are well attested by persons of long experience in the country. I shall first mention the facts as they *might* be recorded with a species of truth, (that is, half the truth, or truth as far as it goes,) and as they often are recorded by the partial observer, who either does not learn the end of his tale, or, if he does, neglects to record it; and then I shall *note* other important circumstances of the different cases, which will give the whole a totally different aspect. I adopt this method, not to censure the credulity of a liberal public, who are, perhaps, too ready to believe what they most devoutly *wish* to be true; nor to censure the too charitable views which the missionary, in the midst of a perverse and gainsaying people, takes of the case of an inquirer, or of a convert; but I wish to caution the Christian public against receiving intelligence from a foreign land without the same limitations with which they would receive intelligence from a distant section of their own country under similar circumstances.

Human nature is radically the same everywhere. The Bible, however, has made an essential difference among men. A person tolerably acquainted with human depravity in a Christian land may, by deducting what has been derived there from the Bible, approximate, in some good degree, to human depravity in a heathen land. It would seem that a person might, by keeping in view a few well known and acknowledged principles in human character, judge pretty correctly what limitations he ought to make when reading accounts of the labors and successes of missions in India. He has been repeatedly advertised that the Hindoos are deceitful, false, selfish, and devoted to the most debasing system of idolatry; yea, he has been assured that the Hindoos are guilty of every sin enumerated by St. Paul in the first chapter of his epistle to the Romans. He reads in the letters and journals of missionaries, that so many thousands of tracts and portions of the Scriptures are distributed; so many villages and towns visited; so many thousands of people for the first time brought under the sound of the Gospel; and so many children in schools reading Christian books, and repeating Christian catechisms, hymns and prayers. He rejoices at these things, and ought to rejoice at them as the most probable means of success. But he is not, on this account, bound to make a compromise with common sense and common experience, and to suppose that these books, which are often so eagerly sought for, and so gladly received, are half of them ever read or valued on account of the truth which they contain; or that all the people who often crowd around the missionary have any respect for the truth he delivers; or that the children in our schools, while they are ostensibly taught Christianity, may not, at the same time, be taught to contemn the very truth which they commit to memory; or that a person who presents himself as an inquirer after the truth, or professes himself a convert, has *necessarily* a regard for the truth, or any intention to practice according to his profession. To suppose that things are otherwise, is to suppose that to be true in a heathen land, in reference to the success of the Gospel, which is not true in a Christian land.

We hope, pray, and labor for the conversion of India; but, till power from on high shall be given to move the idolater's heart, all human means will be despised and rejected of men. In the day of God's power, these same means shall be mighty to the pulling down of the strongholds of idolatry. Reports too favorable may in many instances be made, without attaching any blame to the missionary who makes them. It is impossible for him to fathom the bottomless pit of hypocrisy with which a native's heart is peculiarly filled. Still, he is without apology, if he relate facts, without their accompanying circumstances, in such a way as to lead his absent friends to believe that there exists a state of things which, indeed, has no existence. I might, for example, make an entry in my journal, on a certain day, thus: "Went into the village—preached to a very attentive audience—distributed a thousand tracts—the people were so eager for books, that I was obliged to stand on the steps of the temple, and have persons to keep the crowd from pressing on me, while I made a judicious distribution of the books. I could not supply the demand." All this might be strictly true—not a circumstance exaggerated. But *note:* "Three days after my departure, I was informed that, at the instigation of the Brahmuns, every book in the village was collected and burnt, and the whole village in an uproar." This has often occurred, and too often been overlooked or omitted by the missionary in making out his report. He may fear to develop the whole of the dark side of the picture, lest he should thereby dishearten some timid brother, who might be induced to reinforce the Indian mission. But, on the other hand, who that has witnessed the sad effects which too often follow disappointments arising from decisions made on partial statements or misrepresentations, would not deprecate the thought of increasing the number of laborers on such a principle? Such helpers can be of no great avail.

The method of relating the following anecdotes, which I have chosen, will, if I mistake not, strikingly illustrate the trait of character of which I am speaking. I shall, in the first place, give the facts as they actually occurred, and as they would appear to any person who should regard himself as dealing with honest men; and then I shall *note* the result as it afterwards occurred.

A short time after our arrival at Ahmednuggur, Mr. Graves wished to employ a learned Brahmun to assist in the translation of the Scriptures. Several who, on examination, were found incompetent, were rejected. It was well known to the candidates who offered themselves, that, whoever should be employed, must, as a condition of service, attend Divine worship with us on the Sabbath. A Brahmun was at length taken on probation. After having heard the Gospel preached for one or two Sabbaths, and become acquainted with our mode of worship, both public and private, he declared to Mr. Graves that the sound of the Gospel was perfect melody to his ear; that it was to him good news of great joy; and he esteemed it a peculiar privilege that he had at length met with a man from whom he might daily hear the good words of salvation. He would rather, he said, serve Mr. G. gratuitously, than be deprived of his instructions. *Note:* As soon as this man had secured service in the mission, he manifested, in the absence of Mr. G., a most marked contempt for the Gospel. He often did not even preserve an outward decency, in the midst of the most solemn part of the service; and it was reported that he stirred up the people against us in the town.

Another Brahmun, employed by a member of the mission as a writer, was so pleased to be in the service of a missionary, and to hear the word of God from him, that he declared he would, in case of being dismissed from his present situation, come and sit at the door of the missionary from morning till evening, though he could gain nothing by it, but to be near so good a man. *Note:* This man has given his employer a deal of trouble. As soon as he thought himself firmly settled in our service, he put on the most ridiculous airs of importance. He pretended to be so scrupulous about his own religion, that if a man of low caste came into the house where he was, he was obliged to go out; or if the table were laid for dinner in his presence, he would instantly quit his work, and go away. When it was intimated to him that the business for which he was employed was nearly completed, and his services would not much longer be required, his *feelings* on the subject of Christianity changed for the better immediately. But when he saw his work drawing to a close, and knew he *could* have no farther service, he threw off the disguise, and became so openly contemptuous and indecent, during the service on the Sabbath, that he was discharged before he had finished his work.

Mrs. Read one day sent for the girls of her school to come to her at five o'clock in the evening. Long before the appointed hour, they were all seated on the veranda. I inquired why they had come so soon, as it was then so warm that Mrs. R. could not come out. The teacher said, "he could scarcely restrain them from coming sooner, they were so anxious to meet Madam—that they loved her as their own mother, and could not be persuaded to go for their dinner till they had complied with her request." When she came out to them, they gathered around her with the greatest eagerness—said they were delighted to attend school—were most happy to learn to read, and owed everything to her. *Note:* The girls had come for their *presents*, or, more properly, their *pay* for attending school—the only means by which a girl in Nuggur could be induced to attend school a single day. If one of these girls failed, through delinquency, to receive her present, or lose her allowance of four pice per week, she would instantly be angry, and impudently declare that she will no longer attend school. Her parents support her in this resolution, and she does nothing but rail against the school for about a week, when she returns. Though this was the only stimulant that we could then bring to bear on the minds of either parents or children, we did not despair of seeing good result from them; and especially as they are supported by the voluntary contributions of English ladies at the station, we thought it quite worth our while to sustain them.

Two of the most learned Brahmuns in Ahmednuggur came to Mr. Hervey a few days before his death, and conversed with him in the most flattering manner on the probable success of the Gospel in Ahmednuggur. They said it was well understood by the people that the mission was established here for the express purpose of overthrowing Hindooism, and that every body sat quietly expecting the event. They believed, they said, that in three years the Christian religion would prevail over all others in India, and they wished to cast in their lot with the missionaries. They expressed great gratification in the progress which Mr. H. had made in acquiring their language. They hoped and believed he would very soon be able to speak it with fluency, and be long useful to their countrymen. *Note:* These were two pundits, one in Mr. Hervey's service; and all this nonsense, which cost the two friends an hour's idle talk, was only prefatory to the main object of the visit. The one in service wished to be absent a month to celebrate the nuptial rites of his sister's marriage, a child seven years old; and he feared Mr. H. might employ another man during his absence, who might afterwards be retained. His object was to get a promise that he should be taken into service after his return. They seldom trust to open and fair means. I knew a Brahmun, who came to me every day for a week, professedly to hear the Gospel, (who was at the same time violently opposed to Christianity,) but really, as it afterwards appeared, only to induce me to lend him a rupee, which he probably would never pay.

I might here give scores of similar instances. The two Brahmuns above mentioned are both proud, bigoted priests, and are, we have too much reason to believe, the greatest revilers of Christianity in the place. Such shameless duplicity do the Brahmuns practice.

It is no uncommon thing for Brahmuns of respectability to come and acknowledge their conviction of the truth of our religion, and of the inspiration of the Bible, and to avow the falsity of their own religion and sacred books. They will sometimes be present at our morning service, and not only assent to what we say themselves, but declare to the people that our preaching is good and our religion true. Mr. N——, of the Scottish mission, relates the following fact, which occurred while on a tour in the Deckan: "After we had returned from preaching in the village, a Brahmun came and sat down at our feet. He said, 'I heard you preach in the village; every thing you said is true. Your religion is good, your shastras are divine, but ours are all false.'" *Note:* "All this," says Mr. N., "was but a preamble to an important petition which he had to make. And this petition was no more nor less than for an *empty bottle.*" But when he obtained this, he then begged it might be filled. The only way a Hindoo ever manifests gratitude for one favor is to ask for a greater one.

I had for several mornings observed a Brahmun of very respectable appearance present at our Mahratha service. He appeared to pay profound attention to the reading of the Scriptures, assented by a nod to the remarks which were made, and acknowledged, in the presence of the people, his persuasion of the divine origin of Christianity, and that their own shastras were defective, and in many things false. After prayers, he inquired if Mr. T. (the collector of Ahmednuggur) did not read the Scriptures every morning, and instruct his servents, and others who chose to be present. On being informed that he did, he said he had heard that Mr. T. was a true worshiper of God, and he wished to hear his instructions. But as he was not acquainted with him, he desired a note of introduction. I assured him Mr. T. would be happy to see him in his little assembly, and that if his only object was to hear religious instruction, I would give him a note. He assured me of the sincerity of his intention, took the note which I gave him with much seeming gratitude, and went the next morning according to promise. *Note:* Shortly after I handed him the note, (written in English,) he came and asked me what I had written. I told him I had written what he requested, a respectful application for his admittance to Mr. T.'s domestic congregation to hear the word of God. "Have you not written that I am a very learned man, an eminent Brahmun, and well versed in government business, having been much in the service of Europeans?" No, I told him. He then insisted on my enumerating his qualifications for government service, and nothing but a decided refusal relieved me of his importunity. The truth was, he was out of service, and had, as I afterwards learned, tried every expedient to get employment in some government office. On the second morning he applied for a situation in Mr. T.'s office, making my note and his friendship for me reasons why he ought to be favored in preference to the numerous applicants who had petitioned for office through the proper channels. Being refused, he had no further inducement to go to Mr. T.'s, and accordingly was seen there no more.

A Hindoo woman came one day to Babajee, our converted Brahmun, and said she had heard the good instruction which we daily give to the people, and had become deeply affected by it. She wished to be near us, that she might hear more of our "good words," and was ready to renounce caste and become a Christian. As a proof of this, she ate with Babajee and his wife, attended Mahratha prayers, and evinced an humble, inquiring spirit. *Note:* She was a poor woman, and had come with her two small children. When we told her, after a few days, that we did not hire people to become Christians, and wished none to join us but such as gave evidence of a new heart by walking according to the laws of God, she appeared less anxious to become a Christian. But when informed that, as she was a healthy person, and able to support herself by her labor, we could do no more than to give her some kind of service, which would enable her to remain near us, and receive instruction, she left us without ceremony, not liking the proposal. Not a few are drawn by the loaves and the fishes.

I shall here add a few more anecdotes, somewhat different in their character, but illustrative of the same thing. They relate chiefly to the system of imposition which everywhere characterizes the dealings of natives among themselves. Hence will appear the sad bondage which ignorance and superstition have combined to impose on the poor Hindoo.

I have said the people of India have now for two centures been "devoured by successive flights of birds of prey and passage" from the different nations of Europe. I might also say they nurture, within their own body politic, principles and practices more ruinous to their own interests, and more destructive to their peace and happiness, than all the calamities which their foreign foes have ever inflicted. They are slaves to their own passions, slaves to their customs, superstitions, and prejudices, slaves to their fears, and to every designing person who may possess either the power or the knowledge to impose on them. The will of a superior is their law, and the arm of power only gives right. Like the myriads that people the ocean, they seem destined to prey on each other. Here each superior grade feed on the inferior, and all, united, feed on the weakest. And some of these (as the flying-fish) are not only devoured in the water by their own species, but when they attempt, by flying into the air, to escape this class of pursuers, they are instantly pounced on, and devoured by the birds of prey, which, in hungry flocks, hover over the deep, watching the wars and commotions of its scaly inhabitants, and ready to seize the unfortunate. So it is with the poor ryots (working classes) in India. They are the common prey. When they cannot be overawed by power, they are duped or terrified by their superstitious fears; and what remains to these wretched beings after being fleeced by voracious shoals of hungry Brahmuns and Purbhoos, is devoured by no less voracious foreigners. The following anecdotes will show how easily the common Hindoos may be overreached by designing persons.

When Sir John Malcolm, late Governor of Bombay, was traveling in the upper provinces of India, it is reported that his head servant was in the habit of terrifying the people of the villages through which they passed, by telling them that it was the governor's custom to have an infant child served up daily for his breakfast. The rumor — which, by the way, was not original with the servant, for it was long ago reported, and believed to this day in the remote provinces, that the English, not content with eating *cows*, a heinous sin, actually eat children — produced the desired effect. It spread from village to village; and as the governor approached, the affrighted people flew to the head servant, as is usual, to engage him by bribes and presents to make interest with the governor to spare their children. He would accordingly agree for such a sum as he could get, to appease his master and spare the weeping mothers.

Oomajee was the chief of a band of marauders, who, as late as the year 1830, plundered in the Deckan. He for a long time eluded the pursuit of the British troops by a series of arts and manœuvres, which, if written, would fill a volume. Sometimes he escaped on a poor native pony, in the garb of a woman; sometimes he assumed one disguise, sometimes another; and it was only through the treachery of a Hindoo, who professed to join his band, that he was ever seized. He seldom undertook his excursions at random. He knew beforehand where the intended booty was deposited, what its value, and every circumstance of the place. This information Oomajee would often get himself by visiting the house where he suspected there was treasure or valuable property, in the garb of a religious beggar. Although this mode of deception appears to have been one of the most common, the people manifest little or no suspicion of persons in such a garb. But what is more wonderful, the inhabitants of the very section of country where he had for some years been committing his ravages, and for whose security the government were at great trouble to apprehend him, would neither give information nor assist in taking him; which is supposed to have arisen from a superstitious fear that their assistance in the case would only bring on them the increased vengeance of their almost supernatural foe.

The following may be taken as a very good specimen of Hindoo priestcraft. I extract it from a Calcutta periodical: A missionary, seeing large companies of women strolling about the country, inquires the cause, and is informed that "a Brahmun, residing some miles to the east of this place (Mungurrooh), had lately met a serpent, who directed him to say that all the women of India should forsake their homes two days and a half, which they should spend in begging for the Brahmuns; in default of which, the offender might expect a speedy visit from the serpent. The two days and a half are spent in walking about the streets and roads, and at night they sleep under trees in the vicinity of a temple."

About two years ago, as I was traveling in the Deckan, I chanced to stop in the same bungalow with Judge B. of Poona. He has been in India some twenty years, and possesses a very just idea of native character. He has in his service a great number of natives of the higher castes, and has had an opportunity of forming a correct estimate of Hindoo morality. He related to me a great number of instances of the duplicity, the downright knavery and deception, which the higher orders of the people are constantly practicing on the lower. The following may be taken as a specimen:

A writer of his was in the receipt of a monthly pay, not exceeding thirty rupees. This was the only honorable means which he had for his subsistence. He kept a horse and a buggy, a palankeen and a mistress, besides defraying the necessary expenses of himself and family — the whole, at a very moderate estimate, could not fall short of a monthly expenditure of two hundred rupees. And all this sum he realized from a situation which was honestly worth but thirty rupees. How was this done? Not by embezzling public money, for none passed through his hands; but he obtained it in bribes and presents from natives. A simple man, for example, comes from some back village to prefer a complaint against his neighbor, or to get redress for some grievance. He comes to the magistrate or the judge; but supposes he can only approach the great man through his servants. These drones confirm such a notion, and are at all times ready to engage for the poor and ignorant. Some one, therefore, undertakes; but first secures for himself five, ten or fifty rupees, as the poor man is able to give. He then informs him that he will present his case to the judge, and there can be no doubt of success. And here the affair most probably ends, unless there be a prospect of getting another bribe.

As illustrative of the same thing, I will add one more anecdote, which fell under my own observation a few months ago. While on a preaching tour with Babajee, to the east of Ahmednuggur, a sprightly Hindoo boy came running after us, as we were leaving his village, and begged a tract. He appeared very much pleased on receiving it, and doubtless expressed himself so to the people of his village. But in an hour or two he came again, bringing the tract, and apparently much agitated. We asked him what was the matter? He reached out the book, and begged we would take it back; for he said a Brahmun had told him that, if he kept that book, some dreadful calamity would certainly befall him. Nothing could persuade the poor little fellow to keep his tract.

All these things are done with the most perfect grace. Not an expression, or gesture, indicates the wiles which the deceiver is practicing. To one unacquainted with their character, or who only sees them when they come to pay their respects, as to a great man, the natives of India appear to be the most inoffensive, artless and amiable people in the world. Hence it is that foreigners, on their first arrival in the country, and travelers who pass through the country, with a plenty of money and a large retinue, and those who are high in the service of government, and see the natives only when they approach them as dependents or flatterers, form the most erroneous notion of their character. Were the Governor of Bombay, or any person of high rank, to travel from Bombay to Ahmednuggur, he would, in all places and under all circumstances, find the natives the most respectful and kind. His every wish would be carefully attended to, and the greatest complacency would be manifested in him, both as a man and a functionary of government. He might, as far as he could discern, represent them as a very happy, amiable, unsophisticated people. But suppose a missionary, or any other person with but a servant or two, were to pass the same way a few days after, what would be his report on the same subject? He would tell us that, in one village, he found it difficult to get an humble dinner; in another, he could not get conveyance; and that at almost every stage he experienced some annoyance, arising from the falsity, the indolence or the downright knavery of the people.

It is when they are detected, and charged with a misdemeanor, that they display the insidiousness of their character to perfection. It may be said, and almost without an exception, that a native is never taken by surprise—is never disconcerted, whatever charge is brought against him, and however unexpectedly. "His specious politeness, and astonishing command of temper, leave all European hypocrisy in the shade." The servant, for example, is arraigned before his master, for having defrauded him in his accounts. The man is conscious of his guilt, and knows he is detected; but not a muscle of his face moves: his eye is as placid as the sun-beam. On the spur of the moment, he fabricates the most plausible explanation of the whole matter—says he "*cannot* lie, for God sees him,"—offers "to swear on his master's Bible" that all he has now said is strictly true—proposes to call in his fellow-servants, and to appeal to them if his account is not just. They all, to a man, declare that not an article is charged above the market price, and that not an article is charged which was not actually purchased for the master, and consumed by him. The "unjust steward," to put the matter beyond all question, insists on calling the shop-keeper from the bazaar. He, fully understanding the whole business, very gravely declares that the servant did take of him every article here specified, and paid him precisely what he had charged in the bill presented to his master. The master perfectly well knows that he has not received half the articles for which he is called on to pay, and that the price is some two or three times more than their value. But he has no remedy, or he does not like to seek a remedy. He, therefore, submits to the imposition, or strikes from the bill what he sees fit. The servant very quietly replies, "Just as master please; I pay what I tell master; but never mind, I pay for it out of my own money, if master no pay." Or suppose the master to detect his servant in the very act of stealing his stores, or other articles, the latter would, in nine cases out of ten, not be at all disconcerted. He would instantly give the most specious account for the present suspicious appearances. He was "getting something for master, or looking after master's things."

A native servant of government is charged with embezzling public money, or of receiving bribes. Though guilty of a series of such rogueries for many years past, he expresses no emotion, except a grave surprise that a faithful old servant like himself, who had never been guilty of a misdemeanor in all his life, should now be thought capable of such an act. He appeals to the valuable public services of his fathers; he shows that they had been pillars of state from time immemorial; he appeals to his own fidelity in past years, and appeals to God as a witness to his integrity; he pleads his loyalty to the present government, and feels grieved that a whisper of suspicion could exist any where; and attributes it all to the envy of his fellow-servants. He is convicted, condemned and dismissed in disgrace. He says "*it is fate*," insists on his innocency, and seeks a new field of enterprise. If convicted of a capital crime and condemned to death, he conducts himself in a similar manner. He goes to the gallows as coolly, and launches into eternity as thoughtlessly, as he would go to his dinner. He says "it is fate."

With all due apology for the length of this article, I must add one anecdote more, as illustrative of the above remarks. The subject of the story is now in Poona jail for three years. He converses about his imprisonment with the most inconceivable coolness and composure, says he is perfectly innocent, that his confinement is no punishment, as he has a plenty to eat without any care or expense of his own, and shall at the expiration of the three years go out to enjoy his fortune of three lacs of rupees. His case was this: a survey of the Poona district was being made under the superintendence of a Captain P——, for the purpose of levying the land tax. With the characteristic indolence of "an old Indian," he confided this important business in a great measure to his head writer, a shastree, whom he had, after a long trial, proved, as he supposed, to be a trust-worthy man. Though the captain neglected his duty, the writer did not neglect *himself*. The survey went on, and the lands were all carefully examined as to their quality, agreeably to the orders of government. And what then? Instead of adjusting the amount of the tax to the quality of the land, the shastree adopted another plan. He told the cultivator who held the good land, if he would pay him such a sum, his good land should be registered, and, consequently, taxed as poor land. And, on the other hand, he threatened the cultivator who held the poor land, that, if he did not give him a specified sum, he would cause his poor land to be taxed as good land. In this way he secured large sums from both parties. The holder of the poor land complained to Captain P. But the complainant was only referred to the shastree, who had the whole affair in his hands, and was supposed to manage it with great skill and fidelity. So the roguery went on till the charge of Captain P. fell into other hands. Complaints were then listened to, investigation was made, the fraud detected, Captain P. censured, and the rich shastree delivered up to justice, tried, convicted and imprisoned for three years.

CHAPTER XVI.

Hindoo notions respecting the Female sex—Widowhood—Prohibition of second Marriage—The Death of a Husband—Wailings—The Marriage state.

THE remark is almost too trite to be repeated, that the degradation or the elevation of the female sex may be graduated by the prevalence or the absence of the Christian religion. And it will probably hold no less true that the *degree* of their degradation in heathen countries may again be graduated by the particular system of false religion which prevails, according as it is more or less debasing to the mind. The women of the Parsees, or fire-worshipers, are less debased than those of the Mussulmans in India; while those of the latter class bear less marks of degradation than the women of the Hindoos. In the mind of the Parsee, the Deity is elevated as high as the sun; while the Hindoo degrades him to a stone, or the vilest object that exists. Mohammedanism may in theory contain a more just acknowledgment of God than the religion of the fire-worshiper does; but, in practice, as seen in Bombay, preference must be given to the latter. The Mussulmans are, in all their feelings, superstitions and practices, nothing but idolaters, though they do not stoop quite so low in the objects of their worship as their Hindoo neighbors.

Hence, then, we are to seek, in Hindooism itself, the first and the principal cause of the low condition of females in India. The genius of Hindooism saps, in the heart of man, the very foundation of all those tender and noble affections of his soul, which capacitate him to appreciate and admire those excellencies which are peculiar to the other sex. Hindooism must make its votary selfish, distrustful and brutish. Love, tenderness, spmpathy, weakness, modesty and dependence, which we accord to the female as her appropriate virtues, and which soften our rough souls into congenial passions, are ridiculed, if not despised, by the Hindoo. He marries, or rather buys, his wife as he does his beast of burden, and afterwards regards her in very much the same light. All those little civilities and attentions which females receive in a Christian country are unknown in India. Were a Hindoo to inquire after the health of his neighbor's wife, or of his daughter, the husband and father would instantly be fired with indignation. He would receive it in no other light than as an insult to his honor. Indeed, a native of India will not believe that a gentleman can ever frequent the society of females, or pay them any attention, whether married or otherwise, except it be with designs of lewdness. A Hindoo is never seen to treat his wife with familiarity or fondness. Were he even to be seen walking or riding with her, or caressing her, or engaged in familiar chat, he would be ridiculed by his friends as a silly, effeminate man; he would, tauntingly, be called a *European.*

The following quotations, from one of the sacred books of the Hindoos, will show that female degradation is, in the first instance, chargeable, as I have said, on Hindooism:

"The supreme duty of a wife is to obey the mandate of her husband. Let the wife, who wishes to perform sacred ablution, wash the feet of her lord, and drink the water; for a husband is to a wife greater than Shunuru or Vishnoo. Her husband is her god and gooroo, her religion and its services; wherefore, abandoning every thing else, she ought chiefly to worship her husband. If (after the death of her husband) the wife wishes to worship Vishnoo, let her abstain, or worship him in the character of her husband; and let her always remember her husband as assuming the form of Vishnoo, and denominated Hurree." This implicit obedience of the wife extends to any thing which the husband may choose to command. His will and authority are paramount to any law, human or divine. If he command his wife to lie, steal, or commit adultery, she must obey. "There are several instances on record, of the *best* of women cohabiting with other men, when their husbands bade them."

In tracing the causes of female degradation, then, we are to begin at this point. This blind and unlimited obedience is inculcated in their shastras — it is ingrafted in their religion — it circulates through all the veins and sinews of society — it shows itself in the social and domestic circle — it stamps on the countenance of every female the indelible mark of inferiority. As soon as the father is told that a female child is born to him, his countenance falls, and his neighbors come to condole with him on account of his misfortune. The native cannot believe that Europeans have not the same feelings. Not a year ago, the lady of a missionary in C—— became the mother of a little daughter. A native friend of the husband called on him the next day, and was observed to look unusually sad. The gentleman inquired the cause; when the native, to his no small amusement, increasing the longitude of his physiognomy, said, "I have heard the new-born infant is a *daughter*, and I have come to condole with you in your *hard fate*." To become the father of a son, is regarded the greatest honor and happiness; but the birth of a daughter is a calamity. And thus the girl is, from her infancy, made to feel her inferiority. It appears in every thing. She is regarded as incapable of mental improvement, and is doomed to a servile life. Ignorant and indolent, she, in her turn, becomes a wife, without any choice of a husband, and not unfrequently, sadly against her wishes. If she be of high birth, she is little more than the prisoner of her husband. He immures her within the gloomy walls of his mansion, and watches over her with a most jealous eye. There she wastes away her life in idleness, regarded as only fit to minister to the gratification of her husband. If, on the other hand, she be a person of low caste, she becomes the wife and the drudge at the same time: carrying burdens, laboring in the field, bringing water from the public reservoir, gathering cow dung, kneading it into cakes, and drying it for fuel, are her appropriate departments of labor. Nearly every occupation which nature points out as the sphere of the hardier sex, is, in this country, assigned to the woman, while her appropriate labors are performed by men. Her washing is done by the washerman; her sewing, by the tailor; her milk and butter, and all articles of food which require but little cookery, are purchased in the bazaar. She has no furniture to clean — no floors to sweep and scrub. A coat of the grand solution, cow dung and water, once a week, settles that long account which the industrious house-wife at home has with her floors. Indeed, indolence and dirt at home, or drudgery and disgrace abroad, seem the only alternatives of Hindoo women.

It will here be said, "They must be educated, be taught to knit and sew, and instructed in all the arts of housewifery." Such a remedy would be about as adequate to remove the evil as the prescription which a very knowing native gave to his friend for the removal of a fever. He ordered him to "*scrape his tongue.*" This he thought a very philosophical remedy, because the symptom of fever appeared on that organ. The disease which cankers and corrodes the female community in this country lies too deep to be cheated out of its possessions by such means. Education, and the instruction which I have supposed, may increase their wants, without supplying the means, or creating the moral habits, for gratifying these new wants. It is easy enough to tell a Hindoo mother and her daughter (if you can get access to them) how fine and comfortable a thing it is to have a neat, pretty house, with clean furniture, to sleep on a bed, to sit on a chair, to eat from a table with plate, knife, fork, and spoon, to sew, knit, spin, etc. But it is quite another thing to bring them into a state in which they could either have, or, having, could enjoy such a state of things. This would be to change the whole constitution of society, to change custom and to destroy caste, to exchange Hindooism for Christianity. Hindooism is made up of prejudices, superstitions, Brahminical impositions, customs, usages of caste, and the like; and these are inseparably entwined with all their social and domestic habits. Articles of food, the manner of cooking, divisions of labor, and, indeed, the whole mode of life for a Hindoo, are regulated by relgious injunctions. In order, then, to relieve any class in India, as the females, for example, from the degradation and wretchedness of their present condition, we must first relieve them from Hindooism, and give them the ennobling and beatifying religion of Jesus Christ. In proportion as the force of religious principle (if I may so denominate an attachment to Hindooism) is weakened in the minds of fathers and husbands, in the same degree will the very desirable effects above alluded to follow.

A native, when remonstrated with for allowing his wife or his daughter to remain in a state of ignorance, inferiority, and neglect, very justly replies, that "she is not qualified for the society of the other sex." True, she is not qualified for the society of her own husband. But why is she not? The fault is, again, chargeable on the national religion. Hindooism makes it a crime for a woman to learn to read and write. And the course of life which, in the present state of things, a woman is obliged to follow, renders education, and a knowledge of the arts and comforts of civilized life, unnecessary, and, in a worldly point of view, hurtful. The education of native females (considered as heathen) can confer on them little or no temporal advantage. They have no scope for it, and can have none under the present system. It would be like putting the costly and graceful attire of an English lady, on a poor, dirty, cooly woman. The first basket of brick, or mortar, or cow dung, which she should place on her head, would crush the pretty bonnet, and besmear it with a vile solution, to say nothing of the suffering of her poor head, by substituting so frail a thing for the substantial old rag which answers the double purpose of poising the burden and protecting the head. And the fine dress, too, would suffer no less debasement to its comeliness. Female schools, as far as they may be brought under Christian influence, are the medium of conveying religious knowledge, and may thus be the means of producing that radical change which will permanently ameliorate the condition of Hindoo women. In this sense only, I apprehend, do female schools fall within the limits of the extensive plan of missionary operation. And in reference to this object, they call for the most hearty co-operation of the enlightened female communities in Christendom.

The prejudices of the natives in general against female education are very strong. They seem not only alarmed at the idea of *innovation*, but they fear the consequences which may ensue. Their apprehensions are sometimes supported by reasons which cannot but elicit a smile from the gravest Christian husband. I recollect once hearing a conversation between Mr. A. and a company of men in a country village, to whom the subject of female education was apprently new. Mr. A. pointed out to them the advantages and comforts of a wife's being able to read, write, and keep accounts; it would make her the man's equal and companion, as well as his helper. His auditors listened with a very significant gravity, and no doubt thought it all a very fine theory. One more wise than his neighbors answered: "All this, Sahib, may be very true with your people, but it will never do for us. It would be impossible for Hindoos *to keep their wives in subjection*, if they were to be educated." In vain did their opponent assure them that women of the most refined education, and the most extensive knowledge of human nature, made the most obedient and affectionate wives in the world. They will then, said he, be governed by reason, judgment, and common sense; and regarding the interest of their husband as their own, they will yield a rational and cheerful obedience in those things in which the husband's will ought to have the preference; while, at the same time, he might enjoy the advantage of her better judgment in matters which pertain to her own sphere. They only rejoined, "Our women are not like yours; if educated, they would be refractory; they would no longer carry burdens or collect cow dung."

It will easily be inferred that a woman occupying so subordinate a station, not admitted to the confidence of her husband, and seldom to his company, except it be in a way that must make her feel, more than any thing else, how *brutish* his regard for her is, can only be kept in *subjection* by coercive means. Hence the violence, the beatings, the cuffs and kicks, which many poor wives receive from their husbands. I have in the dead of night heard the alternate blows and screams, till it seemed the defenseless wife must expire under the lash before I could afford her relief. I have seen the same woman the next morning forsaken of her unrelenting husband, and lying outside of her house, so exhausted and bruised that she could not rise from the ground, nor scarcely raise a hand. It is astonishing with what shameless coldness a native will speak of whipping his wife. I recollect an instance of a Brahmun from the continent, who, in conversation with a missionary in Bombay, was speaking of his village, of his own troubles, and the like, when he observed that, for some cause which I have forgotten, he had flogged his wife. "Flogged your wife!" said the missionary. "How is this? Do you think such things to be right?" "Oh, yes," said he, very coolly, "women must be kept in subjection, you know."

Every one is acquainted with the atrocities of infanticide, which have terminated the miseries of thousands of female children annually, and which are still practiced in some provinces of India. The following account of the Gickers, taken from "Dow's History of Mohammedanism in India," portrays this subject in horrid colors: "The Gickers were a race of wild barbarians, without either religion or morality. It was a custom among them, as soon as a female child was born, to carry her to the market-place, and there to proclaim, holding the child in one hand and a knife in the other, that any person who wanted a wife might now take her, otherwise she was immediately put to death. By this means they had more men than women, which occasioned the custom of several husbands to one wife. When this wife was visited by one of her husbands, she set a mark at her door, which, being observed by any other who might be coming on the same errand, he immediately withdrew till the signal was taken out of the way."

The practice of a *plurality* of husbands still exists in some places in the north of India. (See letters from India by Victor Jacquemont, the French naturalist, 1834.) On the Neilghery Hills, in South India, there is a similar custom, the origin of which, not unlikely, might be traced to the above mentioned practice of destroying female children. These *ladies* of the Hills are said to turn the monopoly to their own account. When they travel, "they station their several husbands on the road at a distance of five or six miles. The first husband *carries her* on his shoulder to the next station, where another husband is waiting to forward her in the same manner to the third, and so on to the end of her journey.

There is a practice in some parts of the northern provinces, more degrading, perhaps, to the female sex, than any I have yet mentioned; and what renders it the more wonderful, it is so completely at variance with the extreme jealousy with which husbands in India generally watch over their wives. It is there regarded a mark of hospitality for the host to prostitute his wife to his guest. This extraordinary proffer is not made to their own countrymen, or the people of their own caste only, but to strangers and foreigners. Several Europeans have given this account from personal acquaintance with the fact, and in one instance, I recollect a native of rank was much offended with a European gentleman, whose guest he happened to be, because he did not offer him the same hospitality.

Widowhood is regarded in India as the greatest calamity that can possibly befall a woman. The widow is stripped of her ornaments, compelled to wear white clothing, has her head shaven, may not stain her face with saffron water, nor imprint on her forehead any of the symbols of their caste or worship. She is excluded from all ceremonies of joy; especially that of marriage, where her appearance would be considered an evil omen.

The reader here will cease to wonder why so many Hindoo wives make a *voluntary* sacrifice of themselves on the funeral pile. Besides the *merit* and *future* rewards held out to them as motives derived from their religion, there are inducements of another kind, which probably act on their minds still more powerfully. Religion and custom have rendered widowhood so wretched and disgraceful, that the Hindoo wife, on the demise of her husband, chooses death rather than so miserable a life.

The prohibition of a second marriage, together with the wretched state of a widow after the death of her protector, and the detestation in which she is held by the people, is, no doubt, the true cause of this. Hence the burning of widows, and the burying them alive with the deceased husband. The following remarks from the Abbe Dubois, than whom no one has ever enjoyed better opportunities of becoming acquainted with the domestic habits of the Hindoo, exhibit this subject in its true light. Never do we feel more forcibly than when contemplating such exhibitions of idolatry as the following, that nothing but the Gospel can raise the degraded females of India, and assign to woman her appropriate place among intelligent and happy beings. Let the reader listen to the wild and savage lamentations of a Hindoo woman at the death of her husband, and then tell me if there be no need of a remedy.

"When the husband dies first, just before his parting breath, the wife flies to her toilet; and for the last time in her life, adorns herself with all her jewels, and her finest attire. She is no sooner dressed, than she returns with marks of the profoundest grief on her countenance, and throws herself on the body of her dead husband, which she embraces with loud shrieks. She continues to clasp him fast in her arms, until the relations, who are generally quiet spectators of what is going on, thinking she has acquitted herself sufficiently of this first demonstration of grief, attempt to take her away from the body. She will not yield, however, to any thing but force, and appears to make violent efforts to disengage herself from their restraint, so as to precipitate herself again upon the corpse. But, finding herself overpowered, she must be contented with rolling upon the ground, as if she were bereft of reason, striking her bosom violently, tearing out her hair in handfuls, and giving several other proofs of the sincerity of her sorrow. She is compelled to act in this manner, were it only in dissimulation, and to save appearances, as it is all in conformity with custom, and appertains to the ceremony of mourning.

"After exhibiting these first evidences of despair, she gets up; and, assuming a more composed appearance, approaches the body of her husband. Addressing it, in a style rather beyond the limits of real affection, she demands, 'Why hast thou forsaken me? What evil have I done that thou has left me at this untimely age? Had I not always for thee the fondness of a faithful wife? Was I not attentive to household affairs? My pretty children, whom I have brought thee! what will become of them, and who will protect them, now thou art dead? Did I not neatly serve up thy rice? Did not I devote myself to provide thee good eating? What did I leave undone? And who henceforward will take care of me?' Such pathetic appeals as these she utters in a sad and lamentable tone; and at each demand she pauses, to allow scope to her grief, which then breaks forth in violent screams, and with torrents of blasphemies against the gods, who have deprived her of her protector. The women, who are attending, wait till she has finished her lamentations, which they re-echo nearly in the same dismal tone.

"She continues to apostrophize her husband in this manner, till her wearied lungs can no longer afford her the means of making her afflictions audible, or till her exhausted eloquence has spent all its stores. It is then time for her to withdraw, that she may enjoy some repose, and meditate upon some new harangues to be addressed to the dead body, which they are preparing for its obsequies.

"The more vehement the expression of the widow's grief on such occasions, and the louder her exclamations, so much the more is she esteemed for her intelligence and sentiment. It would be highly discreditable to a woman, under such circumstances, to forbear these expressions of violent sorrow. I was once appealed to by some relations of a young widow, whose stupidity was so gross, they said, that at her husband's death she had not a word to say, but only wept.

"These ceremonies, wailings, and lamentations, have been continued from high antiquity. Very distinct traces of this are visible in the Holy Scriptures; in that passage, for example, (Gen. 23,) which relates to the death of Sarah, the wife of Abraham; and, still more, (ch. 50,) where this kind of ceremony was practiced by Joseph at the interment of his father: 'And they came to the threshing-floor of Atad, which is beyond Jordan, and there they mourned for his father seven days. And when the inhabitants of the land, the Canaanites, saw the mourning in the floor of Atad, they said, this is a grievous mourning to the Egyptians: wherefore the name of it was called Abel-mizraim, that is, the mourning of the Egyptians.'

"It is well known that the Romans hired mourners to attend their funerals, who were paid well, in proportion to the apparent vehemence of their sorrow.

"In like manner, it is the custom in India to engage women for pay, to assist on such occasions, to add to the solemnity of the mourning by their tears and lamentations. These weeping hirelings, when sent for, instantly assemble around the deceased, with hair disheveled, and half their bodies bare, and commence by setting up the loud shout of lamentation in unison; then weep in gentler cadence, and beat time to the measure, by thumping their bosoms with both hands. Sometimes, in mild apostrophe, they reproach the dead for his cruelty in departing, and sometimes join in high eulogiums on the virtues and good qualities which he exhibited in life. Each, in her turn, pours out her measure of reproof and commendation. This assumed grief disappears as soon as the body is carried to its obsequies. They receive their wages, and mourn no longer."

The evils resulting from the prohibition of a second marriage, are, no doubt, as great as have been represented. But whether these same evils would not exist in regard to another class of females, were widows allowed to marry a second time, deserves consideration before we pronounce an unqualified reprobation. It is true, the widow is despised, forlorn, and cast out; but perhaps she is held in no more contempt than an unmarried female would be, who failed of wedlock in her youth. If a certain portion of females must remain unmarried, as the history of almost every nation shows they do, we may very plausibly ask what portion we may more fairly leave to such a lot, than those who have once known the weal or woe of matrimony?

The inquiry has more relevancy with the European than the

American, the surplus of females being much greater in Europe than in America. These remarks, I am aware, are based on the supposition that the unmarried part of the community will become unchaste, and this is the only supposition which can be made in India, without doing violence to almost universal fact. Until some redeeming spirit shall arise for poor India, we may hope that as few evils will arise, by allowing widows to be consigned over to wretchedness and shame, as there would, were we able to change this practice, and in their stead give up the same number of young girls as victims of licentiousness.

A native will assign a more practical reason for this singular prohibition. A Brahmun, in conversation with Mr. Allen, not long since, said he thought the practice a very good one, and necessary to the objects of matrimony, and particularly to the comfort and safety of the husband. Were it allowed, he said, for a woman to marry a second time, it would be impossible to tell what excesses of evil she might commit, when she became dissatisfied with her present lot. She is his cook, but not his companion at the table, and would find it an easy matter to administer poison, quit his house, forsake her children, and involve the family in distress. But while perpetual widowhood, portrayed with disgrace and misery, worse than death itself, is held out as the only prospect of a wife, she is made to feel that the comfort and preservation of her husband is more precious to her than life. It makes me blush for the degeneracy of human nature, to acknowledge that the utility of the practice can be predicated on so humiliating a reason. But I verily believe that the Brahmun spoke the honest sentiment of his heart, and the sentiments of thousands of others in this land of sin. Not long since, a Jewish priest advanced the same sentiment. He said he very much disliked the usages of Europeans on the subject of marriage. With them, he said, a man might not, without difficulty, put away his wife; and that this gives the wife too much advantage over her husband. But among his people, he said, the wife well understands that she holds her present station only on condition of proper subordination, and due attention to her lord.

If the Hindoo wife transgress what her husband chooses to call the bounds of propriety, or neglect to do whatever he may impose, she is forthwith discarded, and her place supplied with another, who, in her turn, is only regarded as a servant, never as a companion, entitled to no attention, and she receives none, not even in familiar intercourse. "To marry and to buy a wife, are synonymous terms in this country. Almost every parent makes his daughter an article of traffic, obstinately refusing to give her up to her lawful husband, until he has rigorously paid down the sum of money which he was bound for, according to the custom of the caste. This practice of purchasing the young women whom they are to marry, is the inexhaustible source of disputes and litigation, particularly among the poorer classes."

Such is an imperfect view of the evil. But the remedy? It is easy, simple, sovereign. It is the Gospel of Jesus Christ. Hindooism must be displaced by Christianity; the Gospel must be preached, heard and believed. For they cannot believe except they hear. Every system of missions, or plan of benevolence, which does not make the *preaching of the Word* the prominent object, which does not look to, and depend on, this as the promised means of success, and hold all others as only auxiliary, will, in the same proportion, fail as a remedy for the monstrous evils of which I have been speaking.

CHAPTER XVII.

Noor Mahal, the Empress of the Great Mogul — Her Origin and Wonderful History — An Extraordinary Woman.

In singular contrast to what we have seen to be the character and condition of women in India in the foregoing chapter, I shall now introduce to the reader an oriental lady, whose beauty, accomplishments, intelligence and influence at the court of the

Great Mogul, and whose romantic history seems more like some fairy tale of Eastern romance, than real life in the more sober West. Such a female character as Noor Mahal would be extraordinary any where, or in any period of the world, but much more extraordinary in India, and more than two hundred years ago.

In all those Eastern countries woman has been, from time immemorial, a mere blank in her social condition. In the family, in society, in the great world, woman has been nothing accounted of. She is a mere drudge, a tool, a matter of convenience. She no where holds a commanding position, or a position of equality with the sterner sex. The chief reason of this fact, so humiliating to the whole sex, is to be sought in the character of the prevailing systems of religion in those countries. Nothing short of Christianity puts woman in her rightful position and preserves her there.

The theatre on which our lady acted so brilliant a part was in the north of India. She was probably the most extraordinary woman that ever lived in Asia. Northern India was at this period the central portion of the empire of the Great Moguls. Lahore, Agra and Delhi were cities of ancient renown, as they are of modern celebrity. Each was in turn the capital of the Mogul Empire, and each would have a history, could it be written, of thrilling interest. If extent of dominion, wars, conquests, unsurpassed military achievements, and regal magnificence, such as even the "gorgeous East" never surpassed, if equaled, are topics for the historian, the Mogul dynasty offers a fertile field. Nor was the court of the Great Moguls less remarkable for its learned jurists, its skillful artists, its great scholars, and men of letters.

The scene of our present tale is Agra. Let us, therefore, pause a moment amidst the monuments of its ancient grandeur, and contemplate scenes of no ordinary interest. On the banks of the Jumna, on which the justly renowned city of Agra stands, may be seen, near the rich and beautiful gardens of Rambaugh, the far-famed mausoleum of Ulha-ma-Dowlah, the revered parent of

Noor Mahal. At the death of her father, the inconsolable daughter proposed, as a proof of her affection and a memorial of her magnificence, to perpetuate his memory by a monument of solid silver. Dissuaded from this, she erected a noble fabric of marble, which still stands in the city of Agra, a lasting memento of a daughter's affection, and a beautiful specimen of oriental architecture.

From the top of this monumental edifice may be seen the blue waters of the Jumna, winding through a rich champaign country, with gardens stretching out on either side of the rippling current. Opposite, the city of Agra, with its bastioned fort, marble palaces, splendid cupolas and broad ghauts, intermixed with trees, stands in all the pomp of Eastern architecture; below, in silvery pride, the lustrous Taaj Mahal is seen, and far as the eye can reach, country houses, decorated with light pavilions, springing close to the margin of the stream, diversify the landscape.

This sepulchral monument, a splendid relic of the house of the immortal Timour, and a lasting memorial of the once august dynasty of the Great Moguls, is here selected to introduce the reader to one of the most remarkable personages that ever wielded the sceptre of India. She did not wield the sceptre directly. She enjoyed a convenient medium in the person of her imperial husband. And here let me remind the reader, as he peruses the character and history of this extraordinary woman, that she lived in an age and in a country in which her sex are, by prejudice, by custom and religion, doomed to a state of ignorance and degradation from which humanity recoils, and over which Christianity weeps. Woman is there deemed incapable of mental improvement, unworthy the companionship of the other sex, and wholly unfit to share in the counsels of the State. She is, indeed, a blank in society, and doomed to drag out a life of animal existence in blind subserviency to the "lords of creation," and ministering only to the grosser appetites of human nature.

Under such inauspicious circumstances, the heroine of our tale appeared at the imperial city. It was about the year 1585.

The renowned Ahbar, surnamed the Great, then swayed the sceptre over the vast Mohammedan Empire in India. Selim was his only son. At the death of his father, he came to the throne, in the year 1605, under the modest title of Noor-ul-Deen Mohammed Jehanghire, Mohammed, the Light of the Faith and Conqueror of the World. He was the husband of the singular personage whose history we shall now attempt briefly to trace. We shall avail ourselves of the authority of the Persian historian, who is almost the only chronicler that has transmitted to us records of those semi-barbarous, but intensely interesting, times.

Chaja Aiass was a native of Tartary. He was descended from an ancient and noble family, which had, by the various revolutions of fortune at this time, fallen into decay. Hence he left his country to try his fortune in Hindoostan. A good education was his whole patrimony. Falling in love with a young woman as poor as himself, he married, but soon found great difficulty in providing for his wife even the necessaries of life. Reduced to the last extremity, he turned his thoughts to India, the usual resource of the needy Tartars of the north. He clandestinely set out for a foreign country, leaving behind him friends who either could not or would not afford him relief. His whole resources consisted of one sorry horse and a very small sum of money. Placing his wife on the animal, which was already laden with a sack containing articles of food and a few cooking utensils, with a sleeping mattress, he walked by her side. She could ill endure so long a journey, for she was about to become a mother. Their scanty pittance of money was soon exhausted. When they arrived on the confines of the great solitudes which separate Tartary from the dominions of the Grand Mogul, they had already subsisted several days on charity. No house was there to cover them from the inclemency of the weather, no hand to relieve their wants. To return was certain misery; to proceed, apparent destruction.

They had fasted three days, and to complete their misfortune, the wife of Aiass was seized with the pains of labor. She begun to reproach her husband for leaving his native country at an unfortunate hour; for exchanging a quiet, though poor, life for the ideal prospects of wealth in a distant land. In this distressed situation she became the mother of a daughter. Here they remained for several hours, in the vain hope that travelers might pass that way. They were disappointed. Human feet seldom tread those deserts. The sun declined apace, and they feared the approach of night. The place was the haunt of wild beasts, and should they escape their hunger, they must fall by their own. In this extremity, the husband placed his wife on the horse, but found himself so much exhausted that he could scarcely move. To carry the child was impossible, the mother could not even support herself on the animal. An agonizing contest now begun between parental affection and necessity. The latter prevailed, and they agreed to expose the child to the highway. The infant, covered with leaves, was placed under a tree, and the disconsolate parents proceeded in tears.

When they had advanced about a mile, the eyes of the mother could no longer distinguish the solitary tree under which she had left her first-born. She gave way to grief, and throwing herself from the horse, exclaimed, "My child! my child!" She endeavored to raise herself, but she had no strength to return. He prevailed on his wife to sit down, promising to bring the child. He approached the spot, and as his eye caught the infant, he stood petrified with horror. A black snake was coiled around it, and Aiass fancied that he beheld him extend his fatal jaws to devour it. The father rushed forward. The serpent, alarmed, retired into the hollow tree. He took up his daughter unhurt and brought her to her mother, and as he was relating the wonderful escape, some travelers appeared and kindly relieved their wants. They proceeded gradually and came to Lahore, where the emperor then held his court.

At the period when our adventurers arrived at Lahore, Asiph Khan attended the imperial presence. He was a distant relative of Aiass, and one of the monarch's omrahs. He received his kinsman with attention and kindness, and to employ him, made him his private secretary. Aiass soon recommended himself to Asiph, and by some happy accident his diligence and ability attracted the notice of the emperor, who raised him to the command of a thousand horse. He became in process of time master of the household; and his genius being still greater than even his good fortune, he raised himself to the office and title of Actimad-ul-Dowlah, or "High Treasurer of the Empire." Thus he, who had almost perished through mere want in the desert, became in the space of a few years the first subject in India.

This daughter of desert-birth received, soon after her arrival at Lahore, the name of Mher-ul-Nissa, or the "Sun of Women." She had some right to the appellation; for in beauty she excelled all the ladies of the East. She was educated with the utmost care and attention. In music, in dancing, in poetry, in painting, she had no equal among her sex. Her disposition was volatile; her wit lively and satirical; her spirit lofty and uncontrolled. Selim, the prince royal, one day visited her father. When the public entertainment was over, and all but the principal guests had withdrawn, the ladies, according to custom, were introduced in their vails.

The ambition of Mher-ul-Nissa aspired to the conquest of the prince. She then sang; he was in raptures. She danced; he could hardly be restrained by the conventional rules to his place. Her stature, her shape, her gait, had raised his conceptions of her beauty to the highest pitch. When his eyes seemed to devour her, she, as if by accident, dropped her vail, and shone full upon him in all her charms. Her timid eye by stealth fell on the prince and kindled all his soul to love. He was silent the remainder of the evening. She endeavored to confirm by her wit the conquest which the charms of her person had made.

Mher-ul-Nissa had been betrothed by her father to Shere Afkun, a Turkomanian nobleman of great renown. Selim, distracted with his passion, knew not what course to take. He applied to his imperial father, but he refused to do such an act of injustice, though in favor of the heir to his throne. The prince retired abashed. Mher-ul-Nissa became the wife of Shere Afkun. Selim, though chagrined, dared make no open attack on his fortunate rival during the life of his father. Shere Afkun, however, suffered severely on this account at court, and retired in disgust. Selim mounted the throne of India. His passion for Mher-ul-Nissa, which had been repressed from respect and fear for his father, now returned with redoubled violence. He was now absolute. No subject could thwart his will or his pleasure. He recalled Shere Afkun from his retreat. Still, he was too much restrained by public opinion directly to seize the wife of the omrah. Shere was inflexible. No man of honor in India can relinquish his wife without disgrace. He was naturally high-spirited and proud; his incredible strength and bravery had rendered him extremely popular; and it was not to be expected that he would yield to public indignity. He had served in Persia with renowu, and during the reign of the illustrious Acbur had distinguished himself in the field, and shared the highest honors of the court.

Shere Afkun was called to the presence, received graciously, and loaded with new honors. Naturally open and ingenuous, he suspected not the emperor's intentions. Time he hoped had erased from his mind the memory of Mher-ul-Nissa. He was deceived. The monarch was still resolved to remove his rival. He appointed a day for hunting, and ordered the haunt of an enormous tiger to be explored. The animal is said to have carried off the largest oxen. This monster was discovered in the forest. The emperor, attended by Shere Afkun and several thousand of his principal officers with their trains, directed thither his march. Having, according to the custom of the Tartars, surrounded the ground, they moved toward the centre. The tiger was roused. His roaring was heard in all quarters, and the emperor hastened to the spot.

"Who among you will advance singly and attack this tiger?" cried Jehanghire to his nobles. They were silent. All eyes were turned on Shere Afkun. He spoke not, imagining that none durst attempt a deed so dangerous. After the refusal of the nobles, he hoped the honor of the enterprise would devolve on him. Three, however, offered themselves for the combat. Not to be outdone, as the emperor had rightly judged, Shere at length addressed the presence: "O Monarch of the World and Light of the Holy Faith, to attack an animal with weapons is both unmanly and unfair. God has given to man limbs and sinews as well as to tigers; he has added reason to the former to conduct his strength." The omrahs objected in vain, "that all men were inferior to the tiger in strength, and that he could be overcome only with steel." "I will convince you of your mistake," replied Shere Afkun; and throwing down his sword and shield, he prepared to advance unarmed.

The emperor, secretly pleased, made a show of dissuading him from so dangerous an enterprise. Shere, however, was determined; and the monarch, with feigned reluctance, yielded. After a long and obstinate struggle, the intrepid warrior, mangled with wounds, laid the savage beast at his feet. His fame was increased, and the base designs of the emperor defeated. But the determined cruelty of the latter did not stop here. Other devices of death were formed against the unfortunate Shere. Again he appeared at court, and again caressed by the emperor, he suspected no guile. But fresh machinations of his imperial awaited him. Orders were at one time secretly given to an elephant-rider to crush him to death in his palanquin, as he passed through a narrow street; and at another, forty ruffians were employed by the viceroy of Bengal, whither he had now retired, to dispatch him in his bed. He overcame the elephant with his sword, and dispersed the ruffians with the most prodigious deeds of daring.

The fame of the last exploit resounded through the empire. The populace thronged around him on every side, and shouted his praises. He retired to Burdwan, where he hoped to live in obscurity and safety with his beautiful and beloved Mher-ul-Nissa. He was again deceived. The viceroy of Bengal had received his government on condition of removing the emperor's rival, and he was not unfaithful to his trust. Under pretense of visiting the dependent provinces, he came to Burdwan. He made no secret of his design to his chief officers. The brave and persecuted Shere met him as a friend, with only two attendants. The mercenary viceroy feigned politeness; but his bloody designs soon became apparent. Shere was insulted by a pikeman; swords were drawn; our hero had no time to lose. He spurred his horse up to the elephant on which the viceroy sat, broke down the amari, or castee, and cut him in two. He turned his sword on his officers. First fell Aba Khan, an omrah of five thousand horse. Four other nobles shared the same fate. A death attended every blow. The other chiefs, astonished and affrighted, fled to a distance, and formed a circle around him. They galled him with arrows; they fired with their muskets; his horse fell under him. Reduced to the last extremity, he challenged his foes severally to single combat, but in vain. He had received several wounds, and now plainly saw his approaching fate. Turning his face toward Mecca, he took up some dust in his hand, and, for want of water, threw it by way of ablution on his head. He then stood up seemingly unconcerned. Six balls entered his body before he fell. His enemies had scarcely courage to come near, till they saw him in the last agonies of death. They extolled his valor to the skies, though in adding to his reputation they detracted from their own.

Mher-ul-Nissa received the intelligence of the fatal combat with fortitude and resignation. She was sent with all possible care to Delhi, where Jehanghire then held his court. Though kindly received by Rokia, the sultan's sultana begum, the emperor's mother, Jehanghire refused to see her. Whether his mind was now fixed on another object, or remorse had stung his soul, authors do not agree. He gave orders to shut her up in one of the worst apartments of the seraglio; and contrary to his usual munificence to women, he allowed her but fourteen annas (about forty cents) per day for the subsistence of herself and several female slaves. Such coldness to a woman whom he passionately loved when not in his power, was unaccountable and absurd. The haughty Mher-ul-Nissa could not brook it. She had no remedy. She gave herself up to grief as for the death of her husband. The hope of an opportunity to rekindle the emperor's former love at length reconciled her to her condition. She trusted to the astonishing power of her beauty, which to conquer required only to be seen. An expedient soon offered.

To raise her reputation in the seraglio, and to support herself and her servants with more decency, she called forth her invention and taste in working some admirable pieces of tapestry and embroidery, in painting silks with exquisite delicacy, and inventing female ornaments of every kind. These articles were carried by her servants to the different squares of the royal seraglio, and to the harems of the great officers of the empire. The inventions of Mher-ul-Nissa so much excelled everything of their kind that nothing was in high esteem among the ladies of Agra and Delhi but the work of her hand. By these means she accumulated a considerable sum of money, with which she repaired and beautified her apartments, and clothed her slaves in the richest tissues and brocades, while she herself affected a very plain and simple dress.

In this situation the widow of Shere continued four years, without once having seen the emperor. Her fame reached his ears from every part of the seraglio. Curiosity at length vanquished his resolution, and he determined to be an eye-witness of what he had so often heard. He resolved to surprise Mher-ul-Nissa; and communicating his purpose to no one, he suddenly entered her apartments, when he was struck with amazement to find everything so neat and elegant. But the greatest ornament of all was Mher-ul-Nissa herself. She lay half reclined on an embroidered sofa, in a plain muslin dress. Her slaves sat in a circle around her, at their work, attired in rich brocades. She slowly arose, in manifest confusion, and received the emperor with the usual ceremony of touching first the ground, then her forehead, with her right hand. She uttered not a word, but stood with her eyes fixed on the ground. Jehanghire remained for some time silent. He admired her shape, her stature, her beauty, her grace, and that inexpressible fascination of mien which it is impossible to resist.

Having recovered from his confusion, Jehanghire at length sat down on the sofa, and requested Mher-ul-Nissa to sit by his side. Astonished at the simplicity of her dress, the first question he asked her was: "Why this difference between Mher-ul-Nissa and her slaves?" She very shrewdly replied: "Those born to servitude must dress as shall please those whom they serve. These are my servants, and I alleviate the burden of bondage by every indulgence in my power. But I that am your slave, O Emperor of the Moguls! must dress according to your pleasure, and not my own." Though a sarcasm on his conduct, this answer was so pertinent and well turned that it greatly pleased Jehanghire. He took her at once in his arms. His former affection returned with all its violence; and the very next day public orders were issued to prepare a magnificent festival for the celebration of his nuptials with Mher-ul-Nissa. Her name was also changed by an edict into Noor Mahal, or the Light of the Harem. The emperor's former favorites vanished before her; and during the rest of the reign of Jehnghire she bore the chief sway in all the affairs of the empire.

Her adroit management for her family was scarcely less remarkable than that for herself. Her father was raised to the first office in the empire; her brothers were made nobles; and a numerous train of relations poured in from Tartary to share in the good fortune of the family of Aiass. All were gratified with lucrative employments; some with high ones. No family ever rose to rank and eminence more suddenly or more deservedly. The charms of the new sultana estranged the mind of the emperor from all public affairs. Easy in his temper, and naturally voluptuous, the powers of his soul were locked up in the pleasing enthusiasm of love by the engaging conversation and the extraordinary beauty of Noor Mahal. She, for the most part, ruled over him with absolute sway; sometimes his spirit broke forth from her control. An edict was issued again to change her name from Noor Mahal, the Light of the Harem, to Noor Jehan, the Light of the World. To distinguish her from the wives of the emperor, she was always addressed by the title of Shahe, or empress. Her name was joined with that of the emperor on the current coin. She was the spring which moved the great machine of the state. Her family took rank immediately after the princes of the blood. They were admitted at all hours into the presence; nor were they excluded from the most secret parts of the seraglio. Indeed, she exercised a complete control over the mind of the emperor. He dared attempt nothing without her concurrence. She disposed of the highest offices at pleasure, and the greatest honors were conferred at her nod. The magnificence of the favorite sultana was beyond all bounds. Expensive pageants, sumptuous entertainments, were the whole business of the court. The voice of music never ceased by day in the steets; the sky was brightened at night by fire-works and illuminations. The magnificent gardens and the rich and stately palaces of Agra and Delhi were alternately vocal with the festivity and joy of a most luxurious court.

Agra, the imperial city, now displayed all the beauty and splendor which eastern wealth, despotism and luxuriance could so readily bestow. The imperial palace, built of the richest white marble, with its spacious hall of audience ceiled with silver, and hung with the most costly tapestry, and adorned with embroidered sofas, gay ottoman's, and furniture of the richest description; with its many suites of marble apartments, decorated with mosaics of flowers executed in many colored agates and cornelians, ovelooking the beautiful waters of the Jumna, was the centre of magnificence and beauty. The tomb of Acbur; the fort, with its lofty walls and turrets; the mausoleum of Aiass, already mentioned; the Mootee Musjid, or the pearl mosque, rivaling in beauty and splendor the Taaj Mahal itself; with gardens, fountains, noblemen's palaces, and the towering domes of a hundred mosques, combined to form the glory of the once renowned seat of Moslem power.

It was at this period that the English embassadors first appeared at the court of the Great Mogul. On several occasions they witnessed the full pomp of this luxurious court. They represent the splendor and extravagance of the court as almost incredible. Precious stones and jewels appeared in the greatest profusion. The person of the emperor, on state occasions, was not only covered, but ladened with pearls, rubies and diamonds; and his elephants, with gilded trappings, had their heads ornamented with valuable jewels. Nothing astonished the foreigners more than the grandeur of the royal encampment when the emperor had taken the field. The imperial tents were surrounded by a wall half a mile in circuit; and the tents of his nobles exhibited the most elegant shapes and brilliant variety of colors. The whole vale, in which they were collected, resembled a beautiful city. Mighty monarchs! Unrivaled beauty and magnificence! Where are they? The haughty race of Timour have passed away like a morning cloud. The peacock-throne is deserted; the proud city has fallen; stately palaces, tombs and mosques are crumbling to the dust. Only a few marble monuments remain to tell how great, how little — how strong, how weak — how vain the Moslems were!

Two centuries have passed, and yet Agra still presents some of the noblest specimens of human art—the sad relics of Mohammedan wealth and greatness. On surveying the ruins of Agra, and contemplating the marble palaces and mausoleums which still remain, a modern traveler, the writer of "Scenes and Characteristics in Hindoostan," says: "The delights of my childhood rushed to my soul; those magic tales, from which, rather than from the veritable pages of history, I had gathered my knowledge of eastern arts and arms, arose in all their original vividness. I felt, indeed, that I was in the land of genii, and that the gorgeous palaces, the flowery labyrinths, the oriental gems and glittering thrones, so long classed with ideal splendors, were not the fictitious offspring of romance. * * * Here the reader of eastern romance may realize his dreams of fairy land, and contemplate those wondrous scenes so faithfully delineated in the brilliant pages of the Arabian Nights."

But to return to the favorite sultana. She had now completed her ascendancy over the mind of the emperor. Her influence at court was supreme. Nothing could stand before her. Her caprices were law; her intrigues for her children for a long period distracted the whole empire; and she never failed to take signal vengeance on all who sought to thwart her wishes. Mohabet Khan, a loyal omrah and faithful adviser of the emperor, at length unhappily crossed the path of this ambitious woman. The machinations of her evil genius were now awakened to remove the troublesome nobleman; for she could revenge as well as fascinate. So powerfully had she wrought on the mind of a weak and credulous prince, that she soon procured his recall from an important foreign service, under the suspicion of conspiracy. He came, found the emperor encamped on the bank of the Jumna, and immediately formed the bold design of seizing his person. He entered the imperial tent with five hundred brave rajpoots, and bore away the imperial spoil. Noor Jehan was with the main army on the opposite side of the river. Enraged at the disaster which had befallen her royal spouse, the fair sultana resolved to make one desperate effort to rescue the emperor. The river was to be forded in the face of the hostile rajpoots. Mounted on an elephant, the "Light of the Harem" first plunged into the river, with her daughter by her side. She exposed herself to the hottest of the battle, and emptied four quivers of arrows on the enemy. The young lady was wounded in the arm, but the mother pressed on. Three of her elephant-drivers were successively killed, and her elephant was severely wounded. The rajpoots rushed into the river to seize her; but the master of her household, mounting an elephant, saved her from their hands.

The battle was long, and desperate, and bloody. Complete victory remained to Mohabet and his invincible rajpoots. The emperor was retained a prisoner; and the flickering "Light of the World," with diminishing rays, retired to Lahore. She was soon recalled by stratagem to the presence of her fallen lord, accused of treason, and her own husband compelled to sign her death warrant. The dreadful message was delivered to the sultana. She heard it without emotion. "Imprisoned sovereigns," said she, "lose their right to life with their freedom; but permit me once to see the emperor, and to bathe with my tears the hand that has fixed the seal to the warrant of death." Mohabet consented to the interview, on condition that it should be in his presence. She entered. She uttered not a word. Her beauty shone with additional lustre through her sorrow. Jehanghire burst into tears. "Will you not spare this woman, Mohabet?" said the emperor; "you see how she weeps." "The Emperor of the Moguls," replied Mohabet, "should never ask in vain." The guards retired from her at the wave of his hand; and she was restored that instant to her former attendants.

The noble Mohabet, having vindicated his character and reduced the emperor to the necessity of granting his own terms, generously liberated his royal prisoners. But the vindictive empress, once chagrined and humbled, ceased not to pursue the man who had spared her life when in his power, till he was reduced to the condition of a fugitive and a beggar. She again governed the empire without control.

But the meridian was passed; our eastern luminary was sinking beneath her horizon. "The Sun of Women," "the Light of the World," continued to wane, till, in the death of Jehanghire, she set to rise no more. Shah Jehan mounted the throne. Another favorite sultana irradiated the harem; and the once beautiful Mher-ul-Nissa, whose charms and brilliant wit and diplomatic intrigue had for many years swayed the most powerful court of which the world could then boast, now ruined in all her schemes of ambition, remained a prisoner at large in the imperial palace at Lahore.

In the mean time, the court at Agra shone in all the splendor of oriental magnificence. New palaces were erected, new and more stately gardens formed, and new inventions of pleasure and new pomp and show marked the reign of this extravagant prince. Even the gorgeous shows and the brilliant festivals of the favorite sultana of the late reign are said to have vanished in the superior grandeur of those exhibited at the court of Shah Jehan. Having assassinated his elder brother, and exterminated every male of the house of Timour, he had assumed the royal umbrella under the pompous titles of "*The Star of the true*

Faith; the second Lord of the Happy Conjunctions; Mohammed, the King of the World!"

A single instance will serve as a specimen of the vanity and splendor of the imperial court at this time: On a festive occasion—the birth of a son to the heir-apparent to his empire—the emperor mounted a new throne formed of pure solid gold, embossed with various figures, and studded with precious stones. This throne had been seven years in preparing; and the expense of the jewels only amounted to one million two hundred and fifty thousand pounds sterling! It was distinguished by the name of the Tuckt-Taous, or the peacock-throne, from having the figures of two peacocks standing behind it, with their tails spread, which were studded with jewels of various colors to represent life. Between the peacocks stood a parrot of the ordinary size, cut out of one emerald. The finest jewel in the throne was a ruby which fell into the hands of Timour among the rich spoils of Delhi.

"The Sun of Women" must at length sink from our view. "The Light of the Harem" was extinguished. Noor Mahal died in her palace-prison at Lahore, in the year 1645. Her power had ceased with the death of her husband; and she was afterward too proud even to speak of public affairs; and, therefore, she devoted her remaining days to study, retirement and ease.

In beauty and grace, she excelled all the women of the East; nor was she less extraordinary in the peculiar features of her mind. She rendered herself absolute in a government in which women are thought incapable of participating. Their power, it is true, is sometimes exerted in the harem; but like the virtues of the magnet, it is there silent and unperceived. Noor Mahal stood forth in public; she broke through all restraint and custom; and acquired power by her own address more than by the weakness of Jehanghire. Ambitious, passionate, insinuating, cunning, bold and vindictive, yet her character was never stained with cruelty; and she maintained the reputation of chastity, when no restraint but virtue remained. Her passions were indeed too masculine. When we see her acting the part of a soldier, she excites our ridicule more than admiration. It seems to detract from the soft charms of the captivating Mher-ul-Nissa, and transcends that goal of feminine delicacy beyond which her sex ceases to please.

CHAPTER XVIII.

Hindoo Holy Days—List of them—Their Character—Their Influence on the People.

I HAD heard it remarked, in Calcutta, on my arrival in the country, that the Hindoo holy days amounted, in all, to the enormous number of three months and five days in the year. I supposed this to be an exaggeration; but a further acquaintance with the observances of this people convinced me that the number of such days was astonishingly great, and perhaps might amount to ninety-five, as asserted. This led to a more particular inquiry; and having in my service an intelligent Brahmun, who had shown an unusual willingness to communicate to me the rites and mysteries of his religion, I requested him to draw up a full account of all the holy days which are observed by the Hindoos in each month of the year. I have carefully translated this paper, and, did space allow, would present it entire. It contains, as the Brahmun said, a complete list of each holy day in every month of the year, in the order in which they occur, the reasons of each, and the manner of its observance. I shall refer to a few as specimens. The reader may readily imagine what must be the social and moral influence on a people, of so large a number of days devoted to pastimes and frivolity.

These holy days are not alike observed by all classes of the people. Some are of a general character, and consequently command the attention of all castes, while others are confined to a particular caste. There is, however, a strange accommodation on this subject. A holy day affords an excuse for idleness and revelry; and none stop to inquire what is the religious design of the day. Hence the Hindoo, the Mussulman, the Parsee, and the native Christian are not unfrequently seen mingled together in the same observance. They mutually observe each other's festivals, so far as to suspend their business, and make them days of pastime and frivolity. The Hindoo, or the Mussulman, or the Parsee, as well as the native Christian, will, if in your service, remind you, on the 25th December, that it is natal day, or Christmas; and he expects a present on that day, and freedom from labor. There is, perhaps, not a more fertile source of the poverty and of the depravity of this people, than their holy days.

The Hindoo year is divided into twelve months, and each month into two parts of fifteen days. The first month of their year commences with the middle of March, and ends at the middle of April, and so on with other months.

CHYTRA, THE FIRST MONTH — FROM 15TH MARCH TO 15TH APRIL.

Prutipuda, New Year's day. — "On this day all the people rub their bodies with unctuous substances, preparatory to ablution; bathe, erect a pole, on which is suspended a cloth and a mango sprig, and worship it. They eat the leaves of the lime-tree, and close the day by feasting Brahmuns and making them presents. On this day commence the festivities in honor of Ram, and the worship of the saints."

Ramunuwumee, the birth-day of Ram, and the 9th day of the light half of the moon.—"On this day, the worshipers of Vishnoo, of whom Ram is an incarnation, celebrate the praises of their god in the temple of Ramschundu, with music, singing, and reciting the names of that deity. After having related the various stories relative to the birth and childhood of Ram, and celebrated his honors for half the day, and given the accustomed presents and blessings, they form processions, and march through the streets. On the next day they, for the most part, feast the Brahmuns; and, on the night of the same day, they have a dramatic entertainment, which consists of songs, beating tomtoms, playing on instruments of music, and throwing the red powder."

The powder used on this occasion is composed of two kinds of grain, bajree and nachunee, dyed with a decoction of red sandal wood.

Shunkust Chutooruthee, the fourth day of the dark half of each month, on which ceremonies are performed for the averting of difficulties and troubles.—"On this day the people observe a fast to Gunputtee, whom they worship at evening. Having presented the accustomed offering of food, they invite and dine as many Brahmuns as they can (from the food offered in sacrifice). It must always be borne in mind that the Brahmun's *mouth* is the way to the god's *belly*. On this day many make vows, that they may obtain a son." *Gunputtee*, which means lord of troops, or god of hosts, is a god very generally worshiped by all classes of people. He is represented as a short fat man, with the head of an elephant. He is the god of wisdom, and the remover of difficulties. Hence vows are made to him in cases of difficulty and distress; as when a person has no male issue, &c. He is also invoked at the commencement of all undertakings, at the opening of compositions, at the setting out on a journey, &c., &c. A Hindoo will not write a note of two sentences without commencing it with an invocation to Gunputtee. To gratify the whim of the natives in this thing, *government* papers, documents, orders and the like, are allowed, by their English governors, to commence with an invocation to a heathen deity.

Shivaratha, the night of Shiva, which occurs on the 14th of the dark half of every month, but more especially observed on the 14th of the month Maghu.—"On this night, fasting, vigils, and other religious ceremonies are observed in honor of Shiva. The people (during the fast, it seems,) eat fruit, parched corn, and the like. On this night the Shukta people worship the Shuktee, and feast." The origin of the observance of this night is given in a well known legend thus: A hunter had climbed up a bilina tree to observe a deer, which he was pursuing. During the whole night, he shook down leaves upon a lingam, which lay hid underneath; and thus, though unintentionally and ignorantly, he propitiated and won the heart of Shiva, who forthwith conferred Moksha on him, and ordered this night to be kept in commemoration of the pious deed. Moksha, that is, final and eternal beatitude, which mean, in Hindooism, the deliverance of the soul from the body, its exemption from further migrations, and its complete absorption in the great Spirit of the universe.

I will give a word of explanation concerning the worship of the Shuktee by the Shuktas. The abominable sect of the Shuktas is the "secret society" alluded to in the commencement of the memoir, to which Babajee once belonged. Shuktee here means the phalic personification of the female, as the counterpart of the lingam, or the phalic personification of Shiva. This sect, in Bombay, is said to amount to 500 persons, principally Brahmuns and natives of the higher castes. The meetings are secret, and their belief and observances little known among the common people. Here the members, of whatever order, carouse and debauch together without distinction of caste. In defiance of all law and custom, they eat beef and drink brandy, professing no longer to be bound by the distinctions and usages of caste, or to be burdened by the rites and observances of their old system of belief. They say they worship in spirit, and hence call themselves *spiritual worshipers*. This sect may not unlikely be taken as a specimen of what the nation would be, if, by any secular process, we were to take away the restraints which caste and other usages of their religion impose upon them, and were not to supply the place of these with the salutary restraints of Gospel morality.

Amawashya, the day of the new moon.—"On this day the people perform the *Shradha* in honor of deceased relatives. They invite a Brahmun in the name of their deceased relative; or if one family be too poor, two unite, feast him, make him a present, and then perform the ceremony of the Shradha." The Shradha is a funeral ceremony, observed at various fixed periods, consisting of offerings with water and fire to the gods, and to the names of the deceased; and gifts and food to the relatives present, and to the officiating Brahmuns. It is especially performed for a relative recently deceased; for three parental ancestors, or for all their ancestors collectively. The ceremony is regarded indispensable to secure the ascent and residence there of the soul of the departed into the world appropriated to the manes. There are many modes of performing this ceremony; and many are its pretended purposes or objects.

JYESHT, MAY—JUNE.

Dushuhara, the tenth day of the month. This is the day on which the Gunga, or Ganges, descended from heaven to earth; and whoever bathes in the sacred stream on this day, is purified from ten varieties of sin.—"On this day the people, according to their respective ability, invite Brahmuns to their houses, and worship them in honor of Vishnoo, distribute to them rice and fruits, and make presents, as far as they are able."

Wutusavitree, the worship of the goddess, or the divinity which is fancied to be in the sacred tree, when worship is paid to it.—"On this day married women worship the large Indian fig-tree, fast, give presents of fruits, sweetmeats, light dishes of food, articles of dress, decorations, &c., to Brahmuns, and to one another, pilfer trifles, dispense charity as they are able, and on the next day feast."

SHRAWAN, JULY—AUGUST.

Nag Punchumee, the fifth day of the first half of the month. Nag, a serpent.—"On this day all the people, men, women, and children, collect and worship the serpent. The women sing songs, make mud images of the serpent, or draw figures of serpents on paper, and worship them. According to their ability, they feast Brahmuns and make them presents." I have twice witnessed this festival at Ahmednuggur. The singing, feasting, and merry-making were, as is usually the case, for the most part, beyond the ken of my observation. In the afternoon of this day, the whole population of the town, as one would suppose, leave their homes, and go into the fields in search of the holes of serpents. The whole immense plain, west of our house, as far as I could see, was but one moving mass of people coming and going.

The chief object of worship on this day is the corbra copella. The hole of this venomous reptile is generally found in the large ant-hills, four or five feet high, which are met with in every part of the Deckan. The people seek out these holes, and there pay their stupid adorations to the fearful reptile, who lives coiled in his burrow as insensible of the honor paid him, as the people who render it are insensible of the duty which they owe to the true God.

Poorneema, the day of the full moon.—"On this day the Brahmuns eat the punchaguvya, (the five sacred products of the cow, viz: the milk, butter, curd, dung, &c.,) make offerings, renew the sacred thread, feast one another, make presents, and tie an amulet to the arm, after having consecrated it to some god. This they do as a preventive against evil spirits. This day is also called *Narulee* (cocoa-nut day); because on this day the people go to the sea-shore, each person carrying a cocoa-nut; and having worshiped the sea, which at this season of the year is generally in awful commotion, throw in their cocoa-nut," for the purpose of quieting its raging billows! The monsoon is now pronounced to be passed, and the boats and native ships put out again to sea. This ceremony performed, presents are made to the Brahmuns.

Junmashtumee, the birth-day of Krishna, the eighth day of the waning moon.—"Krishna was born in the second watch of the night of this day. The Byragees and the Goojurs for the most part conduct the festivities of this occasion." I witnessed a part of the disgusting ceremonies of this celebration about two years ago. I was stopping for the day at the small village of Choke. The day was exceedingly rainy, and the low country in the Concon was covered with mud and water. From an early hour in the morning, we had been disturbed by the loud singing and the carousing of the natives. I went out about eleven o'clock to ascertain the cause; and never did I witness a scene which made me feel so much that I was beholding the sports of infernal spirits loosed from the pit. Some twenty or thirty naked creatures were dancing in the mud, having formed themselves in a circle before the image of the abominable Krishna, singing the praises of this, the vilest of their gods, in a voice and with a mien which would not do away one's first impression that they were from beneath. In this way, different companies of the people spend the day. Towards evening they assemble at the usual place of concourse, put the image of Krishna in a palanquin, and carry him in procession about the village, and finally bring him to a river, or some neighboring pool of water, in which they throw him. The whole scene of the procession is quite as disgusting as the rites of the morning. Brahmuns danced naked before the procession, and the palanquin was accompanied and followed by a rabble of every caste, some adoring the image, and others playing lascivious pranks, and singing bawdy songs, which recount the achievements of this notable god. Mrs. ——, when looking from a distance at the Brahmuns dancing *almost* naked before their god, said she did not wonder that Michal was disgusted when she saw her royal spouse dancing naked before the ark, if he resembled these Brahmuns. David, in what he did in this instance, acted, not unlikely, in conformity with an eastern custom.

BHADRUPUD, AUGUST—SEPTEMBER.

Tritiya Huitalika, the worship of the goddess on the 3d day.—"On this day the married women make sand images of Parwuttee, (the wife of Shiva,) and worship them, and fast. On the next day they cast away these images, and feast!"

Gunash Chutoorutee, the festival of the god Gunputtee, on the fourth lunar day.—"On this day the people make clay images of Gunputtee, feast, and make presents to the Brahmuns, as they are able. Some people observe this day with great festivities. After a few days, they cast these images into the water." This festival continues, in all, ten or fifteen days. Some retain and worship their image of Gunputtee but four or five days, others much longer. The casting the image into the water concludes the festival. The spirit of Gunputte, they say, descends, and takes possession of the clay tabernacle which they have prepared; and while he deigns to favor them with his presence, they worship him, and honor his presence with all sorts of mirth and festivity. When he wishes to resume his seat among the gods, they take his image to the river side, or to the shore of the sea, or some body of water, and throw him in, knowing that he chooses to return through the medium of that "element." For this purpose, different companies may be seen daily, during the continuance of the festival, going in procession to the water side. The procession is as grand as it is possible for the parties to make it. The god is conveyed on a man's shoulder, or in a cart, or a carriage, or in a palanquin, or under a beautifully ornamented canopy, as the persons concerned are able. The equipage of the procession, and the bands of music, depend on the same circumstance. Most of these images are covered with tinsel, and cheap showy ornaments; and some of them are richly ornamented, and covered with an elegant dress. These, however, as far as they are movable, without defacing the image, are taken off before it is thrown into the water; and other decorations are afterwards secured by the boys, who immediately wade or swim in, and rescue the sinking god; and either drag him out whole, or break off a head, or an arm, or a foot, as they choose.

Dusura, the Doorga Pooja, on the 10th day of the month, the day on which Ram marched against Rawuna, king of Ceylon. It is celebrated with great splendor and show. The images mentioned above, as made nine days before, are now cast into the water.—"On this day, the people having performed the unction, bathe. The people, then, acording to their occupation, respectively worship those things by the aid of which they gain a livelihood, or enjoy pleasure; as their tools, instruments, papers, pen, ink, and table, palanquin, horses, &c., &c. Having feasted Brahmuns, friends, and relations, they perform, in a most pompous procession, the ceremony of the Silunguna, (passing the borders as described below.) They then worship the thorn-tree, and return to their houses. The women then take the *owalunee*, a dish containing money and other articles for presents, and go about waving it, and singing, Eda peda jao; Buleechu rajya howo; that is,

> All pain and affliction be gone—
> Let the kingdom of Bullee come;

and then give presents to those for whom they are intended." The ceremony of the Silunguna wears very much of a military character among the Mahrathas in the Deckan. The Mahrathas were from their origin a warlike people. Formerly, they always considered themselves in a state of war, which was their principal source of revenue. On the day of this festival, they prepared for their plundering excursions, by washing their horses, sacrificing to each a sheep, and sprinkling the blood, and eating the flesh. In one year, Sindia, then a Mahratha chief, is said to have slaughtered 12,000 sheep for this purpose. Brahmun chiefs, who are prohibited by their religious creed from taking life, were in the habit of giving their servants money for the purchase of sheep on this occasion. This was to foster a martial spirit. The festival, as now observed, is but a ceremony in imitation of the original one. The people are at present seen to go out into the fields in procession, to ride about, brandish their swords, and go through a mock fight; but it is not practiced now as a preparation for war, as it once was.

Nuruk Chutoordushee, the 14th, the day on which Vishnoo killed the demon Nuruk.—"Before sunrise on this day, the people anoint and bathe. They then eat light food, spend the day at play, invite their friends to dinner, and wave the owalunee, as a charm to drive away evil spirits. At night they illuminate their houses, and display fireworks. This is the festival of the Dewalee." The Dewalee continues for three days. This festival is perhaps the worst in the whole year. Gambling, revelry, debauchery, thieving, lying, roguery, and dissipation of every description are not only tolerated, but are esteemed praiseworthy on this day, and religious acts. And what is still more deplorable, it is *said* that the English Government, or at least some of their public functionaries, exercise a peculiar indulgence towards crimes which are committed on this day.

KARTIK, OCTOBER—NOVEMBER.

Dwadushee, the twelfth day.—"On which is the marriage of the toolsee-tree (or shrub). All the people on this day marry, in due form, the toolsee and Ball Krishna, give presents to Brahmuns, and throw about crackers." The toolsee is the sacred tree, which is reared with great care, and may be seen near the door of almost every native house. Near the tree is always deposited a little smooth black stone, called the shalagram. The origin of the tree, the stone, and of the festival connected with them, is, according to the story, as follows: Ball Krishna had fallen in love with some pretty goddess; but not being able to obtain the object of his passion, he fixed on an expedient that he might spend his life in the presence of his beloved, though he might not lawfully marry her. He struck her with his magic wand, and transformed her into a tree, to which he gave the name of toolsee, and ordered that this tree should be for ever worshiped. Or, as others say, she, in self-defense, invoked the help of one of the gods, who thus transformed her. He converted himself also into a small, smooth stone, which he directed should always be placed by the side of the toolsee, that he might for ever enjoy her presence; and further ordained, that this union with the goddess should be commemorated yearly, by *marrying the stone and the tree.* Hence these are formally married once a year.

PHALUGOON, FEBRUARY—MARCH.

Poorneema, the day of full moon.—"This is the festival of the Holee, generaly called the Shimgah. If the village be small, they prepare but one holee—if large, several. The holee is a pile of wood, or of cow dung. At the close of the festival, the villager, to whom the honor belongs, brings polee, a kind of cake, from his house, sets fire to the pile, worships it, presents an offering, and throws the polee on the burning pile. Then all the people cast on polee. The people also build private piles at their own houses, set them on fire, worship them, throw on cocoa-nuts, and perform the bomba." The bomba is the cry made by bellowing, and at the same time beating the mouth with the palm of the hand. It is the cry of distress, except during this festival, when it is made for amusement. This festival is second in vileness to none, unless we except the Dewalee. Last year I thought it to be the worst of the two. All classes of people participate in it. It is almost impossible to retain a person of any caste in service during these days. All seem infatuated. During the last four days of the Shimgah, the people carouse and debauch both night and day. Processions may be seen at all times of the day parading through the streets, disguised with masks, dressed in the most grotesque manner, and their bodies and faces painted and besmeared with red or yellow powder. They throw yellow dye on each other, bellow through the streets as before described, play the buffoon, and outrage all shame and decency. On the last day of this festival, the women amuse themselves in the streets by throwing mud and dirt at each other.

At the time of the Shimgah, last year, I was at Mahabulishwur Hills. The great day of the festival occurred on Sunday. As I was returning from church, I met a native going towards the village, naked, painted, and spotted, to represent a leopard. A few hours after, a company of natives came to our door to ask the Shimgah *present*. On looking out, a scene, such as I never beheld before, presented itself. The pit, thought I, has surely now been disgorged of its inmates. The most of this band were naked, and painted in the most hideous manner. Some were on all-fours, painted in representation of wild beasts; some wore masks; others were dragging ponderous chains; and all running, dancing and howling most infernally. One or two had their naked bodies and limbs painted and variegated, representing tigers, with great chains about their necks, which were held by their keepers, about whom they clanked their chains and gnashed their teeth. It is a practice among too many Europeans to look on and laugh at such buffoonery, and make the actors presents. It is in consequence of this practice, I have been told, that the Shimgah has become a season of more foolery and dissipation than it formerly was. I have observed, not only here, but in Ahmednuggur, that the main object of these vile companies is to visit the houses of Europeans, and there to exhibit their choicest feats. Nor is this all. Both on this occasion and on that of the Taboot, a Mussulman festival, many Europeans actually contributed beforehand to enable the parties to get up the fete. In one instance, I knew the officers of a regiment to fix on the plan (that there might be an equality) of giving, for this purpose, one day's pay, which, in the case of an ensign or cadet, would be six rupees, or three dollars, and in the case of a colonel five, and, in some instances, ten times as much.

Towards the evening of the same day, another company appeared before my house. These excited feelings far more painful than those in the morning had done. Those had excited my compassion. I pitied them as poor deluded creatures, who had seldom, if ever, heard of a "more excellent way" of worshiping God. They were strangers to me. But these were no other than *the older boys of my school.* For several days previous I had taken much pains to instruct them in reference to the folly of the Shimgah. The whole population was beginning to be infatuated with the Shimgah mania; and I had very particularly pointed out to them the frivolity and the wickedness of such observances, urging them, at the same time, by my wishes on the subject, and by their own interest. I failed, however, as the event would seem to show, to convince them even that such exhibitions would be displeasing to me. They were required to come with their teacher to my house, on the afternoon of a Sunday, to be catechised, and to receive religious instruction. The teacher came at the appointed hour, as usual. I asked him where his scholars were. He said they were near, and he would call them if I wished. Suspecting nothing, I told him to do so; when, to my no small astonishment, they rushed out from a neighboring jungle, transformed into demons. Some were naked, and painted to resemble ferocious beasts; other were clad in the most fantastic style. One, the best scholar in school, who had for some time past distinguished himself in his Scripture lessons, was the leader of the party. He had his body bound about with the skins of wild beasts; and from the ends of these were suspended a great number of bells, some as large as cow-bells, which rung at every step. Fain would I have believed that these were not the boys to whom I had, from day to day, been teaching catechisms, hymns, and the commandments of the one living and true God. I do not suppose they came in defiance, to do violence to the feelings with which they ought to have known I regarded the Sabbath, or to show their contempt of what I had said in reference to the Shimgah. I suppose it to have been no more than an illustration of the utter heedlessness with which they had heard what I had said to them. The Shimgah happened to occur on that day, and they probably only thought to get a present from me, or from some one who would look at their fooleries.

The origin of this festival, like the origin of most of Hindoo holy days, is involved in obscurity. In general, no one can guess their origin, from the contradictory accounts which are given of them by the natives. I have heard two accounts of the origin of the Shimgah; either of which *may* have given rise to some part of the observances. One is, that a certain king, in a rage, murdered his wife, and afterwards burnt her; and hence arose the custom of yearly erecting and burning the pile. The other story is, that the daughter of a king one day threw herself into the fire, when the father, on beholding it from a distance, ran to rescue her, crying out for help, and at the same time beating his mouth with his hand. Hence originated the burning of the pile in commemoration of her tragic death, and the beating the mouth with the hand in imitation of the distressed father.

I witnessed an instance of the celebration of this festival, a few days before leaving Bombay, which may be taken as a *European improvement* of its observance. As I was passing along the street one day, I saw a large concourse of people collected about the house of a rich native. Presuming they were engaged in some Shimgah performance, I turned aside to see what it was, and was not a little amused at the character of the exhibition. Several natives were clad in the garb, and were mimicking the habits of Europeans. Some as military officers, some as soldiers and servants, and others as gentlemen and ladies. The latter performed a European dance, greatly to the amusement of their fellows. Native men and women are never seen dancing together in India. Dancing for amusement, is performed only by women of ill fame, who follow this as their profession, and dance only for pay. The promiscuous dancing of the two sexes, in the manner of Europeans, affords the natives a subject of much ridicule, and, not unlikely, of contempt. In some parts of the East, European ladies will not be seen dancing in public on this account.

It appears from the list, that the number of Hindoo festivals amount in all to one hundred and thirty-four; or, if we include the monthly observance of the sun's passing from one sign of the zodiac to another, (only one of which I have numbered,) we have one hundred and forty-five. That is, ten which occur monthly, and twenty-five anniversaries. And if we would know how large a portion of the Hindoo's time may be consumed in religious observances, or in rites in some way imposed by their religion, we must wade through two or three other catalogues, as tedious, perhaps, as the one we have just closed. I mean, of the observances on account of births, marriages, and deaths. From the first embryo existence of the child till he is consigned to his mother earth, there is probably not a month, perhaps not a week, in which it is not required that some ceremony be performed, when a Brahmun must be called, and presents given. Nor do these vultures yield their prey to death. His manes must be feasted, through a Brahmun's mouth, and offerings be made for his benefit, through a Brahmun's hand.

CITY OF BENARES.

CHAPTER XIX.

Holy Places in India—Their Influence on the People—How kept in Character.

Holy places in India are almost innumerable. To an ignorant and self-righteous people, the idea of a pilgrimage is extremely fascinating, and the subtle priest is not slow to turn this principle of human nature to his own account. There is scarcely a feature in the Hindoo religion which exhibits more Brahminical duplicity, or more popular credulity and infatuation, than the practice of pilgrimage. Not content with the heavy burdens which he has imposed on the people, in the observance of so many holy days, and in the endless train of ceremonies at births, marriages, and funerals, Satan has devised the still more expensive and ruinous practice of pilgrimage. For the sake of an illustration, I will suppose a case, similar to which some thousands, doubtless, occur in India every year.

A family, consisting of a father and mother, two aged grand-parents, and seven children, live in a country village near Bombay. From year to year, they have cultivated their rice-fields, labored hard, and lived in comparative comfort. But instigated by some Brahmun, who, perhaps, had no other design than to secure a fee for consulting the stars, to determine an auspicious day for starting, the father begins to talk of a pilgrimage to Kashee (Benares). All take fire at the happy thought. Their neighbors applaud or envy; the children are pleased with the novelty of the adventure; the father sees himself returned from Kashee, a saint receiving the prostrations of his neighbors; the mother participates in the common joy, and only looks sad and frets, when told that she must remain behind; and the aged pair bless the gods that their days may terminate so happily. They hope to behold the holy city, to bathe in the sacred river, and die on its banks. The farm is mortgaged; the oxen and only cow are sold; a pittance of money is collected, at the expense of the family; a tattoo (small horse) is purchased, and the necessary accompaniments for the journey; an auspicious day is fixed by the Brahmun, the due ceremonies performed, and the father, grandparents, two sons, and a daughter leave their comfortable home, and commence a journey of three months to Benares, at the rate of ten miles a day. One bears before the little company a flag of reddish orange color, suspended on a bamboo; another carries a tomtom, or some rude instrument of music; the decrepit old man hobbles on with his staff, scarcely able to bear his own burden; the old woman is seen riding astride the tattoo, on whose back is first placed a broad pack-saddle, then a bag containing the food and household furniture of the company, and over this the beds, or rather mats, of the whole family. Each person carries a bundle, containing his clothes, cooking-pot, hooker and tobacco.

Thus accoutred, they are soon recognized as pilgrims, and joined by other companies, who are traveling the same way, and for the same purpose. Unskilled in the dark wiles of older pilgrims and mendicants, they hail them as companions of the road, and congratulate themselves on so auspicious an event. One band after another join them, till they amount to a caravan of some hundreds. Among these are some of the most arch villains which India affords. They are clad in the habit of devotees; their oily hair is sprinkled with ashes, and their faces and part of the body covered with the sacred red powder. Their lips drop honey, but gall is in their hearts. Our pilgrims only dream of the happy consummation of their wishes, and look to their saintly companions as their guides and protectors. They hoist more flags, beat louder the tomtoms, turn aside to see every holy place, and to worship every strange god on the road; go on merrily during the day, carouse, dance, tell stories, and sing bawdy songs in the evening; and at night herd together, men and women, married and unmarried, shameless as so many cattle. Any restraints of delicacy which might once have existed in the young female, is now broken down. Not a month has elapsed, when our pilgrims find their pittance of money is exhausted. The ghostly rogues have filched away their last pice. But they are comforted with the very consolatory assurance that these privations, to which they must now be subjected, will only enhance the merit of their pilgrimage. An expedient is fixed on for the supply of the future wants of the caravan. The veneration which they feel for the character of the devotees, and the meritorious end which they propose, quiet all misgivings as to the *means* to be employed. Hence they sometmes beg, as poor and pious pilgrims; and sometimes assuming a more hostile appearance, they enter a village, in a body, and *demand* whatever they require. One beats his breast with his fist, or cuts his flesh with a knife, to terrify the poor villagers by his streaming blood. Another threatens to cut his throat, or to beat out his own brains, invoking vengeance on the man who refuses to comply with his demands. The poor, superstitious creature believes, should he suffer the devotee to kill himself, that he should not only be accountable for the shedding of blood, but the spirit of the devotee would haunt and torment him all his life.

The company move on, sometimes in distress for bread, in almost a continual war among themselves, and often times are as the devouring locust to the villagers. The tattoo becomes lame, and can no longer carry his burden; the old man is sick, and the two sons now become so inured to profligacy, that they neither pity nor relieve their friends; I need not say what the daughter is. But a new disaster awaits them. They are attacked at night by a band of marauders, with which this part of the country is always infested. Resistance is useless; some resist, and are maimed or killed. The Bheels, as they are called, pillage their luggage, take their cooking-pots, drive off their tattoos and bullocks, and strip them of every thing which is worth conveying away. One of the sons is killed, and the father maimed. A long delay follows, during which every possible means is resorted to for the recovery or the replacing of the lost goods.

Our pilgrims, reduced to a state of abject beggary, now proceed. But the aged pair cannot travel. They stop in a wretched shed, and after many days of pain and suffering for the bare necessaries of life, the grandmother dies. Then follows a tumult about her burial. The villagers refuse to bury her without a reward, and they will not believe the son has no money. The Pariahs (men of very low caste, who are obliged to clear away nuisances,) are at length forced to take her away. They again join the caravan, and, after a journey of more than five months, they arrive in sight of the holy city. Their countenances light up with joy as they behold the lofty spires of the temples, and see multitude after multitude descend the sacred steps into the Ganges. They follow on, and bathe in the holy stream. But, alas! what are they to do! They have no money, and no one cares for them. They cannot even get a shed where they can place the poor decrepit old man, or find a night's repose. The holy Brahmuns of the far-famed Kashee, from whose very touch they thought to derive holiness, will not look at them. They have no money. The father in sullen silence says, "It is fate." The daughter is decoyed away by a young Brahmun, and is seen no more. The father says, "It is fate." The ungovernable son has scarcely seen his father since their arrival, and now he has joined a band of strolling players, and gone to Calcutta. The father says, "It is fate," and nothing can be done. The enfeebled old man fast declines, and will soon finish a miserable existence. His son becomes impatient, and determines to return to his once comfortable home. The old man cannot move, and begs his son not to forsake him, or to force him away. He entreats that he may be allowed to die in sight of the sacred river. A council is called, and it is determined that the old man be carried to the river, be bathed in the holy water, then laid on the bank and have his mouth, nose and ears filled with mud, and be left there to die. The advice is followed, and the miserable son now sets his face towards home, with no other consolation than that he has performed a meritorious act in helping his fathar to die by the Ganges. Dying here is considered by the Hindoo one of the greatest blessings he can enjoy. Of our pilgrim family, the father only returns. He subsists on his way by begging; and, after an absence of ten months, arrives at his former dwelling. But how changed! Strangers occupy it. His wife had been unable to cultivate the farm; two of his children had sickened and died; and after struggling with poverty and sufferings a few months, she eloped with a stranger, and no other account could be heard, but that she had "gone beyond the Ghauts."

Such, in its general features, may be taken as a specimen of the incalculable misery inflicted on the Hindoos by long pilgrimages. If the distance be short, the results are consequently less disastrous. They who have read the disgusting accounts of pilgrimages to Jugunath, "of the roads for fifty miles being marked by the skulls of those who have perished on the way," and of the thousands who are left to die on the banks of the Ganges, and they who will take the pains to calculate what must be the probable consequences of a company of people, both poor and unprincipled, leaving their houses for nearly a year, traveling across the country, and visiting the central points of iniquity in India, will not think the picture which I have drawn to exceed the original. The same may be said of a man who has made a pilgrimage to Benares as is said of a pilgrim from Mecca: "Never believe a man who has been to Mecca once; if he has been twice, look out for your pockets; if three times, look out for your throat."

The principal holy places in India are Benares, Hurdwar, Jugunath, and Rameshwur. These are places of general celebrity. People from all parts of the country resort thither; and I know not that the people of one part of India regard them as more sacred than the people of the opposite part do. There are a great number of other places which are held in high estimation, in certain natural divisions of the country, as Pundurpoor and Trimbuck, in the Deckan; and there are a still greater number which are held as very sacred by the people of the neighborhood, but are little known abroad. I shall here confine myself to the sacred places in the Deckan; and of these I shall not speak particularly of any except those I have visited. Pundurpoor, Trimbuck, Nassic, Jejury, Toka, Pyton, and Mahableshwur, are the principal. Wazree Baee, in the Northern Concon, is a place of much resort.

I visited Pundurpoor in the year 1834. This may be regarded as the grand emporium of Satan's dominion in the Deckan. People from all quarters are constantly crowding to this place, to worship the renowned Vithoba, who is said to be the same with Kirshna. Pundurpoor is his residence. The image of this god is the object of the pilgrimage. By what means he has acquired so much celebrity, is difficult to say; though it cannot be doubted that it has been brought about by the dexterous management of those interested. The proprietors of the temple are now said to amount to two hundred Brahminical families. Wonderful stories are of course told of the miracles which have been performed by Vithoba, at this place. No pains are spared to keep up the sancity of the temple. For this purpose a book is kept in circulation at Pundurpoor, which contains the astonishing feats of the god. The image is said, at certain times, to move; has been heard to speak, and, in case of danger, to assume a menacing attitude, and to frighten off an enemy. A story is told, and believed, of course, by all who hear it—(for there is nothing except the *truth* which the Hindoo will not believe, however absurd it may be)—a story is told that, at some former period, a company of Moguls, when making conquests in the Deckan, came to Pundurpoor, in order to violate the temple, and destroy the idol. But on approaching the god, and looking him in the face, they were awed at his visage. He began to assume the most terrific appearance. The sturdy Moguls were affrighted. The vital fluid congealed in their veins; their joints trembled; their knees smote together; they became as dead men, and were happy to make their retreat, and never afterwards attempted to disturb the great and terrible Vithoba.

In this way the character of the god is supported. And in a similar way the reputation of holy places is sustained. The objects of this deception are pride, avarice, and licentiousness. There are connected with the temple a great number of Brahmuns, besides the owners of it, who derive their subsistence, as well as gratify their pride and their passions, by means of the revenue of the temple. There are also connected with all these large establishments, a great number of prostitutes and servants. All these are interested to keep up the reputation of their respective temples abroad, and to draw thither pilgrims. The prosperity of the several parts of the establishment depend very much on the presence and on the money of strangers. No European eye may penetrate into the interior of these haunts of vice. He may not so much as see the image of the god. I was permitted to see, from the top of a neighboring building, some parts of the inside of the temple at Pundurpoor, but could not look into the most holy place, where sits the god. Nor are Hindoos of low caste ever permitted to enter the temple, or to see the object of their adoration. They worship without, and deposit an offering of money at the foot of the steps which lead up to the outer gate. I am unable, from the nature of the case, to state what are the profits of the establishment to its proprietors, or by what means the whole revenue is obtained. I am aware, however, of two sources from which a large income is doubtless realized annually. Every pilgrim is required to bathe at a certain spot; for which privilege he pays a specified sum. And he is also required to make an offering of money, food, and the like, at the temple. If we may judge, on this subject, from the immense multitudes of people who flock to this place from all parts of the country, from the well-known avarice and duplicity of those whose interest it is to impose on the pilgrims, and from the credulity of those who resort to such places, we may infer, without much apprehension of belying the parties, that the poor pilgrims in general are not likely to have the happiness of being told that the measure of their righteousness is full, till their whole stock of money is expended; and hence a great amount must be received by the Brahmuns who keep up the establishment.

Pilgrimages are made to Pundurpoor at all seasons of the year; yet there is a particular season when they are regarded as peculiarly efficacious, and all who can, visit the place at this time. Pundurpoor is still a prosperous town, though much inferior to what it once was. Formerly, it was a favorite residence of the

Peshwa, and of the principal personages of the Mahratha court. Its very dust is accounted holy. As I was approaching at some miles distant, a pilgrim, who was returning, to show the complacency which he felt at my inquiries about Pundurpoor, offered me some of its holy dust. He doubtless supposed this would be very gratifying to me. The Brahmuns assert that the lands about it are so holy, that no grain will grow on them, and that they produce nothing but a consecrated shrub. Here is an enormous car for the god Vithoba, in which he is seated annually, and drawn by men through the streets in the same manner as Jugunath is, on the other side of India. The car is thirty feet high, twelve square, and consists of three stories.

Jejury is also a holy place of much celebrity, twenty-four miles south of Poona. This is a very rich establishment, and, if possible, surpasses Pundurpoor as a haunt of vice. The temple, which is dedicated to Khundoba, (an incarnation of Shiva,) has an income of 60,000 rupees ($30,000) annually. And what is particularly disgraceful to Christianity, two-thirds of this immense revenue is derived from the British Government; not directly, I believe, like the sums which are actually paid out of the government treasury for the support of some other temples which I shall hereafter mention, but by means of the rents of houses and lands, which are allowed to be appropriated to this purpose. The god has horses and elephants kept for him; and he, with his reputed spouse, is daily bathed in rose and Ganges water. The latter is brought over land, a distance of more than a thousand miles. They are also perfumed with the otto of roses, and decorated with gems. It is said there are at present a hundred male and two hundred female prostitutes here. It is stated, on good authority, that there were attached to this temple, in 1792, "two hundred and fifty dancing-girls," who are of the last mentioned class, "and Brahmuns and beggars innumerable." The dancing-girls are probably not a source of expense, but of revenue to the establishment. The two hundred females above mentioned, are called *the wives of the god*. Mothers devote their daughters to the god from their infancy, and when the girls arrive at a marriageable age, they are wedded to the deity, and afterwards reside at the temple and live for the god, and may not marry a mortal. What say you, Christian parents, to this? Is it hard, is it wrong, is it too much that *your* God has required that you set apart your children to his service? Heathen parents have set you an example.

The temple at Jejury has a magnificent appearance from a distance, as you look over the extended plain on your approach. It is built of fine stone, and situated on a high hill in a beautiful country. The access is from the north, by broad flights of stone steps, which are illuminated of a night by lamps attached to stone pillars, and forming rude chandeliers. There is almost a continuous row of beggars seated on each side of the steps. These have congregated here from all parts of the country, for the double purpose of being at a holy place, and of begging from the numerous pilgrims. Some of them are really objects of charity, and tolerably modest in their applications; others are sturdy beggars, and impudent beyond endurance. The whole summit of the hill, consisting of an acre or two of ground, is covered with the temple and its buildings. In front of the temple is a favorite spot, among the Mahrathas, for performing the ceremony of *swinging*. The post is kept constantly standing. I had scarcely entered the temple, when I was assailed by the Brahmuns on all sides for presents in behalf of the god; and I am sorry to add, that they adduced the example of Europeans, as a principal argument why I should give them money. When will Christians cease to abet and support idolatry?

Nassic and Trimbuck-eshwur are two holy places in the vicinity of each other, and about ninety miles north of Poona. Nassic is famous as the seat of Brahminical learning in the west of India, and perhaps in no place this side of Benares are the Brahmuns so haughty and impudent, or so much opposed to the introduction of Christianity. It is a place of pilgrimage for the people of a large extent of country. A *great* pilgrimage occurs here once in twelve years, when the concourse of people is enormous. The cholera, which is almost a constant attendant on such occasions, generally breaks out among the wretched multitude who assemble at this place, and sweeps off, as with the besom of destruction, thousands, and sometimes tens of thousands, of these deluded pilgrims. It may seem strange, and strange indeed it is, that so marked a judgment as this does not arrest their attention, and lead them to search for the cause. But neither judgments nor mercies seem to have any such influence among the Hindoos.

The following anecdote will show to what vile subterfuges the Brahmuns will resort, rather than acknowledge, or allow the people to acknowledge, the hand of God either in his blessings or in his chastisements. In the year 1826, the Rev. Gordon Hall visited Nassic, at the time of the last great pilgrimage. He preached the Gospel to multitudes, and distributed a great number of tracts and portions of the Scriptures. The concourse of people on this occasion was innumerable. Every house was filled, every temple and shed occupied, and every street crowded. Thousands could find no shelter. They were exposed to the heat by day, and to the chilling air by night. Such a multitude, badly fed, badly housed, and naturally filthy, but now from necessity ten times more so, afforded the proper materials for the raging of the cholera. It commenced its havoc, and before Mr. Hall left the place, multitudes were swept off daily. But how did it affect this deluded people? Did they not see the hand of Divine displeasure in it? No: it was only made the occasion of blinding their eyes and hardening their hearts still more. When the people cried — not to God, but to the Brahmuns — for help, because of their sore affliction, mark the wiles of Satan! These subtle priests, in the same quiet, significant way by which they are accustomed to accomplish their purposes, inquired if there was not a cause which had brought the vindictive demon (as they esteem the cholera) among them at that time — if there were not some grievous sin among them which had displeased the gods? The people were aware of no such cause. "Have you not," continued the Brahmuns, "listened to a man of another religion, and taken books from him?" This was enough. The cause of all their calamities was apparent, and they only needed to be told what they should do. The answer was ready: "Go," said the Brahmuns, "and collect all those books and burn them." It was done, and after a few days the plague was stayed. That is, the time of the pilgrimage elapsed, and the pilgrims evacuated the place, as the Brahmuns foresaw they would. The fuel being removed, the fire was extinguished.

These particulars were related to me by a Brahmun from Nassic about a year ago. He did not know, however, that the missionary was Mr. Hall, or that he was of the American mission. I have applied the anecdote to Mr. H. because the date agrees, and no other missionary visited Nassic near that time.

Trimbuck-eshwur is a sacred place within a few miles of Nassic. The two places, in respect to pilgrimages, may be regarded as one. Both are renowned as favorite residences of Mahadeo (Shiva). Trimbuck (eshwur is but a suffix, meaning god) derives its sanctity chiefly from its location at the source of the sacred river Godavery, the Ganges of the Deckan. Every river of any magnitude is esteemed sacred, and the place where it rises is holy ground. There is also at Trimbuck a hill which is declared to be the very *head* of Mahadeo. It has been asserted, and of course believed, that if any one should dare ascend this hill, he would instantly "be reduced to ashes" by the fire issuing from the head of the deity. This has proved quite enough to secure the sanctity of the spot. The spell was, however, broken about two years ago by Captain S——, deputy surveyor-general of the Deckan. He visited this place in the discharge of his official duty, and ordered his flag-staff to be erected and his tent to be pitched on the summit of this hill. Terrified by the well known predictions of the Brahmuns, his servants dared not obey the order. The command was renewed, and the men, foreseeing the displeasure of the officer in case of disobedience, said, "It is our fate," and then attempted the awful ascent. To their utter astonishment, they were, in a few moments, at the top of the hill, and *all live men*. Captain S—— left his flag-staff standing on the hill, as a memorial of his triumph over an inveterate superstition of the Hindoos. The religious establishment at Trimbuck is said to receive from government 6,000 rupees annually.

Toka and Pyton are towns on the Godavery river, and on this account are regarded sacred places. Pilgrimages are made to these places by the people of their vicinity. Toka is a very favorite resort for Brahmuns; it being a town which, on some former occasion, was given as a present to them. Pyton is held sacred as a place of pilgrimage. Mahableshwur is a place of resort for pilgrims. It is sacred to Mahadeo, and is also the source of the river Krishna, and is the supposed source of four other rivers. The Krishna is said to issue here from the mouth of a cow. This is true, but the cow is of *stone*. There are a great number of holy places of minor importance in western India, which need not here be mentioned. They are frequented by neighboring villagers, but are little known abroad. In this list I might enumerate several Mohammedan tombs, as well as the monuments over the graves of some Englishmen, which are worshiped by the Hindoos.

I cannot close this chapter, which introduces the reader so much into the penetralia of Hindooism, without adverting more particularly to the *means* which are adopted to keep up the character of these holy places. I shall here introduce a few extracts from the writings of the Abbe Dubois, for the double purpose of confirming what I have already said, and developing the arts and expedients to which the priests resort, in order to sustain the sacred character of these places. The Abbe may, perhaps, be quoted, on such subjects, with more confidence than any writer on Hindoo customs and superstitions. While I have full confidence in the facts which he states, let it not be supposed that I admit the *conclusion*, which, in one of his late works, he has drawn from his premises. He knew better than any man how corrupt Hindooism is, and how vile is the character of the Hindoos; and hence he drew the conclusion that the Hindoos *can not be converted*. This we cannot for a moment allow, for the power is of God. I do not, however, think that Dubois did, as he is accused, altogether lose sight of the Divine influence in his views of the conversion of India. His opinion was that the day of deliverance for poor India has gone by; and that, on account of her idolatries, and abominations, and grievous rebellions against God, she is given over to hardness of heart and blindness of mind, that she may believe a lie.

In his enumeration of the various methods which the Brahmuns and other interested persons adopt to sustain the reputation of the temples at these holy places, and, in consequence, to support the sanctity of their own characters, and to secure their temporal interests, he says:

"Next to the sacrificers, the most important persons about the temple are the dancing-girls, who call themselves deva-dasi, servants or slaves of the gods; but they are known to the public by the coarser name of strumpets. Their profession, indeed, requires of them to be open to the embraces of persons of all castes; and, although originally they appear to have been intended for the gratification of the Brahmuns only, they are now obliged to extend their favors to all who solicit them.

"Such are the loose females who are consecrated in a special manner to the worship of the gods of India. Every temple, according to its size, entertains a band of them to the number of eight, twelve, or more. The service they perform, consists of dancing and singing. The first they execute with grace, though with lascivious attitudes and motions. Their chanting is generally confined to the obscene songs which relate to some circumstance or other of the licentious lives of their gods.

"They perform their religious duties at the temple to which they belong twice a day, morning and evening. They are also obliged to assist at all the public ceremonies, which they enliven with their dance and merry song. As soon as their public business is over, they open their cells of infamy, and frequently convert the temple itself into a stew.

"They are bred to this profligate life from their infancy. They are taken from any caste, and are frequently of respectable birth. It is nothing uncommon to hear of pregnant women, in the belief that it will tend to their happy delivery, making a vow, with the consent of their husbands, to devote the child then in the womb, if it should turn out a girl, to the service of the pagoda. And, in doing so, they imagine they are performing a meritorious duty. The infamous life to which the daughter is destined brings no disgrace on the family.

"These prostitutes are the only females in India who may learn to read, to sing and to dance. Such accomplishments belong to them exclusively, and are, for that reason, held by the rest of the sex in such abhorrence, that every virtuous woman would consider the mention of them as an affront.

"These performers are supported out of the revenues of the temple, of which they receive a considerable share. But their dissolute profession is still more productive. In order to stimulate more briskly the passion, which their lewd employment is intended to gratify, they have recourse to the same artifices as are used by persons of their sex and calling in other countries. Perfumes, elegant and attractive attire, particularly of the head, sweet-scented flowers, intertwined with exquisite art about their beautiful hair, multitudes of ornamental trinkets, adapted with infinite taste to the different parts of the body, a graceful carriage and measured step, indicating luxurious delight: such are the allurements and the charms which these enchanting sirens display to accomplish their seductive designs.

"From infancy they are instructed in the various modes of kindling the fire of voluptuousness in the coldest hearts; and they well know how to vary their arts, and adapt them to the particular disposition of those whom they wish to seduce."

It is shocking to every sense of modesty to look at the figures which are carved on the walls of the temples at Ellora, and at several other places which I have visited. The arts of exciting the passions are practiced in India, if we may judge from the representations of such things on the walls of their temples, to an extent inconceivable to any person of decent imagination.

"Another contrivance of the Brahmuns, employed with no less success, consists in the public testimony they give to a vast number of pretended miracles wrought by the god of their temple, in favor of numerous votaries, who have shown their faith in him, and brought him abundant offerings. These miracles comprehend the cure of all sorts of disease; of the blind, who have regained their sight; the lame, who have recovered their limbs; and the dead, who have been raised.

"But the miracle which takes precedence of all others, and is always listened to with the highest delight and admiration, is the fecundity conferred on numbers of women who remained in a barren state, till their prayers and their offerings obtained from their divinity the gift of children. We have seen that sterility in India is accounted a curse, and that a childless women is always despised.

"The Hindoos consider a man to be rich only in proportion to the number of his children. However numerous a man's family may be, he ceases not to offer up prayers for its increase. A fruitful wife is the highest blessing in the eyes of a Hindoo; and no misery can be compared with that of a barren bed.*

"The children become useful at an early age. At five or six years old they tend the smaller animals. Those that are stouter, or a little more advanced, take care of the cows and oxen; whilst the adults assist their fathers in agricultural labor, or in any other way in which they can afford comfort to the authors of their being.

"Superstition has a powerful influence in keeping up this vehement desire of having children which prevails among the Hindoos; for, according to their maxims, the greatest misery that can betide any man, is to be destitute of a son, or a grandson, to take charge of his obsequies. In such a state he cannot look for a happy world hereafter.

"In pursuance of this system, we see their barren women continually running from temple to temple, ruining themselves frequently by the extravagance of their donations to obtain from the ruling divinities the object of their ardent desires. The

* It is a maxim with the superstitious Hindooos, that he whom heaven blesses with a son, who digs a tank, and plants a grove of fruit trees, has discharged his duty in this world, and has an indisputable right to eternal happiness hereafter.

Brahmuns have turned the popular credulity on this point to good account; and there is no considerable temple, whose residing deity does not, among many other miracles, excel in that of curing barrenness in women.

"There are some temples, however, of greater celebrity than others in this way, to which women in that state resort in preference. Such is that famous one of Tirupati, in the Carnatic. Sterile women frequent it in crowds to obtain children from the god Vencata Ramana, who presides there. On their arrival, they apply, first of all, to the Brahmuns, to whom they disclose the nature of their pilgrimage and the object of their vows. The Brahmuns prescribe to the credulous women to pass the night in the temple, in expectation that, by their faith and piety, the resident god may visit them, and render them prolific. In the silence and darkness of the night, the Brahmuns, as the vicegerents of the god, visit the women, and in proper time disappear. In the morning, after due inquiries, they congratulate them on the benignant reception they have met with from the god; and, upon receiving the gifts which they have brought, take leave of them, with many assurances that the object of their vows will speedily be accomplished.

"The women, having no suspicion of the roguery of the Brahmuns, go home in the full persuasion that they have had intercourse with the divinity of the temple, and that the god who has deigned to visit them must have removed all impediments to their breeding."

There are a few other facts which have fallen under my observation still more illustrative of that strange propensity of the Hindoos to worship *strange* gods, and, at the same time, of their indifference about *what* they worship. As I was on a tour to the east of Ahmednuggur, I saw one morning, over a beautiful plain, seven miles before me, a temple like that of Jejury, situated on a hill. Its appearance, as I approached, was majestic. My curiosity was of course excited to know to what deity this fine structure was dedicated; and I was told, on my arrival at the village (Merdee), that it was a Hindoo temple, and a place of great sanctity, to which the people of the surrounding villages made an annual pilgrimage. In the course of the day, I went into the temple, and, to my surprise, I found it to be nothing more or less than a Mohammedan tomb over a Mohammedan saint. There was neither idol nor any thing to indicate it to be a Hindoo temple. I made many inquiries, and found the Hindoos habitually worshiped at this tomb, and appeared to regard it as a temple of their own. On the same tour, I saw another Mohammedan tomb, which was called by its proper name; and, notwithstanding, it was made a place of pilgrimage by the Hindoos. On the other hand, there is a house kept in Ahmednuggur by a Mussulman woman, where the people of her religion meet one evening in the week, and enjoy festivities, and practice lewdness, in honor of a Hindoo god. Amalgamations of this character are generally on the part of the Hindoos.

I have not disguised the disgraceful fact, that these haunts of vice and pits of destruction, called holy places, are abetted by the British Government in India. While they have given large sums for their support, without which many of them could not be sustained, they have imposed a tax on pilgrims, and from some of these places they have received, in return, a considerable revenue. But, to the honor of the British name, this unrighteous, cruel system, I am told, is soon to cease. I am unable to give any thing like an entire list of the several appropriations made by government to these places. One establishment in Poona receives 25,000 rupees per annum; another, 3,600; Trimbuck, 6,000; Jejury, 40,000. The revenue of many villages goes to support the temple of the village.

CHAPTER XX.

Hindoo Superstitions—Ceremonies—Omens—The Treatment of Diseases—Eclipses.

I do not promise to give a full exposition of these several extensive subjects within the limits which may be allowed to a single chapter. There is scarcely an occurrence in life, which, to the superstitious Hindoo, is not ominous of good or evil. There is scarcely an hour in the day when he is not bound to the performance of some ceremony, or is not made a slave to some superstition. He leaves his house of a morning; but if he sees a bird fly in the *wrong* direction, or meets an animal of ill omen, or first sees a person of a certain caste, or any object betokening ill, he must return, and relinquish his enterprise, and perhaps may not go out of his house again that day. I shall not attempt to enumerate these endless observances, as I have not a list of them from competent native authority. It is enough to say here, that *everg thing* has a "sign" to it. I shall therefore content myself with giving a few specimens of the general subject.

The cholera morbus is regarded by the Hindoos as a malignant goddess, whom they worship, in order to deprecate her anger. They believe that this goddess wanders to and fro, up and down the earth, afflicting the people in one part of the earth, and then moving off to another place, where she commences the same work without mercy or compassion. In order to propitiate this malignant demon, the people make her offerings of rice, ghee, flowers, fruits, and the like. They sacrifice to her sheep, goats, buffaloes and fowls. I witnessed a large sacrifice of this description at Ahmednuggur. Two or three buffaloes were sacrificed, several sheep and goats, and a great number of fowls, with rice, ghee, (clarified butter,) fruits, flowers, and food of all sorts, as the villagers chose to bring. A temporary altar had been erected in the open field; and this was placed before a rude stone, which was tipped with red paint, and dignified with the name of the goddess Zurree Murree (cholera morbus). The goddess, ornamented with flowers, was placed in a small temple which had been constructed of bamboos, and was covered with the boughs of trees. I did not happen to be present when any of the victims were slain, but I am assured by those who have witnessed it, that there appears a striking analogy between the Hindoo rites of sacrificing, and those prescribed for the Israelites in the writings of Moses.

Some months before leaving India, I happened to be at Wyee, a celebrated Brahminical place, when the cholera was raging with great violence, and sweeping off large numbers of the people daily. On the evening of my arrival, the banks of the Krishna river were illuminated by the fires of the funeral piles of those who had died that day. The bodies which were consuming were only those of the higher castes. The lower orders are not able to burn their dead, on account of the expense; and, consequently, these numerous fires only indicated the daily number of deaths among the former class. The others are quietly conveyed away to the banks of the river, or to the side of some body of water, where they are buried. Coffins are not used by any class of natives. The dead are generally carried out in their ordinary clothing, painted and ornamented with flowers. The body is by some castes of Hindoos deposited in a recumbent position, and by others in a sitting posture; and it is supplied with food for its journey to the eternal world.

The Brahmuns at Wyee had begun the work of propitiation, as they generally do, after the pestilence had nearly spent its violence. The grand sacrifice occurred the next day after my arrival. About ten o'clock in the morning, seeing a large concourse of people collected about a temple, near the river, I went towards the crowd. When at a considerable distance, I was stopped by some Brahmuns, who said I must not proceed, as they were engaged in sacrificing; and the offering would prove inefficacious if I should be present. I asked what they were offering in sacrifice, but they would not tell me. Promising not to disturb them, I insisted on going to the place, and proceeded onward. Seeing me determined to know what they were doing, a Sepoy took hold of my arm, saying, "Sahib, you *must not go.*" He appeared too much in earnest to be resisted, and consequently I yielded, but not till I had approached so near as to see a large heap of rice, not less than two cart loads, placed before the temple of Zurree Murree. On this heap of rice the people were throwing meat offerings of ghee, oil, cocoa-nut, flour, and the like. A dark volume of smoke arose near the temple, but of what the burnt offering consisted, I could not discover. The great earnestness with which they prevented me from witnessing the scene, much excited my suspicion that they might be making an offering, which, if known, would have involved themselves in difficulty with the criminal law. I saw very plainly that they were prepared to use violence, if other means had not succeeded, to keep me at a distance from their rites. I conversed with several Brahmuns on the subject of the sacrifice, but could get no satisfactory account of it.

The demon goddess is not only to be propitiated by sacrifices, but various other means are used to induce her to leave a place where she is unsparingly scattering the arrows of death. In some instances, the Brahmuns have been known to presume so far on the credulity of the people, as to cause a large car to be made, for the purpose of conveying the vindictive goddess out of their village. Wooden figures of horses or elephants are attached to the car, and when the goddess is seated in the vehicle, in compliance with the petitions of the Brahmuns, by whom she is made propitious, the whole is drawn away by the villagers; and the alarms of the people, which, on such occasions, are dreadful, and, no doubt, the predisposing cause of the cholera, are from this time quieted, and the pestilence soon abates. It should be kept in mind, that such measures are seldom, if ever, resorted to, till the cholera has raged for some fifteen or twenty days, about the usual time of its prevalence in one place. Should a few cases occur after the goddess is conducted away, a very plausible reason is at hand: the parties had no faith in the measures, or the goddess had indulged some malignity against the sufferers, because their offerings had not been of sufficient value, or they had, in former days, neglected the Brahmuns, or the gods. And thus the whole affair, which ought to be regarded as a scourge from heaven, is turned to the account of an avaricious priesthood, and serves only to rivet the fetters of superstition and Brahminical tyranny on an ignorant and idolatrous people. Reasons are frequently assigned for the awful visitations of the Zurree Murree; and individuals are sometimes made to suffer severely, as having provoked the goddess to anger. I have, in another article, given an instance of this. In 1826, she poured out her wrath without mixture on the inhabitants of Nassic, on account of their having received Christian books from Mr. Hall. Sometimes the prevalence of the cholera is attributed to the old women, and they are in consequence treated in the most cruel manner. When the cholera raged in Ahmednuggur, as I have before stated, Babajee was branded as the author of it; and the distress which was experienced there by all classes, on account of the failure of the annual rain, was attributed to the establishment of our mission. Before missionaries came among them, they said, they had rain, and fruitful seasons; but now they were about to die of famine.

Consistently with his professed belief, a Hindoo cannot take medicine in case of cholera. The only way for him, is to exorcise the demon. This, it is pretended, may be done by the muntru. All this passes very well in their theory, but, in case of an attack, most natives are very glad to get Eupopean medicine. The cholera is by no means the only disease which is supposed to be the effect of an evil spirit, or to be induced by some animal, or other object, in the stomach, or in the part affected. Not long since, I read a very curious Hindoo book, a part of their shastra, which treats of *diseases*. In this, every disease is represented as possessed of a bodily form. A liver complaint is caused by a crab, which is eating the liver. A cough is occasioned by a large caterpillar, which has taken up his abode in the throax;

a tooth-ache proceeds from the gnawings of a vindictive little worm, which has domiciled himself in the decaying tooth. If proof be wanting of the latter, the native will most proudly produce it; and all the wise reasoning of western sages is put to the blush. A person with the tooth-ache is told to extract the worm by smoking a certain kind of seed. An inverted earthen vessel is placed in a shallow basin of water, and a hole perforated for a tube at the top. The seed is put on a heated shovel, and introduced through the side of the vessel by another hole. Let the patient inhale the smoke through the tube for half an hour, or till the pain ceases, allowing the saliva to fall through the tube into the water below. On examination, it will be found that the water contains the worm of the tooth; or, if the case be an obstinate one, five, ten or twenty may be found. Though often assured that the worm-like appearance is but the germ of the seed, which almost instantly vegetates by means of the heat and water, yet nothing will persuade the native that these are not actually worms from the tooth.

The natives of India, Hindoos, Mussulmans and others, have a very singular superstition about the snake. They regard him, when found about the house, as a kind of guardian deity. As I was one day sitting with my teacher, a great outcry was made at the cook-room, a building but a few yards from the house. We ran to ascertain the cause, when the natives pointed to a large serpent lying over the cook-room door, with his head hanging down. All were at first eager to kill him. Clubs, sticks and stones awaited him on being drawn with a hook. He was partly stupified by an attempt which he was making to swallow a huge rat which he had just caught, and he promised to fall an easy prey; when in an instant every native threw down his weapon and exclaimed, "This is the lord of the mansion! Don't hurt him, don't hurt him!" I smiled at their nonsense, and cried out to have them assist in destroying the reptile. But it was of no use, and the serpent escaped. I was anxious to know what this superstition was, and whence it arose. But I

THE INDIAN BOA.

could ascertain nothing more than this, that they believed the serpent to be the guardian of the premises; and should they wound him, he would avenge himself on them; and should they kill him, some sad calamity would ensue. Whence the superstition originated, I could not ascertain with any certainty. It may arise from the veneration which they have for the serpent on account of his being the support of the world. They believe this earth rests on the head of an enormous serpent. An earthquake is caused by his moving his head.

The Hindoos believe that if they look at the moon on a certain day, they shall be instantly struck dead. Nothing of course will induce a man to raise his eyes to the moon on this day. The common people are acquainted with every omen and sign prevalent among the nations of the West, and many others seem peculiar to themselves.

The following may be taken as specimens of ceremonies, which may, for the most part, be classed under the head of domestic duties and observances. They are taken from a translation of a book from the Sanskrit, in which the wise sages of India hoped to have locked up all the precious arcana of their craft. And so it was for a long time. But in this degenerate age of Hindooism, when every thing seems to be going wrong, when men are found departing from the "old way," to such an alarming degree that "they do not sleep in the right position," "cleanse their teeth with the branches of improper trees," "call in the barber on an improper day," "put on new apparel as soon as it is purchased, without waiting for two or three revulsions of the earth,"—when enormities like these had threatened the stability of their ancient fabric, it was time that the ordinances of the golden age should be promulgated in the vulgar tongue, to remind the men of this iron age of that "glorious period when these irregularities were unknown, and when the gods came down to earth and talked Sanskrit familiarly with the great sages of the East." Such a book we now have, published in the Bengalee language.

The first two pages contain directions for cleaning the teeth The Hindoos use neither brush nor powder, but pluck a little twig from the first tree, strip it of its leaves, and rub the teeth with the bruised end. This must be done at a specified time, and according to prescribed rules. "He who cleans his teeth after the sun has risen, why does he worship Vishnoo?" "Cleanse the teeth with the thumb and the second and third finger, never with the first." "When no twig can be obtained, or on forbidden days, cleanse the teeth with water poured twelve times from the palm of the hand into the mouth." "If a person cleanse his teeth on the day of a shraddhu, or of fasting, those two actions lose their reward." "He who cleans his teeth at the middle or close of the day, the gods receive not his flowers, nor his ancestors the water he offers them." "He who cleans his teeth at the time of bathing, the gods receive not his sacrifice."

The following are regulations on the subject of *bathing* and washing: "Let not the face be washed looking towards the south or west, for fear of eternal punishment." "Bathing in the morning, and clarified butter in the mouths of Wyshakh, Kartik, and Magh, destroy the greatest sins." "He who at the time of bathing rubs his body with his hand, or with any thing besides his napkin, is as though he touched a dog. Let him bathe again." Every portion of the body of a Hindoo is the residence of some god. "He who after bathing neglects to wash his feet, loses a year's merit." "He who bathes at the steps used by a washerman, is as though he killed a Brahmun." Washermen are persons of low caste. "He who, at the conjunction called Narayunee, bathes in silence in the Koorootaya river, raises thirty-three millions of his ancestors to eternal bliss!"

Rules on the subject of cooking and eating: "If, while a Brahmun is cooking, he gives fire to a Shoodru, the whole food is polluted." "Eating with the face to the east, insures long life; with it to the south, celebrity; to the west, wealth; to the north, pecuniary embarrassment." "If, before taking of food, you do not, with your finger, make a circular water-mark on the ground to contain your dish, the demons will devour all the food." "If, at the time of eating, the water-pot be placed on the left hand, the water becomes blood." The right hand is holy, the left unholy; each has its distinct functions. The body, from the naval upwards, being holy, is the province of the right hand; the rest of the body being unholy, is abandoned to the left. Then follows a long list of prohibited dishes, and restrictions on certain kinds of food on particular days. "He who, on Sunday, eats meat, fish, honey, rice, gruel, wood-apple, or ginger, will be childless through seven transmigrations, and wretched through every succeeding birth." "On the first day of the moon, he who eats of a pumpkin, becomes indigent." "Ignorance follows the eating of cocoa-nut on the eighth." "It is sinful to eat beans on the eleventh." And similar restrictions through the month.

"Clothes washed in a shallow pool, or by a woman, or by a washerman, or hung up to dry with the two ends pointing to the south and west, are unholy. He who puts on new apparel on Sunday, becomes poor; on Monday, is afflicted with boils; on Tuesday, is subject to much trouble; on Wednesday, will possess means of purchasing new clothes; on Thursday, will become learned and wealthy; on Friday, will become happy; on Saturday, will become involved in trouble and disputes." And so on, as to almost every action in life. "He who *shaves* on Sunday, becomes miserable; on Monday, happy; on Tuesday, hastens his own death; on Wednesday, accumulates wealth; on Thursday, becomes dishonorable; on Friday, childless; on Saturday, brings on his head every misfortune."

"When any one stumbles, let him who sees him exclaim, Rise! rise! When one sneezes, let the spectator say, Live! live! When a man yawns, let him and those around him snap their fingers." "To sneeze when one is about to sit down, or lie down, or about to eat, or is dressing, or bestowing gifts, or is engaged in a dispute, or in a wedding, is highly inauspicious." "The earth trembles if it be plowed on the day of the new moon, or the full moon, or on the day of a Shraddhu, and during five particular days of Assar." "He who rides to a place of sanctity, loses one half of his merit; he who carries an umbrella over his head, or uses shoes, loses one-fourth of his merit," &c. As to the *reasons* of these, and ten thousand like rules and observances, I know nothing. They are, doubtless, irrevocably buried beneath the vail of oblivion which shuts out from human ken the profound wisdom and holy illumination which is said to have adorned the Brahminical priesthood in the "golden age" of Hindoostan.

Rules relative to ceremonial impurity are as minute as they are puerile and absurd. On the death of a relative, a Brahmun is unclean ten days, and a Shoodru thirty. This extends to the sixth degree of consanguinity. On the birth of a son, the mother is unclean twenty days; of a daughter, thirty. This impurity extends also to all the relatives, to the sixth degree of relationship. "When a Brahmun follows the corpse of another Brahmun of different kindred, he must purify himself by bathing, touching fire, and eating clarified butter. If the corpse belong to one of the military tribe, the Brahmun who follows is unclean one day," &c. "If the smoke of a funeral pile blows on any one, he must purify himself by bathing. He who weeps for another becomes unclean." "The day on which the finger is cut, or a drop of blood shed, the individual becomes unclean, and can perform no religious duty; if blood drop from the tooth, the most essential services of religion are suspended. After tonsure, weeping, touching what is forbidden, or vomiting, a man must purify himself by bathing." "He who has lost caste, a chundalu, (low caste,) a fool, one not perfectly sane, a midwife, a woman for a month after accouchment, a village hog, a fowl, a dog, or an undertaker, are never to be touched."

The Hindoos use the rosary in the same way as the Mohammedans and the Catholics do. The custom is doubtless brought from the East. Nearly every devotee carries a long string of beads. They are not only carried in the hand, and used as a rosary, but they are worn on the arms, the neck, or the body, as amulets. I have seen devotees nearly covered with strings of beads. The Hindoo rosary consists of a hundred and eight beads; the Mohammedan, of a hundred and one.

The natives of India have a very extraordinary superstition regarding a person about to be executed. They believe he imparts a sanctity to every thing he touches. For this reason he throws flowers, fruits, and spices to the crowd about the gibbet, who catch the dying boon as eagerly as the friends of the good old saint hang on his lips in a dying hour, and catch the last accents of his expiring breath. But the comparison seems almost profane. I should have doubted whether a superstition so abhorrent to every better feeling of human nature, and so subversive of all right and justice, could have existed, had I not the most indisputable evidence of the fact. What I am about to relate transpired in Jalna, a large town, not above a hundred miles from Ahmednuggur. I visited the place, where the culprit was executed in the beginning of the year 1834, about fifteen months after it took place, and had confirmed to me on the spot what I had the year previous so often heard asserted.

A camp follower had been convicted of the murder of his own mother, and had been condemned to the gallows. As he was a notoriously vile man — the suspicion of having committed other murders resting on him, and the present one being of peculiar aggravation — his body was condemned to hang on the gibbet exposed to the public gaze, a terror to evil doers. Whether this man dispensed his blessings at the hour of his execution, I do not know. But a few days after the execution, when the humors of the body began to drip on the ground, the Brahmuns reported that there was a healing efficacy in these humors. The sick, the lame, the blind, and the diseased of every description were assembled on the spot. All fancied that they found relief, and their *fancy* no doubt relieved many. The deluded people from every quarter congregated here, and they then began to pay divine honors to the vile remains of the more vile murderer of his mother. A new deity was now created, and, but for the interference of the English authorities at Jalna, he might in a few years have rivaled in celebrity the present renowned Hunnamunt or Gunputtee. This disgusting incident may show how easy it is for a people, who are in "all things too superstitious," to make a new god; and how small a matter is the origin or the character of a god. Many Hindoo deities may not be able to claim a more honorable orign.

Amulets are almost universally worn by the Hindoos for the preventing or the curing of diseases, or the driving off of evil spirits. These are made of different materials, and are worn about the arm, the neck, or the body. Sometimes they consist only of a single thread; sometimes they are made of leather, and set with small shells. Strings of beads form a very common amulet. An instance occurred on our premises at Ahmednuggur, which illustrates, very strikingly, the influence which this superstition has over the mind of a native, and sometimes over his better judgment. Kondooba was a member of our church, and had given very satisfactory evidence of his conversion. He had manifested no lingering confidence in Hindooism, or shown any distrust in Christianity. He was taken ill. He suffered much pain, and found no relief in the medicines we gave him. His native friends advised him to use the charm; and he accordingly allowed them to tie the amulet on his arm. The next day, when the charm was discovered, and he was asked the reason of its being there, he bethought himself of his error, and confessed that he had sinned, in resorting to a charm for the removal of his pain, and not to God. He wept, and grieved, and humbled himself before the Lord. He said he was overcome in the hour of temptation, when in the midst of bodily pain he inadvertenly sought the aid of a false god.

The superstitions, and consequent ceremonies, connected with the muntru, are too prominent in Hindoo mythology to be passed over in silence, but too prolix to be given in detail. The muntru is a mystic verse, or incantation, the repetition of which is declared to be attended with the most wonderful effect. None but Brahmuns, and the higher order of Hindoos, are allowed to repeat it. Shoodrus are prohibited to repeat, or even hear the muntru, on pain of eternal torment. All things are subservient to the muntru. The gods themselves cannot resist it. It is the essence of the Vedas; it is the united power of Brahmu, Vishnoo and Shiva. By its magic power, it confers all sancity, pardons all sin, secures all good, temporal and spiritual, and procures everlasting blessedness in the world to come. It possesses the wonderful charm of interchanging good for evil, truth for falsehood, light for darkness, and of confirming such perversions by the most holy sanction. Indeed, there is nothing so difficult, so silly, or so absurd, that may not be achieved by this extraordinary muntru.

Whenever the wonder-working Brahmun chooses, the natural properties of bodies may be changed only by the repetition of a single mystic verse, the relations of objects destroyed, and the very laws of nature be suspended. Men and brutes become gods; gold, silver, brass and stone, receive the divine spark. A poor Brahmun once came to me to solicit employment. The ragged, filthy cloth with which he attempted to cover his person, was voucher enough for the tale of poverty which he related. After expressing all our pity for his destitution, and informing him how a young, healthful man like myself might find an immediate relief in his necessities, I asked him how it was possible that a *Brahmun* could be so poor as he appeared to be? "Have you not the muntru?" "Yes." "Can you not by means of that do any thing you choose? Can you not expel all these foreigners from your land, take the reins of government yourselves, secure the departing wealth of your country, change stones to gold, and misery to happiness?" "Yes, yes," said he, "such is the power of the muntru, but the muntru fails where foreigners have the dominion." "No, no," answered my pundit, who sat by, and had anticipated my next question, "that is not the reason; the Brahmuns, though possessed of ample power to extinguish the English Government any time they choose, have judged it expedient to humble themselves in the sight of all nations, and to subject themselves and their people to a long penance. Hence they have *allowed* strangers to devour them, in like manner as a man in the performance of the penance called tuppu subjects himself to the most painful austerities. All this, said he, goes to corroborate the idea of the mighty efficacy of the muntru." The valor of British arms, the glory of British possessions, and the duration of British rule, are grants at the will of a few *apparently* impotent Brahmuns, poor, dirty, cringing fellows, who will stoop to almost any servility to gain their bread!

The following declarations are found in the Hindoo sacred books, respecting the efficacy of the mystic verse, or the muntru: "Whoever shall repeat, day by day, for three years, without negligence, that sacred text, shall hereafter approach the divine essence, move as free as air, and assume an ethereal form." "By the sole repetition of this verse, a priest may indubitably obtain beatitude, let him perform or not perform any other religious act." "He who, seated opposite the sun, repeats this verse, is liberated from fear and sickness; misfortune ceases, and unlawful meats, drinks, intercourse and connections, become pure and lawful. Whoever in the morning repeats that invocation which ought not to be communicated to another, becomes prosperous, and obtains every temporal and spiritual advantage; and whoever repeats it continually every morning, noon and night, obtains the fruit of a hundred sacrifices, and passes over the mournful sea of mortality."

The communication of this wonder-working verse, together with the investiture of the sacred thread, is called the Savitree. Nothing can be more wonderful and absurd than the pretended efficacy of these ceremonies on the young Brahmun. He instantaneously becomes a "twice-born," or regenerate man, and is afterwards an object of veneration and worship. The sacred thread is always worn by the Brahmuns over the left shoulder, crossing over the breast to the right, and it is renewed annually.

The investiture is, properly speaking, a sacrament. Besides this, there are several others which may be named in the same connection. In enumerating the ceremonies, or, in other words, the sacraments of the Hindoo religion, I shall not go into detail.

Should I attempt this, I should subject myself to the charge of gross indelicacy. These ceremonies, which by some are said to be eighteen, by others sixteen, and by others twelve, are, according to the last estimate, the following: The sacrifice on or before conception; sacrifice on vitality in the fœtus; sacrifice in the fourth, sixth, or eighth month after pregnancy; giving the infant clarified butter out of a golden spoon at the cutting of the naval string; naming the child on the tenth, eleventh, twelfth, or hundred-and-first day; carrying him out to see the moon on the third lunar day of the third fortnight, or to see the sun in the third or fourth month; feeding him with rice on the sixth or eighth month, or when he has cut teeth; tonsure in the second or third year; investiture with the sacred string in the fifth, eighth, or sixteenth year, accompanied with the communication of the mystic verse; loosing the moonju (sacred thread) from the loins, in preparation for marriage; marriage and funeral ceremonies.

"The most intelligent natives are utterly at a loss to show the moral meaning of most of these ceremonies. They can point, however, to absurd promises connected with them. Many of them refer to such delicate subjects, that I cannot mention them here in any other way than by remarking, that the sex, form of the body, mental and moral constitution of the soul, the felicity or infelicity of the birth, the health, the possessions, the power, the enjoyment, the age, the employment, and even the future destiny of men, are made to depend on a few trifling and absurd ceremonies, performed generally by friends, without the slightest reference to the spirit with which they are conducted." *

The muntru, as might be supposed, is employed very extensively for the removing of pains, for the curing of diseases, the bite of venomous snakes, the sting of scorpions, &c. An instance occurred next door to our own family, too apposite to be omitted. As we were one day at dinner, intelligence came that Mr. B. was suffering very severely from the sting of a scorpion. Mr. A.

* Wilson's Exposure of Hindooism.

and myself hastened to his house, when we found him still in great distress, though partially relieved by holding the hand which had been stung in hot water. When the pain had subsided, and the confusion which had been occasioned by the event had given place to order, Mrs. B. was reminded, by seeing a tumbler containing a little water standing near her husband, of the interest which their pundit, in company with a Brahmun, whom he had called in as soon as Mr. B. began to feel the pain of the venomous reptile, had manifested to effect a speedy cure. He had proposed the application of the muntru; but Mr. B. not seeming to appreciate the kind offer, the benevolent-hearted Brahmun no doubt felt it to be his duty to the distressed man, although he might not *then* appreciate the act. Mrs. B. had seen the two Brahmuns performing some ceremony over that same glass of water, but took no further notice of the thing at the time. They said over the glass of water the magic-working *verse;* then placed it near Mr. B., watching the opportunity when it might be a kindness to attend to his call for water. The *muntrified* water was accordingly offered, and Mr. B., not knowing the design, and almost senseless from pain, gladly drunk it off. The pain being removed, we had our amusement at the joke, and the Brahmuns, no doubt, appropriated to themselves the more substantial satisfaction of having cured the bite of the venomous beast.

Amulets, likewise, are worn for the preventing and the curing of serpent bites. There is a fountain of water near Sattara, which has a high reputation for its efficacy in such cases; and there are also several temples famous for the performance of the same cures. I recollect stopping, about three years ago, in a small village a few miles north from Poona, where the people said the god of their village was much renowned for the curing of serpent bites. If a man or a beast were bitten by a serpent, they said they had only to bring him into the presence of their god and he was immediately cured. No one, they said, had ever died, if he could but be got to the temple. I did not much doubt this; for the chances were, nine out of ten, that if the person or the beast bitten did not die before he could be brought, by the slow process of the Hindoos' movements, to the temple, he would not die of the bite, either there or elsewhere.

It is generally to be remarked, that when the Hindoos apply to us for medicine in case of sickness, in preference to resorting to the muntru, or to some similar remedy, and are cured by our prescriptions, they seldom, if ever, attribute the cure to the medicine which they have taken, and which, under God, has afforded them relief, but to some ceremony which they have performed at the same time. Several instances have come to my knowledge, in which I have known persons to whom I have given medicine, and who were most evidently benefited by it, to get up a procession, employ a band of musicians, and celebrate the praises of their god for the cure. They would neither thank me for my trouble, nor acknowledge the kind hand of God in giving efficacy to the means which were used.

In few respects do the Hindoos suffer more on account of their superstitions than they do in reference to sickness and disease. Many a wretched creature spends "all his living" for the prescriptions of some quack, or drags out a miserable existence and dies in the midst of the charms and the enchantments of a Brahmun. The practice of medicine among the Hindoos is the most downright quackery. Many die without any medical attendance, and thousands are hastening to their graves by the bad treatment of their quacks. The number of blind, lame, maimed, leprous, and diseased, is astonishingly great in India; and no doubt one principal reason for this is the bad treatment, or the want of good treatment, in the original complaint.

An extract from the "Travels of Bernier," a French traveler, and for twelve years a resident at the court of Delhi, as physician to the Great Mogul, Aurungzebe, more than a century and a half ago, will very appropriately close this article. I quote this author with the more pleasure, because he enjoyed the opportunity of minutely and accurately observing, and had the ability to delineate the character and strange customs of the Hindoos in the remote period of his residence among them:

"The eclipse which I witnessed at Delhi seems also very remarkable, from the preposterous notions and superstitions of the Indians. At the time of its appearance, I ascended the terrace of my house, which was situate on the banks of the Jumna, whence I saw both sides of the river, to the extent of a full league, covered with Hindoos, who stood up to their middle in the river, gazing attentively at the sky, that they might plunge and wash themselves the moment the eclipse should commence. The little boys and girls were in a complete state of nudity; the men were likewise so, with the exception of a piece of linen girded about the loins; and the married women, together with the young females, who were not above six or seven years of age, were merely clad with a simple cloth. Persons of rank, such as rajahs, or Hindoo princes, and the shroffs, or money-changers, the bankers, jewelers, and other great merchants, were for the most part gone to the opposite side of the water with their families, and had there pitched tents, and fixed in the river certain kunnauts, (a kind of screen,) to perform their ceremonies, and conveniently to wash themselves along with their wives, so as not to be seen by any body. The idolaters no sooner perceived the commencement of the eclipse than they raised a tremendous shout, and at once plunged themselves into the water, I know not how often in succession; then standing up erect in the water, with their eyes and hands extended to heaven, muttering and praying with apparent devotion, and at intervals taking water in their hands, which they threw towards the sun, bowing their heads most profoundly, moving and turning their arms and hands, sometimes in one fashion, sometimes in another; thus continuing their plunges, their prayers and their fooleries, to the termination of the eclipse, at which time every one withdrew, throwing pieces of cocoa-nut some distance into the water, and bestowing alms on the Brahmuns or priests, who did not fail to be present at the ceremony. I remarked on coming out of the water that they all took new clothes, which were lying ready for them on the land, and that many, the most devout in appearance, left on the spot their old apparel for the Brahmuns. And thus did I view from my terrace this grand festival of the eclipse, which was in like manner celebrated on the Indus, on the Ganges, and on all the other rivers and reservoirs of India; but above all on that of the Zenaiser, where more than a hundred and fifty thousand persons from all parts of India were assembled, its waters on such days being reputed more holy and efficacious than on any other."

I might here quote from the same author several most horrid descriptions of the Suttee, as witnessed by himself. But as this heart-sickening practice has been so often described, and as it will soon, I trust, remain as a subject only to be referred to in history, I forbear.

CHAPTER XXI.

Hindoo Deities—Their Origin—Their Character—Shiva—The Lingam—Krishna—Indra.

VOLUMES might be written on this subject, which would neither repay the writer nor instruct or amuse the reader. I shall only add to what has already been inserted in the memoir on the general subject of the character of the gods, a few specimens, which will better illustrate their particular character. I have selected those deities which are in the highest repute among the people. And here I shall again quote the Abbe Dubois in his descriptions of Shiva, Lingam, Krishna, and Indra.

SHIVA.

"This god is generally represented under a terrible shape, to show, by a menacing exterior, the power which he possesses of destroying all things. To aggravate the horrors of his appearance, he is represented with his body all covered with ashes. His long hair is platted and curled in the most whimsical way. His eyes, unnaturally large, give him the appearance of being in a perpetual rage. Instead of jewels, they adorn his ears with great serpents. He holds in his hand a weapon called sula. I have sometimes seen idols of Shiva, of gigantic proportions, admirably contrived to inspire terror.

"The principal attribute of this god, as we have mentioned, is the power of universal destruction; although some authors also give him that of creation, in common with Brahmu.

"His fabulous history, like that of all the other Hindoo gods, is nothing but a tissue of absurd and extravagant adventures, invented, as it would seem, for the mere purpose of exhibiting the extremes of the two most powerful passions which tyrannize over man—luxury and ambition. They relate to the wars which he maintained against the giants; to his enmity and jealousy in opposition to the other gods; and, above all, to his infamous amours.

"It is related that, in one of his wars, being desirous of completing the destruction of the giants, and of obtaining possession of Tripura, the country which they inhabited, he cleft the world in twain, and took one-half of it for his amour. He made Brahmu the general of his army. The four vedas were his horses. Vishnoo was his arrow. The mountain Mandara Parvata was used for his bow, and a mighty serpent supplied the place of the string. Thus accoutred, the terrible Shiva led his army to the abode of the tyrants of the earth, took the three fortresses they had constructed, and demolished them in a moment. This, and other stories of Shiva, are given at great length in the Bhagawata.

"Shiva had great difficuly in obtaining a wife; but having made a long and austere penance at the mountain Parvata, that lofty eminence was so affected by it as to consent at last to give him his daughter in marriage."

This god, more generally known in Western India by the name of Mahadeo, (the great god,) is almost universally worshiped. The emblems of Shiva are the Lingam, which is described below, and the Nundee Byle (sacred bull). These—the former representing the male organs, and the latter being a representation of the Bull in Shiva's heaven, on which he is supposed to ride—are always placed in front of the god, and are objects of worship.

THE LINGAM.

"The abomination of the Lingam takes its origin from Shiva. This idol, which is spread all over India, is generally inclosed in a little box of silver, which all the votaries of that god wear suspended at their necks. It represents the sexual organs of man, sometimes alone, and sometimes accompanied. The long account given of the origin of this mystery in the Linga-purana, may be thus abbreviated:

"Shiva having one day, in presence of the seven famous penitents, exhibited himself in a state of nature, began to play several indecent vagaries before them. He persisted till the penitents, being no longer able to tolerate his indecency, imprecated their curse upon him. The denunciation took immediate effect, and from that moment Shiva was emasculated. Parvati, having heard of the misfortune of her husband, came to comfort him; but I have not the courage to return to the pages which contain the topics of consolation which she used, or the methods she employed to repair his loss.

"In the meantime, the penitents having more coolly considered the disproportion of the punishment to the offense, and wishing to make all the reparation in their power to the unhappy Shiva, decreed that all his worshipers should thenceforth address their prayers, adoration, and sacrifices to what the imprecation had deprived him of.

"Such is the infamous origin of the Lingam, which is not only openly represented in the temples, on the highways, and in other public situations, but is worn by the votaries of Shiva, as the most precious relic, hung at their necks, or fastened to their arms and hair, and receiving from them sacrifices and adoration."

The Lingam is the ordinary symbol of all the followers of Shiva. That sect spreads over the whole of India, but particularly in the west of the peninsula, where the Lingamites com pose; in many districts, the chief part of the population. The particular customs of the sect have been before noticed; the most remarkable of which are, their abstinence from whatever has had the principle of life, and the practice of interring their dead, in place of burning them, as most other Hindoos do.

"We know not to what excess the spirit of idolatry may lead the ignorant; but it is incredible, it even seems impossible, that the Lingam could have originated in the direct and literal worship of what it represents; but rather that it was an allegorical allusion, of a striking kind, to typify the procreative and regenerating powers of nature, by which all kinds of being are reproduced and maintained in the wide universe."

There is nothing in the whole system of Hindoo abominations so shockingly abominable as the worship of the Lingam. Not only is this vile representation worshiped in their public temples, not only hung about their necks in a silver case, or worn in the manner of ornaments on the arms, but the women may be seen of a morning on the sea shore, or near the river, where the people go to bathe, forming lingams of mud, and placing them in the sand, then bowing down and worshiping them.

KRISHNA.

"Besides the ten avataras of Vishnoo, the Hindoos recognize another, which is that of his change into the person of Krishna. This metamorphosis, and all the fables that accompany it, are contained in the book called Bhagawata, which is scarcely less famous than the Ramayana.

"Krishna, at his birth, was obliged to be concealed in order to avoid the attack of a giant who sought his life. He escaped his enemy under the disguise of a beggar. He was reared by persons of that caste, and soon exhibited marks of the most unbridled libertinism. Plunder and rape were familiar to him from his tender years. It was his chief pleasure to go every morning to the place where the women bathe, and, in concealment, to take advantage of their unguarded exposure. Then he rushed amongst them, took possession of their clothes, and gave loose to the indecencies of language and of gesture. He maintained sixteen wives, who had the title of queens, and sixteen thousand concubines. All these women bore children almost without number; but Krishna, fearing that they would league against him, and deprive him of his power, murdered them all. He had long and cruel wars with the giants, with various success. At last, his infamous conduct drew upon him the curse of a virtuous woman, the effects of which were soon apparent in a wound, of which he died."

It seems scarcely credible that a people should hold up to admiration so vile a character as that ascribed to Vishnoo, when regarded merely as a man; and yet more wonderful that they should ascribe such a character to a god, a popular object of their worship. They unblushingly descant on Radha, his principal mistress, of his sixteen wives, his sixteen thousand concubines, and the sixteen hundred milk-maids, with whom he used to dance and commit all manner of fooleries and abominations — how he stole a girl that was betrothed to another and married her. His tricks, jokes, thefts, and deceptions form the most common themes of amusement for story-tellers and loungers in every place of public resort.

And his worship is of a piece with his reputed character. Many of the rites performed at the poojas of Vishnoo are shockingly indecent. "These nightly poojas are connected with the greatest impurities." While the pooja is going on within the house or temple where celebrated, singing, dancing, reveling, and every kind of indecency may be witnessed outside. Youth dressed up to represent Vishnoo and his mistress Radha dance together. Thieves, gamblers, and and all sorts of vile characters are prominent actors in the scene. "It is amazing," says one long a resident in the country, "how much this scene looks like an English race-ground. Here I have seen gray-headed idolaters and mad youths dancing together, the old man lifting his withered arms in the dance and giving a kind of horror to the scene, which idolatry itself, united to the vivacity of youth, would scarcely be able to inspire."

Allusion to a single scene in the annual pooja performed in honor of this vile god, will suffice to give an idea of the character of the whole. Before the house where this pooja is to be celebrated, "a hole is cut in the ground, and filled with water to make mud. Into this, oil, sour milk, and tuamerick are thrown and mixed up with the mud. Afterwards, the crowd begin the play, by seizing first one person and then another, and rolling them in the mud; others roll themselves in it. To this is added music, dancing, singing of obscene songs, and all kinds of revelry." In this frenzied manner, dancing through the streets, they go to some pool of water, or to the river, wash themselves, and thus ends the festivity.

Such worship commends itself as at least suitable to the character of such a god, and appropriate to the character of his worshipers. We might select scenes in worship of the goddess Doorja quite as revolting. After feasting Brahmuns, and making offerings to the gods, and revelings and songs obscene, the pooja closes with a finale quite in keeping with what has gone before. "Many rich men engage a number of prostitutes to dance and sing before the idol. Their songs are exceedingly obscene, and their dances very indecent. The clothes of these women are so thin that they are almost the same as naked; the hair of some is thrown loose, hanging down to the waist; they are almost covered with ornaments. While these dances are going forward, the doors are shut to keep out the crowd. Europeans are carefully excluded."

INDRA OR DEVENDRA.

"This god, as we have before stated, is king of the inferior deities, who sojourn with him in his paridise called Swarga, or seat of sensual pleasures; for in this voluptuous abode no other are known. All who are admitted into it have a supply of women equal to the most inordinate concupiscence; and their vigor is so increased as to render them capable of perpetual fruition.

"It will be naturally supposed that the history of a god who rules over a society like this, must be disgusting, and filled with nauseous obscenity; and it certainly would be a cruel task to be obliged to submit to the perusal of what the Hindoo books contain on the subject of Devendra, and of the detestable gratifications in which the votaries who are admitted into his paradise indulge.

"It makes me blush even to allude to such obscenities; and the shame they occasion restrains me from entering into an enlarged detail of the fables relating to the divinities of India, which are replete with allusions equally abhorrent to modesty and reason."

Indra was once among the most celebrated of Hindoo deities, but at present he appears to be much out of vogue. His importance now is merely nominal. Similar revolutions no doubt are continually occurring in reference to other deities. Brahmu, once a superior deity, and still the first person of the Hindoo trinity, is now, through his indecent behavior, expelled from the society of gods. No temple is now built to him, no one pays him divine honors, no one repeats his name; while Hunumunt, a god of yesterday, a monkey, a general of a monkey army, is worshiped throughout all Western India, and very generally throughout the whole country. His temple is to be seen in every village, and his name is in every one's mouth. New gods are constantly springing into existence, which will in their turn throw the divine monkey in the back ground, and become the principal divinities of the country. Within the last two years, several instances of this nature have occurred to my own knowledge. A new divinity has within this period been created in Bombay, which promises fair to supplant some of his more honored predecessors. A rich native by the name of Darkjee Dadajee, built and adorned a superb temple, and set up in it a god, whom he called *Darkeshwar*—a name derived by substituting Eshwar, an appellation of the Supreme Being, for *jee*, the honorary post-fix of his own name. Thus, by joining to his own name the name of the Supreme, he has given to the world a new divinity.

I have already, in a preceding chapter of this volume, given an account of the creation of a god at Jalna. But for the timely interference of the English, the murderer of his mother might have become as renowned as Ram or Krishna. The monument of Col. Wallis, in the burying-ground at Seroor, is worshiped by the Hindoos, in the same way as the Mussulmans worship the tombs of their saints. A light is kept constantly burning before the tomb, and natives of all classes bow before the monument as they do at their temples. The colonel, who was much esteemed by the natives while living, is now enrolled in the canon of their saints, and not unlikely he will yet find a place in the Hindoo pantheon. Similar honors are likewise paid to the tomb of Lord Cornwallis, in Bombay.

I might here name another instance which fell under my own observation at Ahmednuggur. It is not very similar to the examples above, but not less indicative of the stupid propensity of the Hindoos to worship any thing but the true God which chance throws in their way. Captain M——, of the British army, at the death of his mistress, a Hindoo woman of low caste, indulged the extraordinary whim of erecting a tomb over her remains. The architect, a Hindoo, brought him the plan of a temple, which seems to have pleased him so well, that he allowed the architect to follow it. When it was completed, it was supplied with images by the same person. These were at once recognized by the people to be legitimate gods, and received their adoration. And had not the temple been abused, and the deities profaned, by some European soldiers, whose indignation seems to have been excited by the outrage which decency as well as Christianity received, this place would in all probability have become the resort of idolaters for many generations to come.

It would, perhaps, be impossible, were it of any utility, to trace out the origin of most of the Hindoo pantheon. There are legends extant, which profess to give the origin of some of these deities. But they are probably sheer fabrications. As a specimen, we may take the story of Gunputtee, a god almost universally worshiped. He is said to be the son of Pawuttee, the wife of Shiva, though not by natural birth. While Shiva was one day absent on a hunting excursion, his wife seized the opportunity of bathing in her own house. But fearing her husband might suddenly return, or she be otherwise interrupted, she desired to place a porter at her door. Having no one near, she hit on the following happy expedient: She took the dirt which she had washed from her person, and formed a sepoy. At her will the *clay* became animated, and was placed for a guard at the door. Shiva soon after returned; but on attempting to enter the house, he was repulsed by the unexpected sentinel. Enraged at this affront, he drew his sword, and severed the young man's head from his body, and went in pursuit of his wife. She, surprised and astonished at his appearance in spite of her porter, demanded how he had entered. He replied "that he had killed the impudent fellow at the door." She exclaimed, in an agony of grief, "You have killed my son, you have killed my son!" Her excessive grief softened the rage of the infuriated husband, and he promised to make her amends. He accordingly went out and decapitated an elephant, and placed the head on the trunk of the unfortunate son of Pawuttee, and restored him to life; and at the same time ordained that he should, under the name of Gunputtee, or Gunesh, (which means the lord of armies,) be worshiped throughout the whole world. He is, accordingly, every where adored, as the god of wisdom, and the remover of obstacles. Hence he is invoked at the commencement of every undertaking. He is represented as a short, fat man, with the head of an elephant.

I am aware this is not the only account which is given of the origin of Gunputtee. Like most things in Hindoo mythology, not only the traditions, but the written accounts contained in the shastras, are so contradictory, that it is impossible to know what the Hindoos themselves believe in reference to these matters. Concerning the deified man, Tukaram, of whom it is written that he was taken up bodily into heaven, there are, in different Hindoo books, no less than six different places specified from which he ascended, and these places far distant from each other.

The above account of Gunputtee was given to me by Babajee; and I have no doubt it is as worthy of credit as any account extant.

Since writing the above, I have read with much interest the "Travels of Bernier," a French physician, in Upper India. His remarks, or rather the opinions of others, which he details, respecting the Hindoo triad, are so curious, if not well founded, that I am induced to extract them. Speaking of the three principal deities of the Hindoos, he says: "With respect to these three beings, I have seen several European missionaries who were of opinion that the Hindoos have some conception of the mystery of the trinity, and said it was expressly declared in their books to consist of three persons in one God. For my own part, I have repeatedly argued with the pundits, but they explain themselves so ambiguously, that I have never been able exactly to comprehend their ideas on the subject. Nay, I have heard them declare that there are three most perfect beings whom they call Divityus, but without clearly explaining what they imply. In this they resemble the ancient idolaters, who never defined the words *genii* and *numina*, which is, I think, the same as Divityu among these idolaters. I have also conversed with the more learned pundits, who, it is true, assert that these three beings are really one and the same god, viewed under three different attributes, viz: the creator, the preserver, and the destroyer of all things. Moreover, I have discoursed with the reverend Father Kou, a German Jesuit, a missionary at Agra, well versed in the Sanskrit, who maintained that, not only did their books declare the existence of one God in three persons, but the incarnation nine times of the *second* person of their trinity. I will relate what a certain Carmelite of Shiraz communicated to the reverend father above mentioned, when traveling through that city on his way to Rome:

"'The Hindoos,' says he, 'do aver that the second person of the trinity was nine times incarnate, and that he delivered the world from its *manifold sin* and *iniquities*. But the eighth incarnation is the most celebrated, inasmuch as they entertain the notion that the world, being subjected to the *power of giants,* was *redeemed* by the *second* person, *incarnated,* and *born* of *a virgin,* at midnight; the *angels chanting praises* in the air, and the heavens showering down flowers during the whole night. This incarnate god slew first of all a *giant,* who flew in the *air,* and who was so hideous and monstrous as to obscure the sun, and, by his fall, to cause a convulsion of the earth, into which he penetrated so deep that he descended into *hell.* That this god incarnate being *wounded on the side,* in the first conflict with this giant, fell, but *by his fall routed,* and *put his foes to flight;* that after he had *raised himself* again, and *redeemed* the world, he ascended into heaven; and that, because of his wound, he is commonly denominated, *Wounded in the side.*' "

I must not here omit a reference to one other deity, whose office is of a more *practical* character than any yet named. I refer to *Vishwakurma,* called the son of Bruma, and the architect of the gods. He presides over all the arts and manufactures of mortals; and, consequently, occupies an important position in the regards of all laborers, artizans and business men, who worship this wonderful god at least once a year, that they may obtain success in their business.

Vishwakurma is painted white, with three eyes, holding a club in his right hand, wearing a crown upon his head, a necklace of gold, and rings on his wrists.

Each class of artificers performs this worship through some of the implements of its trade. The joiners, for example, set up their mallet, chisel, saw, and hatchet, as a representative of their god, painting them, putting flowers on them, then worshiping them with the usual ceremonies. Weavers make use of their shuttle, putting it into the hole in which they put their feet when they sit at their work. The weavers have one curious way of knowing whether their worship will be attended with much profit. They get a new piece of cloth, oil it well, and then set it on fire, holding it up with a stick. If it blaze briskly, they promise themselves much business. The barber worships his razor; the potter, the wheel on which he turns his pots; the mason, his trowel; the washerman, his beetle, or stamper, or his smoothing iron; the blacksmith, his hammer and bellows; the farmer, his plow. Women who spin, worship their wheel; the shoemaker bows down to his awl and his knife. Each craft chooses the principal tool or instrument with which he works, and makes it his god.

Thus, instead of raising their minds to the Great Source of all good, they are taught to worship the tools belonging to their trades as the cause of their temporal happiness. "They sacrifice to their net, and burn incense to their drag, because by these their portion is fat and their meat plenteous."

One class, at least the potters, abstain from labor a whole month previous to the time of performing this pooja.

The worship itself is not long; but the festival is prolonged by getting up as good a feast as their ability will allow, and inviting as many Brahmuns as they can feed. At the close, the worshipers make all kinds of merriment, going on the river in boats, singing songs, playing on different instruments of their rude music. Some of the better sort sit in companies, make and tell stories; others resort to houses of gambling and ill fame.

The mechanics and laborers regard their tools as the proper representative of the god which they now worship. They look upon him as the original inventor of all the mechanical arts.

I have alluded to the *origin* of Hindoo deities. I may speak of the origin of one other, which further exhibits the genius of that singular system of priestcraft. We meet in Hindoo mythology a god called Hurree Hurru. This is a union of Vishnoo and Shiva in one body. Hurree means black; Hurru, white. The image has four arms and two feet.

The origin of this image is as follows: Lukshmee and Dooga, wives of Vishnoo and Shiva, were once sitting together, when the former said that Vishnoo, her husband, was greater than Shiva. Dooga contended for the pre-eminence of *her* husband. Lukshmee contended that her husband must be greatest, because for the reason that Shiva had worshiped him. In the midst of this conversation, Vishnoo came up and overheard the words of Lukshmee. Shiva was already present. Vishnoo, therefore, to convince Lukshmee that both were equal, immediately entered the body of Shiva, and they became one. Hence the name Hurree Hurru. When Lukshmee saw this, she begun to pay honor to Vishnoo and Shiva, and to acknowledge that both were equal.

When the unsanctified mind of man once cuts loose from the simple teachings of revelation, and the heart wanders from the guidance of the blessed spirit, we need not wonder at any vagaries into which man may fall, in respect to religion. Its maythology will be peopled by gods to suit the fancy and inclinations of its votaries, and its modes of worship will correspond. Vain would be the attempt to enumerate, much more to describe, the many and various acts of worship and the no less singular devices by which this people hope to render propitious their gods, and accumulate merit which shall avail them hereafter. At one moment you see them walking for hours around a temple, or circumambulating the image within; next, the stupid devotee is drinking the water in which an image has been bathed or a Brahmun has dipped his foot. Another act of merit among the Hindoos is that of reading a book, not a word of which do they understand.

But among all the singular acts of religious merit performed by the Hindoos, that of teaching parrots to repeat the names of a god is the most singular. This device, it must be confessed, has not, in this our labor-saving age, received its due meed of praise. The Hindoos, even centuries before this new world had emerged from the great western ocean, had out-Yankeed the Yankees!

And this invention, too, has another merit. "It is considered as bringing great merit both to the teacher and his scholar." The parrot goes to heaven as well as his master. Numbers of Hindoos, particularly of a morning and evening, may be seen in the streets waking about with parrots in their hands, which repeat after them, Radha-Krishna, Radha-Krishna, Krishna,

Krishna, Radha, Radha, or Shiva Dooga, or Kalee Tararou, or the name of some other god. Six, twelve, or eighteen months are sometimes employed before the parrot has learned his lesson. The merit lies in having repeated the name of a god so great a number of times.

CHAPTER XXII.

Hindoo Atonements for Sin — Penances — Sacrifices — Mortifications — Bodily Inflictions — Transmigration and Punishment for Sin.

I HAVE incidentally mentioned many of the rites and observances by which the votaries of Brahmunism seek to atone for sin. They may be said to abound in atonements. Holy bathing, reading the shastras, pilgrimage, fasting, giving to the Brahmuns, feeding devotees, building temples, digging tanks, with the endless routine of sacrifices, penances, and religious austerities, which make up a very important part of Hindooism, have been alluded to above, and some of them have been briefly described. I shall here add a few anecdotes, which will serve to illustrate the subject better than could be done by a tedious exposition.

I have already referred to the wonderful effects of the *muntru* in procuring the pardon of sins of every description, and conferring final beatitude. The repetition of this mystic verse at once sets the offender free, and assures him all the blessedness of the upper world. But this wonder-working crucible, in which sins of the most obstinate cast are fused and poured out as a pure oblation to the gods, is kept exclusively in the hands of the Brahmuns. Whether the common people are not able to pay for the transmutation of their baser metals into gold, by the very easy method held out to them by this philosopher's stone, or whether they practically have misgivings in respect to its efficacy, I know not; but so it is, that they resort to an endless routine of atonements, some of them very expensive, and most of them attended with great bodily mortifications.

A man in Bombay has been performing a penance of a very painful character for sixteen years. He sits in a miserable shed, holding on his left hand a vessel of perhaps ten pounds' weight, which contains the sacred shrub. His whole arm is withered, and the finger nails have shot out like ram's horns, five or six inches in length. It is confidently affirmed by the people about him, that he never leaves this spot, nor gives himself a moment's respite from his burden, either night or day. But, notwithstanding the precautions which are used by those who are interested to keep up the farce, this man has been seen from his post, though not in such a manner as to forfeit, in the estimation of the people, his character for sanctity. He is considered the most holy man in Bombay—there is no doubt he is the proudest man there. In a village not two miles from Ahmednuggur, there is an ascetic, who is said to carry his austerities to still greater perfection. His friends assert of him that he has actually subsisted *without food* for several years.

In the same vicinity I knew a man, about two years ago, to sit in the jungle for three months, almost naked, during the coldest part of the year. He selected his station on a small knoll, at a considerable distance from any dwelling, drew a circle with his stick about eight feet in diameter, and seated himself in the centre. He sat there in a perfect state of listlessness, (or, as the people say, in a state of the most profound meditation and absorption in the divinity,) exposed by day to the heat of a tropical sun, and by night to the chilling winds. I have seen him late of an evening and early of a morning, and I am much inclined to believe that he seldom, if ever, overstepped the narrow limits of his circle. He subsisted on the free-will offerings of his visitors. They took this mode of making themselves partakers of the merit of his austerities. I will not disgust the reader by attempt-

21

ing to describe the appearance of this man, or of the place which he occupied, as I beheld it at the expiration of three months. The reader may fancy what must have been the accumulation of filth, both on his body and in the circle about him. The recollection of his unshorn and uncombed hair hanging about his shoulders, matted with oil and dirt; his tattered old cloth, glazed with the accumulated dirt of months, and perhaps years, and alive with vermin; and the place where he sat covered with the filth of three months' residence, revive in my mind, even at this distant period, the idea of one of the most disgusting scenes I ever beheld.

Passing a rod of iron through the tongue; hanging suspended by the legs from a tree over a slow burning fire, inhaling the fumes and sparks; leaping on a plank set full of sharpened plates of iron; lying on a bed made of a plank set with iron spikes; looking at the meridian sun for whole days in succession; supporting heavy objects with the extended arm, till it becomes withered; measuring a specified distance with one's length; swinging through the air suspended from a hook; and penances too numerous and too foolish to be enumerated, are resorted to as expedients for taking away sin, and accumulating righteousness.

An extraordinary instance of "measuring the length," fell under my observation about two years ago, on the road between Poona and Ahmednuggur. The subject of this penance was a poor, decrepit old man. When he had once prostrated himself, he had scarcely strength to raise his body from the ground. I watched him as he fell on his face, and marked with a short stick where he was to place his foot at the next prostration, and then struggled to rise; and never have I witnessed a scene which excited my pity more. Never have I beheld a more deluded Pagan, or one apparently more honest in his delusion. An old man, just tottering over his grave, a worshiper of idols for more than half a century, an inhabitant of a village where the light of the Sun of Righteousness had not yet gleamed; one who, seemingly, had never before heard the efficacy of the hollow rites of Brahmunism to take away sin called in question, now stood before me. He had settled all his worldly affairs, and come to the determination to measure his length to Pundurpoor by Poona, a distance of more than a hundred and fifty miles; and had now come seven miles, at the rate of one mile a day. I interrogated him as to the object of his pilgrimage, and the motives which led to it. I remonstrated with him on the folly, as well as the temerity of the undertaking, and offered him some money to defray his expenses if he would return to his family. I told him he could never expect to reach Pundurpoor now, at the commencement of the monsoon, and feeble as he was, but he must expect to die on the way. All this was in vain. He said it was the same to him, whether he lived or died. If he died, he said, it was in a good cause. I have never met with so striking an instance of delusion in India. It would be curious to analyze the motives which prompted to this undertaking. I can easily conceive that the poor, ignorant man, in the evening of life, began to feel some vague dissatisfaction with his past religious observances, and was at length led, either by his own reflections or by the advice of his gooroo, to adopt this plan to make up at once for all past delinquency, by a most severe penance. How far he believed such service would be acceptable with God, it is impossible to say. Still, I can suppose him convinced that he was performing a service pleasing to God, and really beneficial to himself.

Hook-swinging I mentioned as another expedient. While on a tour in the Deckan, I witnessed the following instance of this penance. I arrived in the village of S—— about eight in the morning. When I had breakfasted, and recovered a little from the fatigue of a hot morning's ride, I sought an interview with the people; but, to my no small disappointment, I found that the villagers were either absent or in such a state of excitement as to preclude all hope of being able to gain their attention that day. On inquiring the cause, I was informed that there was to be a *buggard* (hook-swinging) that day, in the vicinity; and all the people were, on that account, half infatuated. Babajee and myself at once determined to witness the scene, and persuade the devotee, if possible, from swinging; or, at least, to point out to the multitude a more excellent way. We accordingly set off. The post was erected on the top of an oval hill, near the temple of Kundooba, about two miles from the village. Our road lay over an extensive plain, which was covered with a moving mass of people, winding their way, from every direction, towards the hill. There were not less than a dozen villages within sight from the place of exhibition. From all these, and others at a greater distance, the inhabitants, men, women, and children, emerged in swarms, until every road and every by-way were filled with the passing multitude, and the whole plain seemed moving towards the hill in its centre. One feeling seemed to pervade every heart. It was the feeling which predominates with the rabble at a fair in England, or with the heterogeneous mass seen at the grog-shops and about the carts at a general muster in America. Amusement, frivolity, and dissipation are the apparent objects of pursuit. Not the semblance of devotional feeling, not the decency of religious propriety, is any where to be discovered.

We ascended the hill. It was already literally covered with people. A procession was at that moment moving slowly about the temple. A band of native musicians preceded them with the loud tomtom, and other rude minstrelsy, which grated no less horribly on the ear. Next followed the devotee who was about to swing. He was naked, save a stripe about his loins. About his neck was a garland of flowers; his body, face, arms, and hair were besmeared with the sacred powder, and in his hand he carried a poignard, on the end of which was fixed a green lime. Over his head was spread a coarse canopy, supported by four men. The procession came around to the front of the temple, where they halted, and the devotee prostrated himself before the god, in honor of whom he was about to swing. Thence they proceeded to the post, which had been erected twenty yards in front of the temple. After circumambulating this, the devotee was presented to the officiating person, to receive the hooks in his back. We embraced this opportunity of remonstrating with the deluded man, and of addressing the no less infatuated multitude. All availed nothing towards dissuading them from the performance of the disgusting rite. They soon became impatient, and we found it prudent to desist. The officiator (not a Brahmun) then presented the hooks, and an instrument for piercing the skin and flesh, for their more easy insertion. He first demanded and received some pice from the devotee, as his fee; then, bringing the ear of the man to his mouth, he gave a most terrific scream — enough to stun the poor fellow; and, after performing some other trifling ceremonies, he took up some dust from the ground, directly behind the devotee, and marked the parts of the small of the back where the hooks were to be inserted. The flesh was cut and the hooks inserted. One end of the traverse beam, which turns on a pivot, and from which a rope is suspended, was brought down, and the hooks made fast to the rope. The beam was then brought to a level, by means of a rope suspended from the other extremity, which consequently brought the devotee into the air, and set swinging by persons employed for the purpose. With one hand he supported his head and the upper part of the body in an upright posture, by holding fast to his cloth, which had been suspended before him for this purpose from the traverse beam, and with the other hand he scattered spices, nuts, and flowers to the multitude, who joined with him in shouts of exultation.

After swinging till he appeared to be exhausted, he was let down. And then ensued a ridiculous scene. He had no sooner reached the ground than the coolies who swung him made a very hasty and rather a violent demand on him for their *pay*. Whether their demands were exorbitant, or whether the devotee thought to make a cheap business of his penance, I know not. The crowd at this moment became so great as to press me beyond hearing distance. Perhaps the poor fellows knew the difficulty of collecting debts for such service, and therefore embraced the present as a favorable opportunity. Be this as it may, a tumult and confusion ensued. The vociferation of a dozen voices at once, concentrated for the first time the attention of the multitude to the spot of exhibition. It all ended in words, and a payment of the price. This being arranged, the man retired with his friends to receive their congratulations. After a few moments I followed him. He swung in fulfillment of a vow made when dangerously ill. But a very small part of the vast multitude manifested the least interest in the swinging. They were buying and selling, eating, drinking, smoking, chewing the betel-nut, laughing, talking, singing, and playing. Every nook and corner contained some one who sold fruit, sweetmeats, pan-suparee, and the like. Every one kept the holiday in as merry a way as he could. If viewed as a carousal, it was barbarous; if viewed as a religious act, it was disgusting and abhorrent to every right feeling of the human heart.

Other atonements, or expedients for gaining merit, relate to practices of impurity, which belong peculiarly to the religious code of the Hindoos. A Hindoo, who is not himself a proselyte to these particular opinions, might not say that *he* should, under present circumstances, be benefited, or be justified, in resorting to such atonement, as I have mentioned; while at the same time he would contend that these practices are not only lawful, but truly beneficial to those who, in conformity to their religious creed, addict themselves to them. It is taught in the Pooranus and Tuntrus, and known to be acknowledged and practiced by the Hindoos, that, in the presence of some of the most celebrated idols—among which is Juggunath—"all distinctions of sex and caste are abolished, and that men may, in this situation, gratify their evil lusts with impunity; and that they permit men to violate the laws of chastity under the pretence of blunting the passions."* The Abbe Dubois mentions several temples, where

* Wilson's Exposure of Hindooism.

public prostitution before the idol is practiced as the most effectual method of propitiating the deity.

Too much has, perhaps, already been said on this disgusting subject. The reader will excuse me, for it is the *atonement* by which every system of salvation must be judged, and by which it must stand or fall. And in thus exhibiting the Hindoo doctrines of atonement for sin, I effectually introduce the reader into the very spirit and essence of Hindooism.

But the Brahmuns shall be allowed to speak for themselves, that I may escape the imputation of abuse or misrepresentation. The following are a few specimens of the daily prayers used by the Brahmuns. "These," says a writer in the Calcutta Christian Observer, "were compiled by certain pundits from the Pooranus and other shastras, held sacred by the Hindoos. The character of these petitions, the objects to whom they are addressed, and the expected efficacy of such services, form a very correct criterion by which we may judge of the method of atonement and forgiveness of sins which is inculcated among the Hindoos.

PRAYER TO BE USED WHEN BATHING.

"O Jahnavi! that didst issue from the feet of Vishnoo in three channels, and whose streams are sacred, *remove my sin.*

"I am sin, I commit sin, my nature is sinful, I am conceived in sin. O Hurree! do thou deliver me from sin."

PRAYER AFTER BATHING.

"Reverence to Gunga, (Ganges,) O goddess! queen of all the goddesses. O Bhagawata! O Gunga! thou art the savior of the three worlds, the cause of motion in the sea; thou dwellest in the head of the Sunkar; O thou pure being, *may my mind repose at thy feet.*"

"O Bhagnathi! source of joy, O mother! thy praise is recorded in the Negama shastras. I cannot utter thy praise; *deliver me from my ignorance.* O Gunga! pure as the cold moon and fair as the pearl are thy waters. *Remove far from me the weight of my sin,* and convey me across the ocean of this world."

"Such is the purity of thy waters, that those who drink thereof will be promoted. O mother! those who trust in thee *shall not see death.*"

"O Jahnavi! thou deliverest from hell: thou destroyest sin. Thy waters are mighty; thy form is radiant, O Guuga! O victorious Jahnavi! O sacred river! thou glancest with an eye of pity on the devoted worshipers. The pearl in the crown of Hurree reflects its lustre on thy feet. Thou bestowest sons and conferrest prosperity on those who seek thee. O destroy within me disease, grief, sin, anger, and all other evils. Thou art the essence of three worlds! thou surroundest the world as a garland. They who in their heart put their trust in thee, will always enjoy bliss and freedom. The words of these prayers impart bliss to the soul, they drop as honey from the honeycomb."

PRAISE TO GUNGA.

"Gunga effectually removes sin, quickly destroys sorrows, gives joy and freedom, and is our chief refuge. Having repeated this, the worshiper bows to the river."

"They who repeat the names of Gunga within a hundred yojunas (900 miles), obtain emancipation and pardon of all their sins, together with admission into the heaven of vaicantu."

Here follow many others of similar import. But it is useless to transcribe them. The ground of their atonement is *works.* The river Gunga, or any other imaginary god or goddess, grants absolution to all who repeat his names.

Works of supererogation likewise are allowed a place in the expiatory system of the Brahmun. By works, a man may not only atone for his own sins, and secure a sufficiency of righteousness for himself, but he may accumulate a stock of merit, which may, if well paid for, be transferred to others.

I have heard different natives repeat the following anecdote of Bajee Row, late Peshwa at Poona. As it furnishes an extraordinary example of this kind of traffic, I will relate it. The Peshwa was a very profligate character. Business and dissipation gave him no time, if ever he had the inclination, to go through the tedious routine of austerities which the most liberal Brahmun would have pronounced necessary to the expiation of such a man's sins. On a certain occasion, the Peshwa adopted a summary way of liquidating the whole debt at once, and still reserving in store a stock for future emergencies. It was reported to him that a devotee of very extraordinary sanctity had come to Poona, and was there performing marvelous acts of mortification. Bajee Row immediately requested an interview with the reputed saint, and soon struck a bargain for his whole stock of righteousness, for which he gave the moderate sum of 25,000 rupees.

This same Bajee Row was without issue. This, with a common Hindoo, is a subject of endless regret; but with the usurper of the throne of the Deckan, it was infinitely more lamented. Offerings had been made to every idol famed for remedying such calamities, pilgrimages performed, the muntru tried, and all the ordinary expedients resorted to, but in vain. When all devices had failed, when Brahminical ingenuity was almost exhausted, one, more sagacious than his fellows, declared to the Peshwa that the circumambulating of two mountains, not a great distance from Poona, by a great number of Brahmuns, would be an undertaking of extraordinary merit, and in all probability would prove efficacious in the case in question. A great number of Brahmuns, some hundreds it is said, were accordingly called, their labor defined, their wages appointed them, and they were sent forth to their work. One of these mountains was eighteen miles in circumference, and the other nine. Each Brahmun was to make one circuit around his respective mountain daily. They continued their task for a long time, received their pay, but the Peshwa remained childless. There was some defect in the proceedings. Probably the Brahmuns had not all been duly purified, or the Peshwa had no faith. No one, I believe, ever doubted the efficacy of the transaction, or its adaptation to accomplish the desired end.

The above story was related to me by Babajee, who was himself one of the Brahmuns employed to circumambulate the mountains.

Such acts and penances are performed at the instigation of the Brahmuns; and I need not say the object of them is their own emolument. Nor are these *modest* priests satisfied to risk the enforcing of their pretended claims on the fragile foundation of temporal penalties and bodily inflictions. Future rewards and punishments are almost entirely made to depend on the observance or the non-observance of Brahminical injunctions. A falsehood told for the benefit of a Brahmun is meritorious; to injure a Brahmun in any way, is one of the most heinous sins. I have selected the following as a specimen of the kind and the degree of punishment which is threatened on the poor Hindoo for comparatively trivial offenses, when committed against a Brahmun — offenses which, in other cases, are, in this country, considered perfectly justifiable:

"An author in a Hindoo book (I quote the Abbe Dubois) declares, among other things, that he who breaks his word with a Brahmun, or occasions him any detriment, directly or indirectly, in his temporal concerns, will be condemned in his second birth to become a devil. He will not be permitted to dwell on the earth or live in the air; but will be obliged to make his abode in a thick forest, among the branches of a bushy tree, where he shall never cease to groan by night and day, cursing his unhappy lot, and deprived of all aliment but stinking toddy, mixed with the slaver of a dog, which he shall drink out of the skull of a death's head.

"It is in this way that offenses, imaginary or of small account, are menaced with endless punishment after death, by the direction of the popular faith; while adulterers, perjurers, and robbers, and other real offenders, are absolved by the Brahmuns of their actual crimes, for selfish objects, and assured of a recompense after death, which should pertain exclusively to virtue."

CHAPTER XXIII.

Religious Orders—Ascetics—Mendicants—Beggars—Their Character and mode of Life—Their Influence over the People.

The reader of foreign intelligence, I am well aware, often feels a difficulty arising from the use of unknown terms, which are sometimes carelessly and sometimes unavoidably used by the writer. He speaks of a puntojee, a pundit, a bungalow, and the like, as familiarly as a writer at home would use the corresponding terms, a teacher of languages, a schoolmaster, and a house; while many of his readers are completely non-plussed at these *sonorous* words. I do not propose here to supply the reader with a glossary of terms in general; but having before me a paper prepared by a learned Brahmun, which contains an explanation of the several appellations, practices, and employments of the different orders of Hindoo devotees and ascetics, I shall translate it for his benefit, giving him timely notice not to proceed, unless he have the interest or curiosity to bear with a few more hard names. We hear of yoogees, gosawees, byragees, etc., and, for the want of some distinctive idea, we get no idea at all of this important and extensive class of Hindoos. The majority of our readers may wish only to know that they are a kind of bigot, or hermit, or hypocrite; while others, who regard the Hindoos as they really are, a large and interesting portion of the human family—an open volume, from which he may read human nature in its most deplorable form—and those who regard Brahmunism as the most extraordinary monument of priestcraft, of wordly wisdom, and human folly which the world ever witnessed, will be happy to avail themselves of any farther means of becoming acquainted with so essential a part of Hindoo mythology.

Ascetics are divided into different orders, says the Brahmun, according to their caste. I shall here mention their respective castes, offices, habits, and modes of life. The first four classes are of the Brahmun caste. The life of a Brahmun is divided into five parts: First, childhood, or the period till the investiture with the sacred thread. This period may, on an average, be reckoned at about twelve years. Second, Brumuchuree, another period of twelve years from the investiture. This is the period for study, and the acquisition of a knowledge of the shastras. During this period, the young Brahmun is required *sacredly to abstain from women*, to give himself exclusively to the study of the vedas, and *to speak the truth*. A Brumuchuree is also a Brahmun, who religiously abstains (professes to abstain) from sexual commerce through life.

The next Brahminical grade is the Gruhusth. The Brahmun may now marry and look after his domestic affairs, always remaining intent, however, on the worship of the gods, and inviolably speaking the truth. This period continues twelve years. Then follows the Wanprusth, when the Brahmun must abandon his house, his wife, and family, and betake himself to the jungle, absorb himself in contemplation, exist on roots, nuts, and wild fruits, and continually worship God. The principal thing to be obtained now, is the subjugation of the passions. This is done by the practice of the "six duties," viz: shumu, (apathy, stoicism;) dumu, (government of senses and animal appetites;) tupu, (the practice of mortification and austerities;) tiliksha, (patience, sufferance, endurance of the good and evil of natural life;) shudda, (reverential faith in the shastras;) and summadhan, (restraining the mind from external objects, and fixing it steadfastly in contemplation.)

These six duties are doubtless intended as counterparts to six radical evils of human nature, which every Brahmun will tell you "flesh is heir to," viz: kam, krodh, lobh, mohu, mudu, mutsur, or lust, anger, covetousness, the pride of life, intoxication, and envy. We are not told by the sages of India how the Brahmun, at this period, is to dispose of his wife and family. Every Brahmun is bound by his religion to pursue this course. But, happily for their families and for society, this injunction, like most of the precepts of their sacred books, is unheeded. All these things yield to inclination and circumstances.

The last stage of the Brahmun's life is that of the *sunyasee.* He is now to make a final renunciation of all worldly hopes, put on the red-ochre colored clothes, take his staff and his earthen cup, and wander about as a mendicant, devoting himself wholly and constantly to Narayun (a name of Vishnoo). He must have no fixed habitation, pursue no occupation, nor receive the necessary supplies of food and clothing in any particular place, nor remain constantly in any one village. He must now be entirely devoted to the performance of the "six duties."

Every Brahmun is supposed to be consecrated to religion, and nominally belongs to one of the above-mentioned orders, according to his age; while, at the same time, those who wish to devote themselves to another order, either for life or for a definite period, are at liberty to do so. Accordingly, there are Brahmuns among the Gosawees and other orders of ascetics, as will be seen below.

Gosawees, among Brahmuns, are those who gain their livelihood by chanting the names and celebrating the praises of Hurree (Vishnoo); who, with repentance for sin, remain constant in the worship of the deity, and who regard not the favor of man. But Gosawees, among Shoodras, are somewhat different. They are worshipers of Shiva, and dress in dirty ochre-colored clothes, or go naked. They abandon their homes and families, go from country to country, visit every holy place and sacred stream, and profess to devote themselves wholly to the service of their god. Some of these live on charity, and lead a life of great austerity, while others enjoy the revenue of certain towns and villages, which have been made over to them on account of their reputed sanctity, and which descend from father to son by virtue of inheritance. Shoodra Gosawees are divided into a great number of classes, as the Giree, the Poree, the Bharutee, the Gorkhpuntee, &c., which differ only in some minor peculiarity of dress or mode of life. The general characteristics of a Gosawee are the ochre-colored dress, the long, uncombed, dirty, matted hair, the staff or bar of iron set round with rings, and the earthen or metallic vessel.

Byragees are worshipers of Vishnoo. They must renounce lust, anger, and hope, wander about, sometimes naked, sometimes clad, and visit holy places and sacred streams. They subsist by begging, and professedly continue constant in the worship of the deity. Some of them enjoy the revenue of villages, given as above mentioned, and some are Yogees.

Yogees are those who, suspending the breath, abstracting the mind, and restraining all natural desires, absorb themselves in Brahmu, or Universal Being; and by destroying all human feelings and desires, by abstract meditation and self-forgetfulness, they seek absorption in the divine nature. The merit of all performances depends very much on the attitudes and postures in which the devotee stands or sits. Of these, no less than eighty-four are mentioned.

Jungums are followers of Shiva, and worshipers of the Lingam. They may be regarded as the Gooroos of the Lingites, and are said to be in a state of hostility to all castes, but especially hate the Brahmuns. They do not wear the tuft, or lock of hair on the top of the head, which is common to the Hindoos; and, Shiva excepted, they acknowledge no deity. They live by begging, and carry in their hands a metallic image of the bull, which possesses the wonderful property of deciphering men's destinies.

Duwures are the worshipers of Bhyruwu, and mendicants who live on charity, and dance and carouse in honor of their deity.

Gondhulees, who devote themselves to the worship of the goddess, which they perform by the observance of tumultuous festivities. They beg in the name and for the honor of the goddess.

Nonukuputee, ascetics devoid of hope and desire; morose beggars, who go about in the garb of a Fakir, (Mohammedan saint,) repeating the names of the gods. They carry in their hands the tipuree, (a small vessel,) which they present from house to house, and from shop to shop, to receive pice.

Bootyas—devotees of the goddess of Bhuwanee. They go about begging, decorated with shells, their clothes soiled with oil, and a torch in their hand.

Bhoopees are worshipers of the goddess, who make a vow to subsist on the eleemosynary contributions which are voluntarily made to them. But they must not beg.

Wangees are devotees of Khundoba, and do not regard caste. They carry about tumeric powder in the skin of the wag, (tiger,) which they give to the people, declaring it to be a mark of the divine favor. They worship Khundoba, and ask alms in the name of Mullaree, a form of Khundoba. Among these devotees are to be classed those females who, when young, are devoted by their parents to this god; and such, also, as in after life leave their husbands, and give themselves up to him. Such are the women at Jejury, who have been mentioned under the head of holy places. They are called Bhaweenee, from the god Bhawu, Faith! And if I may judge from the Hindoo proverb, they are the most *common prostitutes* in the country. Of a thing which is so common that any one may take it up and use it without asking the consent of the owner, the Hindoos say, "*It is Bhaweeneecha kasota*," that is, common as the *lower garment* of the Bhaween. These women, after quitting their husbands, are dedicated to the god, by pouring oil over their heads, from the lamp before the idol.

Gooruwus are worshipers of Shiva or Hunooman, who do the service of the temple; such as sweeping it, attending on the idol, etc. They live on offerings made to the god. In small villages they are usually Shoodras; in towns, Brahmuns.

Some persons become ascetics by inheritance, and, in consequence, enjoy cetain revenues; some become such through necessity; others, on account of their extraordinary sanctity and abstraction from the world, as they fain would have it; others, on account of a vow, devote themselves to a religious life. Most of them pretend to be gooroos, religious teachers. The Hindoos entertain the notion, not peculiar to them, however, that religion is some wild vagary, attainable only by priests and devotees, but not practicable for people in common life and engaged in the business of the world. I have often heard Brahmuns ask Babajee how it was that he professed to be a worshiper of the invisible God, and to be possessed of a knowledge of divine things, and still he lived in his house, enjoyed the comforts of domestic life, and wore the turban and the common dress. "If you will be religious," said they, "*take your staff and your gourd-shell*, and put on the devotee's garb."

The following quotations from Dow's History of Hindoostan will form a good practical supplement to this article. While they impart a few additional facts, they will also illustrate and corroborate what I have already said:

"The Sunyasees," by which he denominates devotees in general, "are a set of mendicant philosophers, commonly known by the name of Fakirs, which literally signifies, poor people. These idle and pretended devotees assemble sometimes in armies of ten or twelve thousand, and, under pretense of making pilgrimages to certain temples, lay whole countries under contribution. These saints wear no clothes, are generally robust, and convert the wives of the less holy part of mankind to their own use, upon their religious progresses. They admit any man of parts into their number, and they take great care to instruct their disciples in every branch of knowledge, to make the order the more revered among the vulgar.

"When this naked army of robust saints direct their march to any temple, the men of the province through which their road lies very often fly before them, notwithstanding the sanctified character of the Fakirs. But the women are, in general, more resolute, and not only remain in their dwellings, but apply frequently for the prayers of these holy persons, which are found to be most effectual in case of sterility. When a Fakir is at prayers with the lady of the house, he leaves either his slipper or his staff at the door, which, if seen by the husband, effectually prevents him from disturbing their devotion. But should he be so unfortunate as not to mind these signals, a sound drubbing is the inevitable consequence of his intrusion.

"Though the Fakirs enforce with their arms that reverence which the people of Hindoostan have, naturally, for their order, they inflict voluntary penances of a very extraordinary kind on themselves to gain more respect. These fellows sometimes hold up one arm, in a fixed position, till it becomes stiff, and remains in that situation during the rest of their lives. Some clench their fists very hard, and keep them so till their nails grow into their palms, and appear through the back of their hands. Others turn their faces over their shoulder, and keep them in that situation till they fix for ever their heads looking backwards. Many turn their eyes to the point of their nose, till they have lost the power of looking in any other direction. These last pretend to see what they call the sacred fire; which vision, no doubt, proceeds from some disorder arising from the distortion of the optic nerve.

"Some of these men are really what they seem, enthusiasts; but others put on the character of sanctity as a cloak for their pleasures [and their crimes]. But what actually makes them a public nuisance, and the aversion of poor husbands, is, that the women think they derive some holiness to themselves from an intimacy with a Fakir.

"Many other foolish customs besides those we have mentioned, are peculiar to these religious mendicants. But enthusiastic penances are not confined to them alone. Some of the vulgar, on the fast of *Opposs*, suspend themselves on iron hooks, by the flesh of the shoulder blade, to the end of the beam. The beam turns round with great velocity upon a pivot, on the head of the pole. The enthusiast not only seems insensible of pain, but very often blows a trumpet, as he is whirled above, and at certain intervals sings a song to the gaping multitude below, who very much admire his fortitude and devotion. This ridiculous custom is kept up to commemorate the sufferings of a martyr, who was in that manner tortured for his faith."

In another part of the same history, the author gives a most ludicrous account of an army of these Fakirs, headed by an old woman, attacking the great Mogul, at Delhi. "The security," says he, "which Aurungzebe had acquired by the defeat of so many formidable rivals, was disturbed from a quarter which added ridicule to danger. In the territory of the prince of Marwar, near the city of Nuggur, there lived an old woman who had arrived at the eightieth year of her age. She possessed a considerable hereditary estate, and had accumulated by penury a great sum of money. Being seized with a fit of enthusiasm, she became all of a sudden prodigal of her wealth. Fakirs and sturdy beggars, under a pretense of religion, to the number of five thousand, gathered around her castle, and received her bounty. These vagabonds, not satisfied with what the old woman bestowed in charity, armed themselves, and, making predatory excursions into the country, returned with spoil to the house of their patroness, where they mixed intemperance and riot with devotion. The people, oppressed by these holy robbers, rose upon them, but were defeated with great slaughter.

"Repeated disasters of the same kind were at last attributed to the power of enchantment. The ridiculous opinion gaining ground, fear became predominant in the opponents of the Fakirs. The banditti, acquiring confidence from their success, burned and destroyed the country for many leagues, and surrounded the castle of the pretended enchantress with a desert. The raja marched against them with his native troops, but was defeated; the collectors of the imperial revenue attacked them, but they were forced to give way. A report prevailed, and was eagerly believed by the multitude, that, on a certain day of the moon, the old lady used to cook, in the skull of an enemy, a mess composed of owls, bats, snakes, lizards, human flesh, and other horrid ingredients, which she distributed to her followers. The abominable meal, it was believed by the rabble, had the surprising effect of not only rendering them void of all fear themselves, and inspiring their enemies with terror, but even of making them invisible in the hour of battle when they dealt their deadly blows around.

"Their numbers being now increased to twenty thousand, this motley army, with the old woman at their head, directed their march toward the capital. Bistumia (for this was her name) was a commander full of cruelty. She covered her route with murder and devastation; and had her rear in the smoke of burning villages and towns. Having advanced to Narnoul, about five days' journey from Agra, the collector of the revenue attacked her with a force, and was totally defeated. The affair had now become serious, and commanded the attention of the emperor. He found that the minds of the soldiers were tainted with the prejudices of the people, and he thought it necessary to combat Bistumia with weapons like her own. The emperor, in the presence of the army, delivered to his general billets written with his own hand, which were *said* to contain *magical enchantments.* His reputation for sanctity was, at least, equal to that of Bistumia; and he ordered a billet to be carried on the point of a spear before each squadron, which, the soldiers were made to believe, would counteract the enchantment of the enemy. The credulity which induced them to dread the witchcraft of the old woman gave them confidence in the pretended charm of Aurungzebe.

"The Fakirs, after their victory at Narnoul, thought of nothing but the empire for their aged leader. Having rioted on the country for several days, they solemnly raised Bistumia to the throne, which gave them an excuse for festivity. In the midst of their intemperate joy, Sujait, the imperial general, made his appearace. They fought with the fury of fanatics; but when the idea of supernatural aid was dispelled from the minds of the imperialists, the Fakirs were not a match for their swords. It was not a battle, but a confused carnage—a few owed their lives to the mercy of Sujait; the rest met the death which they deserved. Aurungzebe, when he received Sujait after his victory, could not help smiling at the ridicule thrown on his arms by the opposition of an old woman at the head of a naked army of mendicants."

And here I must again quote Bernier. His description of Yogees is much to the life, and possesses the further merit of exhibiting the manners of this class of people as they were nearly two centuries ago, and as they now are, that I do not hesitate to extend this article a few paragraphs.

"Among the infinity and great diversity of devotees of India, there are numbers who inhabit a kind of convent, in which there are superiors, and where they make vows of chastity, poverty and obedience, and who lead so strange a life, that I know not whether you will be inclined to believe it. These are commonly distinguished by the appellation of Yogees; a great number of whom are to be seen parading about, or sitting almost naked, or lying down night and day on ashes, and generally under the branches of large trees, which are on the borders of tanks or reservoirs, or else in the galleries which surround the temples. Some have their hair hanging to their very knees, twisted or plaited together like the hair of our spaniels. There is no one of the fairies of hell so horrible to behold as these people all bare, with their black skin, long hair, spindle arms, and in the posture I have mentioned, with their immense crooked nails.

"I have often met in the country, chiefly in the territories of the rajas, whole bands of these Fakirs in a complete state of nudity, and quite appalling to the sight. Some hold their arms extended; others had their hideous hair hanging in disorder about them, or else bound round their heads; some had a kind of Herculean club in their hands; others had large, dry, stiff tigers' skins over their shoulders. Thus I beheld them pass, with the most shameless audacity, through the midst of the village. I could not but admire the cool indifference with which the men, women and children regarded them: with no other emotion than when so many hermits pass through the streets; and how devoutly the women presented to them alms, considering them, no doubt, in the light of holy personages, and wiser and superior to the rest of mankind.

"I saw, not very long ago, a famous one at Delhi, called Sarmet, who went naked through the streets, and who had rather suffer his neck to be severed from his body than permit himself to be clothed, what promises or threats soever the Emperor Aurungzebe might make him.

"I had seen several, who, through devotion, went long pilgrimages, not only altogether bare, but loaded with large iron chains, similar to those, though not so heavy, which are put about the feet of elephants; others who, from a particular vow, stood for the space of seven or eight days successively erect on their legs, which became, in consequence, swollen as large as their thigh; others, again, stood for whole hours on their heads, without wavering, with their heads down and their feet upward, and so many other constrained and extravagant postures, that we have no tumblers who could imitate them in their feats of activity; and all this, it seems, through devotion and through motives of religion, of which, however, one cannot discover even the bare resemblance.

"All these extraordinary and novel exhibitions so much amazed me, that I was in a complete dilemma what to think of them. Sometimes I considered them as the remains, or rather as the authors, of that ancient and infamous sect of cynics; but I could discern nothing in them but brutality and ignorance; and they appeared to me so many automata, rather than rational creatures. At another time I regarded them as enthusiasts, though I could not perceive a shadow of true piety in all their actions. Sometimes I thought that the idle, lazy and independent life of a beggar might have in it something attractive. Sometimes I imagined that the vanity which is to be found in every condition of life, and which is perceptible as well under the patched mantle of a Diogenes as under the comely garment of Plato, might be the motive that actuated these machines; and, then, reflecting on the miserable, austere life they lead, they set at defiance all my conjectures.

"Among those that I have mentioned, there are some who are believed to be true saints, illuminated, perfect Yogees—that is, perfectly united to God. These are men who have forsaken their relations and the concerns of this life, and sequester themselves in some remote spot or forest, like hermits, without ever approaching the city. If any food is conveyed to them, they receive it; if not, it is believed they can exist without, and subsist by the special grace of God, in perpetual fasting and prayer, and absorption in profound meditation. I say absorption; for they carry this meditation to such an extreme as to pass whole hours in it, beholding all the time (as they affirm) God himself, like an effulgent, ineffable light, with an inexpressible joy and satisfaction, associated with an utter contempt and abandonment of the world.

"This is not all: when two or more Yogees of eminence happen to meet, and you can manage to pique them on the superiority of their skill, they perform such wonderful feats in emulation of each other, that I know not if Simon Magus could excel them. They divine our thoughts; cause the branch of a tree to blossom and bear fruit in the space of an hour; hatch eggs in their bosom in less than a quarter of an hour; and produce whatever birds you demand, which are made to fly *instanter* about the chamber, and numerous other such prodigies. I am always attempting to discover whether the thing might not have been done by some deception, artifice or legerdemain; and am sometimes so unfortunate (or, if you will have it, so fortunate) as to detect the cheat."

CHAPTER XXIV.

Miscellaneous Explanations of various Practices, Customs, and Vices, existing among the Hindoos, as referred to by Babajee, in the articles prepared by him for the Moral Society.

On reading the articles drawn up by Babajee for the formation of a Moral Society, it seems to the writer that the simple *allusion* there made to so many singular habits and vices, will leave the inquiring, and especially the curious reader, to ask a further explanation concerning them. As such an explanation will introduce the reader more fully into the *society* of the Hindoos — if society there may be, where *confidence*, the bond of the social compact, scarcely can be said to exist — or it will, more properly speaking, introduce the reader more fully to the social habits of that people, I shall add a few explanations and remarks on each of the twenty-three articles. As the object is not the exposition of the articles, but to make them texts, from which to delineate local character, there is no occasion to repeat them, but only to refer to them numerically.

1. "Ardent spirits" are manufactured in India, and are also brought, as an article of commerce, from England, America, and other places. Drunkenness, however, is not a common vice among the native population. The use of wine and strong drink is forbidden, both to the Hindoos and to the Mussulmans, by their respective religions. Consequently, no one among these two largest portions of the natives of India but an *irreligious* man, or an *outcast*, or an *infidel*, would dare to use ardent spirits. The Parsees of Bombay, the descendants of the ancient fire-worshipers of Persia, who fled to India for conscience's sake when the infatuated followers of Mohammed invaded the country, use wine, beer, and brandy immoderately. This they do, not with the sanction of their religious books, but on the same principle as they eat *ham* — swine's flesh being prohibited. They call it *mutton*, and eat it without asking any questions. The Parsees, being comparatively a small portion of the population, do not furnish a great number of drunkards. The ranks of this loathsome band are left to be filled up by *Christians*.

The intoxicating liquor drunk by the common and poorer classes of the natives, is called arrack. This is a cheap, *fiery* liquor, produced by fermentation or distillation from the *tadee* of the cocoa-nut tree. A branch, or, more properly, a stem of the tree is cut off, and from the end of the newly cut stem there oozes a kind of sap, of a milky color, and a saccharine taste. This is a wholesome, pleasant beverage, not intoxicating when taken fresh from the tree; but the liquor produced from it is highly intoxicating, and is said to be more injurious than the intoxicating drinks of Europe. It will be seen that the first resolution was aimed at an existing evil, against which converts from Hindooism need to be fortified.

2. "Heathen sports, shows, jugglers' feats, and the like," are so common among the Hindoos, and so exactly adapted to their taste and to their habits, and have so constantly furnished them amusement, it would not be strange should converts to Christianity here meet a strong temptation to spend much of their precious time in the same indulgence. It would be needless, were I able, even to enumerate these. They are more numerous than in Europe or America; some equal in interest to idle gazers, and many inferior and very frivolous. The cry of *Tumashee*, (sport or exhibition,) never fails to collect the idle rabble. Whatever be its character, it will answer the end of gratifying a vitiated taste, and of killing a few hours of time. Pictures representing the feats of their gods, the achievements of their heroes, the greatness and goodness of their priests, the sensual joys of heaven, and miseries of the nether world, and a thousand other things calculated to arrest the attention of an indolent people, are every where exhibited and minutely explained by the exhibitors. I once stopped, as I was passing a crowd of people in the street, to look at one of these pictures, which happened to be a representation of the two conditions of the future world. I mention one of the explanations that were given as an example. The exhibitor had unrolled his long canvass, on which were delineated in opposite rows the state of the happy and the miserable, as fixed after death. He then pointed to one figure, saying, "You there see a man seated on an elephant, reclining in the easy *howda*, which is hung with such rich trappings, and so shining with gold. You see one attendant in rich livery, holding over his head the *chutree*, a large and splendid umbrella, to prevent a hot ray of the sun from striking him; and another servant is gently waving the chowrie to refresh him, or to drive away the flies. You see his retinue of servants, and camels, and horses, and palanquins?" "Yes." "Well, that man was

INDIAN JUGGLERS EXHIBITING TAMED SNAKES.

once like one of *you*. But he honored the gods by worship and sacrifices; he made *large presents to the Brahmuns* and gooroos, and faithfully performed the duties of our religion; and now he is rewarded as you see. He revels in eternal youth; his strength is increased to a degree that he may live in the perpetual gratification of every appetite; and no means are wanting to the consummation of all his desires. You see on the opposite side, do you not, that poor fellow, half starved, naked, terrified by serpents and loathsome reptiles, stung by scorpions, and tormented by little devils thrusting into him sharp-pointed spikes?" "Yes." "Well, there is a man who would not worship his gods, nor perform the rites of his religion. He ate, and drank, but did not feed the Brahmuns, or the religious beggars. And now he has his reward."

Comic and dramatic performances are every where common, but indifferent. Tumbling, boxing, and all sorts of buffoonery, are performed by the numerous companies of strolling players which traverse the country continually. Dancing women entertain the great, and *dancing bears*, the vulgar. Monkeys, playing the soldier, the friend, the rogue, or the lover; tigers, leopards, parrots, and different kinds of beasts, and birds, and serpents, are exhibited. Jugglers, of all grades and descriptions, are common. Their feats are attributed to some supernatural power; as is the case in India with every thing, the reason of which does not at once appear obvious.

3. "Buffoonery, jeering, and the derision of others," are perhaps more sadly characteristic of human nature in India than the same unlovely qualities are in a Christian land. To this list I may add scandal, tale-bearing, and slander. A Hindoo is altogether governed by self-interest; and these are instruments by which he often attempts to bring about his selfish purposes. The reputation of a neighbor, or a brother, is never considered, when it stands in the way of his own preferment or advantage; nor does he hesitate to fabricate the most vile report, if it is likely to be for his own benefit. Railing, reproach, ridicule, jeering, and abuse begin when deception, flattery, and low cun-

ning end, or, rather, when they have failed to accomplish their objects. And these are often followed by horrible execrations, such as the cursing of one another's mothers, or their dead relations.

4. "Heathen festivals" are the source of endless evils to the people. Their number and character have been described in a preceding chapter, from which it will be seen how demoralizing must be their influence on the minds of the people. The good people of this Christian country think that our two or three annual festivals, when observed only as days of mirth and frivolity, produce more moral evil than as many weeks or months will repair. The consequences, then, of *one hundred and forty-five* heathen festivals, annually, must produce an inconceivable amount of dissipation and vice on the Hindoo nation. Were these festivals but Irish wakes, or English fairs, or American celebrations of independence, with "bonfires, cannon, excessive mirth, and conviviality," or were they what they pretend to be, days of worshiping heathen gods simply, they would be less debasing to the nation than they now are. They have no redeeming quality. They foster no sentiment of patriotism, or friendship, or social virtue; they encourage no art or science, or bring any advantage to any one; while on the other hand, they encourage idleness, propagate vice, corrupt the youth, perpetuate the sins of the more advanced in life. They are fascinating to all classes of the people of the East, and present a powerful temptation to unstable and ignorant converts, on account of their former habits. The resolution which our native friends at Ahmednuggur made, not to observe such festivals, was not needless.

5. "Lucky and unlucky days," among the Hindoos, are, like many things of a similar nature, too endless to be described, and the account, if made out, would be too tedious and frivolous to be read. There is a labyrinth of intricacies about them, which no one but a *Hindoo priest* can see through, and he is oftentimes put to his wit's end, as he would have the people suppose, and obliged to consult oracles, and get supernatural aid, before he can always determine on the day, or the particular part of the

day, when a particular kind of business may be commenced, or when some *important* ceremony may be performed. But as they are paid for their very essential services in these matters, and as they can, by having all these important secrets in their own hands, control almost any event to their own liking, they are not much to be pitied, if they should sometimes torture their poor brains in vain, in order to meet an exigency. The common people know, in general terms, that some days are lucky, and others unlucky; but it is quite impossible for them to know the detail of this difficult matter; and hence the necessity of calling in a Brahmun. A certain day may be lucky for the commencement of one kind of business, and not for another; or one part of the day may be propitious for a certain purpose, and another part of the same day unpropitious.

6. "The singing and hearing of songs" is a favorite amusement among the Hindoos. Men, and sometimes women, go about the country, and sing songs as their profession. They are much run after by all classes of people, yet I should judge but poorly paid. They not unfrequently amuse their auditor the whole night, alternately singing and reciting. At every interval, the hearers applaud the song and the singer, or indulge in loud peals of laughter, if there be wit or obscenity in the song. These songs are generally of a most vile character; and their singing or recitation is attended with corresponding lascivious tones and gestures. The feats and tricks and the debaucheries of their gods are the most common subjects of their songs. Others relate to affairs of gallantry among mortals. A few are religious, and a few historical. The manner of singing is in a *sing-song* tone, most rude and unmusical.

7. "Story-telling" is but another part of the same amusement. There is a set of men who are professed story-tellers. They travel from place to place, like those who sing or play the buffoon, or exhibit shows, or play the part of the juggler or the conjurer. All these characters are essential accompaniments to a place of pilgrimage, or to the proper celebration of their holy days. I once went to a place of pilgrimage in the Southern

Concon. Multitudes of people were assembled, to pay their devotion to a certain god or goddess, I have forgotten which. A large inclosure had been made, by means of curtains suspended in front of the temple of the deity now to be honored; and a great concourse of people were crowded about it. Wishing to ascertain what was the matter, and the manner of worship on the present occasion, I penetrated through the crowd, that I might see what was doing within the temporary inclosure, and in front of the temple; when, to my astonishment, the principal character there was a common story-teller, amusing the people with the love-stories of departed worthies, the achievements of imaginary heroes, and the silly fooleries of reputed deities. This comical genius, who was a mimic, a mountebank, a buffoon, a singer, and a story-teller, seemed to form the principal centre of attraction for the pilgrims.

The character of the stories which they relate, is similar to that of the songs as mentioned above. They often consist of legends, traditions, and the most incredible fictions respecting their forefathers, or the giants, or ancient sages and warriors; but more generally they relate to the *miraculous* fooleries of their gods. The indispensable qualities which go to constitute a *good story* among this people, are the *marvelous*, the *obscene*, and the *lascivious;* and the principal qualifications in the actor are impudence, an evil imagination, and a talent to fabricate. There is scarcely a feature in Indian society which so much vitiates the public taste, and turns the heads and corrupts the hearts of the people so effectually, as that of story-telling. The character of these stories contributes in an astonishing degree to the formation of the character of the youth of the nation.

8. "We will not use abusive or obseene language." A partial acquaintance with Hindoo society will show that such a resolution as this is not made at random, or without a current and a very prevalent vice for its object. What is called obscenity is, I am aware, to some extent a *comparative* vice. Custom, and habit, and education, have pronounced a thing to be impure in one nation, which is not regarded as impure or obscene in an-

other. The delicacy of one recoils from the mention of a thing which conveys to the mind of another, differently educated, no indelicate allusion. It is no doubt desirable that our own imaginations and thoughts should be so pure, and the public taste so truly chaste, that we might speak of and discuss many topics which are now forbidden. The danger, taking human nature as we find it, is undoubtedly on the side of too much laxity. Yet there may be a *squeamishness* of taste which is exceedingly inconvenient for all parties, and really prejudicial to the cause of moral purity. There is something like a national standard in these things, a departure from which is regarded by the people of each nation as a deviation from the rules of delicacy. This may be illustrated better by an example. Take, for instance, that member of the body which an *American* lady would call a *limb* or the *lower member* of the body. An English lady would call it by its proper name, and speak of it as she would of the arm or the head, apparently without the remotest suspicion that there could be any thing indelicate in doing so. The French lady also calls it a leg, and never thinks to dishonor or be ashamed of so necessary a member of the body; while the Hindoo female speaks of this member, and treats it as familiarly as she does her arms or her neck. She wears a dress which exposes the whole or a part of it; and neither she nor any one sees or feels any impropriety in the exposure. It is hard to know where, in these four cases, we may lodge the charge of indelicacy with the greatest propriety. In the former instance, there *may* be the most fastidiousness, while there may *not*, in the latter instance, be the most indelicacy of thought and imagination.

We must not, therefore, suppose that every deviation of the Hindoo from *our* standard of propriety, is a transgression of the rules of real decorum. Yet there are other things which the respectable of all nations unite in pronouncing indelicate and obscene, and which, in their nature, are so. And after making all the allowances which we can on the score of national taste, we find in the language, as well as in the conduct of the Hindoos, an obscenity, and a degree of filthy communication, which is quite shocking to all our feelings of propriety or delicacy. The common slang of the people is full of it; and it seems to abound among all ranks of the community. And when it is employed in reproach, and in angry and abusive conversation, and in quarreling, it becomes tenfold more horrible. The Hindoos seldom, if ever, fight so as to come to blows. Indeed, I never saw one Hindoo strike another. Their anger is often excited to an awful pitch, and, did you not know their cowardly habits in this respect, you would suppose they must undoubtedly annihilate each other in their wrath. Not a blow, however, will be struck. But such torrents of abuse, and such execrations and maledictions as you never before conceived of, supply the place of broken heads and bruised limbs. The belligerent parties spare no terms of reproach. Each abuses and curses the mother and the deceased relations of the other, and they provoke one another by the foulness of the epithets which they apply. No disrespect, however, is meant to the poor mothers or the dead relations who are so unmercifully execrated. It is only a *customary* way of abusing an adversary.

9. "Custom," with the Hindoo, is every thing. He believes, not because his reason is convinced, or he approves of his system of religion, as well pleasing to his god, or suited to his circumstances as a sinner, but because it is the custom of his people to believe so, and his fathers believed so before him. Nor does he practice the rites and ceremonies of his religion on any more rational grounds. The same remark will apply to almost every act in common life. He does not seem to do any thing from reflection, but from habit and custom. Innovations and improvements are, of course, never thought of, much less adopted. But the article in question does not refer to the ordinary customs of common life. As Christians and missionaries, we do not care whether our converts wear hats or turbans, coats or ungrikas; sit on the floor, and eat with their fingers from a leaf, or sit on a chair and use knife, fork, spoon, and plate; whether they, like the Hindoos, mount their horses on the right side, or, in a more Christian-like manner, mount on the left. Respecting these things,

they have our example, and wherever we believe they could be benefited by an exchange, we advise and counsel. It is only in a moral point of view that we seek to change customs and laws. It is the "custom" for the Hindoo to speak the truth or falsehood, to make a show of fairness, or to resort to knavery, just as he judges shall best suit his own selfish purposes. It is a "custom" to cheat, to deceive, to overreach, whenever there be an opportunity; and to live in the indulgence of the carnal appetites. When I reprove the Hindoo for any of these sins, he answers: "Such is our custom." Custom neutralizes every thing: it is the grand apology for every sin. It is a difficult task to teach a Hindoo that *custom itself* may be wrong. It is hard to convict him of guilt contracted only by following the beaten path of custom. In *theory*, the Brahmun will talk, for example, of *continence*, as a virtue that should be practiced. But in *practice*, he will tell you there is not, and there cannot be, any such thing. An Utopian view of virtue, he says, teaches self-denial, while custom allows of free indulgence; and he sees, as he pretends, all men following the dictates of custom. He will not, therefore, believe that any one ever practices the opposite virtue, except through necessity or restraint. Hence it will be seen that a resolution, "not to observe Hindoo customs which are opposed to the Christian Scriptures," was neither useless nor unmeaning, in reference to Hindoo converts in a heathen land. And well it might be for Christian converts, in a Christian land, to make and keep a resolution that they will observe no *Christian custom* which is opposed to the *Christian Scriptures.*

10. The Hindoos are every where proverbial for their "indolence." Labor is always regarded as a sore evil. To eat to shameful excess, to smoke, gossip, to hear and tell stories, and to sleep more than half of the twenty-four hours, is regarded by the Hindoo as the *summum bonum* of happiness. Perhaps nothing would sooner attract the attention of the foreigner on his arrival in India, than the immense crowds of idle people which every where throng an eastern city. So limited are the actual wants of the people, and so few the incentives to industry, and such

the institutions of caste, that probably not above a fourth part of the inhabitants of any given place are at the same time engaged in any employment; and those that are employed do not generally labor more than six hours a day. Hence the multitude of idle people which may always be seen lounging about the bazaars, the temples, and other places of concourse. The standard of industry among a people is generally formed on the real or imaginary wants of that people. These wants may be necessary in themselves, or become so by the customs of society. In either case, they are incentives to industry; and whatever promotes the industry, promotes the virtue of a people. For an idle people have never yet been a virtuous, a moral or a religious people. The wants of the Hindoos—I mean of the great mass of the people—are absolute wants. A bare subsistence is all they seek or expect, and this may be gained by a very small amount of labor. Hence the divisions and sub-divisions of labor, and much of the nonsense of caste, and the moral corruption of the people. Each caste of people has its prescribed departments of labor; and if a person of one caste be found doing a kind of work which belongs to another caste, he will be persecuted and compelled to abandon it. Therefore, while a man adheres to the rule of caste, and while his *wants remain so very few*, he is doomed to a life of comparative idleness. But the convert to Christianity is neither bound by caste, nor ought he to confine his wants barely to a miserable subsistence. He should be taught to acquire, to appreciate, and to enjoy the good things of this present life. The temptation to indolence is doubtless increased, in some degree, by the heat of the climate.

11. "We will not do or say any thing against the Christian church." Such a resolution may be of more practical utility among Hindoo converts than the reader would at first imagine. Scandal and detraction seem to be the common ingredients in the composition of the Hindoo's character; and these unlovely traits are most unsparingly exhibited whenever an occasion is offered. There are many ways in which the unwarrantable expectations of a convert to Christianity may be disappointed, or he may be restrained, chagrined, admonished, or suspended.

MANUFACTURING INDIGO.

And as he has not been in the habit of feeling moral restraints, and is accustomed to treat all who for the moment *seem to him* to oppose his interest or his gratification as enemies, and, exercising neither reflection nor self-command over his unreasonable feelings, he will unsparingly deal out reproaches, sarcasm and abuse against the church, and the missionaries, and Christianity. During these intervals of petulance and dissatisfaction, he seeks no explanations, nor does he ever seem to think that any explanations could be made. He forgets all past kindnesses, magnifies his imaginary wrongs, and is not scrupulous to whom he unbosoms his griefs. The evil done, the missionary at length is informed of his grievances, and redresses them by word of explanation. All is again quiet, and the poor ignorant creature, who *imagined* he had just occasion for all his hard speeches against his patrons and protectors, now exercises in them the most implicit confidence. Hence it will appear that converts are in danger of acting and speaking against the church.

12. "Wandering about from place to place," and killing time by every species of dissipation, is but the legitimate fruits of the idle habits of the Hindoos. When out of service, as I have shown that more than three-fourths of the people are, the Hindoo rises in the morning, saunters for an hour or two about in the bazaar, loiters with every company of loungers, returns at ten or eleven o'clock to his breakfast; his indulgence is there generally limited by his inability to get more; smokes his goodee-goodee, and then gives himself over to sleep till three or four in the afternoon. He then properly begins his day. Laborers have, by this time, completed their daily task; servants, writers, teachers, and men in different employments, are now at leisure; and the vast multitude of idlers are beginning to leave their respective lairs, and to congregate for the evening's entertainment. You may see them now arranged according to their castes. The company on the platform, under yonder tree, with red turbans, and comparatively clean and white clothes, are Brahmuns. They manifest the superiority which they claim, by the important manner in which you see them conversing together, and by that pe-

culiar and significant toss of the head. The company which you see seated on the steps of the temple, and in front of it, with enormous, large, dark-red turbans, and so intent in conversation on apparently weighty matters, is composed of native merchants and banyans, many of whom are rich, and all are misers. There is sitting another circle of men about a fire, made by the burning of the straw and refuse of the streets. These men are very black, poorly clad, and dirty. Some are without turbans, others have but a coarse cloth about their heads, and the whole group is ill-looking and wretched. They are the Mhars, the lower order of working-men and coolies. But look beyond all these groups, and you may see different companies of women and girls, gossiping in circles, according to their respective castes. Sometimes they are good-naturedly gossiping, and sometimes there is a little *jarring* in their community. And then, what eloquence! what epithets! what torrents of abuse! what flood-gates are opened, and what a noise of the many waters! Would you see "how great a matter a little fire kindleth," and how great a commotion may be excited by the "little member"—would you learn what unsurpassed achievements the tongue is capable of performing, you must see and hear two Hindoo women, when sharply quarreling.

Among these different idle groups which I have been showing you, the well-dressed, light-brown complexioned, well-formed Parsee, with his spotted turban, may be seen walking. And there goes the tall, well-formed Arab, or the haughty Mussulman. These different groups will, doubtless, if they can find entertainment, spend the whole night in this manner. Thus is time squandered and morals corrupted. Thus does the idler drag out life amidst a multitude as idle and corrupt as himself.

13. "Neglecting to hear the word of God on the Sabbath," is not a sin peculiar to the Hindoo convert, nor is he the only one that needs to enforce this duty by a *resolution*. Yet the Christian in India is very much prone to this sin. He fancies he is sick; his head aches from Saturday night till Monday morning; he is astonished to have fever on him all Sunday; he dares not leave his house on Sunday for the fear of rogues, though he has found

it secure during the past six days. Many, and often very frivolous, are the excuses which he has for his absence from our regular religious services. Babajee traced the whole to "slothfulness," and indifference to the word of God, and formed a resolution to counteract the evils.

14. "The customs of servants." And what are these? I have spoken of the absolute authority of "custom" in general. But domestics, servants, and dependents of every description, have customs and usages peculiar to themselves, which they appeal to as affording sanction for practices that would otherwise be very reprehensible. To receive a per centage on all money paid out by the master, to overcharge (in their accounts of purchases made for their master) perhaps double or treble, to appropriate his property to themselves, to defraud him in any way they can, and to take bribes from others for the privilege of defrauding him, and a thousand such like practices, are regarded by servants as legitimate measures when dealing with their masters. Servants of every grade have their peculiar perquisites, which are sometimes considerable when compared with their monthly pay; but the steward is the person who shares the most largely in the profits of their *customary* system of defrauding. When engaging in the service of a "rich man" and a great household, his wages are a consideration of no consequence, when compared with the perquisites of his situation. While he is content with a moderate per centage, his master has patience with him; but, when he becomes more avaricious, as he generally does after a short time, and begins to "waste his master's goods," by appropriating to himself a great share of what is committed to his care, the master is offended, calls the steward to an account, and discharges him from his service, or "puts him out of his stewardship."

An understanding has all along existed between the servant and the marketmen, shopkeepers, and others with whom he has had dealings. Bôth the real and the nominal price of every article is agreed on, that the servant and the shopkeeper may tell the master the same story. In this way, a systematic course of deception and fraud is carried on, under the sanction of *custom;* and in like manner pilfering, and downright thieving, is practiced to a most shameful extent. Converts to Christianity, if engaged in a family as servants, have before them a powerful temptation to practice what are called the "servant's customs."

15. "Administering to the sick," visiting the fatherless and widows in their afflictions, feeding the hungry, and clothing the naked, are not the attributes of Hindooism. They are the free and rich streams which flow from the fountain revealed in the Gospel. Christianity is charity; Hindooism is cold selfishness. Thousands and tens of thousands of wretched beings are annually left to die without medicine, without attendance, and without pity. If a man sickens from home, and if he be without money, as in most instances would be the case, and no one *interested* in him were near, he might suffer and die alone. He could expect nothing on the score of charity. I have in another place mentioned several descriptions of diseased persons, who are discarded on account of their diseases as soon as they become incurable. The "tender mercies" of the heathen are "cruelty." An anecdote will best illustrate this subject, and at the same time explain another point. A Brahmun by the name of Myral had for some time been in the service of the mission, as a pundit. We knew him to be a married man, but without children; and we were of course astonished to hear of his second marriage, knowing that his wife was still living, and that Hindooism does not allow of a plurality of wives. I informed him, one day, that I was knowing to his second marriage, and asked him how he, a pundit and a gooroo, could so far transgress the laws of God and of Brahmunism as to marry again, while he had a wife living? He said that, in ordinary cases, it would be wrong to marry under such circumstances; but that in his case it was right and lawful. I asked him why? He replied, "My wife is sickly, and unable to discharge the duties of a wife." You have no right to cast her off on that account, but ought rather to support, cherish, and comfort her, and to treat her, in every respect, as kindly, and as conjugally, as if she were vigorous and healthy. "What

BURNING A PRIEST IN SIAM.

you say, Sahib, is good; but my wife is *very* ill, she can do nothing—she is no wife to me." But you have no right to neglect her and take another, said I. "Never mind that, Sahib; she cannot live long, she *will die* in two or three months."

16. The Hindoos "bury" or burn their "dead," according to caste and circumstances. Burning is the most honorable; but it is too expensive for the poorer classes of the people. The funeral pile must consist of a sufficient quantity of wood, or of dried cow-dung, to consume the body completely. Burying is attended with very little expense. Coffins are never used, and little or no clothing is deposited with the body; and if any be allowed to remain on the body, it is only the ordinary clothing of the deceased. There is, properly speaking, no religious service at a Hindoo funeral. There is a savage howling, and shrieking, and inconsolable wailings. The "mourning women" encompass the house of the afflicted, and express all the signs of the most sincere grief. The tears trickle down their cheeks, they smite their breasts and wring their hands for anguish. Their distorted, woeful countenances seem the true index of an agonizing heart. But, except the mourning of a few near relations, and the hollow ebullitions of these hirelings, there is no seriousness, no solemnity in a Hindoo funeral. The bearers of the deceased are hirelings; the Brahmuns who may officiate only think of their fee, and the bystanders appear as perfectly thoughtless and vacant as if the body of an ox or horse had been carried by. Death and the grave never seem to teach a lesson of mortality to the living in India. No voice is heard to say, "Be ye also ready."

17. I do not think the Hindoos are particularly prone to the "use of harsh or unkind language." When in a passion, the lower orders of the men, and the women especially, deal out their invectives with an unsparing hand, alias tongue. But irritability and anger are less prominent characteristics of the Hindoos than subtlely and dissimulation. The Brahmuns, in particular, have acquired an astonishing command over their tempers. They can disguise their real feelings to an extraordinary extent, and they are shrewd, artful, obsequious, *good-natured*

fellows. And the people, in general, are rather supine than irritable; but, when excited, there is a grossness and a severity in their manner and conversation. There is a harshness of sound in the Mahratha language which at first gives the foreigner the idea that all who use it are angry.

18. The Hindoos, to some extent, use "intoxicating drugs, as opium and bhang." Opium-eaters are not common among the Hindoos. Many Mussulmans in India use opium to a shameful excess. The *bhang*, or preparation from the seed of the hemp, is more commonly used; but this is not so general as to make it a national habit. Smoking tobacco in the hukar, and chewing the pan-sooparee, are almost universal. The pan is an astringent leaf, and sooparee is the bedel-nut, which, with a little *chunam*, (a preparation of lime,) are chewed by all of every age and sex. They color the teeth red. When smoking, persons of the same caste form a circle, sitting in a row on their heels; the hukar is then passed around; each man takes but one whiff, and hands it to his neighbor.

19. "The giving of instruction" is, with the Brahmun and the gooroo, a mere matter of selfishness. They teach whatever will promote their own interest and gratification, and they suppose that these can only be promoted by the mental bondage and the ignorance of the people. And hence the "instructions" which they have to give are generally "bad" for their disciples, and their "advice" is often pernicious. I have shown for what reason holy places are sustained, why pilgrimages are enjoined, and for what reasons penances and austerities are prescribed. All these things are "advised" or commanded to profit or aggrandize the priesthood.

20. "The muntru and tuntru" are charms and mystic ceremonies, to which is attributed an unlimited influence in the cure of diseases, in the removal of difficulties, and in the accomplishment of anything which the Brahmun, who alones possesses this marvelous power, may wish. I have spoken on this subject elsewhere, but may here farther say, that such is the confidence of the common people in this manner of removing diseases, that

MARRIAGE PROCESSION OF A BRIDE IN LEBANON.

they are universally prone to resort to it. The Brahmuns, by their clever management in this species of roguery, so well *time* their manœuvres, that they often *seem* to be successful; and if they fail, the failure is readily attributed to a want of faith in the people, or some extraneous circumstance.

21. I have already alluded to the "usages" which the Hindoos practice at "births and funerals." The "marriage ceremonies" are still more burdensome and expensive. The wedding garments, the numerous processions, the musicians, the feastings, the illuminations, and all the attendant rites and ceremonies of these occasions, render a Hindoo wedding a season of great dissipation and expense. The marrying season continues about three months, during which the whole community participate in the hilarity, at least so much as to find in it a standing excuse for a holiday. The marriages of the rich are truly splendid. No expense is spared by the fathers of the bride and of the groom to render their respective entertainments grand and imposing. The common classes of the people try to imitate the more wealthy, and spend all they have and all they can get on credit at the marriage of a son or a daughter. Debts thus contracted are handed down from father to son, as his patrimony; and thus a poor man may be paying twenty-five per cent. interest for money borrowed at his great grandfather's marriage.

22. "Games of chance" are common in India. Cards and chess are well known, and much used. People of all ranks spend much of their time at their different games, sometimes simply for amusement, but not unfrequntly for money. Many of the natives are very skillful players; and it is remarkable that the Hindoos have long been acquainted with most of our western games, and they have several which are peculiar to themselves.

23. "We will do evil to no man"—a resolution worthy of the best Christian in the 19th century, in any part of the world. Christianity is the only religion which pretends to a power sufficient to emancipate its votaries from selfishness. Its motto is, "Peace, good will towards men." To do evil to no man, neither in word, deed, or thought—never to advance our own interests

to the prejudice of our neighbor, is a consummation in holy living devoutly to be wished. This negative virtue, so excellent, and so hard to practice, is the legitimate fruit of Christianity. Hindooism can pretend to no such excellence. Her votaries are full of maliciousness, envy, murder, debate, deceit, malignity, whisperers, backbiters, proud, and inventors of evil things. They devise evil against their neighbor, and do not hesitate to sacrifice his interest and his comfort to their own. May that wisdom which is from above, full of mercy and good fruits—may that charity which suffereth long, and is kind, which envieth not, which vaunteth not itself, is not puffed up, which seeketh not her own, thinketh no evil, and rejoiceth not in iniquity, guide and possess the heart of the poor selfish Hindoo.

CHAPTER XXV.

The Moral Character of the Hindoos no ground of Discouragement to Missionary Efforts among them—The Result of such Efforts as Great as the Present State of the Church Warrants us to Expect—Much may be Expected when the Right Spirit shall Pervade the Church.

In concluding this volume, the thought occurs that an unwarrantable inference may be drawn from the unlovely character which I have given of the Hindoos. Should it be inferred from the account which I have given of the character of that part of the heathen world, and of the success which has hitherto attended all endeavors to ameliorate their condition, that they *cannot be converted* to Christianity, the inference does not, necessarily, go to impeach the veracity of my account of them. It rather reflects on the *Christian logic* of those who draw the inference. In the *Christian's* philosophy, the *badness of moral character* can never be predicated as a ground of discouragement, or a reason for the want of success. If so, where would be our personal hopes of salvation? where our hopes of the conversion of the world? Nor can the want of success among a particular portion of the heathen, at a given time, and under given circumstances, be taken as an indication that such a portion of the heathen world cannot be converted. There may be some grand defect in the application of the means.

I am aware that I have portrayed the darker shades of the Hindoo character, and that I have pursued a similar course in regard to missionary labors in that country. But this I have not done unadvisedly. It is more agreeable to give the more brilliant colors to a picture. It is more agreeable, in missionary operations, to reflect upon and to describe the *little which has been done*, and what facilities and encouragements there are for our future progress, than to speak of the *much* which remains to be done, and of the obstacles and discouragements which every where stare us in the face. Hence this has been done by others. It therefore seemed to devolve on me to fill up the picture, by supplying the darker shades. The difficulties, I trust, have neither been overrated nor the Hindoos belied; nor any motive actuated the writer, except that of presenting the friends of missions with an impartial view of the work which they have to do, hoping by this means that they will pray more *understandingly*, as well as more fervently, and give more liberally, and devote themselves to the work more freely.

The patrons of foreign missions have, if I mistake not, often indulged in feelings of despondency in reference to our mission in Western India. They say the mission has been established more than forty years; that the Gospel has been preached during nearly all this period; that great quantities of tracts and portions of the Scripture have been circulated; that schools have been established and supported; that a great number of youth have been taught the rudiments of Christianity; that great sums of money have been expended there; that much precious health has been sacrificed, and many valuable lives lost, and hitherto little *apparent* success has followed.

Such is the view which many good people have taken of that mission; and hence there has been a reluctance on the part of the candidates for missionary labor to engage in that field, and no doubt a corresponding doubting, and hesitation, and luke-warmness on the part of Christians in general. What I wish principally to show in this chapter is, in the first place, that the obstacles in the way of the conversion of India, and the supposed want of success in missionary labors, have been overrated; and in the second place, that the real want of success may be owing to a wrong state of feeling in the churches at home.

The "*romance* of missions" has not yet entirely given place to that sober, deliberate, common-sense, dependent, and prayerful state of mind which Christian experience teaches is the only safe, and proper, and effectual way of conducting so important an affair as the propagation of the Gospel. There is a vail of mystery—a mist—a dusky cloud between Christians in this country and the heathen world. They see men there as trees walking. They look through a medium which presents a double refraction in reference to missionary labors; but it presents no form at all when they contemplate the character of the heathen. They do not consider that depravity is radically the same there; that the missionary has to contend with the same hatred to divine things, the same obduracy of heart and pervisity of will which try the patience and exhaust the energies of the minister at home; that all the corruptions of human nature which are to be met with in a Christian land, and which here meet a rebuke in an enlightened public sentiment, present a bold, unblushing front to the missionary, sanctioned by custom, confirmed and familiarized by habit, and authorized by the current system of religion. The worshiping of an uncarved stone, or a loathsome reptile, is so repugnant to their own feelings, and to common sense and reason, and so absurd, and so dishonoring to the majesty of Heaven, they seem to suppose that the poor benighted heathen need only be pointed to a "more excellent way," and they are ready to embrace it. They wonder at the tardiness of the heathen, they are astonished that they can vindicate the worship of idols, and are half inclined to think that such blindness and stupidity warrant us to abandon them to their fate. They expect more from the application of the same quantity of means in a heathen land, than is expected or experienced in a Christian land; whereas they ought to expect much less.

Missionaries are sent out at the rate of about one to a million of the heathen. They must speak in a strange tongue; supply the whole country with books; they are expected to take on themselves the education of the youth of the nation; to change customs, and laws, and prejudices; to overthrow a system of religion which has held the public mind in absolute bondage for many centuries; to civilize, refine, and Christianize a whole nation, and all this in a few short years. That is called an "unsuccessful mission," where the missionary can only report, after ten or twelve years, that the work is but *begun;* that only a few have as yet been converted; *but* that Christianity has been extensively preached; that a great quantity and a great variety of Christian books have been prepared, published, widely circulated and read; that a great number of children are in the process of a Christian education; and that all the *means* which we are commanded to use are in operation, and are, we confidently hope, preparing the way for a glorious result. We, as missionaries, have a right to claim the same indulgence, on account of our own frailty and insufficiency, as is allowed to ministers of the Gospel at home. We have a right to demand, in reference to our labors, the same indulgence, with regard to the perversity and obduracy of human nature, as is conceded to the religious teacher in a Christian land, and the same as has been allowed to all reformers.

Experience has shown that the reformation of the world has *never* been an easy task. Noah, and Lot, and Abraham, and Moses, experienced very serious difficulties in their efforts to reform their respective cotemporaries. The prophet Isaiah grieves and laments that so very few regarded his message: "Who hath believed our report, and to whom is the arm of the Lord revealed?" When he had toiled through a long life, and worn out his body in unwearied labors for the salvation of his countrymen, and breathed out his soul in anxieties and lamentations for a nard-hearted and stiff-necked people, he uttered the desponding lamentation, "I have labored in vain, and spent my strength for nought and in vain."

The tender-hearted prophet Jeremiah met with no better success. He deplored the universal degeneracy of his people; he grieved over their hardness of heart; his spirit sunk under the accumulated burden of his trials and his labors; and in an hour of despondency he cried, "O that my head were waters, and mine eyes a fountain of tears, that I might weep day and night for the slain of the daughter of my people. O that I had in the wilderness a lodging place of a wayfaring man, that I might leave my people, and go from them." Disconsolate prophet! how he sunk under the discouragements of his ministry. After an afflictive ministry of half a century, he was called to his reward above, leaving his ungrateful and depraved countrymen almost as bad as he found them.

All the prophets experienced the same difficulties. They found it no easy matter to reform men. They prophesied, as it were, to a valley of dry bones. They preached to a people who, having ears, would not hear, and having eyes, would not see; nor would they understand, and turn and be healed. Their thrilling eloquence was for the most part spent on the desert air. The apostles and the ministers of the primitive church had the satisfaction of seeing but few of their hearers embrace the doctrines of the cross. The multitude rushed on to death and everlasting ruin. Nor do the present generation of Zion's watchmen report that men are now *naturally* more favorably disposed toward the truths of the Gospel. With all the auxiliaries which the present day affords for the communication of the truth—with all their unwearied labors on the Sabbath, in the Bible class and the Sabbath school, in the room of the sick and at the bed of the dying—they have the happiness of seeing only a few, out of the multitudes to whom they preach, savingly benefited. How many carefully prepared and excellent sermons are preached, to which we can trace no visible utility; how many Bibles and tracts are circulated, which are not read; and how much religious instruction is wasted, for aught we can see, on the passing wind?

What marvel, then, if missionary operations must be weighed in the same balance? Why should it be thought a thing incredible? Why esteemed as if a "strange thing" had happened, if evangelical labor among the heathen should meet the same unwelcome reception that it does in a nominally Christian land? Missionaries are sent to "a people of a strange speech, and of a hard language." Like the preacher at home, they have to contend with all the natural opposition of the human heart, with this addition: that the sins of the heathen are, for the most part, nurtured by ignorance and superstition, and sanctioned by the prevalent system of religion. They lift up their voice in the streets; in the chief places of concourse, in the openings of the gates, in the city and in the village they cry, "How long, ye simple ones, will ye love simplicity, and scorners delight in their scornings, and fools hate knowledge?" They seize on every occasion, try every motive, and ply every argument; they employ all their eloquence, and exhaust their minds for arguments to refute the errors of the idolater, and persuade him to embrace a pure and holy Gospel. They preach on the Sabbath, and during the week, at their stated places of worship. In weariness of body and mental lassitude, occasioned by the debilitating influence of a tropical sun, they translate the word of God into a strange tongue, and prepare tracts and books, grammars and dictionaries. They are "in journeyings often" for the preaching of the Gospel and the distribution of the word of God. As they travel from place to place, lodging in sheds or open temples, and sometimes in want of the most common comforts of life, they every where contend for the Christian faith. But so averse is the Pagan's heart to Divine truth, so blinded is he to all the dictates of reason and common sense, and so infatuated is he by a system of false religion, which satisfies that natural propensity to have some religion, and, at the same time, leaves him the full enjoyment of all his carnal propensities, that, if he deign to turn aside for a moment to listen to the tender entreaties and the precious promises of the Gospel, he hears the story of the cross as it were an idle tale. Now and then one receives the Gospel gladly, and it proves to him a savor of life unto life; while the vast majority who hear (as is the case in a Christian land) go on with the multitude to do evil. They behold, wonder, despise, and perish!

Thus must the missionary toil in an unfriendly climate, far from home and friends, and all that had become endeared in his native country—thus must he exhaust his strength and pour out his life, struggling with ill health, and expecting an early grave. His soul must be tortured by the abominations of idolatry; his faith staggers at the mountain-like discouragements which surround him on every side, if, for a moment, he lose sight of the Divine promises. The demands which are made on his *patience* by the stupidity, the ignorance, the dissimulation, the treachery, the falsehood, the dishonesty, and the general perverseness and obduracy of the heathen, oftentimes threaten to overwhelm him in the vortex of despair. His nerves become unstrung, disease preys on his vitals, and not unfrequently he finds an untimely grave. And what is the result of such sacrifices, such labors and trials? It is, with fewer exceptions than may at first be supposed, just what the result of the sacrifices, labors and trials of the patriarchs and prophets was, and just what the result of the labors of the ministers of the Gospel of the present day is. The *few* hearken to the voice of the Son of Man, and live; while the multitude pass on to death and everlasting destruction.

A review of the *apparent* success which a preached Gospel has met in the world for eighteen centuries past, is, by no means, flattering to the moral character of man. It is not my design here to discuss this forbidding subject; but I have alluded to it to show that the difficulties which the missionary has to contend with are not *peculiar* to *his* labors. They are common to all the benevolent efforts which have ever been made. And the same course of reasoning which many adopt, in reference to missionary labor among the heathen, if applied to benevolent enterprises at home, would discourage the stoutest hearts and enfeeble the strongest hands. The grand difficulty lies in the perverse will and in the obdurate heart of man. The reason why the Gospel has had so little apparent success, either in this country or in heathen lands, is, because *men love darkness rather than light.* Licentious man does not like *the straight and narrow way.* We experience, in general, the same obstacles to the truth in India; and, in its general character, the same success which is experienced in a Christian land. There are important specific differences; but these do not change the general character of the work. Depravity there flourishes in its own native soil; its features are the same as in a Christian land; and it presents the same opposition to the light and to the truth.

What is our conclusion, then? Shall we say that the word of God has taken none effect? What if some, yea, what if many have not believed? Shall their unbelief make the faith of God without effect? By no means. We can only say, in reference to these obstacles and discouragements, that man is "desperately wicked—the carnal mind is enmity against God—not subject to the law of God, neither indeed can be."

But supposing the obstacles to be as great, and the success of missions to India as limited as many have supposed, what influence ought such facts to have on our benevolent enterprises? Ought they to *dishearten us*, and to lead us *to abandon the work* of the world's reformation? or ought they *to clothe us with humility, to bring us for help to the foot of the cross*, and to quicken our diligence?

It is evident they ought not to dishearten us. Our motto in discouragements is, "Paul may plant, and Apollos may water, but God giveth the increase. He that planteth is nothing, and he that watereth is nothing, but God that giveth the increase." Our sufficiency is all of God. The work is vast, the enemy against whom we contend is formidable and potent; but the weapons of warfare are not carnal, but *mighty, through God*, to the pulling down of strong holds. There can be no failure on the ground of the potency of the enemy, or of the weakness of our armor, or of the insufficiency of our Leader. There is no want of promises on the part of God that he will bless our labors, nor any want of ability in Him to fulfill his promises. We may then rest assured, that no well-directed, pious efforts of ours shall be suffered to go without a reward, or shall fail to accomplish some glorious end in the kingdom of our Redeemer.

The *very thing* which *we* desire, may not be accomplished just in the *way* we had supposed; and the thing which God sees to be desirable, and which he has determined to do, may not be accomplished at that very *point* of *time* when *we* think best. But he is certain to do it in the *best* time and in the best manner. This point is beautifully and forcibly illustrated by the following simile: "For as the rain cometh down from heaven, and returneth not thither, but watereth the earth, and maketh it bring forth and bud, that it may give seed to the sower, and bread to the eater; so shall my word be that goeth forth out of my mouth; it shall not return to me void, but it shall accomplish *that which I please*, and it shall prosper *in the thing* whereto I sent it." We, as Christians and as loyal subjects to our heavenly King, need only know *what is commanded*, and we are bound to do that, whether we can fully understand the reason of it or foresee the result or not. The real success of missionary labors may be great when the apparent success is very limited. The leaven may be secretly at work, and the "whole lump" may be soon leavened.

But is it true, as some have supposed, that the success of the Gospel, in some heathen countries, has been decidedly less than has been experienced from the same amount of means in a Christian land? If the circumstances of the two cases were duly considered, and the means employed, and the consequent success were measured by the same standard, I suspect the disparity, if there be any, would not be found on the side of the foreign field. Take a district of country in New England, containing ten parishes; or take, for an example, ten churches in the city of New York. Estimate the whole amount of supporting Christian institutions within the boundaries of these ten congregations. Put into the account the salaries of ten ministers; the building or annual rent of ten churches; the cost of a supply of books for the people; the whole expense of schools; the expense in money and time for Sabbath schools and Bible classes; and every thing, indeed, which goes to aid the general cause of religion or of moral improvement. And put in an opposite column the whole amount of expense requisite to carry on the operations of a mission where there are ten missionaries; and not only the *amount* of the first will be the greater, but, I believe, the impartial observer will be obliged to allow, that the success of the latter will *not* be found to be the less.

There is, therefore, nothing in the present aspect of our Indian missions which ought to dishearten us; and, consequently, in the second place, nothing which should lead us to abandon the work. Difficulties and discouragements there indeed are; and some of these appear, to human ken, to be insurmountable. But when we compare the obstacles in the way of the diffusion and acceptance of the Gospel in a heathen land with the corresponding obstacles in a Christian land, and, especially, when we look to the right source for help, we see no reason for despondency. "He that observeth the wind shall not sow; and he that regardeth the clouds shall not reap."

Had our blessed Redeemer commanded us to go into all the world, and *convert* every creature — to change men's *vile hearts* — purify their motives — to rectify their consciences, and to do all this by human agency, we might well despair. But we have no such command. The injunction is, "Go into all the world, and *evangelize* all nations" — that is, *preach* to them; afford them the *means* of salvation; spread out the Gospel feast, and invite them; declare to them the precious promises to obedience, and proclaim the awful threatenings against the disobedient. Set life and death before them in all the terrors of the one, and in all the loveliness of the other. Pray for them, and use every means to reclaim them from a state of sin and wretchedness, and to bring them into the light and liberty of the sons of God. More than this we cannot do — more than this we are not required to do.

Wherever, therefore, we may use these means, there is, as far as we are concerned, a promising and a desirable field.

A mission, then, may be called *unsuccessful* only when we are prohibited from *using the means.* This is not the case with regard to our missions in India. We can there preach the Gospel, unobstructed, over a section of country containing millions of people, and to any extent we please. We can distribute Christian books as extensively; and no limits are set to our system of schools but our inability to support and superintend more. These schools are not so efficient, not so thoroughly Christian as we wish; but they are the best that we can have. They are supplied with Christian books, which are daily read; and they are visited by the missionary, who enforces the truth contained in the books, and imparts, in the course of the year, a great amount of religious instruction.

When, in his wise designs, God has determined to cause the seed thus sown to vegetate, spring up, and bear the fruits of righteousness, is beyond the precincts of human sagacity to discover. We have a plain duty to do, and an opportunity is now afforded to do it. But we cannot expect success even in doing this duty, if we are not willing to commit the result entirely to God, and freely to surrender to him all the glory for its accomplishment. We have assurances enough that our labors *shall not be in vain;* although we may for a time *seem* to labor in vain, and to spend our strength for nought. What though the heathen do rage, and the people imagine a vain thing; the kings of the earth set themselves, and the rulers take counsel together, against the Lord and against his Anointed? Shall not He that sitteth in the heavens laugh? Shall not the Lord have them in derision? Shall He not speak to them in His wrath, and vex them in His sore displeasure? Shall He not give to his Son — either in judgment to destroy, or in mercy to save — the heathen for his inheritance, and the uttermost parts of the earth for a possession? What though we preach to a people who oftentimes appear as hardened and as stupid and senseless as the idols they worship? What though we contend with their unprincipled, subtle, avaricious and scoffing priests. What though we prepare and publish books, some of which are read, some thrown aside as useless and some destroyed? What though, for a time, the people persist in the rejection of every measure we may adopt? Must we abandon such a nation to their own wretchedness? May we forestall the judgment of God by pronouncing *our* judgment of condemnation upon them? Shall we withdraw from them the flickering lamp of life, just at the time, perhaps, when God may be about to light it up into a mighty flame?

Such notions of despondency are founded on a wrong principle. They exalt the judgment and the will of man; but degrade the judgment and the will of God. They assume that Christians must walk by *sight.* They demand that missionaries should at all times be able to point out something which *they have done*—something tangible—something *describable.* It is human to err thus; and God, as it would seem, out of indulgence to our infirmities, has condescended to give a share of *visible* success to most of our endeavors to do good. This he may have done to afford us a visible token of his approbation, and to give us a pledge of what he will do.

Thus much, at least, has been vouchsafed to the Mahratha mission. We have not there been left without a witness. A succession of *converts,* though their number has never been great, has borne testimony, by their professions and their practice, that the grace of God can and will transform a wayward, vile Hindoo into a consistent, devout Christian. And such has been the character of our converts, in respect to rank, as to show us that caste and custom present no obstacle to the conversion of the heathen when once the Spirit of God takes hold on the heart. We have had converts from almost every caste; from the arrogant, hypocritcal Brahmun down to the poor degraded Pariah; each exemplifying, in a greater or less degree, and according to their several abilities, and in their different spheres, the graces of Christianity. We may regard these as specimens of what God can do, and as pledges of what he will do, and as encouragements to our weak faith. Let Christians at home — let missionaries abroad — *do their duty*, and trust to God for the result, and the result *will be good*.

There may, doubtless, be reasons connected with the human instrumentality *why* God withholds his blessing from our several labors. The instruments may be of a wrong spirit, or the means may be too partial, or they may be applied without faith and a due dependence on God, or they may be unaccompanied with the prayers of God's people; and hence very little or nothing may be accomplished.

Similar reasons may, perhaps, be assigned why the Mahratha mission has not been more abundantly blessed. I am ready to appropriate to myself a share of the reproach; I am willing to suppose that another share may fall to my brethren of that mission; but I would *suggest*, whether the church, collectively, and Christians, individually, must not share with us the reproach of ill success, which the enemies, if not the friends of missions, have attributed to our operations in India? Missionary labor among the heathen is the appropriate work of Christ's church. Missionaries are their representatives. The responsibility of the work rests not only on the church as a body, but on every member that composes this body; and in proportion as *individuals* throw off this responsibility, in the same proportion the work is hindered among the heathen. The streams must dry up in proportion as the fountain fails. You cannot, Christian friends, expect missions to prosper, unless *you* are engaged for their support; for you are, under God, their main pillar.

Could I, for once, look in upon you, on the evening of the *first Monday of the month*, I could judge pretty correctly how much reason *you* have to expect that missions will prosper. The churches have very wisely set apart this evening to pray for the descent of the Holy Spirit, for the success of missions among the heathen, and for the general prosperity and enlargement of the Redeemer's kingdom. On this evening, intelligence from different and distant parts of the world is communicated, and information may be obtained respecting the success of the Gospel abroad.

It is but fair to suppose that all who feel, as they should, a personal interest in the prosperity of Zion—all who really and heartily pray, "Thy kingdom come"—will desire to be present; and, if not from unavoidable necessity detained, *will* be present, on this occasion, to mingle their prayers with the thousands of God's people, who meet at this hour to invoke the Divine blessing on so sublime an object. Suppose a church of two or three hundred members were to present, at this monthly prayer-meeting, but two or three dozen of her members, would this not be an alarming indication that such a church possessed very little interest in the extension of Christ's kingdom, and very little sympathy for her missionaries, who have gone out from her to do her work in an inhospitable climate, having relinquished all their rights and privileges in their native land, and voluntarily submitted to a state of exile and trial to which the happy people of this country are strangers? Such churches there are in America, and not a few, I fear. *These churches*, whatever others may do, have no right to complain of the ill success of missions. They themselves furnish a reason for ill success. They prevent "many mighty works" being done among the heathen.

It cannot be urged that a monthly prayer-meeting for foreign missions is a burdensome imposition on the church. One, or at most *two* hours, in the month, is but a short time to spend in a transaction of such vast magnitude. This, when compared with the allotments for other meetings, and for other religious duties, is but very little. And no pious man will say that these allotments are greater than their several objects deserve. Pastors of churches are, doubtless, very faulty in not giving this meeting more prominence, both in their public notices of it, and, more especially, in their preparation for it.

Let ministers *do their duty*—let every member of the church do his duty—let him possess the spirit of his Divine Master, and there will appear no reason to be disheartened, or to abandon the work. Relying on God for help, all will press forward, assured that, in due time, they shall reap, if they *faint not.*

Nevertheless, there is cause for *humiliation.* It has been shown that there is a mysterious withholding of the Spirit from some of our missions—a paucity of converts, and a defection among these converts. We have seen that the fault lies in the instrumentality, not in the agency—with man, not with God. The difficulty appears in man's depravity, not in any want of efficiency in the Gospel. It appears not only in the heathen's opposition to the truth, but it appears in that *cold indifference* which many, perhaps a majority of Christians, manifest in the prosecution of their benevolent enterprises. So things *appear;* but could we scrutinize *motives*—could we look into the *heart*—could we stand by the treasury of the Lord, and there see how much is given ostentatiously, how much grudgingly, how much faithlessly; and could we determine exactly what proportion of our benevolent operations has its origin in selfishness, or in obstinacy for private opinions, or from ambition, or a love of notoriety, we should, doubtless, see less reason than we now do for any thing like complacency in our own works. Our boasting would vanish, our self-confidence would forsake us, and we should oftentimes regard ourselves rather as obstacles than as co-workers with God in the conversion of the world. Our song would be, "Not unto us, O Lord! not unto us, but unto thy name give glory." "Not for your sakes do I this, saith the Lord, be it known unto you."

And yet, although God claims the exclusive glory, and declares the *agency* in the accomplishment of every good thing to be his own, he says *he will be inquired of by his people to do this for them.* What humility, then, becomes us! We should be clothed with it as with a garment of sackcloth, laboring, praying, and doing all those things which are commanded us; and after all confess, "We are unprofitable servants; we have done that which was our duty to do."

The simple fact, so prominently expressed, that *God will be inquired* of by his people, enforces the duty of prayer with a tremendous emphasis. To expect that Christianity will prosper and diffuse itself throughout the world, without the fervent and the effectual prayer of the church, is to expect that God will contradict his own word, and work in a way of which he has given us no intimation.

Hence it appears, that we can find relief in our difficulties and our discouragements, in the work of evangelizing men, only at the foot of the cross. Help must come from an omnipotent arm!

We look abroad upon the world as upon a waste-howling wilderness. We see the earth covered with darkness, and the people with gross darkness. We see an array of wickedness like a mighty army; composed of principalities, and powers, and the rulers of the darkness of this world, and spiritual wickedness in high places. We quake, we fear, we begin to despond; we cast our eye toward Calvary, and thence hear a voice, saying, "Be strong; be of good courage; stand fast in the faith; quit yourselves like men; for all power is given unto me in heaven and in earth"—"Lo! I am with you." We go to Calvary. There renew our strength—derive fresh courage—drink in new supplies of faith and patience—put on our armor—acknowledge and receive our Leader, and return to the combat. There we become assured of the all-sufficiency of the Gospel to reach and subdue the *hearts of men.* We there find the grand remedy for sin prepared for, and exactly suited to, the disease. Wherever it has been applied, it has proved efficacious. It is a sovereign cure in all climates, and among people of every nation and variety of character. If once rightly applied, and cordially received, it will purify the heart of all its vileness, and restore spiritual health to the soul, in spite of long-established custom, or caste, or superstition, or deep-rooted prejudice, or an enthralling system of priestcraft.

Where, then, is the nation so vile, so degraded and ignorant, so superstitious and depraved, that she may not be benefited by the Gospel? Is India that nation? No. I have already adduced instances of conversion among the Hindoos, which go to show that God can transform the Hindoo into a Christian as well as he can the European. I have not, it is true, presented, in this volume, a pleasing character of that people. Call my report from that land a sad and disheartening account, if you please; yet, be assured, it is no worse than the reality. But what does this unfavorable account of the Hindoos go to show? Some say it shows that so vile a people can never be converted; some say this is proof enough that we ought forthwith to abandon them to their fate; others infer that the missionary must be discouraged, and would gladly give over the enterprise of attempting to reclaim so depraved a people.

As these *three gratuitous* inferences have been drawn, to the prejudice of that mission, I may be allowed to draw *two* inferences from the same premises in its favor. And the first shall be, *the worse the disease, the more urgent the necessity of a remedy.*

It will be admitted by all who have read the foregoing chapters, that I have proved the Hindoos to be bad enough. There can be no room for vacillating, because the disease has not reached such a crisis as to require medical advice, and to demand an immediate remedy. Its symptoms are positive. I have shown that the depravity of the Hindoos, as a moral disease, is universal; that it has manifested itself there in all its varied forms; and that it is inveterate enough. It is as old as the nation—it has been fostered by all the civil and the religious institutions of the country—it has insinuated itself into all the veins and arteries of society, and given a sickly hue to the whole face of the community—it has polluted the fountain of moral principle, and caused it to send forth its poisonous streams to vitiate the teeming mass of immortal souls who inhabit that great continent—it has enslaved, in mental bondage, and reduced to degradation and misery, a fifth part of the population of the globe; and it has sent down to death and everlasting ruin countless millions of these blind votaries of idolatry.

And it will be admitted, that all the attempts which the wise men of that nation have made to find out a remedy for this disease have proved abortive. A remedy has, indeed, been applied from the beginning; but the application has only served to lull the patient into security, while it nourished the disease in his v als. It is the remedy which has done the most mischief — which has spread such a moral desolation throughout that land, and blighted every enjoyment which this life affords, and extinguished every hope of a glorious immortality beyond the grave.

If such be the disease, and such the failure of every attempt to remove it; and if we have in our hands a sovereign cure, and if it is made our imperative duty to apply it, I can see no reason why we should not apply it; and I can see no reason for the apprehension that it will not prove efficacious in this case, as it has in all other cases. And I can see no reason for delay. The disease will never heal itself. It will continue to wax worse and worse under its present treatment. Nor may we indulge the hope that any remedy, except the one intrusted to us, will ever be found for its removal. There is, therefore, an urgent necessity of affording the Hindoos the means of salvation immediately.

The second inference which I draw from the bad moral character of the Hindoos is, that *it ought to quicken our diligence.*

The time which we have to labor is short; the laborers are few, and the work is vast. Life is a vapor — a span — and much of this limited period is necessarily taken up with cares for the body and attentions to worldly interests. But a small portion remains to be devoted to our own immortal souls, or to the spiritual benefit of others. When we begin to live, we die. Death hastens on apace, and seals up our accounts to the great day. How forcible the exhortation in our Savior's remark, *I must work the works of him that sent me while it is day: the night cometh when no man can work.* How careful ought we to be that the brief space of time which is allowed us should be filled up in usefulness to our fellow creatures.

The laborers, too, are few. The multitude which throng the broad road to destruction is vast. But *they* will not help us. They care not for their own souls, and how shall they care for the souls of others? How can they enter into our plans of benevolence to rescue a perishing world? This is all foolishness to them. They neither understand the nature of such plans, nor feel the necessity of them. The "earth" may help the "woman," and we should gladly receive such aid; but we must not reckon on such precarious assistance. On the other hand, how small is the number of the truly pious! *Because straight is the gate and narrow is the way which leadeth to life, and few there be that find it.* And among those who have professed to surrender *all things* into the hands of their Redeemer, that he may use them *just as he please*, and who have, by the solemnity of a covenant, given themselves into his hands, with this unconditional surrender, *Lord, here we are, do with us as it seemeth good in thy sight*, among such only a *part* seem to recognize these awful obligations and responsibilities which rest upon them. The majority consider not the case of the destitute, nor feel nor act for a perishing world. What, therefore, we want in numbers, we must make up in diligence.

The work is one of vast magnitude. The grand object of Christianity is to revolutionize the world. The spirit of missions is a spirit of depredation. Their object is to subdue, to recover, and bring back to allegiance those nations that have thrown off the authority of their rightful Sovereign, and chosen to serve the creature rather than the Creator. Sin has perverted every thing. It has changed the customs and habits of men, corrupted their maxims, monopolized the use of their property, absorbed their minds in vanity, blinded their eyes, and corupted their hearts. It is the mother of all the vile habits, the vicious practices, the degrading superstitions, and the false religions with which our world is afflicted. It has entailed on the human family disease, and woe, and death. And how deep-rooted are all these effects of sin! It is the design of Christianity to eradicate all these evils, and to restore to human nature its pristine beauty and dignity.

But how arduous the undertaking! how mighty the enterprise! The "strong man armed" will keep his place and watch his goods till a stronger than he shall come upon him, and overcome him, and take from him all the armor wherein he trusted, and divide his spoil. "The stronger than he," is the Lord Jesus Christ, as revealed in the Gospel. But the conquests of the Gospel must be effected through human instrumentality; and the whole responsibility of this work rests on professing Christians. However much men of the world may contribute to its accomplishment, Christians must stand responsible for it. God will require it at *our* hands. Yet he has not laid on us a greater burden than we are able to bear. He has kindly considered our infirmities, and has only required us to act as instruments in his hands, to the extent of the ability which he has given us. The injunction laid on us, is *to use the means.* The extent of our duty and of our responsibility is, forcibly and clearly, exhibited by the prophet Ezekiel, in these words:

"If thou do *not* speak to warn the wicked from his way, that wicked man shall die in his iniquity, and his blood will I require at *thine hand.* Nevertheless, if thou *warn* the wicked of his way to turn from it; if he do not return from his way, he shall die in his iniquity, but thou hast delivered thy soul."

Nothing unreasonable is required of us—we have no reason to complain, none to despond. All murmuring, all unbelief, all fretting about success, while we are faithfully and perseveringly applying the means, is useless, it is sinful, it is rebellious, it is setting up our puny judgment in the place of the unerring judgment of God. We need only to quicken our diligence; to use to the best advantage the time, the influence, the talents, the property, which God has given us; to let our personal example be such as to recommend the religion we profess; and to be fervent in our supplications, that all our efforts may be crowned with the divine blessing, and all our labors will be followed by a glorious result—whether it be that *particular* result which we desire, or that more stupendous one which God sees to be best.

But I am to show in the conclusion that the success which has hitherto attended our attempts to propagate the Gospel has been as great as the state of the church has ever warranted us to expect; and that the present state of the church does not warrant us to expect more than we now realize.

We have seen how great are the obstacles in the way of the advancement of the Gospel; we have seen how universal, how obstinate, is the disease to which we are called to apply a remedy. We see how vast is the work, how few are the laborers, and how short the time allotted to us for its accomplishment. We see, on the other hand, a remedy provided and well adapted to the cause, and a power sufficient to render it efficacious. But we find that the presentation of this remedy must be made by *men*, and but *few*, comparatively but a handful of the human family, have a heart to engage in this work; and many of these engage in it with a reluctance, and hesitation, and indifference which paralyze all their efforts. We find, too, that the power which alone can give efficacy to all human endeavors, *must be sought*, by fervent and believing prayer. How few these efforts, how doubting the prayers which are offered up for this object! How inadequate the means to the accomplishment of the end!

When we take an impartial survey of the different missions under the patronage of the American churches, we are obliged to confess that the success which has attended them, as a whole, *has not* been such as the *promises of God* warrant us to expect. The well-known character of God; his willingness to grant the influences of his Spirit—on which alone we depend for all our success—his delight in the enlargement of the Redeemer's kingdom; the manner in which he has always guarded the interests of his church, are our best vouchers of his readiness to bless all the efforts of his people, if they were put forth in the right spirit. The question then recurs, Why is it that God does not more abundantly bless our foreign missions? Is it because Christians do not *desire* the conversion of the heathen? No: their *good wishes* are abundantly expressed on this subject. Is it because they do not *pray* for this object? No: they pray, "Thy kingdom come." Nor do I believe that Christians are unwilling to give their money for the support of missions. But still, there is something that hinders the blessing; and, as professed disciples of the blessed Redeemer, we ought honestly to search out the causes of the divine displeasure, and speedily to remove them if in our power. I will suggest what *may* be some of these causes.

1. *The spirit of piety in the church may be too low*, to allow of

the prosperity of the Gospel at her outposts. The church of Christ is a fountain, or a well of water, in the midst of a desert; alluding to the fact, that in the East a field is barren and parched with the heat for the most part of the year, if it be not artificially watered. If there be a good fountain in the midst of it, the field, which would otherwise be a "wilderness and a solitary place," is made "glad," it smiles with a fresh and beautiful verdure, and the "desert rejoices and blossoms as the rose." All this is owing to the fountain, which sends forth its streams into every part of the field, and fertilizes the whole. If the fountain be full, it propels its streams to the remotest parts of the field, the whole is irrigated, and is covered with a luxuriant vegetation. But if the fountain be not full, the streams become small and feeble, they flow but a short distance, the remote corners of the field are not irrigated at all, the vegetation looks sickly, and dies. So with the church. She is the fountain, but she is not full; she does not abound in the Christian graces. Her streams attempt to flow, but they want the propelling power at the fountain. The seed is sown; it springs up, but the plants wear a sickly hue.

2. The propagation of the Gospel among the heathen is not allowed that *prominence* in the minds of Christians, in general, which it deserves. It is made a secondary thing by most of Christians, or a matter of convenience; whereas, in the New Testament, and in the example of the apostles, it is made the very genius of Christianity, and the first and the indispensable duty of every Christian. A grand characteristic of the Gospel is its tendency to diffuse itself; and a willingness to forsake all for the sake of making known the Gospel, is made a test of discipleship. We cannot, therefore, expect to hear of any very signal triumphs of the Gospel till Christians shall approximate somewhere near the Gospel standard, in relation to foreign missions.

3. Christians do not, individually, feel a *personal responsibility* for the conversion of the heathen. They throw the responsibility on the church, or on a missionary society, or on the body of missionaries—all ideal creations, if we exclude the idea of in-

dividual responsibility. Every Christian is bound to go in person to the heathen, if he be not unavoidably hindered, either for the want of the proper qualifications, or on account of other circumstances; in which case he must do his duty to the Pagan world by proxy.

4. The principal reason, I apprehend, why missions to the heathen are not more abundantly blessed is, that there is a great reluctance on the part of Christians to consecrate to the Lord, in this cause, their most *precious possessions.* God now requires of his people, as he did of old, the *best* they have. The sick, the lame, the maimed, the old, that which had a blemish, or that which among the flock was lightly esteemed, was forbidden to be offered in sacrifice to the Lord. This was no doubt intended as a test to the Jews of their loyalty to their Divine Sovereign. Our love to our Savior is to be tested in a similar way. We act on this principle in our earthly attachments. In making *presents* to a highly esteemed friend, we feel the propriety, both in honor to ourselves and in respect to our friend, to offer the *best* we have. We may contribute most bountifully in support of foreign missions, and yet at the same time be withholding that which God demands, and that, too, without which God will neither bless us in giving nor add his blessing to that which we give. Our offerings may be such as cost us little or nothing. They may be made of what we can spare, without inconvenience or self-denial; and they may be but the surplus of what we employ in our worldly business. We cannot expect that God will accept and honor such gifts.

But to apply these remarks: Christians at the present day are willing to give their silver and their gold; some will give a portion of their time and of their influence to a promotion of the cause, as far as it may be done in this country; many are willing to give up *their countrymen* to go to the heathen; and others are willing to spare *their own personal friends.* All are willing to *talk* and *hear* about foreign missions, many to pray for them, and most persons are willing to contribute most largely and freely of *their good wishes.* But *their own precious selves*—ah! here is the test. Now they go away "sorrowful," for they have "great possessions" in these *precious selves.* They are willing to do any thing, to give any thing, to go any where, except it be to *give themselves to go to the heathen.* In this one thing they *must be excused.* What pity that talents like *theirs* should be wasted on "the desert air" of a Pagan land! What pity that attachments, and relations, and prospects like *theirs* should be sacrificed for a people who may ill appreciate their benevolent motives, and who may but ill requite their disinterested and laborious endeavors. They fancy that the church at home cannot dispense with their very valuable services here. They call this fancy of theirs "the finger of Providence;" they now see the path of duty clearly, and decide to spend their lives in their own native land. If I am not greatly mistaken, there are a great number of theological students in our seminaries at this moment, and a much greater number of clergymen in America, who have no better reason for *not* engaging personally in the foreign service of the church, than I have supposed above.

But there is another aspect to this subject. Those who are bound together by the very dear ties of consanguinity, are not willing to sacrifice the pleasures of this relationship. They will give any thing else, but they cannot give their very dear kindred. Brothers and sisters cannot part; fathers cannot give up their own children; mothers cannot dissolve those tenderest ties of which human nature is capable. Ask *any* thing else, say they, and we will give it; but do not ask for *our children.* Here is the tender chord. How painfully it will vibrate; but it must be touched. The "great possessions" of the young ruler were his idol; he could not follow Christ till he had given up them. So missions to the heathen may not be expected to prosper greatly, till Christians are willing to devote to them their *best* offerings, their "great possessions" which they have in their children.

What means the present demand for Christian laborers? A single foreign missionary society ask for a *thousand,* and say they *must* have more than a *hundred,* in order to sustain and "strengthen existing missions, and to form new ones," so far as to be able to secure the fruit of previous labors. If it does not mean that the most untiring pains must be taken to search out and educate pious young men for the ministry—that candidates for the sacred office must offer themselves, as embassadors for Christ among the Gentiles, in a tenfold greater proportion than they ever have done, and that *parents must make a free-will offering of their children* to this work—if it does not mean this, then I cannot divine what it does mean. Whenever the people of God will consecrate to the Lord their most precious possessions, then we may expect Zion to prosper throughout the whole earth.

We have seen what is wanting in order to this consummation so devoutly to be wished. No impossibilities are required of us; nothing inconsistent with our spiritual interests, and nothing inconsistent with our temporal interests. In giving, a man is only required *to give according to that which he hath, and not according to that which he hath not;* and in devoting ourselves or our friends to the work, we are only required to pay a just debt. For we are *bought* with a price, and are debtors to the heathen. We are bound *to offer ourselves a living sacrifice, holy, acceptable to the Lord.* This is a "reasonable service;" a service which, if cheerfully performed, will yield to ourselves the greatest possible happiness.

Let the love of Christ *constrain* his people; let the moving fact that the *whole world*, for whom Christ died, *are dead* in sin; let the touching fact that he died for them, that they who live should not henceforth live to themselves, but to *Him* who died for them, and rose again, take hold on their hearts, and would they not act more vigorously, and give more liberally, and pray more fervently, than they now do? This is all that is wanting. Let such a state of things exist, and Zion will rejoice at home, and missions will prosper abroad. Sin shall then loose his giant grasp on this wretched world, and people out of every kindred, and tongue, and nation shall be redeemed. The ransomed of the Lord shall return and come to Zion with songs and everlasting joy upon their heads; they shall obtain joy and gladness, and sorrow and sighing shall flee away.

TIGER HUNTING.